Fundamentals of Computer Science Using Java

David Hughes
Brock University

JONES AND BARTLETT PUBLISHERS
Sudbury, Massachusetts
BOSTON TORONTO LONDON SINGAPORE

World Headquarters
Jones and Bartlett Publishers
40 Tall Pine Drive
Sudbury, MA 01776
978-443-5000
info@jbpub.com
www.jbpub.com

Jones and Bartlett Publishers
Canada
2406 Nikanna Road
Mississauga, ON L5C 2W6
CANADA

Jones and Bartlett Publishers
International
Barb House, Barb Mews
London W6 7PA
UK

Library of Congress Cataloging-in-Publication Data

Hughes, David (David John Frederick), 1952-
Fundamentals of computer science using Java / David Hughes.
p. cm.
ISBN 0-7637-1761-4
1. Computer science. 2. Java (Computer program language) I. Title.

QA76.H789 2001
005.2'76—dc21 2001029710

Chief Executive Officer: Clayton Jones
Chief Operating Officer: Don W. Jones, Jr.
Executive V.P. and Publisher: Robert W. Holland, Jr.
V.P., Design and Production: Anne Spencer
V.P., Manufacturing and Inventory Control: Therese Bräuer
Editor-in-Chief: J. Michael Stranz
Production Manager: Amy Rose
Marketing Manager: Nathan Schultz
Associate Production Editor: Tara McCormick
Editorial Assistant: Theresa DiDonato
Cover Design: Kristin Ohlin
Composition: Northeast Compositors, Inc.
Text Design: Mary McKeon
Printing and Binding: Courier Westford
Cover Printing: John Pow Company, Inc.

This book was typeset in Quark 4.1 on a Macintosh G4. The font families used were Adobe Garamond, Univers, and Prestige Elite. The first printing was printed on 50# Courier Opaque.

Printed in the United States of America
06 05 04 03 02 10 9 8 7 6 5 4 3 2 1

To my wife Chris, for all those times I was too busy with "the book."

Preface

Why this Book

In the summer of 1996, our Computer Science department made the decision to use Java as the core language for our Computer Science program, beginning that fall. Although there were many Java books available, we soon discovered that most were "trade" or "hobby" books, not designed for university courses and certainly not intended to serve as introductions to Computer Science. It became clear to us that someone needed to write a "Fundamentals of Computer Science Using Java" book, and I thought, "why not me?" And now, after years of researching, testing, and writing, I can provide the book that we searched for years ago: a truly Java-based introduction to Computer Science.

In a first course in Computer Science, the primary goal is to teach the fundamentals of the field. Basic concepts are introduced with the help of a programming language that is often viewed as simply a medium through which algorithms are expressed. From that perspective, it does not matter which language is used in an introductory course, because any would suffice. In practice, however, the language can have a profound impact on the students' learning experience. First, the style of the language constrains the way and the order in which topics can be introduced. Further, the language taught in the first course must support the rest of the curriculum. For these reasons and more, a language-defined text is an important component in an introductory course.

Object-oriented languages in particular are useful in introductory textbooks and are certainly appropriate at this time. Having an object-oriented language as the core programming language supports many courses at the higher level (e.g., software engineering, user interfaces, databases). The question is, then, which object-oriented language?

Our decision to use Java was based on a number of factors. First, we recognized Java as a pure object-oriented language, as opposed to C++, which is a hybrid, and thus does not allow the programmer to fall back into procedural habits. Further, it has a relatively clear and common syntax that can be understood without having to learn a large class hierarchy. Finally, Java has compilers available on a great many platforms that are inexpensive, not overly resource hungry, and the code is platform-independent. All of these things make Java ideal for a first university course.

The approach taken in this book is what might best be called an "object-based" approach. It is my belief that students need to master the skill of method writing before they can craft meaningful classes. Objects occur right from the start. The student's code, however, is written as a client of another class, and thereby makes use of objects through the delegation model rather than the inheritance model.

The text introduces methods as early as possible and then introduces the control structures and types necessary for writing methods. When classes are fully introduced, the students are completely capable of writing the methods for a class and are familiar with writing one class as a client of another. They soon master writing a class as a supplier. Once classes are available, the text introduces object-oriented software development using classes for the decomposition. Responsibility-based design is also introduced using CRC cards as the design methodology.

The pedagogical approach applied to this text is grounded in the idea that the learning process can be facilitated through the use of examples. Each new topic is introduced through a number of complete program examples. Examples are kept as simple as possible to illustrate important concepts. At the same time, the examples are realistic, and allow for meaningful use of new constructs. Students can often use the examples as a starting point for coding of assignment problems.

What is Covered and What is Not

Java, like any programming language, is fairly large and this book does not attempt to provide complete coverage of all Java topics. As an object-oriented language, Java has many standard class libraries and many other APIs, and therefore it would not be possible to provide complete coverage of the language even if I so wished.

The first decision I made was to exclude inheritance. This might seem like heresy, however, I stand by this decision and believe it is appropriate to exclude inheritance from an introductory course. In my experience, students have trouble understanding the true meaning of inheritance, and this often leads them to use inheritance as simply a mechanism for code borrowing. This is very evident in the structure of many books that introduce Computer Science in an object-oriented language. In an attempt to make the first programs interesting, these texts can overuse subclassing. Code reuse through delegation is a much simpler, and often more desirable, approach. In a first course, I prefer to foster in my students a clear understanding of the basic principles, and I leave inheritance and subclassing for a later course. In our program, inheritance and polymorphism are introduced in the second year.

One possible objection to excluding inheritance is that without it we cannot write applets. This is a small loss, as it would be nice if the student's programs could be demonstrated using a web browser. The level of programming necessary for writing applets, however, is really too advanced for an introductory course, since it requires the use of graphical user interfaces to do anything reasonable. To allow interesting first programs, the class library TurtleGraphics is used. This class library supports the turtle graphics model introduced in the programming language Logo.

The AWT and Swing are also not covered in this book. GUI programming requires an event model for programming that allows apparent non-linear flow of control. This is confusing for first-year students. Instead, the I/O class library BasicIO is used. This I/O class library provides a class for prompted input via the dialog box ASCIIPrompter and provides output to the scrollable window ASCIIDisplayer.

Even though inheritance is not covered, classes definitely are. Classes are the fundamental decomposition mechanism in object-oriented design. Of course, without inheritance the design model is incomplete; however, designing with inheritance is difficult and better learned when a student's programming skills are more mature.

Exceptions are also a difficult concept for beginning students to grasp because they introduce a second path of execution. Since Java requires that any exception (other than RunTimeException) be caught or thrown by the method, code dealing with exceptions obscures the expression of the algorithm. The most common occurrence of exceptions is in I/O. To remove the need to deal with exceptions too early, the BasicIO library does not throw exceptions.

Use of the Book

At Brock, the material presented here forms the substance of a half-year (twelve-week) course meeting three hours per week. The lectures are supplemented by a one-hour tutorial, which is primarily a question and answer period, and a two-hour laboratory where the students work on programming assignments. The primary goal of our course is to introduce basic computer science concepts, while introducing language concepts as needed.

Chapter 1 includes a brief history of computing and computing technology, and then describes the basic hardware and software organization of computer systems. The material in Appendix A may be used to supplement this coverage, or can be introduced at a later time for a clearer understanding of the low-level execution of programs. Chapter 1 also provides a preview to the software development process, and the phases included in this chapter are repeated in the Case Studies of later chapters.

Chapter 2 begins the coverage of Java. It introduces the Java syntax notation so that students will be able to read the syntax descriptions that define the language. Turtle Graphics are used to enhance the early examples. Programs are written as clients of

Turtle objects and make use of simple looping and nesting of loops to produce interesting graphics.

Chapter 3 introduces computations and the basic arithmetic operators of Java. Since results of computations must be stored, it also introduces variables and assignment.

Chapter 4 covers methods as a mechanism for procedural abstraction. It covers simple methods, method invocation, parameter passing, and method results, as well as scope issues.

Chapter 5 covers I/O, specifically the BasicIO package. It describes streams as an abstraction of I/O and covers input and output streams and output formatting. The stream concept is consistent with the java.io package, and so many of these concepts are transferable.

Chapter 6 introduces control structures. Some control structures have already been used in their simplest form, but here they are described in detail. The chapter spends its time on the important structures, while only mentioning the less frequently used structures.

Chapter 7 covers the boolean and char types and emphasizes the difference between primitive and reference types. Boolean expressions are explained here in detail, building from their use in Chapter 6. Some of the basic services of the Character class are introduced.

Chapter 8 describes classes. Classes have been used throughout the text, however, prior to this chapter, example programs involved a single class as a client of one or more library classes. Here programs make use of multiple classes. Additionally, class interaction and information hiding principles are explained.

Chapter 9 introduces software development. Classes are used as the decomposition mechanism using a responsibility-based approach to design. The traditional seven phases of the software development life cycle are described.

Chapter 10 covers the String class and special processing for text manipulation.

Finally, Chapter 11 covers arrays, including both single- and two-dimensional arrays, and describes standard array processing techniques.

Each chapter represents approximately one week, or three lecture hours, of material. Chapters 1, 4, 9, and 11 generally take a bit longer, while some of the other chapters take slightly less time. By emphasizing or de-emphasizing certain material, the text can easily accommodate a ten- to thirteen-week course. The sections marked with a star (*) are optional and can be omitted without loss of context in later chapters. The material in Appendix A can be used to augment Chapter 1 if this is seen as desirable.

The presentation is sequential and most chapters depend on material presented in previous chapters. Some of the material from Chapter 1, specifically the sections on computer software and social issues, may be deferred and introduced wherever convenient. Similarly, the section on syntax in Chapter 2 can be de-emphasized as long as the syntax descriptions in later chapters are explained as they are introduced.

Features

The text incorporates a number of features to aid the educational process.

Java Syntax The syntax for each new construct is described using the notation of the Java Language Specification in special boxes called Syntax Boxes. The complete syntax of Java is found in Appendix B.

Turtle Graphics Early examples and exercises use the Turtle Graphics class library. With this application, first programs are made interesting and challenging for the students.

Style Tips Periodically, tips regarding programming style are included to help the student adopt good programming style and become familiar with Java programming conventions. These Style Tips are marked with a special symbol in the margin.

Case Studies Although examples are used throughout the text, most chapters include an additional extensive example that is presented as a case study. The case studies are developed following the software development process described in Chapter 1 and detailed in Chapter 9.

Programming Patterns At appropriate times in the text, I introduce what I call programming patterns. These are inspired by design patterns as described in *Design Patterns–Elements of Reusable Object-Oriented Software*[1], and represent commonly used patterns of programming language text applicable in a variety of programs. Like design patterns, these provide larger, abstract components out of which a program can be constructed. The programming patterns are marked with a special notation in the margin and are collected and described in detail in Appendix C.

Students can use programming patterns as templates in writing program code. Through nesting and merging, patterns can be used to develop fairly sophisticated code. Programming patterns can also be used by those who have learned another language prior to Java to help them become accustomed to the Java style of program expression.

Debugging Techniques Many constructs require special consideration in testing and debugging. When such new constructs, methods or control structures for example, are introduced, a section on testing and debugging is included to guide the student in techniques that can be used to make this process easier.

Memory Models and Flow Diagrams To help explain the concepts of variables, assignment, reference versus value semantics, and similar issues, the text uses a simplified model of memory that diagrams the way information is stored. Similarly, when control structures are introduced, the flow of control is described by flow diagrams.

---

[1] Gamma, E., et al; *Design Patterns–Elements of Reusable Object-Oriented Software*, Addison-Wesley, Reading, MA; 1994

Website The source code and Custom Package for this text can be found at: http://computerscience.jbpub.com/cs_resources.cfm.

Definitions New terms and concepts are written in bold within the text when they first occur. The more important terms are highlighted in blue and their definitions appear in a box in the margin. All introduced terms are collected with their definitions in a Glossary in Appendix D.

Chapter Objectives, Review Questions, and Exercises Each chapter begins with a list of objectives that are the educational outcomes expected of the chapter. To help the student judge his/her progress, each chapter ends with a set of review questions, the answers to which are found in Appendix F, and a set of programming exercises that can also be used as weekly programming assignments.

Acknowledgements

I would like to take the opportunity of thanking the many people who helped bring this book to successful completion. First, many thanks to Michael Stranz at Jones & Bartlett for his confidence in my abilities as an author, and also to Bobbie Lewis and Amy Rose for all of their work.

Thanks are also owed to the reviewers who reviewed my early manuscript and made suggestions that much improved the final product: Claude Anderson, Rose-Hulman Institute of Technology; John Beidler, University of Scranton; Robert Burton, Brigham Young University; John Connely, California Polytechnic State University; Craig Graci, State University of New York at Oswego; Ananth Grama, Purdue University; Pamela Lawhead, The University of Mississippi; Ray Lischner, Oregon State University; Thomas Mertz, Millersville University; Carolyn Schauble, Colorado State University; Dale Skrien, Colby College. My co-instructors in COSC 1P02, Dave Bockus and Sheridan Houghten, provided many insights, examples, review questions, and exercises, for which I am forever indebted.

Finally, special thanks go to the students of COSC 1P02 over the last two years who test-drove the manuscript and provided feedback and insights.

Dave Hughes

Contents

1 Computing Fundamentals

CHAPTER OBJECTIVES

- To become familiar with the early history of computers and computing.
- To identify the four generations of computer hardware and the technology behind them.
- To recognize the four categories of computers.
- To understand the function of the five basic components of computer hardware.
- To be aware of how information is stored in binary form in computer memory.
- To differentiate between system and application software.
- To become aware of the seven phases of software development.
- To identify the four generations of programming languages and how they are executed.
- To understand the program preparation cycle.
- To gain an appreciation of the social issues surrounding computer use.

This book is an introduction to computer science. Computer science is the study of computer hardware, algorithms, and data structures and how they fit together to provide information systems. Each of these topics can be studied at various levels. For example, physicists study the properties of matter that allow hardware components to be designed, electrical engineers study how the components can be combined to produce circuits, and computer engineers study how circuits can be combined to produce computers. Most computer scientists do not need a detailed understanding of the properties of matter, circuit design, or computer design, but rather a basic understanding of how the hardware operates with respect to the design of algorithms. The **algorithm**—a clearly defined sequence of steps to achieve some goal—is a key programming concept covered throughout this book.

An **ALGORITHM** is a clearly defined sequence of steps to achieve some goal.

During your career as a computer science student, you will be introduced to the three main areas of the subject at a variety of levels. In this book, we will briefly consider computer hardware from a functional viewpoint, and then introduce algorithms and programming. This will only be an introduction; there is much more to learn! In fact, you will go on learning for the rest of your career as a computer scientist. Computer science is probably the most quickly changing of all subjects. Computers, programming languages, and even computing concepts of twenty, ten, or even five years ago are rapidly replaced by new, improved versions.

This chapter will serve as an introduction to computer science, with a brief history of the discipline, an introduction to the functional components of a computer, an introduction to the program development process, and some of the social implications. In subsequent chapters, you will be introduced to computer programming in the Java programming language as a foundation upon which to build a computer science career.

When discussing programming, we need a language in which to express the algorithms. The most convenient means is to use an actual programming language. Each language has its own drawbacks. It may be that the language will be out of date in industry in a few years' time, or the language may not support all of the concepts that should be discussed. We have to live with these drawbacks. **Java** is the language we have chosen for this book; it is a relatively new language that is object-oriented. It supports most of the concepts currently viewed as leading to good programming style without having many of the inconsistencies of languages such as C++ or the complexities of Eiffel or Smalltalk. Even if you go on to program in another language, the Java concepts are transferable, even if the specific notation is not. In this text we are really discussing the concepts and using Java as a medium to discuss them.

JAVA is a modern (1990s) object-oriented programming language developed by James Gosling et al at Sun Microsystems.

A computer is a special kind of machine. Unlike machines of the past like a circular saw or an automobile that could do only one task (such as cut wood or deliver people and goods from point A to point B), computers are able to perform a wide variety of different tasks. Computers are **programmable**; they can be

A device (such as a computer) is **PROGRAMMABLE** if it can be instructed (programmed) to perform different tasks.

instructed to do a variety of different things. The program applies the computer to a particular task. Instead of working on physical materials, computers work on **data**—facts, figures, and ideas. Computers synthesize these data into **information**—reports, summaries, and animations. Computers are therefore information-processing machines, and the computer programs are information-processing systems.

DATA are items (e.g., facts, figures and ideas) that can be processed by a computer system.

INFORMATION is processed data (e.g., reports, summaries, animations) produced by a computer system through computation, summary or synthesis.

1.1 A BRIEF HISTORY OF COMPUTING

Computers as we know them are a modern development, evolving from the 1940s to the present day. However, humankind has had to perform calculations since the dawn of civilization.

From Counting to Computing

Counting was first needed to determine the size of wild herds or the number of domesticated animals. Then a notation for numbers was developed to record this information. Finally, arithmetic was developed for people to be able to divide resources among several individuals. Here was the dawn of algorithms. Arithmetic methods such as long division are clearly algorithms.

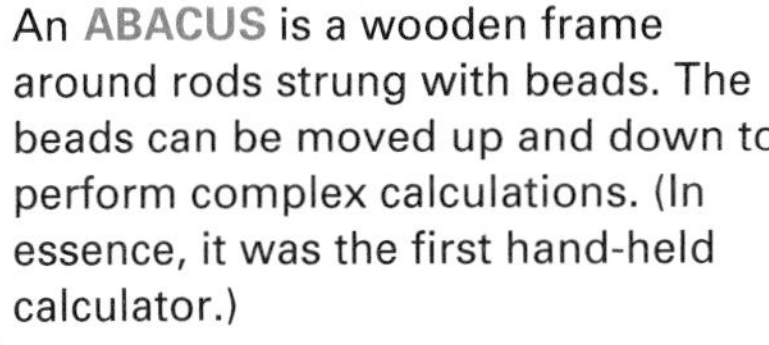

An **ABACUS** is a wooden frame around rods strung with beads. The beads can be moved up and down to perform complex calculations. (In essence, it was the first hand-held calculator.)

As civilization evolved and humankind had the luxury of academic pursuit, some philosophers (as they were then called) studied arithmetic processes. Euclid is credited with the first written algorithm—his description of how to find the greatest common divisor of two integers. An Arab philosopher named **Mohammed ibn Musa Al-Kowarizmi** (ca. 850) wrote at length about arithmetic processes and lent his name to the subject, algorithm.

Calculation by hand was, of course, tedious and error-prone. One early device that aided in calculation was the abacus, which has long been used in China (ca. 1300). A wooden frame around rods strung with beads that could be moved up and down, the **abacus** could be used to perform complex calculations. In essence, it was the first hand-held calculator. However, the user performed the actual arithmetic algorithm.

Blaise Pascal
Reproduced by permission of University of Calgary

In 1617, the English mathematician **John Napier** developed a tool (called **Napier's bones**) based on logarithmic tables, which allowed the user to multiply and divide easily. This evolved into the slide rule (Edmund Gunther, 1621), which was the mainstay of scientists and engineers until the recent development of the hand-held calculator. **Blaise Pascal** (after whom the programming language Pascal is named) developed a fully mechanical adding machine in 1642. The user didn't have to perform the algorithm; the machine did it all. The mechanization of computation had begun.

The **ANALYTICAL ENGINE** was designed by Charles Babbage in the 1840s. This machine was the mechanical forerunner of modern computers. Just like computers of today, there was a means of entering data (input) and receiving results (output) via dials, a place to store intermediate results (memory), an arithmetic mill (the part that did the computations, what we call the processor) and a mechanism for programming the machine.

Still, with one exception, all of the computation devices developed over the next two or three hundred years were just simple machines, not computers. The one exception was the design of the **Analytical Engine** by **Charles Babbage** in the 1840s. Babbage was a mathematician and inventor who was very interested in automating calculations. He had partially developed a machine called the **Difference Engine** (1822–42) which would be able to automatically calculate difference tables (important for preparing trajectory tables for artillery pieces) under contract to the British Government. He had much grander plans, however, for a machine that could do any calculation required—the Analytical Engine. This machine was the mechanical forerunner of modern computers. Just like computers of today, there was a means of entering data (input) and receiving results (output) via dials, a place to store intermediate results (memory), an arithmetic mill (the part that did the computations, what we call the processor) and a mechanism for programming the machine. The program instructions were punched as holes into wooden cards (an idea borrowed from the automated weaving loom previously developed by **Jacquard**, 1804–6).

Charles Babbage

Unfortunately, Babbage was a perfectionist and a bit of an eccentric. Between the inability of the manufacturing process of the day to mill parts with the required tolerances, Babbage's tendency to go on to new ideas rather than complete what he started, and his inability to get along with the government officials for whom he was developing the device, the Analytical Engine was never completely built. However, for the 200th anniversary of his birth, a replica of the Difference Engine was built and is currently in the Science Museum in London, England.

Ada Augusta King
Reproduced by permission of University of Calgary

Ada Augusta King, the Countess of Lovelace and daughter of the poet Lord Byron, was an amateur mathematician and avid handicapper of horses. She was introduced to Babbage by her mother and became quite interested in the practical use of the Analytical Engine. She wrote programs for the Analytical Engine and is regarded as the first programmer. The programming language Ada is named in her honor.

The Modern Era

For a machine to be considered a computer, it must be programmable. The **stored program concept**, as defined by the mathematician **John von Neumann** (1945), is now considered essential to the notion of a computer. That is, a computer must have a memory in which instructions are stored and which can be modified by a program itself. Babbage's Analytical Engine fulfilled this criterion.

The mathematician John von Neumann defined the **STORED PROGRAM CONCEPT**—that a computer must have a memory in which instructions are stored and which can be modified by the program itself.

The modern age of electronic computers really begins in the 1940s (with a push from the war effort), although credit for the

Difference Engine
Reproduced by permission of University of Calgary

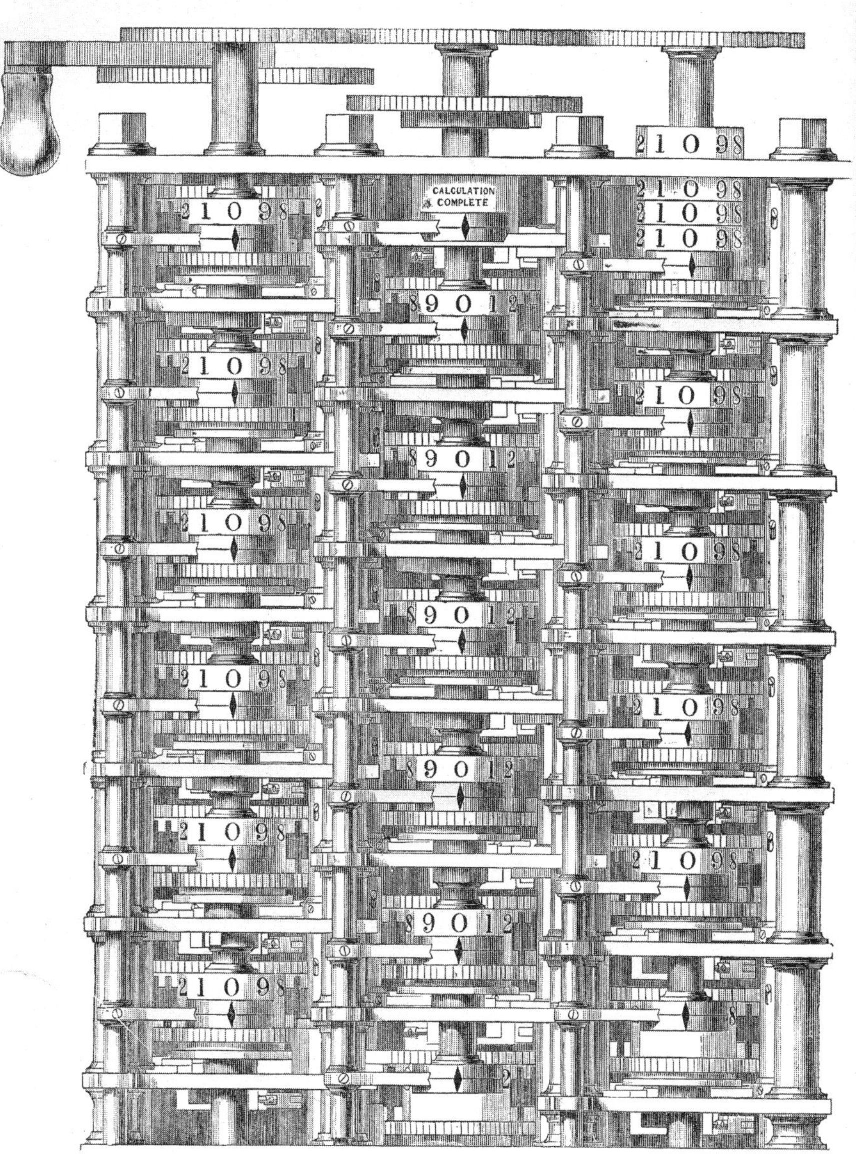

B. H. Babbage, del.

Impression from a woodcut of a small portion of Mr. Babbage's Difference Engine No. 1, the property of Government, at present deposited in the Museum at South Kensington.

It was commenced 1823.
This portion put together 1833.
The construction abandoned 1842.
This plate was printed June, 1853.
This portion was in the Exhibition 1862.

Konrad Zuse
Reproduced by permission of University of Calgary

development of the first electronic computer is not clear. Throughout the 1940s several electronic computing devices were developed, but none was fully electronic and programmable.

One development, of which we have little information since much was lost after the end of World War II, was the work in Germany by **Konrad Zuse** on a series of computing devices culminating in the Z3 (about 1941). Reportedly, this machine was electronic and programmable. Zuse also developed a notation for programs called **Plankalkül** (1945), which is regarded as the first programming language.

Generations of Computers

The basic components of an electronic computer are electronic switches. Computers can be classified into generations based on the technology used for these switches. The older electro-mechanical computers used relays, but the first electronic computers (**first generation**, 1944–58) used vacuum tubes. A **vacuum tube** is an evacuated tube of glass that can be used as an electronic switch. Today we don't see vacuum tubes very often except as the picture tube of televisions and computer monitors.

The **second generation** of computers (1959–63) began with the development of the transistor. A **transistor** is a solid state device that functions as an electronic switch. Because transistors are small and can last indefinitely, this meant that second-generation computers were much smaller and more reliable than first-generation computers.

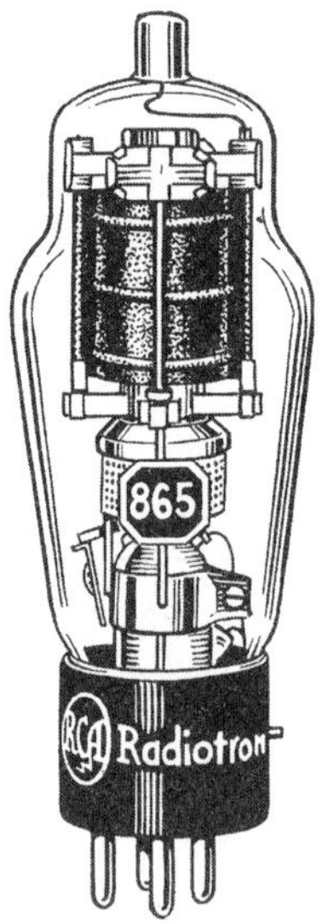

Vacuum Tube
Reproduced by permission of University of Calgary

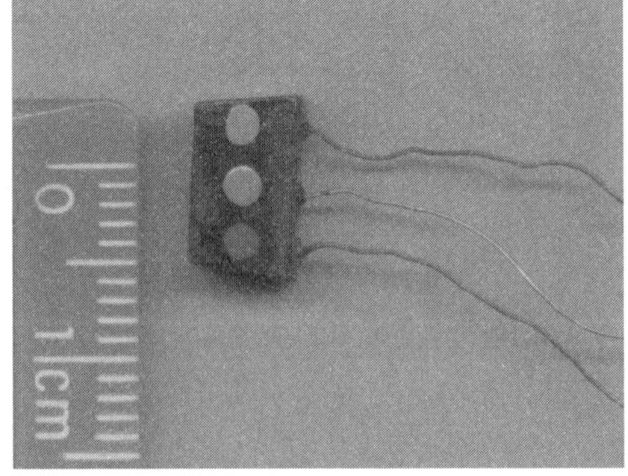

Transistor
Courtesy of Dr. Andrew Wylie

The development of the integrated circuit brought about the **third generation** of computers (1964–70). Essentially, an **integrated circuit** is a solid-state device on which an entire circuit—transistors and the connections between them—can be created (etched). This meant that a single integrated circuit chip, not much bigger than early transistors, could replace entire circuit boards containing many transistors, again reducing the size of computers.

Integrated Circuit
Reproduced by permission of University of Calgary

From here, the evolution of computing technology has been an ever-increasing miniaturization of the electronic circuitry. The **fourth generation** (1971–) is typically considered to be **VLSI** (very large-scale integration). Currently, it is possible to place many millions of transistors and the accompanying circuitry on a single integrated circuit chip.

By the mid-'70s, it was possible to put the complete circuitry for the processor of a simple computer on a single chip (called a **microprocessor**), and the **microcomputer**

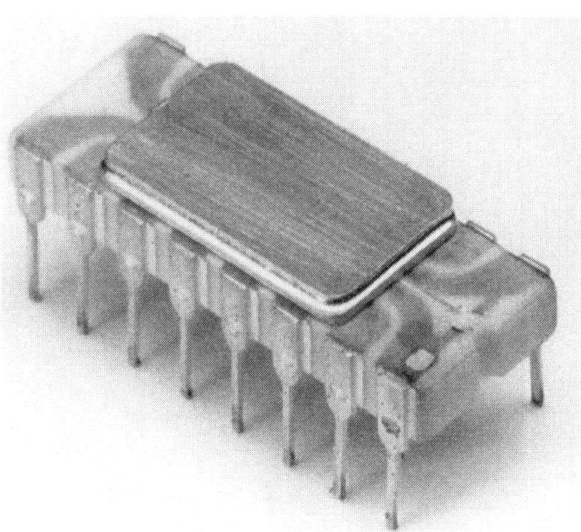

Microprocessor
Reproduced by permission of University of Calgary

was born. In 1977, a small garage-based company called Apple Computer marketed the first commercial **personal computer** (PC)—the Apple II. In 1981, IBM released its version of a PC, expecting to sell a few thousand worldwide. They didn't want to have the hassle of maintaining an operating system, so they sold the code to Bill Gates (a small-time software developer), and Microsoft was born. In 1984, Apple released the "computer for the rest of us," the Macintosh, designed to be so easy to use that it could be used by people without special training. Based on the research done at Xerox's Palo Alto Research Center, the Macintosh was the first commercial computer to use a mouse and a graphical user interface (**GUI**). The modern era of computers had arrived.

1.2 COMPUTER SYSTEMS

A **computing system** consists of user(s), software, procedures, hardware, and data that work together to produce an outcome. The **user** is the individual that uses the system to produce a result such as a written report or calculation. Typically, this is not someone trained in computer science, but s/he most likely is trained in computer use. The **software** refers to the computer programs (algorithms expressed in a computer language) that allow the computer to be applied to a particular task. The **procedures** are the steps that the user must follow to use the software. This is usually described in the **documentation** (either a printed book or online documentation that is read on the computer). The **hardware** is the physical computer itself. Finally, the data are the facts, figures, ideas, and so on that the program will process to produce the desired information.

In this book our focus is on software, that is, with programming. However, we need to have a general understanding of the hardware of a computer to be able to write software.

> A system (e.g., a **COMPUTING SYSTEM**) is a collection of entities that work together to produce an outcome.
>
> A **USER** is an individual that uses a computing system to produce a result (e.g., produce an essay). Typically this is not someone trained in computer science, but s/he most likely is trained in computer use.
>
> **SOFTWARE** are the computer programs (algorithms expressed in a computer language) that allow the computer to be applied to a particular task.
>
> **PROCEDURES** are the steps that the user must follow to use the software as described in the documentation.
>
> **DOCUMENTATION** is instructions (either as a printed book or on-line documentation that is read on the computer) for the user describing how to make use of the software.
>
> **HARDWARE** are the physical components (e.g. processor, monitor, mouse) of the computer itself.

Computer Hardware

There are a great variety of different kinds of computers used for different purposes. Typically, we divide computers into categories based on their power (that is, how fast they can do computations), physical size, and cost. Four categories are usually described:

- **Microcomputers**—Smallest, single-user. Examples: workstations, desktops (PCs), laptops, notebooks, and pocket PCs
- **Minicomputers**—Refrigerator-sized, handle 20–50 users, business use

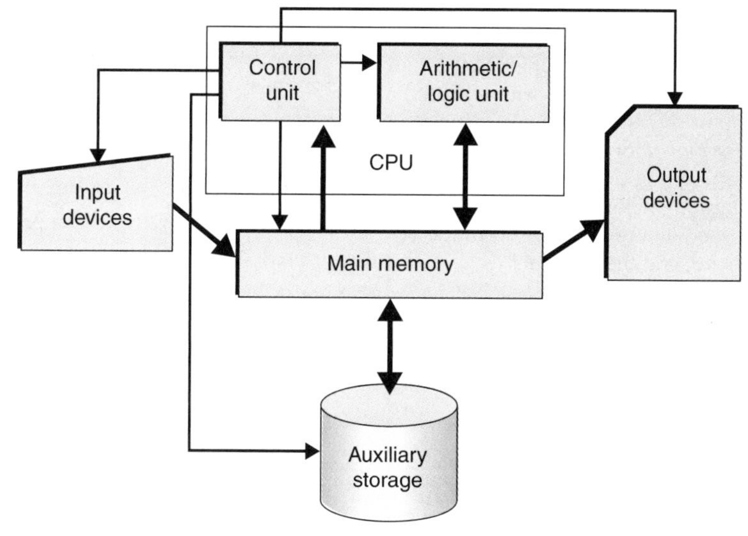

FIGURE 1.1 Hardware components

- **Mainframes**—Larger, room-sized, used by big businesses such as airlines and banks
- **Supercomputers**—Large, very complex, used in research for large amounts of computation, such as in weather forecasting

> The **CENTRAL PROCESSING UNIT (CPU)** contains the circuitry that allows the computer to do the calculations and follow the instructions of the program. The CPU is divided into two main parts: the control unit and the arithmetic/logic unit.
>
> As part of the CPU, the **CONTROL UNIT (CU)** controls the components of the computer and follows the instructions of the program.
>
> As part of the CPU, the **ARITHMETIC/LOGIC UNIT (ALU)** performs the arithmetic (e.g., addition) and logical (e.g., comparison of numbers) functions of the computer.

The division into the four categories is somewhat subjective, and the categories overlap. Certainly, the mainframes of yesterday (such as an IBM 360) may have much less power than a workstation or even an expensive PC of today.

Regardless of the size, power, or category, however, all computers work in essentially the same way and are made up of the same general components: central processing unit, main memory, input devices, output devices, and auxiliary storage (see Figure 1.1).

The heart (or brains) of the computer is the **central processing unit** (CPU). The CPU contains the circuitry that allows the computer to do the calculations and follow the instructions of the program. The CPU is divided into two main parts: the control unit and the arithmetic/logic unit. The **control unit** (CU) controls the components of the computer and follows the instructions of the program. This is described in more detail in Appendix A. The **arithmetic/logic unit** (ALU) performs the computer's arithmetic functions (such as addition) and logical functions (such as comparison of numbers). A microprocessor has the entire CPU on a single chip.

The **main memory** (or RAM—**r**andom **a**ccess **m**emory) is the place where the computer remembers things. The data being processed, the results or information produced, and the program instructions themselves must be present in memory while they are being used. When power to the computer is lost, the contents of memory cannot be relied upon. We therefore say that main memory is **volatile**. This means that main memory can only be used for short-term storage.

Input devices are the components that the computer uses to access data that is present outside the computer system. Input devices convert the data coming from the real world into a form that the computer can process. Examples of input devices are keyboards, scanners, swipe card readers, and sensors.

Output devices are the components that present results from the computer to the outside environment. They convert the computer representation to the real-world representation. Examples of output devices include monitors, printers, plotters, and speakers.

Since it is necessary to store programs and data for long periods of time and main memory is volatile, we need some form of long-term (nonvolatile) memory. These are the **auxiliary storage devices**. They include floppy disk, hard disk, CD-ROM, DVD, and tape units.

Although not traditionally considered one of the basic hardware components, **communications devices** are common on most computer systems today. Computer systems must be able to communicate with other computers to exchange information. Communications devices unite computers into networks (including the Internet). This is the way that applications such as web browsing and electronic mail are provided. A common communications device on a microcomputer is a cable or digital modem, which allows cable television or telephone lines to be used for computer communication.

> The **MAIN MEMORY** (or RAM—**r**andom **a**ccess **m**emory) is (as the name implies) the place where the computer remembers things (much like our own short-term memory). Everything that the computer is working on (including data being processed, the results or information produced, and the program instructions themselves) must be present in memory while it is being used.
>
> **INPUT DEVICES** are the components that the computer uses to access data that is present outside the computer system. Input devices perform a conversion from the form in which the data exists in the real world to the form that the computer can process.
>
> **OUTPUT DEVICES** are the components that present results from the computer to the outside environment. They perform the conversion from the computer representation to the real-world representation.
>
> **AUXILIARY (SECONDARY) STORAGE DEVICES** are non-volatile storage devices used to store information (i.e., programs and data) for long periods of time since main memory is volatile.
>
> **COMMUNICATIONS DEVICES** are devices that allow computers to exchange information using communications systems (e.g., telephone, cable). Communications devices unite computers into networks (including the Internet).

*1.3 DATA REPRESENTATION

We have seen that computer hardware is made up of basic components that are essentially electronic switches. A switch is called a **bi-stable device** because it has two states: open (no current flowing) or closed (current flowing). Since memory is comprised of these switches, data in memory must be represented in terms of two states. In Mathematics, the number system that has only two digits is called the **binary** (or base-2) **number system**. The two digits are 0 and 1. This corresponds to the situation in computer memory, so computers have adopted the binary number system as their basic representation.

In Mathematics, the number system that has only two digits is called the **BINARY** (or base two) **NUMBER SYSTEM**. The two digits are 0 and 1. This corresponds to the situation in computer memory (which is made up of bi-stable devices), so computers have adopted the binary number system as their basic representation.

The binary number system is similar to our common decimal (base-10) number system, in that it is a **positional number system**. In a positional number system, a number is written as a sequence of digits (0 through 9 for base-10), with digits in different positions having different values. For example, the decimal number 107 represents the number composed of 1 hundreds, 0 tens and 7 ones or one hundred and seven. The digits (starting at the decimal point and moving left) represent ones (10^0), tens (10^1), hundreds (10^2), thousands (10^3), and so forth. Note that these are the powers of the base, 10. A binary number works in the same way, except the digits are restricted to 0 and 1 and the base is 2. Thus the binary number 1101011 represents 1 sixty-four (2^6), 1 thirty-two (2^5), 0 sixteens (2^4), 1 eight (2^3), 0 fours (2^2), 1 two (2^1) and 1 one (2^0) or also one-hundred and seven.

A **BIT** is a single *bi*nary dig*it*. The term is used to differentiate them from the decimal digits. Each switch (transistor) in computer memory represents one bit and thus the bit is the smallest unit of measure for storage.

A group of eight bits is called a **BYTE**, and is the basic unit of storage on computers. In many coding schemes, a byte can represent a single text character.

A **MEGABYTE** (MB) is a million bytes (actually 2^{20} or 1,048,576 bytes). Main memory size is usually measured in megabytes, so a microcomputer might have 256MB of RAM.

To distinguish the binary digits (0 and 1) from the decimal digits (0 through 9), we give them the name **bit** (**bi**nary dig**it**). Thus each switch in computer memory represents one bit. To represent information, bits are grouped together. A single bit can represent two possible distinct values (0 and 1); two bits together represent four possibilities (00, 01, 10, 11). In general, a group of n bits can represent 2^n possibilities as summarized in Table 1.1. A group of eight bits is called a **byte**, and is the basic unit of storage on computers. Memory itself is usually measured in **megabytes** (one million bytes, MB), so a microcomputer might have 256MB of RAM (or about 256 million bytes of memory[2]).

*This section represents optional material.

TABLE 1.1 Powers of 2

Number of bits	Values	Number of possibilities
1	0, 1	2^1=2
2	00, 01, 10, 11	2^2=4
3	000, 001, 010, 011, 100, 101, 110, 111	2^3=8
4	0000, 0001, 0010, 0011, 0100, 0101, 0110, 0111 1000, 1001, 1010, 1011, 1100, 1101, 1110, 1111	2^4=16
8	...	2^8=256
16	...	2^{16}=65,536
32	...	2^{32}=4,294,967,296

An **ADDRESS** is a number identifying a location in memory. Information in memory is accessed by specifying the address at which it is stored (its address).

STORING (sometimes called writing) information is recording the information into main memory at a specified address by changing the settings of the bits at that address.

We can think of memory as a set of boxes or cells, each of which can hold some data. To distinguish one box from another, the boxes are labeled with (binary) numbers called **addresses** (much as houses on a street). When the program needs to remember a value for future use, it **stores** (places) the value in a cell at a particular address. Figure 1.2 shows a model of memory. The addresses label each cell. The number 27 (here written in decimal since binary numbers get very long) has been stored at address 0010. Later the program may recall the value

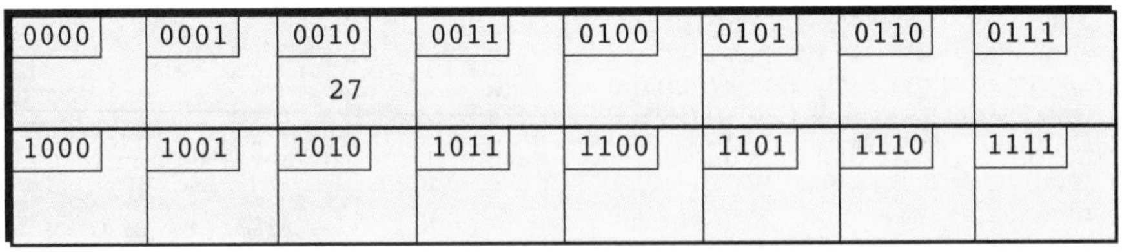

0000	0001	0010 27	0011	0100	0101	0110	0111
1000	1001	1010	1011	1100	1101	1110	1111

FIGURE 1.2 Memory model

[2] Actually, like everything else on computers, a megabyte is defined in base-2, not base-10. A megabyte is actually 2^{20} or 1,048,576 bytes. We commonly use the approximation of one million for convenience.

READING (sometimes called fetching) information is obtaining the settings of the bits at a particular address in main memory.

DIGITIZATION is the process of encoding data (e.g., a picture or sound) as sequences of binary digits. For example, music can be coded as a sequence of binary numbers each representing the height of the sound wave measured at particular sampling intervals. This is the way music is stored on audio CDs.

by **reading** the value from the cell with the given address. Only one value can reside in a cell at any one time. Reading a value doesn't change what is in the cell, whereas writing (storing) replaces the old value with a new one, rendering the old value lost.

Ultimately, every kind of data that a computer processes must be represented as a sequence of bits. To make it convenient to process information, the same number of bits is used for the values of any one kind. For example, in Java, integral values (numbers without fractions) are represented using 32 bits (see Chapter 3). Numbers are represented naturally in base-2. Text characters are assigned binary numbers according to a coding scheme (see Chapter 7) and typically are represented as one byte (8 bits) per character. Other kinds of information must be coded somehow as sequences of binary digits in a process called **digitization**. For example, music can be coded as a sequence of binary numbers, each representing the height of the sound wave measured at particular sampling intervals. This is the way music is stored on audio CDs.

1.4 COMPUTER SOFTWARE

SYSTEM SOFTWARE is software that manages the computer system and consists primarily of the operating system (e.g., Windows 2000).

APPLICATION SOFTWARE are programs (e.g. Word 2000) that allow the computer to be applied to a specific task (i.e., word processing).

The OPERATING SYSTEM (OS) is a set of programs that manage the resources of the computer. When the computer is first turned on, it is the operating system that gets things started and presents the user interface that allows the user to choose what s/he wishes to do.

READ-ONLY MEMORY (ROM) is non-volatile memory that comes from the computer manufacturer loaded with a program called the bootstrap loader.

Software is often divided into two categories: system and application. **System software** refers to software that manages the computer system and consists primarily of the operating system, as in Windows 2000. **Application software** refers to programs like Word 2000 that allow the computer to be applied to a specific task such as word processing.

System Software

The **operating system (OS)** is a set of programs that manage the resources of the computer. When the computer is first turned on, it is the operating system that gets things started and presents a user interface that allows the user to choose what s/he wishes to do. The control unit starts fetching instructions from a special kind of memory called **read-only memory (ROM)**. This memory is nonvolatile and comes from the manufacturer loaded with a program called the **bootstrap loader**. This is a simple program that starts loading the operating system from the hard disk into RAM and then instructs the control unit to start fetching instructions of the operating system.

The operating system then checks out the system to make sure all components are functioning correctly and presents the user interface. This interface is the so-called **desktop**, which mimics an office desktop and consists of pictures called **icons** that symbolize the hard drive, file folders, and programs themselves. When the user indicates that s/he wishes to do word processing, the operating system loads the designated program into memory and then instructs the control unit to fetch instructions from it.

The operating system typically assists the application programs in doing common tasks such as reading from disk or drawing on the screen. It also keeps track of where files are located on the disk and handles the creation and deletion of files. When the user asks a word processing program such as Word to open a file, Word, in turn, asks the operating system to locate the file and load it into memory. When the user is editing the file, Word is simply modifying the copy in memory. This is why, if you don't save the file and your computer crashes or there is a power failure, you lose what you have done. Finally, when the user asks Word to save the file, Word requests this operation of the operating system. When the user quits Word, it instructs the control unit to continue fetching instructions from the operating system, which can then go on to a different task. When the user shuts down the computer, the operating system makes sure everything that must be remembered is written to disk and then shuts down.

Application Software

Application programs work with the operating system to apply the computer to specific tasks. The kinds of application programs available are only limited by programmers' imagination and, of course, market conditions. We have already mentioned one of the most common application programs—**word processing** programs such as Microsoft Word or Corel WordPerfect. These are designed primarily for creating text documents. Other applications include **spreadsheets** (as found in Microsoft Excel or Corel Quatro Pro), for doing numerical calculations such as balancing a checkbook and **database** systems (such as Microsoft Access, Corel Paradox, or Oracle), for keeping track of interrelated data such as student registration and grade information at a university. Although complex in their own right, application programs are written to require little knowledge of computer science on behalf of the user. Rather, the user must have significant **domain knowledge**, that is, knowledge of the area in which the program is applied.

SOFTWARE DEVELOPMENT ENVIRONMENTS (sometimes called interactive development environments, or IDEs) are programs that are used by programmers to write other programs. From one point of view, they are application programs because they apply the computer to the task of writing computer software. On the other hand, the users are computer scientists and the programming task is not the end in itself, but rather a means to apply the computer to other tasks. Often software development environments are grouped under the category of systems software.

Software Development Environments

There is one kind of program that doesn't fit well in the above categories. These are **software development environments**—the programs that are used by programmers to write other programs. From one point of view, they are application programs because they apply the computer to the task of writing computer software. On the other hand, the users are computer scientists and the programming task is not the end in itself, but rather a means to apply the computer to other tasks. Often software development environments are grouped under the category of systems software. We will talk more about software development environments later in this chapter when we talk about program preparation.

1.5 SOFTWARE DEVELOPMENT

Development of software (sometimes called software engineering) involves the analysis of a problem and the design and development of a computer program to apply the computer to that problem. We will study the software development process in detail in Chapter 9. In this section we give an overview of the process so we can begin developing simple programs.

As discussed earlier, a computer program is an algorithm expressed in a special notation called a programming language and an algorithm is a sequence of steps to achieve a specific task. To be effective, an algorithm must cover all the possibilities that might occur. It must be expressed unambiguously so that it is clear what must be done. The process must also terminate, that is, it cannot go on forever. When we develop programs, we must keep these requirements in mind.

Software Engineering

Development of large-scale software is a very complex task typically carried out by a team of software development professionals. Although there are a number of different methodologies for software development, they share common phases: analysis, design, coding, testing, debugging, production, and maintenance.

Before a software system can be developed, what is required must be clearly understood. This is the task of the analysis phase: to develop a requirements specification that clearly indicates what is (and sometimes what is not) required of the system. Although senior team members typically perform **analysis**, even in our early stages of learning computer science it will be important to be clear about what is to be done. Even if we develop a fabulous system, if it is not what was required, it was a wasted effort.

> In software development, **ANALYSIS** is the process of determining what is actually required of a proposed software system.
>
> **DESIGN** is the phase in software development in which decisions are made about how the software system will be implemented in a programming language.

Design is the determination of an approach to solving the problem. Again, this is typically done by senior team members and involves dividing the problem into a number of pieces that will be developed by individual team members. Even when we are developing small programs, it will be important to decide on an approach and to break the task up into smaller, easily manageable tasks to allow us to come to a solution in reasonable time.

Coding is the actual expression of an algorithm in a programming language. Here the programmers (now including the more junior team members) tackle the individual pieces of the problem as set out in the design and develop a solution. We will spend most of our time discussing this phase; it is necessary if we are going to carry out any of the others, so we learn it first.

CODING is the phase of software development in which the classes defined in the design phase are implemented in a programming language.

TESTING is the phase of software development in which the implemented classes are executed, individually and in groups, to determine whether they meet the specifications.

When a class or program doesn't perform according to specification it is said to contain a bug. **DEBUGGING** is the phase of software development in which it is determined why the class(es) fail and the problem is corrected.

PRODUCTION is the phase of software development in which the developed system has been tested and debugged and is made available to the user community.

MAINTENANCE is the phase of software development in which bugs detected in the field are corrected and new features are analyzed and implemented.

When a system has been developed, we want it to perform as specified in the analysis. How do we know it will? This is the responsibility of **testing** (one of the most overlooked phases of development—just consider some of the software you have used). Each part of the system, starting with the individual pieces developed by the programmers, must be tested to see that it functions according to the design. The pieces are then combined to build up the system, which must ultimately be tested to see that it conforms to the requirements specification. Whenever we develop a program, even if it is a simple program as an assignment in our first programming course, we must test the program to ensure that it does what is required.

Unfortunately, since we are all human, programs don't usually perform as they are required to on the first try. This is where **debugging** comes in. When, in testing, it is determined that the program doesn't do what was expected, we must correct the problem. The problem can arise from a number of sources, including: not really understanding what is to be done, not fully understanding the details of some feature of a programming language, or an invalid assumption or oversight in our development of the algorithm. Careful design of the tests that we use in testing can help us pinpoint the error and ultimately correct it.

Finally, the system does what it is intended to do (or at least what we are convinced it does). Now the system is released to the people who are expected to use it (the users). This phase is called **production**.

But it doesn't end here! Even the most carefully designed and tested software will contain undetected errors (bugs). Users' requirements change. A system has to be made available on new hardware and operating systems. The phase in which the system is re-analyzed, re-designed, and re-coded, resulting in a new version of the system, is called **maintenance**. Typically, this phase is much longer that the phases leading up to it, so it is very important to perform the earlier phases with this in mind.

We will return to the software development process in more detail in Chapter 9, when we have a repertoire of programming constructs to draw on. However, the requirements of these phases will guide our steps to that point. Before we begin writing any program, we will try to have a clear understanding of what is required and a plan of how to approach the problem (analysis and design). We will look at techniques for determining exactly what it is our program is doing (or doing wrong) as we look at methods in Chapter 4 and control structures in Chapter 6. This is the start of debugging. We will consider the types of inputs to use in testing our programs when we introduce input and output in Chapter 5. Throughout, we will consider ways to make our programs easier to understand and thus to maintain, through the use of naming and documentation conventions. Through a disciplined approach, we will learn that complex software can be developed in reasonable time and with a minimum of undetected bugs—the primary goals of all software developers.

Programming Languages

We generally use natural language such as English to express algorithms to other people. But English statements are often ambiguous and rely upon the listener's common sense and world knowledge. Since computers have no common sense, it is necessary to be unambiguous. For that reason, natural languages are not used for programming, but rather specially designed **computer programming languages** are used instead.

Generations of languages. Like computers themselves, computer programming languages have evolved through a number of generations. At the beginning, programmers wrote their programs in **machine language** and each operation was written as a separate instruction as a sequence of binary digits. These early languages are known as the **first-generation languages**.

But writing long series of `0`s and `1`s was, at best, tedious. It was decided that the computer itself could help things if a program could be written that would automatically convert an algorithm written in a symbolic notation into machine language. Each operation (opcode) was given a name and the operands (addresses) were expressed as a combination of names and simple arithmetic operations. These **second-generation languages** were called **assembly languages**. A portion of a program written in assembly language is shown in Figure 1.3. Each assembly language instruction still corresponds to one machine operation; the difference from machine language is the use of symbols for the opcodes and addresses.

Since the computer does not understand assembly language, running the assembly-language program requires two phases: (1) translation of the **assembly program** into machine language (called **assembly**) and then (2) running of the resulting machine-language program (called **execution**).

> **MACHINE LANGUAGE** is a binary representation of the instructions understood by the control unit. Since the instructions are the way we communicate the algorithm to the computer, they form a language.
>
> In a second-generation language or **ASSEMBLY LANGUAGE** each operation (opcode) is represented by a name and the operands (addresses) are expressed as a combination of names and simple arithmetic operations. Each assembly language instruction still corresponds to one machine operation.
>
> **ASSEMBLY** is the process of translating the assembly language instructions into machine language prior to execution.
>
> When the machine language version of a program is being executed by the processor, we say the program is being **EXECUTED** (is in execution).

```
BEGIN:   MOV #MSG,R5
SEND:    MOVB(R5)+,R0
         EMT 341
         BCS .-2
         CMP R5,#MSG+5
         BNE SEND
         EMT 350
MSG:     .ASCII  /HELLO/
         END
```

FIGURE 1.3 Assembly language

An **ASSEMBLER** is the program that reads an assembly language program and produces and stores an equivalent machine language program.

The entire process is described in Figure 1.4. The cylinders represent information stored on disk. The rectangles indicate a machine-language program being executed by the CPU. In the assembly phase, a program called an **assembler** reads the assembly-language program, and then produces and stores an equivalent machine-language program. In the execution phase, the resulting machine-language program is loaded into memory and executed, reading its data and producing its results. Of course, once the program has been assembled (phase 1), it can be executed (phase 2) any number of times. In fact, the assembler itself may have been originally written in an assembly language and translated into machine language by another assembler.

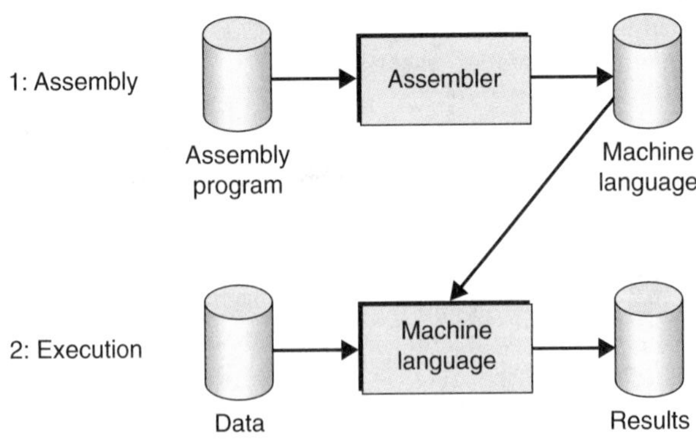

FIGURE 1.4 Executing an assembly-language program

A **LIBRARY** is a collection of pieces of previously written (and previously compiled) code saved on disk that can be used in building a program.

LINKING is the third phase in program preparation where pieces of machine-language code produced by a compiler or assembler are combined with machine code from libraries.

A **COMPILER** is a program that translates (compiles) a program written in a high-level language into machine language.

A **SOURCE PROGRAM** (source code) is the original program written in a high-level language that is being compiled.

OBJECT CODE is the machine-language code produced by compiling a high-level language program.

Although they were a significant improvement over machine language, assembly languages were still tedious for writing programs. Thousands of instructions had to be written to do the simplest things. What was needed was a more natural language. The new languages that were designed allowed the development of programs for specific application domains such as scientific and business processing. These languages are called **problem-oriented languages** or simply **high-level languages** and are the **third generation** of languages.

As programs get bigger, it is more efficient to build them up using pieces of previously written and previously compiled code saved in **libraries**. The program that puts the pieces together is called a **linker**. Again, since the computer doesn't understand the high-level language, a translating program called a **compiler** is needed. The compiler translates (compiles) a single high-level language instruction into many machine-language instructions.

The process of executing a high-level language program is shown in Figure 1.5. In phase 1, the compiler compiles the **source program** written in a high-level language into machine-language code called **object code**. In phase 2, the linker combines the object code and code stored in libraries into executable code in machine language. Finally, in phase 3, the resulting machine-language code is

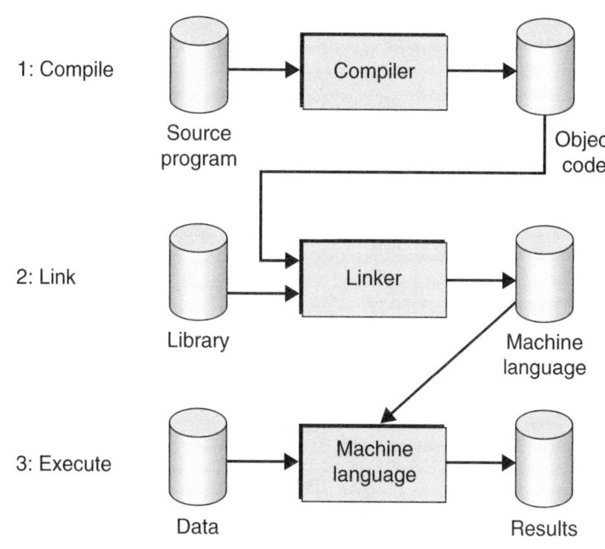

FIGURE 1.5 Executing a high-level language program

executed. As for assembly, the compile and link phases can be done once, in advance, and then the execution phase can be repeated whenever the program is to be run. This is exactly what happens when you execute an application program like Word 2000. The previously compiled and linked code is simply loaded into memory by the operating system and executed. In fact, the only code that is distributed is the machine-language code.

As we will see in Chapter 2, the execution of a Java program is a bit different from this typical model for high-level languages. This is due to Java's requirement for platform independence. However, the phases of program processing are essentially the same for Java as for other languages.

From FORTRAN to Java. Hundreds of high-level languages have been developed since the 1950s for a variety of different application domains. The first high-level language to have widespread use was FORTRAN (short for **for**mula **tran**slation system). Released in 1954 by IBM, FORTRAN was designed for scientific (mathematical) programming and allowed mathematical formulas to be written in a notation similar to that used in algebra. COBOL (**co**mmon **b**usiness-**o**riented **l**anguage), developed in 1959, was designed specifically for business applications. The 1960 definition of the language ALGOL (**algo**rithmic **l**anguage) was the first to include a formal mathematical language specification. Pascal, developed by N. Wirth in 1968, was designed to support teaching good programming techniques in computer science. C was designed in 1972 as a systems programming language and has become one of the most successful programming languages. Ada was developed in 1980 for the U.S. Department of Defense and named after Ada Augusta King, the first programmer. Java, our language of choice, was developed in 1990 at Sun Microsystems and has rapidly become the programming language of the Internet.

Producing executable code during program development involves a repeating sequence of operations—edit, compile, link, execute—called the **EDIT-COMPILE-LINK-EXECUTE CYCLE**.

Program Preparation

Once an algorithm has been developed in a high-level programming language, a number of steps must be completed to produce the desired executable code. This is called the **edit-compile-link-execute cycle**, consisting of four steps.

Step 1. The first step is **edit**. Here the programmer uses a special program called a program **editor** (similar to a word processor, but designed for programming languages instead of natural languages) to type in, correct, and save a source (high-level language) program.

Step 2. In the **compile** phase, a compiler is used to translate the program into object code. Often, the program hasn't been correctly expressed and contains errors in grammar known as **syntax errors**. If the compiler detects a syntax error, the programmer uses the editor to correct it and then recompiles the program.

Step 3. When the program is free of syntax errors, the linker is used to **link** the generated object code with library code. If a **link error** occurs, perhaps because a name has been mistyped, the programmer re-edits the source program, recompiles, and relinks.

Step 4. Once the program is successfully linked, the program is **execute**d to test that it does what is desired. The program may try to do things that are unreasonable (such as divide a number by zero), or it might execute but produce incorrect results. These situations are called **execution errors**, **logic errors**, or **bugs** and must be corrected, resulting in the source program being re-edited, recompiled, relinked, and finally executed again.

> Software development environments (sometimes called **INTERACTIVE DEVELOPMENT ENVIRONMENTS** or **IDEs**) are programs that are used by programmers to write other programs. From one point of view, they are application programs because they apply the computer to the task of writing computer software. On the other hand, the users are computer scientists and the programming task is not the end in itself, but rather a means to apply the computer to other tasks. Often software development environments are grouped under the category of systems software.

This cycle of edit-compile-link-execute continues until the programmer is satisfied that the resulting code works as desired. Since most real-world programs typically are composed of many separately developed pieces of code, the cycle begins again with another piece, and so on until the entire software system is completed.

Today, most programmers use software development environments or **interactive development environments (IDEs)** to perform the edit-compile-link-execute cycle. The IDE allows the system to be developed as a number of separately created pieces called files. When the programmer has modified one or more pieces, the IDE determines which pieces must be compiled and linked so that the system can be tested. This means that the programmer may not be aware of the complete cycle as it is occurring.

Programming is a time-consuming task that must be approached in a careful and structured manner to be successful. The rest of this book deals with this process.

*1.6 SOCIAL ISSUES

The use of computers has significantly changed our society. We have moved from the Industrial Age to the Information Age. Information is now one of our most valuable commodities. Few companies could survive the loss of their databases, and most go to great lengths to prevent unauthorized access. Information exists about each and every one of us in a variety of databases in government and industry. These changes have both their benefits and their liabilities.

The widespread use of computers has displaced many workers but, at the same time, has created many new jobs. Unfortunately, the jobs that have been displaced are typically low-skilled jobs, while the jobs created tend to require highly skilled workers. This creates a significant social problem that requires significant retraining of the workforce.

With the proliferation of database use, individual privacy is also a concern. There are vast quantities of information about every individual in a large number of databases. There are companies that will, for a fee, search public and private databases to compile a dossier about any particular individual. Credit bureaus search credit records to build financial profiles of applicants for credit cards, loans, and mortgages. While the data in individual databases may be reasonably innocuous, when combined with information in other databases, it is amazing how detailed a profile can be established.

Many people use electronic mail for daily communication both within companies and privately. When electronic mail is composed, a copy of the message is saved on the machine being used. This copy is then transmitted and copied on all machines from the originating machine to the receiving machine. Along the way, unscrupulous individuals may be able to access the message. For this reason, it is a good idea not to put in electronic mail anything that would be considered private. It is not even clear, legally, who owns the messages as they are transmitted from machine to machine. Some companies have successfully argued that, since they own the computers that employees' e-mail is saved on, they own the messages themselves and have the right to read them. E-mail has been used successfully in making a legal case against employees.

Most people also think that they can surf the Internet without concern of anyone determining where they have visited. This is also an unfounded assumption. When a web page is downloaded for viewing, the server knows where the page is being sent. This information could be used to build records of who has visited particular sites.

Another concern is electronic commerce. More and more, companies are providing Internet-based shopping. Since the messages requesting a purchase must, like e-mail messages, be transmitted across the Internet, it is possible that they could be intercepted. Including one's credit card number in an unsecured message is a very dangerous practice.

Currently, significant effort is being made to make Internet use more secure. Many companies are working to provide secure e-commerce and others are providing encryption facilities to ensure that only authorized individuals can read a message. As these facilities are put into place, many concerns about Internet use will be relieved.

Since the Internet allows anyone with a computer to provide information on the Net, there are the conflicting concerns about freedom of expression and censorship. Hate literature, pornography, and other normally prohibited information abounds on the Internet. Policing these areas is very difficult since the Internet crosses political boundaries and is under the control of no single jurisdiction. A related concern is bogus information being presented as factual. This has been a major problem in the public health area with fraudulent medical information mixing with valid information. In all of these scenarios, the individual must take responsibility. Sources of information taken from the Internet should be checked to ensure that they are valid. Programs exist to allow parents to prevent the Internet browser on their machines from accessing questionable sites unsuitable for their children. Schools are beginning to teach students how to use the Internet effectively and to separate the valid information from the bogus.

Another area of concern with the proliferation of computers as a distribution medium for information is intellectual property rights. It is very easy to make copies of anything recorded in digital form. This includes documents, pictures, videos, music, and, of course, programs themselves. Copyright laws have protected intellectual property in the past; however, they are not easily enforceable in an age when a perfect copy can be produced in seconds. Currently, **software piracy** (i.e., illegal copying of software) is reportedly costing software manufacturers billions of dollars every year. As more music and movies are available in digital format (such as CDs and DVDs), copying these without loss of quality is also easy and these industries are beginning to experience losses as well. New and different ways of ensuring that creators of intellectual property are able to benefit from their creations are required to deal with the new digital reality. One example is the law that will place a surcharge on blank recordable CDs with the proceeds being divided amongst the artists.

Computer use also has a direct effect on our quality of life. A number of health concerns have been associated with computer use, such as carpal tunnel syndrome and computer vision syndrome. Carpal tunnel syndrome and other repetitive strain injuries (RSI) are often the result of lengthy use of computing equipment. **Carpal tunnel syndrome** is an inflammation in the carpal tunnel—the small opening in the wrist through which the ligaments, blood vessels and nerves serving the hand pass. This inflammation places pressure on the nerves, causing tingling in the fingers and, in extreme cases, severe and unrelieved pain in the hand and wrist. Like most RSI injuries, carpal tunnel syndrome can be prevented through proper posture, supports such as a wrist rest, and frequent breaks and range-of-motion exercises during extended periods of computer use.

Computer vision syndrome occurs from extended viewing of a computer monitor. Computer monitors, like television screens, actually flicker or pulse at a fairly high frequency. This places considerable strain on the eyes and, after time, leads to headaches and eye fatigue. Proper lighting, monitor refresh frequencies, and rest periods help prevent this problem.

Internet addiction is becoming a mental health concern. There are many reported cases of individuals who have established a dependency on surfing the Web that is a true addition. Like any other addict, they suffer withdrawal if deprived of access and typically allow the rest of their lives, such as family and employment, to suffer in pursuit of their habit. Internet addiction must be treated the same way as any other psychological addition.

Computers also have an indirect effect on the environment. Computers require electrical power to function. Although each microcomputer does not draw significant amounts of power, the large number of PCs in use does place high demands on the power supply. Since power is not generated without environmental effects, reducing the power use of computers would have an environmental benefit. So-called **green PCs** are designed to reduce electrical consumption by, among other things, putting the monitor into a lower power stand-by mode when the computer display hasn't changed for a period and only rotating the disk drive when files are actually being accessed.

Since technology is changing at such a fast pace, computers become obsolete quite quickly. This leads to large numbers of microcomputers being taken out of service each year. If these obsolete computers are simply placed into landfill sites, this creates a significant problem. In addition to the amount of space used, computer hardware often contains materials that are hazardous to the environment. There are companies that recover materials from old computers to reduce the amount of material disposed and eliminate the hazardous material. Another technique is computer recycling. When a computer becomes obsolete for one purpose or user, it can often continue to be useful for a user with lower demands. Certain agencies will collect old computers and distribute them to other users, sometimes in third-world countries.

As a society, we rely heavily on computers to manage much of the information that makes our daily lives easier. We use services such as electronic banking and credit cards. Any threats to the correct functioning of these computers are potentially disastrous. The threats can be to the physical computers themselves or, and often more disastrous, to the data they store. Physical threats include things like power supply problems, natural disasters, civil strife, and criminal activity. Threats to data include errors, technological failures such as disk failure, and malicious damage.

Since most data is entered from a keyboard, there is a high likelihood of errors in data entry or **dirty data**. Frequent breaks for data entry clerks or direct data entry using scanners and other devices can help reduce this problem. Still, any data entered must be verified to ensure its validity.

Malicious damage is also a serious problem. A **virus** is a program that has been written by someone with considerable knowledge of an operating system. It can make copies of itself onto a floppy disk inserted into an infected machine or transmit itself along with a program being downloaded from the computer. Once on the machine, the effect of the virus can range from fairly benign, such as displaying a message on a particular date, to malicious, such as erasing the contents of the hard disk. Programs called **anti-virus software** exist that will check to see whether a computer is infected with a virus and remove it if it does not exist.

Security of data is also a concern. Computer criminals called **hackers** attempt to break into computer systems by guessing passwords to accounts and, once connected, can cause all manner of damage from simply stealing data to deleting or modifying it. This kind of crime can be very hard to detect or to trace once it is detected. Quite often the criminals are employees or ex-employees who have an "axe to grind" with a particular company. Improved security measures, in the form of both physical and restricted accessibility, are the best solution to these problems. Computer crime is frequent and costly enough that most large police jurisdictions have specialists dealing with computer crime.

Widespread computer use is a two-edged sword. While it has provided many advantages that we now take for granted—and many new advances are on the horizon—there has also been significant social impact. Being aware of the potential problems is one way to prevent them. Professionals and organizations must subscribe to a code of ethics in computer use. Governments must enact appropriate laws to ensure the privacy and security of personal information.

SUMMARY

In this chapter we have seen that computers as we know them have a brief history (from the 1940s to the present day). However, algorithms and computing devices date back to the time of the Greeks and to the early part of the last millennium, respectively. Modern computers can be classified into four generations based on the technology used for their primary electronic components.

Computer systems are comprised of a number of parts including hardware and software. Although computer hardware can be classified by size and power into categories from microcomputers to supercomputers, the five functional hardware components are still the same. All information in a computer is represented, in some manner, using the binary number system. The instructions that control the computer, represented in a binary code, are called the machine language of the computer. Computer software is classified into system software and application software.

Our primary emphasis in this text is on software development. Software engineering typically involves a seven-phase process, only one phase of which is programming (coding). Modern computer systems are written in high-level programming languages that must be translated into machine language so that computers may understand the instructions. A programmer follows a four-step cycle (edit-compile-link-execute) to proceed from concept to an executable program in machine language.

REVIEW QUESTIONS

1. T F Second-generation computers are based on integrated circuits.
2. T F A mainframe computer would likely be used for an airline reservation system.
3. T F Main memory is for long-term storage.
4. T F Digitization is the process of encoding information into binary.
5. T F The bootstrap loader is stored in the CD-ROM drive.

6. T F Domain knowledge is knowledge in the area of application of the application software.
7. T F An e-mail message can be considered as secure as a letter mailed through the post office.
8. T F Encryption is used on many e-commerce sites.
9. T F Assembly language is a first-generation language.
10. T F FORTRAN is a second-generation language.
11. Which of the following is **not** associated with Charles Babbage?
    a) Analytical Engine b) Plankalkül
    c) Ada Augusta King d) Difference Engine
12. Which of the following is **not** a basic hardware component?
    a) CU b) IDE
    c) RAM d) ALU
13. The Arithmetic/Logic Unit (ALU) is responsible for:
    a) controlling the other units. b) doing arithmetic.
    c) decoding instructions. d) both a and c.
16. Which of the following is not normally considered application software?
    a) word processor b) compiler
    c) spreadsheet d) e-mail program
17. Dirty data is:
    a) data that has been read by a hacker.
    b) the method used by a virus to transmit itself.
    c) information obtained from an illegal web site.
    d) data that has been incorrectly entered.
18. The first programming language was:
    a) FORTRAN. b) BASIC.
    c) Plankalkül. d) Ada.
19. The program that translates a high-level programming language program into machine language is called:
    a) an assembler. b) a translator.
    c) a compiler. d) a linker.
20. The program development cycle consists of the following phases:
    a) edit, compile, link, execute b) open, edit, run, save
    c) design, code, compile, debug d) try, bomb, cry, recover

EXERCISES

1. From your instructor or the computing center at your institution, obtain documentation on the use of the computer systems in the laboratories you will be using in this course. Learn how to obtain access to the Internet, send and receive e-mail, and how and where to save your work on your programming assignments.

2. Using the library, the Internet, and reference books, write a brief biography of some of the following important individuals in the history of computing:

Charles Babbage	Ada Augusta King	Allan Turing	John von Neumann
John Backus	Grace Hopper	Allan Kay	James Gosling

3. From the box cover, reference manual, or online documentation, determine the version and release number and the hardware requirements for one of the pieces of software available in the laboratory or on your home computer. The software might be a word processor, Java compiler, or Internet browser.

4. Using the library, the Internet, and reference books, research one of the following issues of computer use:

privacy laws	repetitive strain injuries (RSI)	computer crime

2

Java Programs

CHAPTER OBJECTIVES

- To gain a reading knowledge of the notation for describing Java syntax.
- To become familiar with writing a program as a client of a library class.
- To be able to write programs to do graphics using Turtle Graphics.
- To recognize the fundamental parts of a class definition.
- To be able to write a class as a main class of a program.
- To make use of a countable repetition loop to provide repetition in a program.
- To use composition or nesting to produce programs of increased sophistication.
- To understand how Java programs are executed while providing platform independence.

This book is primarily about the construction of computer programs. As we have seen, computers only understand programs expressed in their natural language—machine language (a system of `0`s and `1`s). This notation is, however, very difficult for human programmers to use for writing programs, so high-level or problem-oriented languages were developed. Java is one such language, and we will use Java to express our programs.

2.1 JAVA

A programming language is not a natural language that has evolved, like English, but rather one defined for a specific purpose—writing computer programs. However, like any language, Java has grammatical rules that must be followed. So that all those involved in Java programming, from compiler writers to programmers, have a clear understanding of the rules, these rules are expressed in a formal notation. To help us fully understand Java, we will learn to read this notation. We will then begin our main task, learning to write Java programs.

Java: Platform Independent

Java was developed at the beginning of the 1990s by James Gosling *et al.* at Sun Microsystems. Initially, the language (then called Oak) was to be used for the development of consumer electronics, especially set-top boxes for interactive television. Such systems are usually what are called **embedded systems**, in which the software is just one part of a larger system. Commonly, as market conditions change, these systems require a change of processor. Since each different processor has its own machine language, an early design criterion for Java was **platform independence**. That is, the code generated by the Java compiler would be able to run on any processor. This feature is now called "write-once-run-anywhere" and allows us to write our Java code on a Macintosh or PC (or other machine) and then run it on whatever machine we desire.

> **PLATFORM INDEPENDENCE** is the property that the code generated by a compiler (e.g., Java) can run on any processor.
>
> An **APPLET** is special kind of Java program that runs within a browser (e.g., Internet Explorer) and provides the executable content to a web page.

Java happened to come along at about the same time as a new use of the Internet: the World Wide Web. A web browser, such as Netscape Navigator, might run on any machine and download a web page from a server (another, possibly different, kind of machine). The browser would then display the page. A platform-independent language called HTML describes the web page. Originally, web pages were static and simply showed text and graphics like a page in a printed book. However, it was soon realized that dynamic content—pages with which the viewer could interact—would be much more interesting. What was needed was a programming language whose code could run on any machine. Java was an obvious answer. A special kind of Java program (called an **applet**) runs within a browser and provides the executable content.

This has lead to a great deal interest and a lot of hype about Java as the programming language for the Web.

Java: A Modern Language

Our interest in Java is neither as a web programming language nor as a language for embedded consumer electronics, but as a general application programming language. Java was designed to be a modern language. As such, it embodies the object-oriented paradigm of programming. It was also designed to be simple and safe. Like C++, it borrows from the programming language C much of its structure, but it has also improved many of the features that make C++ difficult to use. This makes it a good language for learning computer programming as well as a reasonable language for application development.

In **OBJECT-ORIENTED PROGRAMMING**, a program is designed to be a model of the real-world system it is replacing.

In **object-oriented programming**, a program is designed to be a model of the real-world system it is replacing. The program contains **objects** that represent real-world entities (such as customers, students, reports, and financial transactions) that interact with each other. Many useful objects are provided in libraries to reduce the code that a programmer has to write. In our initial programs we will simply write the code describing one object and make use of other objects from the libraries. Later we will develop larger programs that use many objects, some from libraries and some that we write ourselves.

Drawing a Square

Figure 2.1 shows a listing of a simple program that uses a drawing environment called Turtle Graphics to draw a square. In doing so, it makes use of an object called a `Turtle` from the `TurtleGraphics` library. The object we develop is called a `Square`; it draws a square. To the left of this program listing is a series of numbers. These are not part of the program itself, but are simply for our reference in the description that follows.

A **COMMENT** is a piece of commentary text included within the program text that is not processed by the compiler but serves to help a reader understand the program segment.

In a Java program, we must specify the libraries that we are going to use. This is the function of the `import` statement in line 1. Since programs are meant to be read by people as well as by a compiler, the language allows **comments** to be included within the program text (lines 4–8 and 16). **Comments** begin with the characters `/**` (as in line 4) and end with the pair `*/` (as in line 8). A second form of comment is found on lines 13, 32, and 38. This kind of comment begins with the pair of characters `//` and ends at the end of the line. The compiler ignores all comments when translating the program into machine code. Additionally, for the convenience of the human reader, **white space**—empty lines such as lines 2, 3, 9, 11, and 12 and tabs for indentation—may be inserted as desired.

The actual specification of the `Square` object spans lines 10 through 38. The `Square` makes use of a `Turtle` object, which we name `yertle` (line 13). The

```
import TurtleGraphics.*;


/** This program uses TurtleGraphics to draw a square.
 **
 ** @version1.0 (May 2001)
 **
 ** @author D. Hughes                                       */

public class Square {


    private Turtle  yertle;      // turtle for drawing


    /** The constructor draws a square using TurtleGraphics. */

    public Square ( ) {

        yertle = new Turtle();
        yertle.penDown();
        yertle.forward(40);
        yertle.right(Math.PI/2);
        yertle.forward(40);
        yertle.right(Math.PI/2);
        yertle.forward(40);
        yertle.right(Math.PI/2);
        yertle.forward(40);
        yertle.right(Math.PI/2);
        yertle.penUp();

    };  // constructor


    public static void main ( String args[] ) { new Square(); };


}   // Square
```

FIGURE 2.1 Example—Draw a square

A software system (program) **TERMINATES** when it is no longer executing (i.e. being executed by the CPU).

execution of the program consists of the creation of a new `Square` object (line 35). Once created, the `Square` object does its task (lines 18–32), creating the `Turtle` object (line 20), and then asks `yertle` to draw the lines making up the sides of the square (lines 21–30). When this is complete, the program itself has finished execution (**terminates**).

Java Syntax

A programming language is a mechanism for communication similar to a natural language such as English. Of course, in English the communication is usually between two people. In computer programming the communication is between a person, the programmer, and a computer program, the compiler.

To allow clear, unambiguous communication, certain rules must be followed. In a natural language these rules are called grammatical rules, which we all learned formally or informally as we learned the language. These rules specify how we may use words, punctuation, and other basic elements of the language to compose sentences. They specify, for example, that a sentence must have a subject and a verb and may have an object. They also specify that a period must be placed at the end of an imperative sentence. Implicit from the construction of the sentence and the actual words used is the meaning of the sentence.

The **SYNTAX** of a programming language specifies how the basic elements of the language (tokens, e.g. identifiers, keywords, and punctuation) are used to compose programs. It is described by a set of rules called syntax rules or grammar.

The **SEMANTICS** of a programming language specifies the meaning (i.e., effect of executing the program) of a correctly composed program.

Similarly, a programming language has a set of grammatical rules (its syntax) and a set of rules about meaning (its semantics). The **syntax** specifies how the basic elements of the language are used to compose programs. In Figure 2.1 the syntax specifies the placement of identifiers (names) like `yertle`, keywords like `class`, and punctuation like `;` and `)` in the program. The **semantics** specifies the effect of the program when it is executed.

The grammar of Java is expressed in *The Java Language Specification*[1] using a formal notation. In this notation, the grammar is described by a set of rules. At the beginning of the rule there is a word followed by a colon (such as *`sentence`*`:` in Figure 2.2). This is the name of the rule. Following this line are one or more lines representing alternatives. Each alternative consists of a sequence of words and symbols that are to be written in order. Words written in italics are names of other rules. Words and symbols written in plain font may be of three types: (1) **punctuation**, such

[1]Gosling, J., Joy, B. & Steele, G.; *The Java™ Language Specification*; Addison-Wesley; Reading, MA; 1996.

```
sentence:
      subject verb object .
subject:
      noun-phrase
object:
      noun-phrase
noun-phrase:
      article noun
      noun
verb:
      likes
      has
article:
      a
      the
noun:
      John
      Mary
      book
      Java
```

FIGURE 2.2 Simplified English grammar syntax

as `;`, (2) **keywords**, such as `class`, that have a specific meaning and are defined by the language, and (3) **identifiers**, such as `yertle`—words coined by the programmer.

As an example, the rules in Figure 2.2 specify a simple English grammar.

The grammar specifies that a *sentence* consists of a *subject,* followed by a *verb,* followed by an *object,* followed by a period. A *subject* can be a *noun phrase*, as can an *object*. A *noun phrase* can be either an *article* followed by a *noun* or just a *noun*. A *verb* is one of the words `likes` or `has`. An *article* is one of the words `a` or `the`. Finally, a *noun* is one of the words `John`, `Mary`, `book`, or `Java`. An English sentence can be composed (**derived**) by writing sequences of symbols, starting with the name of the first rule, `sentence`. The derivation proceeds by substituting and alternative for a rule name, until there are no rule names left. Figure 2.3 demonstrates the derivation of the sentence "`John has a book.`" according to this grammar.

This grammar can be used to derive a number of sentences, including those in Figure 2.4. Not all of these are meaningful sentences. The semantic rules of the language would specify which are meaningful and what those meanings would be.

```
sentence
subject verb object .
noun-phrase verb object .
noun verb object .
John verb object .
John has object .
John has noun-phrase .
John has article noun .
John has a noun .
John has a book .
```

FIGURE 2.3 Example—Derivation of an English sentence

```
John likes a John .
John likes a Mary .
John likes a book .
John likes a Java .
John likes the John .
John likes the Mary .
John likes the book .
John likes the Java .
John likes John .
John likes Mary .
John likes book .
John likes Java .
       ⋮
```

FIGURE 2.4 Example—English sentences

To make the rules a little easier to write (and read), a few notational conveniences are used. A rule of the form:

```
noun-phrase:
        article noun
        noun
```

may be written as:

```
noun-phrase:
        article_opt noun
```

where the subscript *opt* following the name *article* means that the inclusion of *article* is optional. A rule of the form:

```
noun:
        John
        Mary
        book
        Java
```

may be written as:

```
noun: one of
        John Mary book Java
```

where the special phrase *one of* written on the first line of a rule means that the symbols on the following line are really alternatives. Finally, a very long alternative can be written on more than one line, with the subsequent lines indented substantially.

Within the Java syntax definition, there are rules of the following form:

```
SomeUnits:
        SomeUnit
        SomeUnits SomeUnit
```

This kind of rule implies that one or more occurrences of *SomeUnit* may be written. If just the first alternative is used, one instance of *SomeUnit* occurs. If the second alternative is used first followed by the first alternative, two instances occur, and so forth. In this book, to make the rules simpler to read, these rules will be omitted and the existence of a plural symbol will imply one or more occurrences of the symbol.

The complete set of syntax rules for Java is collected in Appendix B.

2.2 TURTLE GRAPHICS

Turtle Graphics was first introduced with the language Logo.[2] The metaphor is that there is a turtle that is sitting on a piece of paper, holding a pen. The turtle can be instructed to move either forward or backward, to turn left or right, or to place the pen on the paper or lift it from the paper. If the turtle moves with the pen on the paper, a line is drawn. This motion provides a basic drawing (graphics) facility.

A library package called `TurtleGraphics` has been created to provide this facility in Java. It is not one of the standard Java packages, but rather was defined to provide a framework for introduction to programming in this book. The complete specification of the `Turtle` class (the only class in the `TurtleGraphics` library) can be found in Appendix D.

To use the Turtle Graphics facility, the `TurtleGraphics` package must first be imported (line 1 in Figure 2.1). A `Turtle` object may be declared (line 13) and then created (line 20), having its own pen and paper.

[2] Abelson, H. & diSessa, A.A.; *Turtle Geometry*; MIT Press; Cambridge, Mass; 1980.

TABLE 2.1 Turtle methods

Method	Meaning
`penDown()`	Place the pen on the paper
`penUp()`	Raise the pen from the paper
`forward(units)`	Move forward number of `units`
`backward(units)`	Move backward number of `units`
`left(radians)`	Turn left number of `radians`
`right(radians)`	Turn right number of `radians`

The turtle starts out in the middle of the page facing to the right with the pen up. Subsequently, the turtle may be directed to place the pen down on the paper (line 21) and to move forward (line 22) a certain number of drawing units (the number in parentheses; the page is 200 drawing units square), causing a line to be drawn.

The turtle is directed to turn to the right (line 23) some number of radians. A radian is a unit of measure of rotation around a circle. There are 2π radians around a complete circle. A right-angled turn (1/4 around a circle) is thus $\pi/2$ and is expressed in Java as `Math.PI/2`.

After drawing the other three sides of the square (lines 24–29), the turtle is directed to lift the pen from the paper (line 30). The requests to which a turtle will respond are summarized in Table 2.1.

The result of executing the `Square` program of Figure 2.1 is the window shown in Figure 2.5.

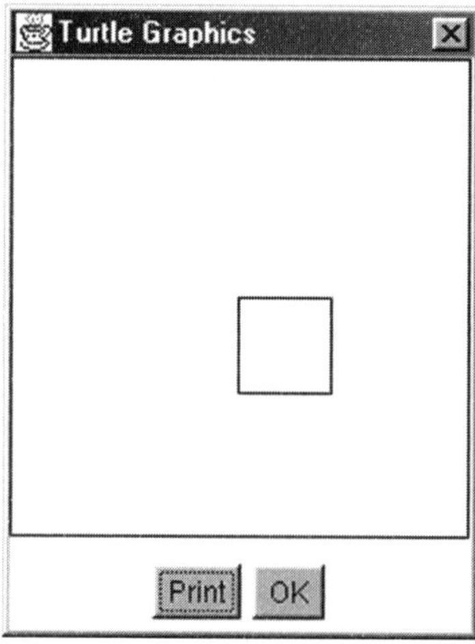

FIGURE 2.5 A square

2.3 CLASSES

Classes are the fundamental building blocks in object-oriented programming. Each represents some kind of entity in the real-world system that the program is modeling. In Java, a program is a collection of classes (including those written by the author and those from libraries). The square program consists of two classes: the class `Square`, as written, and the class `Turtle`, as imported from the `TurtleGraphics` library.

> **CLASSES** are the fundamental building blocks in object-oriented programming.
>
> A **CLASS DECLARATION** is the specification of a class in a Java program that defines a set of possible objects.
>
> A **CONSTRUCTOR** a sequence of steps to be performed when a new object is created in order to initialize the object to a valid state.

In Java the syntactic unit we write and have the compiler compile is a **class declaration**. A class declaration serves to define a set of possible objects. Think of the class name as a generic noun like dog or house. These nouns describe the set of all possible objects (dogs, houses). Actual objects that will be used in a program such as my dog Rover are created from this declaration through the use of a **constructor** (line 20 of Figure 2.1, creating a new `Turtle` object, and line 35, creating a new `Square` object). It is these actual objects that interact to perform the tasks required of the program. In this simple program to draw a square, there is only one of each kind of object—one `Turtle` and one `Square`. However, in larger systems, there may be many kinds of objects and many of each kind.

A class declaration is the only unit that the compiler will compile. All code we write will be contained in some class.

STYLE TIP

Preceding a class declaration, we write a comment to describe the class. This makes it easier for other programmers to figure out what the class does. There is a special kind of comment called a JavaDoc comment, which begins with `/**` and ends with a `*/`. As far as the compiler is concerned, this is just a comment—it begins with `/*`. However, there is a special program called JavaDoc that reads a program containing this kind of comment and automatically produces web-based documentation for a program such as that found in Appendix E for the Brock packages.

The comment preceding a class should include a description of what the class represents and then some additional special lines. The line beginning with `@version` should indicate the version number of the class (see Section 9.1) and the date it was last modified. The line beginning with `@author` should list the author(s) name(s).

A simplified version of the syntax of a class declaration is given in Figure 2.6. Following this syntax, the class declaration for `Square` begins with an optional *`Modifier`*. **Modifiers** describe properties of classes, such as where they may be used. This is called **scope** and is described in Chapter 4. In this case, `public` means that the class may be used by other classes.

> **MODIFIERS** describe properties of classes, such as where they may be used.

Look back at Figure 2.1. The modifier `public` in line 10 is followed by the keyword `class`. Next is *`Identifier`*—a word cho-

SYNTAX

```
ClassDeclaration:
      Modifiers_opt class Identifier ClassBody
ClassBody:
      { ClassBodyDeclarations_opt }
ClassBodyDeclaration:
      ConstructorDeclaration
      FieldDeclaration
      MethodDeclaration
```

FIGURE 2.6 Class declaration

A **CLASS BODY** is an optional sequence of one or more lines enclosed in braces.

sen by the programmer to serve as the name of something. Here it is the name of the class (`Square` in line 10). Finally, a class body appears. A **class body** is an optional sequence of one or more *`ClassBodyDeclarations`* (lines 11–37), enclosed in braces (see `{` and `}` in lines 10 and 38). The *`ClassBodyDeclarations`* consist of a *`FieldDeclaration`* (line 13), a *`ConstructorDeclaration`* (lines 18–32), and a *`MethodDeclaration`* (line 35). We will not discuss the method declaration at this time. Every program will include a line similar to line 35, which serves to create one object of the class being written. This, in turn, executes the constructor for the object, which is where the actual work of the program is done.

STYLE TIP

In Java, identifiers are sequences of letters, digits, and the underscore character (_). An identifier must begin with a letter and must not be the same as a reserved word (see Appendix B). Identifiers are case sensitive, that is, the case of the letters used is significant. Identifiers with the same letters, but in different cases, are considered to be different identifiers.

Identifiers are used to name many things in Java including classes, variables (see Section 3.3), and methods (see Section 4.2). By convention, class identifiers are nouns or noun phrases and begin with an uppercase letter. The remaining characters are lowercase, except for the first letter of subsequent words in the phrase, which are uppercase. For example, the following might be class names:

```
Square    Student    SalariedEmployee
```

Identifiers should be descriptive but should not be excessively long.

Constructors

Objects can be considered intelligent entities that have a memory and can perform tasks requested of them. When they begin life (are created), they start out doing something. In Java, we specify this initial activity using a **constructor declaration**. A simplified version of a constructor declaration is given in Figure 2.7.

SYNTAX

ConstructorDeclaration:
    Modifiers$_{opt}$ *ConstructorDeclarator ConstructorBody*

ConstructorDeclarator:
    Identifier (*FormalParameterList*$_{opt}$)

ConstructorBody:
    { *BlockStatements*$_{opt}$ }

FIGURE 2.7 Constructor declaration syntax

In our program, the constructor for the `Square` class is found in Figure 2.1 in lines 18–32. The *`Modifier`* is the keyword `public`. As for classes, modifiers can be used to indicate the properties of a constructor. The modifier `public` indicates that the constructor can be used by other classes. Next is the *`Identifier`* `Square` naming the constructor. A constructor always has the same name as the class itself. The *`FormalParameterList`* is omitted, and so there is an empty pair of parentheses following the identifier. Finally, there is an optional sequence of *`BlockStatements`* enclosed in braces (lines 20–30). These are called the **body** of the constructor.

The **BODY** of a constructor or method is the sequence of statements that specify the action of the constructor or method.

When a new `Square` object is created (line 35), the statements in the constructor body are executed (performed) in turn. In our case, this accounts for the complete execution of the program.

STYLE TIP

If you consider Figure 2.1, you will see that the constructor header is indented one tab from the left margin where the class declaration starts. Similarly, the statements in the constructor body are indented two tab positions—one more than the constructor header. The closing brace of the constructor body is indented just one tab, so that it aligns with the constructor header. All this makes it easy to see where the constructor begins and ends.

A constructor declaration is preceded by a comment, in JavaDoc style, describing the effect of the constructor. Placing a comment (using //) on the closing brace that is the end of the constructor body also helps pinpoint the end of the body.

Fields

Every object has a memory and can "remember things." This memory is represented in Java by some number of fields. In Figure 2.1 there is only one field; it is declared in line 13. A **field** can be a reference to another object, just as a person object can remember a friend who is also a person object. A field can also remember a value. For example, a person can remember their height of 180 cm. Our `Square` objects can remember the

A **FIELD** is a named memory location in which an object can store information. Typically, it is an instance variable.

SYNTAX

```
FieldDeclaration:
    Modifiers_opt Type Identifier ;
```

FIGURE 2.8 Field declaration syntax

An **INSTANCE VARIABLE** is a field of a class that is declared without the modifier `static`. It represents a storage location that the object (instance of a class) uses to remember information. Each object (instance) has its own memory (instance variables).

`Turtle` they are using to draw the square. A simplified form of a **field declaration** is given in Figure 2.8.

In line 13 of Figure 2.1, the *`Modifier`* is the keyword `private`. This means that the field cannot be used by other classes. The `Type` is the class name `Turtle`, indicating that a `Turtle` object is being remembered. Finally, the `Identifier` is the name `yertle`. The field declaration states that each `Square` object remembers a `Turtle` object by the name `yertle`. Fields that are declared without using the modifier `static` are called **instance variables**. Thus `yertle` is an instance variable.

STYLE TIP

Again, looking at Figure 2.1, you will notice that instance variable declarations are indented one tab from the left margin to mark them as being contained in the class declaration. A comment (using //) is placed at the end of the declaration, describing what the instance variable represents.

Instance variable identifiers are, by convention, nouns or noun phrases, and begin with a lowercase letter. Each subsequent word in the identifier begins in uppercase.

Statements

A **STATEMENT** is the specification of a single action within a program.

A **statement** is the specification of some action to be performed. In our program, there are two kinds of statements: one assignment (Figure 2.1, line 20) and ten method invocations (lines 21–30). An **assignment** has the syntax given in Figure 2.9. In line 20, the *`LeftHandSide`* is the instance variable `yertle` and the *`AssignmentExpression`* is the invocation of the `Turtle` constructor, creating a new `Turtle` object (`new Turtle()`). An assignment statement is the way an object commits something to memory. In this case, the `Square` is remembering a new `Turtle` object by the name `yertle`.

SYNTAX

```
Assignment:
    LeftHandSide = AssignmentExpression
```

FIGURE 2.9 Assignment syntax

SYNTAX

```
MethodInvocation:
        Primary . Identifier ( ArgumentList_opt )
```

FIGURE 2.10 Method invocation syntax

A **method invocation** is the way that an object asks another object to perform some operation. The syntax is given in Figure 2.10. *`Primary`* is the instance variable referring to the object that is being asked to perform the operation. (In each of lines 21–30, this is the `Turtle` object named `yertle`.) Following the period is the name (*`Identifier`*) of the method that the object is being asked to perform (for example, `penDown`, `forward`). Also, there is an optional *`ArgumentList`* enclosed in parentheses. For methods that require no additional information, like `penDown` and `penUp`, this list is omitted and only the parentheses are written. For methods that require additional information, such as a distance to move for `forward` and `backward` or an amount of rotation for `left` or `right`, this value is supplied as the *`ArgumentList`* inside the parentheses.

2.4 LOOPING—THE COUNTABLE REPETITION PATTERN

The example in Figure 2.1 is about as simple as a Java program can get. However, it can be made shorter. Notice that lines 22–29 are repetitious; the same pair of statements is repeated four times to draw the four sides of a square. There is a mechanism in Java called a **loop** that allows us to repeatedly execute a sequence of statements. The statement we will use is a `for` statement (see Section 6.4). The complete syntax of the `for` statement is fairly complex so we won't describe it here. However, we can describe one particular pattern of use of the `for` as our first programming pattern in Figure 2.11.

A **LOOP** is a sequence of statements that is repeated either a specific number of times or until some condition occurs.

A **programming pattern** is a commonly used pattern of programming language statements that solves some particular kind of problem. It serves as a guide to writing some part of a program. The items written in plain font are written as-is, and those items in italics are replaced as needed according to the particular problem at hand.

The countable repetition pattern is a loop that repeats some operation(s) a definite number of times. To make use of the pattern, the number of repetitions is substituted for *`times`* and the statements representing the sequence of operations to be repeated is

Programming Pattern

```
for ( index=1 ; index<=times ; index++ ) {
    statementList
};
```

FIGURE 2.11 Countable repetition programming pattern

substituted for *statementList*. Additionally, a new int variable (we will define what this is later) must be declared and its name substituted for *index*. To make use of this pattern to draw a square, the number of times is 4, and the statements to be repeated are the forward and the right turn. We will use a variable called i as the index. With the substitutions we have:

```
for ( i=1 ; i<=4 ; i++ ) {
    yertle.forward(40);
    yertle.right(Math.PI/2);
};
```

The effect of this use of the pattern is that the pair of method invocations (forward, right) are executed four times in succession. Putting this together into a program gives us a second version of the square program in Figure 2.12.

```
import TurtleGraphics.*;

/** This program uses TurtleGraphics and a for statement to draw a
 ** square.
 **
 ** @version 1.0 (May 2001)
 **
 ** @author D. Hughes                                              */

public class Square2 {


    private Turtle  yertle;      // turtle for drawing


    /** The constructor draws a square using TurtleGraphics.    */

    public Square2 ( ) {

        int i;

        yertle = new Turtle();
        yertle.penDown();
        for ( i=1 ; i<=4 ; i++ ) {
            yertle.forward(40);
            yertle.right(Math.PI/2);
        };
        yertle.penUp();

    };  // constructor


    public static void main ( String args[] ) { new Square2(); };


}   // Square2
```

FIGURE 2.12 Example—Draw a square using a countable repetition pattern

This program is essentially the same as the one in Figure 2.1. The class name has been changed to `Square2` in the class declaration, constructor, and constructor invocation. (Actually, this isn't necessary since we can call a class anything we like. The only reason for the change is to differentiate it from the previous version.) The countable repetition pattern has been substituted for the sequence of pairs of `forward`, `right`. The only other change is the inclusion of a declaration of the index variable (`i`) at the beginning of the constructor. We will discuss variable declarations in Section 3.3. The output of this program is exactly the same as shown in Figure 2.5.

Drawing a Hexagon

The principle of Figure 2.12 can be used to draw any regular closed figure (such as a hexagon or octagon). Basically, we have some number of sides to draw (via `forward`) each rotated from each other by some angle (via `right`). The angles between the sides essentially have to make a complete rotation (2π radians), so the angle is just 2π divided by the number of sides ($2\pi/6$ or $\pi/3$ for a hexagon). We can draw the figure by repeating the pair of method invocations the proper number of times (six for a hexagon). Figure 2.13 uses this methodology to draw a hexagon as shown in Figure 2.14.

```
import TurtleGraphics.*;

/** This program uses TurtleGraphics to draw a hexagon.
 **
 ** @version    1.0 (May 2001)
 **
 ** @author D. Hughes                                       */

public class Hexagon {


    private Turtle  yertle;     // turtle for drawing


    /** The constructor draws a hexagon using TurtleGraphics.              */

    public Hexagon ( ) {

        int i;
```

FIGURE 2.13 Example—Draw a hexagon

```
        yertle = new Turtle();
        yertle.penDown();
        for ( i=1 ; i<=6 ; i++ ) {
            yertle.forward(40);
            yertle.right(Math.PI/3);
        };
        yertle.penUp();

    };  // constructor


    public static void main ( String args[] ) { new Hexagon(); };

}   // Hexagon
```

FIGURE 2.13 (Continued)

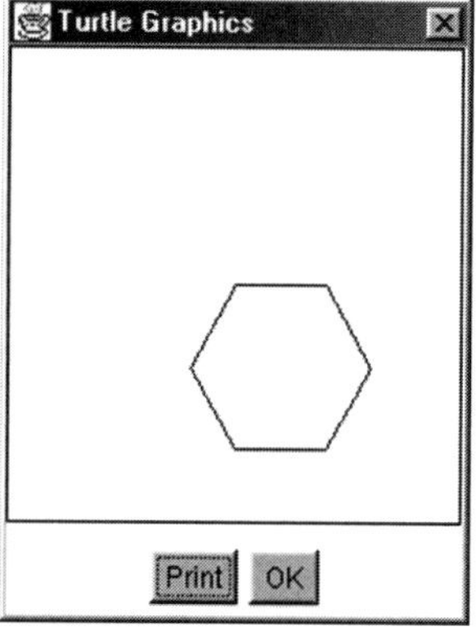

FIGURE 2.14 A hexagon

CASE STUDY Drawing Eight Squares

Problem

As a first case study, we will draw a more complex picture as shown in Figure 2.15. It consists of eight squares with a common corner at the middle of the page, each rotated π/4 from each other, making a complete rotation.

Analysis and Design

The complete picture consists of 32 lines; however, these lines are organized and we can capitalize on the organization to make the problem simpler. Consider that there are eight squares to be drawn. If we assume for the moment that we can figure out how to draw the squares, the problem can be represented by the following pattern:

```
repeat 8 times
    draw a square
    position for next square
```

Now we can turn our attention to drawing a square. We have already seen that this can be accomplished via the following pattern:

```
repeat 4 times
    draw a line
    rotate π/4
```

To ensure that the program will draw the desired figure, we must know where the algorithm for drawing the square leaves the turtle. If we consider the algorithm for the square, the turtle returns back to the exact place from which it started, pointing in the same direction. Thus, positioning for the next square simply requires rotating the turtle π/4 radians.

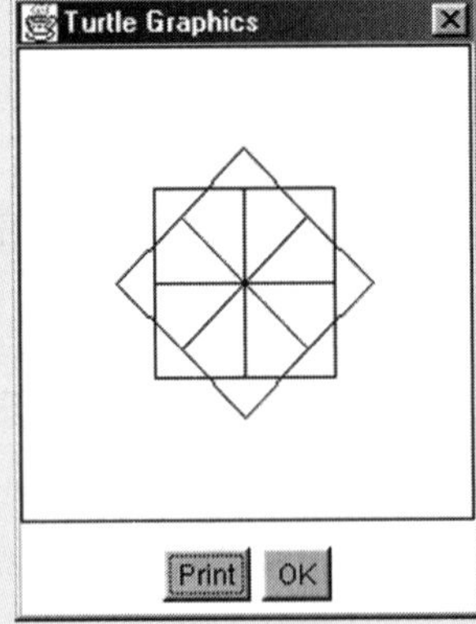

FIGURE 2.15 Eight squares

Coding

Using the countable repetition pattern, we can develop the following code for drawing the picture:

```
for ( j=1 ; j<=8 ; j++ ) {
    draw a square
    yertle.right(Math.PI/4);
};
```

Here we are using the countable repetition pattern with index variable, `j`; number of times, `8`; and the repeated operations consisting of drawing a square and then rotating $\pi/4$ radians to the right. The code for drawing the square is the same as in the previous use of the pattern. Since that code draws the first side of the square in the direction the turtle is currently facing and leaves the turtle facing in the original direction at the original corner, rotating $\pi/4$ radians between each square means that the next square will share the same corner. However, the first side will be rotated $\pi/4$ radians. When this has been done eight times, the last rotation of $\pi/4$ radians will leave the turtle facing in the original direction and at the original starting point—the center of the page, facing right. The code will be:

```
for ( j=1 ; j<=8 ; j++ ) {
    for ( i=1 ; i<=4 ; i++ ) {
        yertle.forward(40);
        yertle.right(Math.PI/2);
    };
    yertle.right(Math.PI/4);
};
```

Note how we have constructed a more complex program out of simpler pieces; that is, we developed the program considering the drawing of a square as a single operation and then substituted the complete code for the drawing of the square. This technique is called **composition** or **nesting** (the placing of one piece of code within another). This is a very common method of developing computer programs. We have been careful to use two different index variables for the two uses of the countable repetition pattern. When we nest this pattern, there is now no confusion about what we are counting. It, of course, requires that we declare two index variables rather than just one. If the uses of the countable repetition pattern are not nested, we may use the same index variable without confusion. The complete program is found in Figure 2.16.

> **COMPOSITION** or nesting is a method of programming in which one piece of code (e.g. loop) is placed within the body of another to achieve the combined effect of both.

Testing and Debugging

This program either works or it doesn't, so testing simply involves running the program to see the result. If it doesn't work, the problem might be obvious from the picture drawn. If not, one technique to determine the problem is to comment out the outer loop by placing comment symbols (//) at the beginning of each line, turning them into comments, as follows:

```
import TurtleGraphics.*;


/**  This program uses TurtleGraphics to draw eight squares each
 **  rotated around the corner.
 **
 **  @version1.0 (May 2001)
 **
 **  @author D. Hughes                                        */

public class EightSquares {


    private Turtle  yertle;      // turtle for drawing


    /** The constructor draws eight squares using TurtleGraphics.      */

    public EightSquares ( ) {

        int i;
        int j;

        yertle = new Turtle();
        yertle.penDown();
        for ( j=1 ; j<=8 ; j++ ) {
            for ( i=1 ; i<=4 ; i++ ) {
                yertle.forward(40);
                yertle.right(Math.PI/2);
            };
            yertle.right(Math.PI/4);
        };
        yertle.penUp();

    };  // constructor


    public static void main ( String args[] ) { new EightSquares(); };


} // EightSquares
```

FIGURE 2.16 Example—Draw eight squares

```
// for ( j=1 ; j<=8 ; j++ ) {
    for ( i=1 ; i<=4 ; i++ ) {
        yertle.forward(40);
        yertle.right(Math.PI/2);
    };
//  yertle.right(Math.PI/4);
// };
```

The program is then compiled and run again. Since these lines are treated as comments, the program only contains the inner loop which is supposed to draw a square. If a square is drawn, we know the problem must be either with the transition between the squares, or with the outer loop itself. This should help us remedy the situation.

*2.5 EXECUTION OF JAVA PROGRAMS

As mentioned in Section 2.1, one of the goals of the design of Java was platform independence—that the code generated by a Java compiler would run on any platform. This is necessary if a Java applet is to be transmitted as part of a web page and then executed, even though the browser might be running on any machine, perhaps an IBM PC or a Solaris workstation. In Chapter 1, we saw that each processor family has a different machine language. An IBM PC doesn't understand Solaris machine language and vice versa. Since, as described in Section 1.4, a compiler generates machine language, how is platform independence possible?

> **JAVA BYTECODE** is a platform-independent binary language similar to machine language that is generated by a Java compiler. This code must be executed by a Java interpreter.
>
> A **JAVA INTERPRETER** is a program (i.e. machine language) which inputs and executes Java bytecode program code. This is how a Java program is executed and how Java achieves platform independence.

To achieve the goal of platform independence, the Java designers specified that a Java compiler, instead of generating actual (native) machine code, would generate a special machine code-like binary language called **Java bytecode**. Since the processor does not understand bytecode, a special program, called the **Java interpreter**, is written for each platform. This interpreter, like a compiler or linker, is a program in native machine language that executes the bytecode on the actual target platform.

Figure 2.17 shows this process in a diagram similar to Figure 1.11. The Java compiler translates the Java source program, as Java code, into the binary Java bytecode. The linker combines this bytecode with bytecode for library classes to produce an "executable" bytecode. In the execution phase, the Java interpreter is loaded into memory and executed. It inputs the bytecode for the program and the data used by the program and executes the bytecode instructions, producing the output.

The result is that, even if the Java program is compiled and linked on a Solaris machine, it can be executed on any other machine, such as an IBM PC—platform independence achieved! However, this does require that a Java interpreter is available for the target machine. Typically, browsers such as Netscape Navigator or Internet Explorer

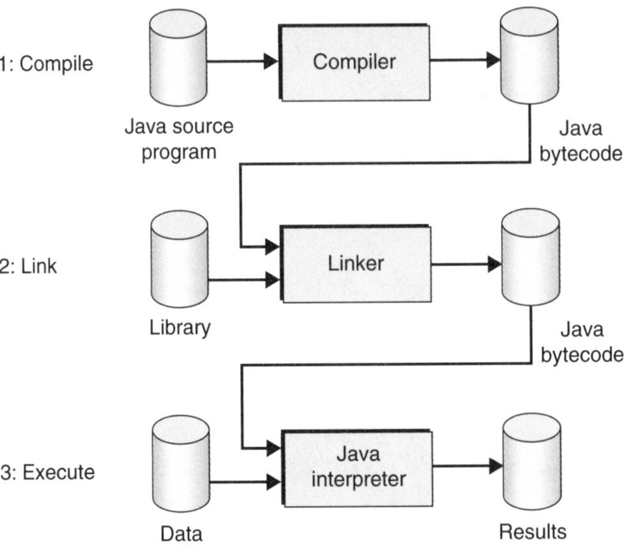

FIGURE 2.17 Executing a Java program

have a Java interpreter built in so that Java applets may be executed. To run a Java application program outside a browser, it is necessary to acquire, install, and run an appropriate Java interpreter.

■ SUMMARY

Programming in a high-level language is more productive than using machine language. We will use the language Java, a recent, object-oriented language. The grammar of the Java language is specified by a set of rules called the syntax rules.

A Java program consists of a number of classes, some written by the programmer, some reused from libraries. Classes consist of declarations of fields, constructors, and methods. An object is an instance of a class, created via the operator `new`. When an object is created, its constructor is executed. Fields—specifically, instance variables—serve as memory for the object and methods, and constructors specify actions the object may perform. Assignment statements allow the object to commit things to memory, and method invocation statements allow the object to make use of services provided by other objects.

Turtle Graphics, as provided by the `TurtleGraphics` library, is a facility for doing line drawings on the screen. A `Turtle` object can be requested to move or rotate, and movement with the pen down draws a line.

A countable repetition can be used to repeat a sequence of statements a number of times. For example, it can be used to draw a square by repeatedly drawing a side and turning the corner. Countable repetitions can be nested to produce complex drawings.

To achieve platform independence, a Java compiler generates bytecode instead of machine language. For a Java bytecode program to be executed, a program called a Java interpreter must be run.

REVIEW QUESTIONS

1. T F In an embedded system, additional hardware is integrated into the computer's processor.
2. T F Java provides platform independence.
3. T F The semantics of a programming language are the set of rules that describe the meaning of a correctly composed program.
4. T F Every `Turtle` object (from the `TurtleGraphics` library) starts out at the middle of the page, facing to the right, with its pen up.
5. T F A program must include a class declaration for every class it uses.
6. T F A class is a type of object.
7. T F The following is an example of a field declaration:

```
private   Turtle   yertle;
```

8. The syntax of a language specifies:
   a) the set of symbols used in the language.
   b) the grammatical rules (how the basic elements may be combined).
   c) the meaning of a correct sequence of basic elements.
   d) all of the above.
9. Which of the following is a valid sentence according to the grammar?

   noun-phrase:

   article$_{opt}$ *noun*

   article: *one of*

   a the

   noun: *one of*

   John Mary book Java

   a) a the
   b) John Mary
   c) a book
   d) Mary book John
10. Which of the following is not a class of terminal symbols in a programming language grammar?
    a) punctuation
    b) identifier
    c) keyword
    d) all are terminal symbols

11. The following line:

```
Yertle.penUp();
```

is an example of:

a) a field declaration.
b) an assignment statement.
c) a method invocation.
d) a programming pattern.

12. In the following line of code

```
yertle.forward(10);
```

a) `yertle` is an object and `forward` is a class.
b) `forward` is an object and `yertle` is an identifier.
c) `yertle` is an object and `forward` is a method.
d) `yertle` is a class and `10` is an argument.

13. The following sequence of statements draws what figure?

```
yertle = new Turtle();
yertle.penDown();
for( i=1; i<=3; i++ ) {
    yertle.forward(40);
    yertle.right(Math.PI/3);
};
yertle.penUp();
```

a) a triangle
b) a square
c) a hexagon
d) none of the above

14. The following:

```
for( j=1; j<=8; j++ ) {
    for( k=1; k<=4; k++ ) {
        yertle.forward(40);
        yertle.right(Math.PI/2);
    };
    yertle.right(Math.PI/4);
};
```

is an example of:

a) composition.
b) nesting.
c) countable repetition.
d) all of the above.

15. How many lines would the turtle draw (`forward`) in the following code?

```
for ( j=1 ; j<=6 ; j++ ) {
    for ( i=1 ; i<=3 ; i++ ) {
        yertle.forward(10);
        yertle.right(Math.PI/6);
    };
    yertle.forward(20);
};
```

a) 24
b) 19
c) 6
d) 3

EXERCISES

1. Modify the example of Figure 2.13 (`Hexagon`) to draw a pentagon (regular five-sided closed figure) with sides `40` units long. The exterior angle of a pentagon is $2\pi/5$.

2. Modify the example of Figure 2.13 (`Hexagon`) to draw a pentagram (as shown below, regular five-point star) with sides `80` units long. The exterior angle from one side to the next is $4\pi/5$, which in Java is written `4*Math.PI/5`.

3. Write a program to draw a cube, in perspective, as shown below. The sides of the cube should be `40` units long. Use any reasonable means to draw the figure. It cannot simply be drawn using a single countable repetition, but must composed of a number of parts. The `Turtle` can be moved from one place to another without drawing a line if the method `penUp` is used before the `forward`. (Don't forget to put the pen down again.)

4. Modify the example of Figure 2.16 (`EightSquares`) to draw the following figure, a poppy, which consists of four equilateral triangles with side `40` units, exterior angle $2\pi/3$ (`2*Math.PI/3`), each rotated $\pi/2$ from the other.

5. Write a program to draw a honeycomb (shown below) as a series of six pentagons with sides of 20 units joined at consecutive corners. After drawing each hexagon, move to its next corner by going forward the length of a side.

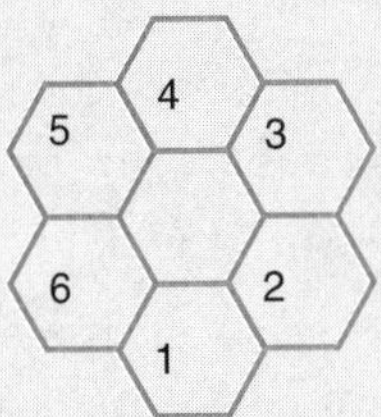

6. Write a program to draw a picket fence (shown below) as series of 13 pickets (boards), each a rectangle 10 units wide and 80 units high. The pickets should be spaced 5 units apart.

7. Write a program to draw a picture frame:

The frame is essentially a square 90 units on a side, except that each side is replaced by a sequence of 6 connected pieces consisting of 7 lines drawn as shown:

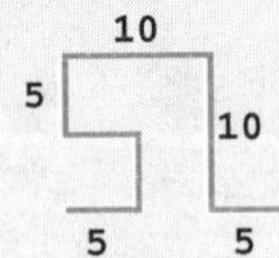

To make the frame bold, use the `Turtle` method `penWidth(2)` before drawing the lines. This sets the width of the drawing pen to 2 units.

3

Computations

CHAPTER OBJECTIVES

- To be able to decide which numeric type to use in a program.
- To understand operator precedence and its effect on writing expressions.
- To recognize mixed-mode expressions and be able to determine the conversions that will occur.
- To know how to declare variables and use them to store results of computations.
- To understand the difference between local and instance variables.
- To be able to determine whether an expression is assignment-compatible with a variable.

As we saw in Chapter 1, computers are very good at performing computations with numbers. In fact, that is about all that the ALU can do! Everything else that a computer does, from word processing to animation, ultimately requires that the words, pieces of a picture, or other information be represented in numeric form as binary numbers or bit strings. Although we will consider the representation of a variety of information, the first we will consider is the native information that computers process: numbers.

Numbers can be used for a variety of things, such as counting or recording measurements. In programming languages, therefore, there are a variety of different types of numbers (numeric types). The processing of numeric information involves computation using arithmetic operations. These computations are represented in programming languages as expressions using a notation similar to algebra.

3.1 NUMBERS

The computer represents all numeric information in binary form. Binary, however, is very tedious and difficult for humans to work with. The compiler comes to our aid. In most programming languages, we represent numbers in our usual base-10 (decimal) notation and the compiler handles the conversion into binary.

Computers typically have two different kinds of numeric representations: fixed-point and floating-point. **Fixed-point numbers** are exact values and roughly correspond to integers in mathematics. **Floating-point numbers** are approximations and correspond roughly to rational numbers. In mathematics, the sets of numbers are infinite, but computer memory is finite. For that reason, there is a bound on the size of both fixed-point and floating-point numbers, as well as a limit on the precision of floating-point numbers.

> **FIXED-POINT NUMBERS** are exact whole number values that roughly correspond to the integer domain in mathematics.
>
> **FLOATING-POINT NUMBERS** are approximations to mixed-fractions that correspond roughly to the rational domain in mathematics.
>
> A **NUMERIC TYPE** is a type that represents numeric values (fixed or floating-point). In Java this includes the types `byte`, `short`, `int`, `long`, `float`, and `double`.

Numeric Types

In Java, there are four different versions of fixed-point numbers and two different versions of floating-point numbers, yielding six **numeric types**: `byte`, `short`, `int`, `long`, `float`, and `double`. These are type identifiers in the Java syntax. The types, their storage requirements, and the range of values for each are summarized in Table 3.1.

Fixed-point types. The four fixed-point types (`byte`, `short`, `int`, and `long`) represent exact integral values in the ranges given. They are numbers without fractional parts. The most commonly used is `int`, giving the best combination of storage space, range, and speed. `byte` and `short` are used only in specialized cases in which very large numbers of integral values of small range are needed, and we will not discuss them further.

TABLE 3.1 Numeric types

Type	Kind	Storage	Minimum value	Maximum value
`byte`	fixed-point	1 byte	−128	127
`short`	fixed-point	2 bytes	−32,768	32,767
`int`	fixed-point	4 bytes	−2,147,483,648	2,147,483,647
`long`	fixed-point	8 bytes	−9,223,372,036,854,775,808	9,223,372,036,854,775,807
`float`	floating-point	4 bytes	−3.40282347E+38	3.40282347E+38
`double`	floating-point	8 bytes	−1.79769313486231570E+308	1.79769313486231570E+308

`long` is used when it is known the range provided by `int` is not sufficient. We will use `long` sparingly; for example, if we need to represent the time within the year in milliseconds. There are 31,536,000,000 milliseconds in a year!

Floating-point types. The ranges of values for the floating-point types require some explanation. The notation used is like that of scientific notation, where a measurement is written as a fraction multiplied by 10 to some power. In Java, a notation such as `E+38` or `e+38` (called **e-notation**) at the end of a floating-point number means "times 10 to the 38th power." Thus the range for `float` written in e-notation in Table 3.1 is the same as the following in scientific notation:

$$-3.40282347 \times 10^{38} \ldots 3.40282347 \times 10^{38}$$

Remember that floating-point values are approximations. `float` has about 8 digits of precision whereas `double` has about 18. Note also that the possible range of values is much greater for `double`. Floating-point values are used whenever we must represent numbers with a fractional part or whenever very large or very small numbers are possible, as in scientific computing. We will commonly use the `double` type in our programs.

Numeric Literals

When we wish to write an explicit value such as 10 in a Java program we use a **numeric literal**. Since all numeric values have one of the six numeric types described above, each numeric literal also has a unique type.

A **NUMERIC LITERAL** is a notation (token) in a programming language that represents a numeric value.

Fixed-point literals. **Fixed-point literals** are written in the natural base–10 representation as a sequence of decimal digits optionally preceded by a sign. If the value is within the range of the `int` type, the literal is considered to be of type `int`. If it is outside this range, it is considered to be of type `long`. To write a literal that is within the range for `int` but to be considered `long`, we follow the digits of the literal with the letter `l` or `L`. There are no literals of type `byte` or `short`.

Floating-point literals. **Floating-point literals** are written as a sequence of decimal digits, optionally preceded by a sign and followed by either a decimal point and a number of additional decimal digits or an exponent (in e-notation), or both. Note that if the sign in the exponent is positive, it can be omitted. If an `f` or `F` follows the floating-point literal, it is considered to be of type `float`; otherwise, it is considered to be of type `double`. Examples of numeric literals and their types are given in Table 3.2.

3.2 EXPRESSIONS

Expressions are used in programming languages to describe numeric computations. The notation used is similar to that used in algebra.

> An **EXPRESSION** is a sequence of operands (variables and literals) and operations (operators and method calls) that describe a computation.

- *Identifiers* (words) are used as variables (similar to single letters like *x* in algebra).
- *Literals* are used to represent constant values.
- *Operators* are used to represent operations.

Basic Java Operators

In Java there are quite a few operators but, for the time being, we will consider only the basic ones. The list of basic numeric **operators** is given in Table 3.3. Note the use of * for multiplication. In algebra, there are a number of notations for multiplication, includ-

TABLE 3.2 Numeric literals

Literal	Type
`0`	`int`
`0L`	`long`
`0.0`	`double`
`0.0F`	`float`
`0E0`	`double`
`0E0F`	`float`
`-2147483649`	`long`
`-2.375E-10`	`double`

TABLE 3.3	Basic Java operators
Operator	**Meaning**
+	addition
-	subtraction
*	multiplication
/	division
%	remainder

ing juxtaposition (for example, ab means a times b), the · (dot) as in A·B, and the × as in A× B. Since early input devices did not support the raised dot and the raised cross, the symbol * was adopted, being close to a raised cross. Similarly, there are a number of different notations for division in algebra (/, ÷, and placing the numerator and denominator on consecutive lines separated by a horizontal line). In Java, the slash (/) is used.

An **OPERAND** is a component of an expression which represents a value in a computation. Operands include literals and variables.

Expressions, then, consist of a sequence of **operands** (literals and variables) separated by operators and using parentheses for grouping. For example, the algebraic expression:

$$\frac{x^2 + 3x}{y^2 - 2y}$$

could be written in Java as:

```
(x * x + 3 * x) / (y * y - 2 * y)
```

One further note should be made concerning the operators / and %. In Java, if you divide one fixed-point value by another, the result is always a fixed-point value with any remainder ignored (this is called **integer division**). For example, 6/2 yields 3 as expected; however, 5/2 yields 2. It is possible to determine the remainder of division by using the **remainder operator** (%). 6%2 yields 0 (6/2 is 3 with remainder 0), whereas 5%2 yields 1 (5/2 is 2 with remainder 1). If this form of division is not desired, it is possible to get a floating-point result via conversion, as we will soon see in the section on Computing Pay, which appears later in this chapter.

INTEGER DIVISION is division of integral (fixed-point) values that produces an integral result without remainder.

Order of Operations

A question arises with the writing of expressions in the order in which the operators associate with the operands, that is, about the order in which the computation is done. For example, does the Java expression:

```
a - b * c
```

TABLE 3.4 Operator precedence

Operator	Precedence
- (negation)	high
*, /, %	middle
+, -	low

mean that b is to be subtracted from a and then the difference multiplied by c, as in

```
(a - b) * c
```

or does it mean that b is to be multiplied by c and the product subtracted from a, as in

```
a - (b * c)
```

Clearly, for most values of a, b, and c, there is quite a difference. As in algebra, there are rules of **operator precedence** that make the meaning clear. Each operator has a **precedence level**; higher-level operators bind to the operands more tightly than lower-level ones. Operators of the same level bind left to right. This gives an implicit grouping of operators and operands that can be overridden through the use of parentheses. The operator precedence levels for the basic numeric operators are found in Table 3.4.

Table 3.4 tell us that the expression:

```
a - b * c
```

would be interpreted in Java as:

```
a - (b * c)
```

since * has higher precedence than – and that operation is done first. If the other meaning of the expression were desired, the grouping would have to be explicitly indicated through the use of parentheses as:

```
(a - b) * c
```

Table 3.5 shows a number of Java expressions along with the completely parenthesized form, that is, the implicit grouping made explicit.

Computing Pay—An Example

Companies often pay their employees based on an hourly pay rate for the number of hours they have worked in a pay period. The formula is:

$$p = r \times h$$

If we wanted to write a program to do this computation for the company, we would need to include an expression based on the particular hours worked and pay rate and the

TABLE 3.5 Sample expressions

Java	Fully parenthesized form	Algebra
`a - b + c - d`	`(((a - b) + c) - d)`	$a - b + c - d$
`(a - b)/(c - d) * e`	`(((a - b)/(c - d)) * e)`	$\frac{a-b}{c-d}e$
`(x - y)/2 + (1 + m)/n`	`((((x - y)/2))+((1 + m)/n))`	$\frac{x-y}{2} + \frac{1+m}{n}$
`(c - (a + b))/d * e/f`	`((((c-(a + b))/d) * e)/f)`	$\frac{\frac{c-(a+b)}{d}e}{f}$
`(-a * x * x + b * x + c)/(a - b)`	`((((((-a) * x) * x) + (b * x)) + c)/(a - b))`	$\frac{-ax^2+bx+c}{a-b}$
`4.0/3.0 * Math.PI * r * r * r`	`((((4.0/3.0) * Math.PI) * r) * r) * r)`	$\frac{4}{3}\pi r^3$

above formula. For example, if the employee worked 25 hours at a pay rate of $8.95, we would use the expression:

```
8.95 * 25.0
```

Note that we are using `double` values here since the amounts are in dollars, with cents being a fraction of a dollar.

The program is going to have to report the result of the computation to the user of the program somehow. This requires a mechanism to do output. The `BasicIO` library is a library (like the `TurtleGraphics` library) that provides a mechanism for doing input and output (I/O). It is covered in detail in Chapter 5. To do output, we make use of the `BasicIO` library and create an `ASCIIDisplayer` object. (`ASCIIDisplayer` is a window on the screen that displays text rather than graphics as the `TurtleGraphics` window does.) Then we use methods of the `ASCIIDisplayer` to display the value desired. The program is shown in Figure 3.1 and the output in Figure 3.2.

The program imports from the `BasicIO` library instead of the `TurtleGraphics` library. It declares a variable `out` to remember an `ASCIIDisplayer` object. It creates a new `ASCIIDisplayer` object and remembers it as `out`. Next, it uses the method `writeDouble` to display the value computed by the expression in the displayer window, and then the method `writeEOL` to mark the end of the output line. Output in the displayer window consists of a number of lines of text, in this case only one. Finally, the program uses the method `close` to indicate that the displayer is no longer going to be used.

```
import BasicIO.*;

/** This program computes the pay for an employee paid at a rate
 ** of $8.95 per hour for 25 hours worked.
 **
 ** @author D. Hughes
 **
 ** @version    1.0 (May 2001)                              */

public class PayMaster {

    private ASCIIDisplayer      out;     // displayer for output

    /** The constructor uses an ASCIIDisplayer to display the
    **  pay for the employee.                                   */
    public PayMaster ( ) {\

        out = new ASCIIDisplayer();
        out.writeDouble(8.95 * 25.0);
        out.writeEOL();
        out.close();

    };  // constructor

    public static void main ( String args[] ) { new PayMaster();};

}   // PayMaster
```

FIGURE 3.1 Example—Pay calculation

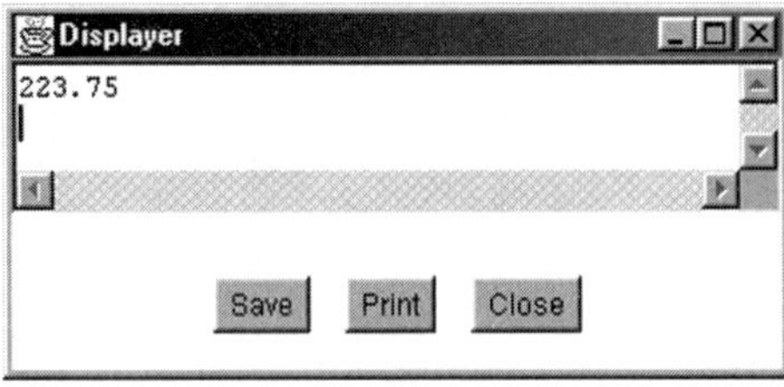

FIGURE 3.2 Pay calculated

Modes of Arithmetic and Conversion

The ALU of the computer can only perform operations on values of the same type. For example, it can add together two `int` values or divide two `double` values. The result of a computation also is of a particular type, usually the same as the two operands. This means that every operand (literal or variable), the result of every operation, and ultimately every expression has exactly one type. An expression involving all `int` operands is an `int` expression and produces an `int` value as a result, and likewise an expression involving all `double` operands is a `double` expression and produces a `double` value as a result. The type involved in the expression is called the **mode** of the expression. For example, `int` and `double`, respectively, are the modes in the examples above.

> The **MODE** of an expression is the type of the value that the expression produces (e.g. an integer mode expression is one that produces an integral result).
>
> A **MIXED-MODE EXPRESSION** is one in which the sub-expressions are not of the same mode (type).
>
> A **CONVERSION** is a change in the type of a value—often implying a change in representation—within an expression.

But what happens if the types of all the operands are not the same? An expression where all the operands are not of the same type is called a **mixed-mode expression**. In such an expression, a mechanism called **conversion** is used to change the types of the values involved in an operation to the same type so that the operation can proceed. The conversions occur in the order defined by the order of operations. Each conversion is what is called a **widening conversion** where, loosely, a value is only converted into a larger type—one that can still represent the complete value—so that no information is lost. The conversions are summarized in Table 3.6. More than one conversion may have to take place in order to make the two operands into the same type.

`byte` and `short` values are always converted to `int` in any expression, even if all operands are of the same type. Fixed-point types are converted to floating-point when the other operand is floating-point. Similarly, the shorter types (`int` and `float`) are converted to the longer types (`long` and `double`) when the other operand is a longer type.

TABLE 3.6 Conversions

From	To	Method
`byte`	`int`	Add high-order 0 digits.
`short`	`int`	Add high-order 0 digits.
`int`	`long`	Add high-order 0 digits.
`int`	`float`	Add a 0 fractional part.
`long`	`double`	Add a 0 fractional part.
`float`	`double`	Add low-order 0 digits to fraction.

Sometimes the order in which the expression is written is makes a difference in conversion, even though the order is irrelevant mathematically. For example, `4/5*1.5` yields `0.0` (that is, `4/5⇒0, 0*1.5⇒0.0*1.5⇒0.0`), while `1.5*4/5` yields `1.2` (`1.5*4⇒1.5*4.0⇒6.0, 6.0/5⇒6.0/5.0⇒1.2`). Remember, the conversions occur as necessary following the order of operations, which, in this case, is left to right. The last example in Table 3.5 could not have been written as `4/3*Math.PI*r*r*r` since `4/3` will be done using integer division yielding `0` and this would not produce the desired result.

> A **CAST** is an explicit direction to the compiler to cause a conversion. A cast, in Java, is specified by writing the desired type in parentheses in front of an operand.

It is possible to force a conversion using a cast. A **cast** is an explicit direction to the compiler to cause a conversion. A cast is specified by writing the desired type in parentheses in front of an operand. A cast has higher precedence than the operators. This means that the operand is cast to another type before it associates with an operator. Thus `(double)4/5*1.5` yields `1.2` (`(double)4⇒4.0, 4.0/5⇒4.0/5.0⇒0.8, 0.8*1.5⇒1.2`). Since the cast binds first, it doesn't apply to the entire expression; therefore `(double)1+4/5` yields `1.0` (because `(double)1⇒1.0, 4/5⇒0, 1.0+0⇒1.0+0.0⇒1.0`). A cast can also be used to force a **narrowing conversion** from a larger type to a smaller type. This conversion might possibly lose some information, such as the fractional part in a floating- to fixed-point conversion. Thus, `(int)(4.0/5.0)*1.5` yields `0.0` (because `4.0/5.0⇒0.8, (int)0.8⇒0, 0*1.5⇒0.0*1.5⇒0.0`).

Centering the Square—An Example

Say we wanted to draw a square in Turtle Graphics centered on the point where the turtle starts. Assuming we desire the same orientation of the square and wish to start drawing from the top-left corner, we could do this by moving upward half the height of the square and then left half the width of the square using the following code:

```
yertle.left(Math.PI/2);      // face up
yertle.forward(20);          // move up half the height
yertle.left(Math.PI/2);      // face left
yertle.forward(20);          // move left half the width
yertle.right(Math.PI);       // face right
```

We could then draw the square as before. However, there is a more direct way. If we move from the center point directly to the top-left corner, we can also then draw the square. Figure 3.3 shows the geometry.

We can thus reposition the square using the code:

```
yertle.left(3*Math.PI/4);              // face to left corner
yertle.forward(40*Math.sqrt(2)/2);     // move to left corner
yertle.right(3*Math.PI/4)              // face in original
                                       //   direction
```

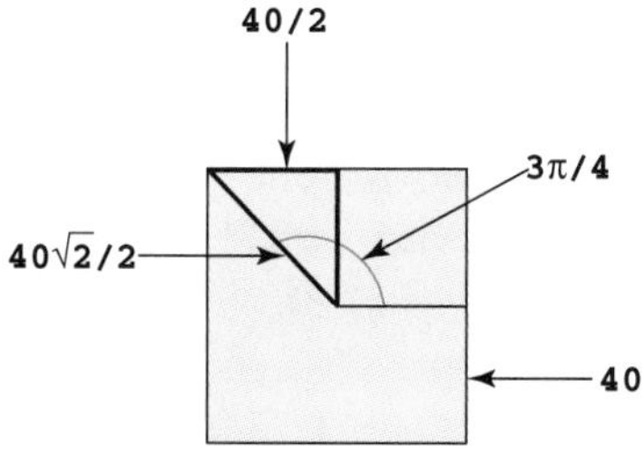

FIGURE 3.3 Geometry of a square centered on the turtle

These three expressions are carefully written to ensure that no information is lost due to conversions. The value of π given by `Math.PI` is a `double` value. Therefore, the `3` is converted to `3.0` before the multiplication, and the `4` is converted to `4.0` before the division, and we get the desired result. Note that `3/4*Math.PI` would have given us an angle of `0.0` radians.

In the second statement above, the operand `Math.sqrt(2)` is the way we express the square root of `2`. This is something called a function method invocation, in which you place an expression in the parentheses (as a parameter) and the function yields the expression's square root. (We will discuss function methods in Chapter 4.) In our drawing of a square, the value the function yields is a `double` value, so the `40` is converted to `40.0` before the multiplication, and the `2` is converted to `2.0` before the division. The result is a `double` value. (Since this distance is not an exact integer, this is desirable.) In this case, the order of writing the code didn't matter; however, if the width of the square was not divisible by 2, the order would have a significant effect.

This gives us the program in Figure 3.4, which produces the picture shown in Figure 3.5.

STYLE TIP

Note the code after the drawing of the square; it serves to put the turtle back where it started at the center of the square. Restoring the initial position is a good idea since, if we are drawing a picture made up of a number of figures, it is easier to determine where the next figure is to go if we know the starting position of the turtle.

```
import TurtleGraphics.*;

/** This program uses TurtleGraphics to draw a square centered
 ** on the starting position of the turtle. It leaves the
 ** the turtle in its original position.
 **
 ** @version    1.0 (May 2001)
 **
 ** @author D. Hughes                                    */

public class CenteredSquare {

    private Turtle  yertle;     // turtle for drawing

    /** The constructor draws a square using TurtleGraphics.    */

    public CenteredSquare ( ) {

        int i;

        yertle = new Turtle();
        yertle.left(3*Math.PI/4);
        yertle.forward(40*Math.sqrt(2)/2);
        yertle.right(3*Math.PI/4);
        yertle.penDown();
        for ( i=1 ; i<=4 ; i++ ) {
            yertle.forward(40);
            yertle.right(Math.PI/2);
        };
        yertle.penUp();
        yertle.left(3*Math.PI/4);
        yertle.backward(40*Math.sqrt(2)/2);
        yertle.right(3*Math.PI/4);

    };  // constructor

    public static void main ( String args[] ) { new CenteredSquare(); };

}   // CenteredSquare
```

FIGURE 3.4 Example—Draw a square centered on the turtle

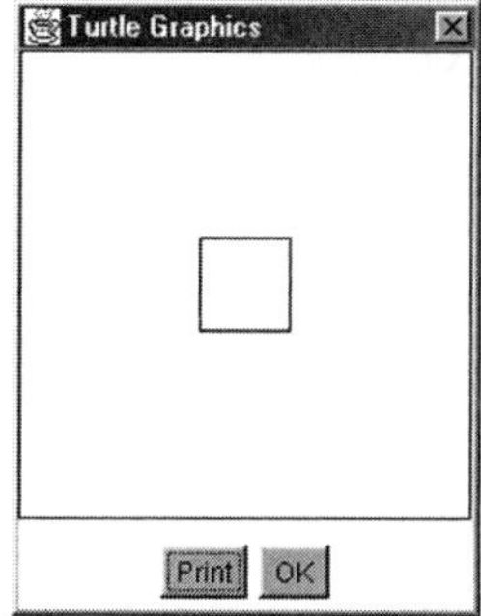

FIGURE 3.5 A square centered on the turtle

3.3 VARIABLES

As we have seen, computers have a specific hardware component called memory in which information can be stored. At the hardware level, cells in memory are referenced via addresses, and the ALU can retrieve the contents of a cell or store a result into a cell via its address. At the programming language level, variable identifiers, or **variables** for short, are used instead of addresses to refer to information stored in memory. We can think of a variable as a name associated with some cells in memory, which the compiler translates into an address.

Declaring a Variable

Whenever some information must be remembered, a variable identifier is chosen. Since the programmer makes up this name, it must be **declared** (defined) using a construct called a **declaration**. This is sort of like writing a dictionary. Whenever we make up a new word, we must give a definition of that word. We will, in fact, sometimes refer to the series of variable declarations in a piece of code as a **variable dictionary**.

> A **DECLARATION** is a construct in a programming language through which a variable's type and scope are defined.

Java restricts the choice of identifiers to a sequence of letters and digits, beginning with a letter. The identifier may be composed of a number of words, but there must be no spaces in the identifier. Java reserved words such as `class`, `for`, and `int` must not be used as identifiers. (A complete list of reserved words is found in Appendix B.)

We have already seen one form of declaration, a field declaration, which can be used to declare instance variables. For example, in Figure 2.1 the `Square` object had to remember the `Turtle` object that it was using and so declared an instance variable called `yertle`. Similarly, in Figure 3.1 the `PayMaster` object had to remember the `ASCIIDisplayer` object it was using for output, so it declared an instance variable called `out`.

SYNTAX

```
LocalVariableDeclarationStatement:
      Type Identifier ;
```

FIGURE 3.6 Local variable declaration syntax

Local Variables

Some information is remembered as long as the object lives. For example, the `Square` object always knows a `Turtle` object. Sometimes, however, the information isn't part of an object's permanent knowledge, but is just a piece of information to be remembered temporarily. Instance variables (declared in a field declaration) are long-term memory. Variables used to remember information temporarily are called **local variables** and are declared within a constructor (or a method, as we will see in Chapter 4). A local variable is declared by using a *`LocalVariableDeclarationStatement`* as defined in Figure 3.6.

> A **LOCAL VARIABLE** is a variable used to temporarily store a value within a method or constructor. In Java, its scope is the body of the method or constructor.

Here the *`Type`* indicates the kind of information being remembered and the *`Identifier`* indicates the variable identifier to be used. We have already seen declarations of this form, such as:

```
int i;
```

in Chapter 2 in the examples for drawing a square using a loop and drawing eight squares. There the *`Identifier`* was `i` and the *`Type`* was `int`, indicating that one integer value would be remembered using the name `i`.

A variable can be used to remember a particular kind of information as defined by the *`Type`* in the declaration. References to other objects can be remembered by a variable declared using a class name as the *`Type`*, as in the declaration of `yertle`. The numeric results of computations can be remembered by a variable declared using a numeric type name as the *`Type`*, as in the declaration of `i`. The amount of memory required to store the information is determined by the *`Type`* and is 4 bytes for an object reference and from 1 to 8 bytes, as shown in Table 3.1, for numeric types.

3.4 ASSIGNMENT STATEMENT

As mentioned in Chapter 2, the statement that is used to commit something to memory is called an **assignment statement**. Its syntax is repeated in Figure 3.7. The *`LeftHandSide`* is a variable that has previously been declared. It can be either an instance variable identifier or a local variable identifier. The *`AssignmentExpression`* is an expression, either a

> An **ASSIGNMENT STATEMENT** is a statement through which the value of a variable is changed or set.

SYNTAX

```
Assignment:
      LeftHandSide = AssignmentExpression
```

FIGURE 3.7 Assignment syntax

numeric expression as described in Section 3.2 or the creation of an object (a *ClassInstanceCreationExpression*) as seen in Chapter 2.

The function of the assignment statement is to replace the information currently stored in memory using the variable given as the *LeftHandSide* by the information computed by the *AssignmentExpression*. It is important to remember that this is a replacement and that any information previously stored in that variable is lost. This is clear if we remember that a variable is essentially a name for a cell in memory, that a cell can only hold one piece of information at a time, and that assignment is the storage of a value in a cell. The corresponding operation of retrieval does not destroy information because we are only looking at it, not removing it from the cell. The use of an identifier as an operand in an expression indicates information retrieval only.

Assignment Compatibility

As we saw earlier, every expression has a type that the expression computes. Likewise, every variable has a type that is the *Type* in the declaration. An assignment statement is said to be *valid* if the type of the expression (right-hand side) is assignment-compatible with the type of the variable (left-hand side). If the assignment statement is not valid, the compiler will indicate this by issuing an error message. The types are **assignment-compatible** under the following three conditions:

> In Java, an expression of type B is **ASSIGNMENT-COMPATIBLE** with a variable (or array or field reference) of type A if: (1) A and B are the same, (2) B is a subtype of the A, or (3) A can be converted to B using a widening conversion.
>
> A type `B` is a **SUBTYPE** of another type `A` if `B` is a specialization ("special kind of") of `A`. In Java a class is a subtype of any class it (directly or indirectly) extends or any interface it (directly or indirectly) implements.

1. If the two types are the same, they are considered assignment-compatible.
2. If the right-hand side is a **subtype** of the left-hand side, they are assignment-compatible. (A subtype is a "special kind" of another type, much as a poodle is a special kind of dog.) We will see this in Chapter 8.
3. If the type of the right-hand side can be converted to the type of the left-hand side using a widening conversion, the two types are assignment-compatible.

Thus the `Turtle` object reference produced by the *ClassInstanceCreationExpression*:

```
new Turtle()
```

is assignment-compatible with the `Turtle` identifier `yertle`. Similarly, an `int` expression is assignment-compatible with an `int` variable or a `double` variable (via conversion).

Suppose we are given the following declarations:

```
short          s;
int            i;
double         d;
Turtle         t;
ASCIIDisplayer o;
```

Then Table 3.7 shows a number of valid (assignment-compatible) and invalid (not compatible) assignment statements.

Note that widening conversions can occur across an assignment (as in `d = 8`), but narrowing conversions cannot (as in `s = 1`) and must be explicitly done in the expression before assignment (as in `s = (short)1`). Note also that the conversion across the assignment happens after the expression has been evaluated, so that `d = 8 / i` causes `1.0` to be assigned to `d`. The expression evaluates to an `int` using integer division and then the `int` is converted to `double`.

The example `d = d / i` shows two different uses of a variable identifier. When a variable identifier is used on the left-hand side of an assignment, it indicates a location into which a value is to be stored. When a variable identifier occurs on the right-hand side, it represents the value currently stored in the location (that is, a retrieval). Since the right-hand side is always evaluated first, this expression replaces the old value of `d` (`8.0`) with a new value (`1.6`), and the old value is lost.

TABLE 3.7 Assignment compatibility

`i = 5;`	valid	`i` assigned the `int` value `5`
`d = 8;`	valid	`d` assigned the `double` value `8.0` (conversion)
`s = 1;`	invalid	literals are `int`; cannot convert `int` to `short`
`s = (short)1;`	valid	explicit narrowing allowed
`d = d / i;`	valid	expression is `double` (value assigned is `1.6`)
`d = 8 / i;`	valid	expression is `int` (value `1`) converted to `1.0`
`i = i / d;`	invalid	expression is `double`, cannot convert to `int`
`i = (int)(i/d)`	valid	explicit cast from `double` to `int` (value assigned is `0`)
`t = new Turtle()`	valid	`t` refers to a newly created `Turtle` object
`o = new Turtle()`	invalid	a `Turtle` is not an `ASCIIDisplayer`

Pay Calculation Revisited

Figure 3.8 shows the pay calculation program (Figure 3.1) rewritten using local variables to store the worker's hours, pay rate, and amount paid. Note that we use complete words for the variable names instead of single letters (as in mathematics) as this makes programs

```
import BasicIO.*;

/** This program computes the pay for an employee paid at a rate
 ** of $8.95 per hour for 25 hours worked using variables.
 **
 ** @author D. Hughes
 **
 ** @version    1.0 (May 2001)                              */

public class PayMaster2 {

    private ASCIIDisplayer      out;     // displayer for output

    /** The constructor uses an ASCIIDisplayer to display the
     ** pay for the employee.                               */
    public PayMaster2 ( ) {

        double  hours;       // hours worked
        double  rate;        // hourly pay rate
        double  pay;         // amount paid out

        out = new ASCIIDisplayer();

        rate = 8.95;
        hours = 25.0;
        pay = rate * hours;
        out.writeDouble(pay);
        out.writeEOL();

        out.close();

    };  // constructor

    public static void main ( String args[] ) { new PayMaster2(); };

}   // PayMaster2
```

FIGURE 3.8 Example—Pay calculation using variables

easier to read. Since rate and pay are both in dollars, double is used to store dollars and fractions of dollars. It is possible that an employee could work fractions of an hour, so double is also used for hours. After the displayer is created, the values for rate and hours are stored in the appropriate variables, and then the pay is computed and stored in the variable pay. Finally, the current value of pay that was just computed is displayed in the output window. The output is the same as shown in Figure 3.2.

STYLE TIP

Local variable declarations, like statements in a constructor, are indented one extra tab so they appear inside the constructor. Like instance variable declarations, a comment is placed at the end of the declaration to describe what the variable represents. You might note that we haven't included a comment on loop index variables (such as i in Figure 3.4). There isn't usually anything useful that can be said about a loop index variable.

Like instance variable identifiers, local variable identifiers are usually nouns or noun phrases beginning with a lowercase letter. Each subsequent word in the identifier begins in uppercase. Loop index variables are traditionally called i, j, k, and so on.

Memory Model

To help understand the effect of assignment, we use a model for the behavior of the program with respect to memory. This is known as a **memory model**. For Java, an effective model is to consider each object as having its own region of storage. We will diagram it as a box, labeled by the class name. There are cells for each of the object's instance variables, labeled by their identifiers, and separate subregions for the constructor (and methods, as we shall see in Chapter 4). These subregions are boxes labeled by the word constructor (or the name of the method) and contain cells for each local variable, labeled by the variable identifier. Initially, we don't know the value stored in the cell. Actually, there is always some value, we just don't know what it is. Therefore, we place a question mark (?) in the cell to indicate this unknown value. For example, the memory model for the program in Figure 3.8, just as it begins to execute the constructor, is found in Figure 3.9.

A **MEMORY MODEL** is a model (notation) of the behavior of the program with respect to memory.

The effect of an assignment statement is to replace the information in the appropriate cell, as indicated by the variable on the left-hand side. It is replaced by the value of the assignment expression, the right-hand side. A numeric value is simply written inside the cell. An object reference is represented by an arrow to the memory model for that object. For example, before the assignment statement assigning the value to pay, the memory model will look like Figure 3.10. The assignment to out created a new ASCIIDisplayer object represented by the box labeled ASCIIDisplayer. out that now refers to this new object. The other two assignment statements have assigned 8.95 to rate and 25.0 to hours, respectively. No value has yet been assigned to pay.

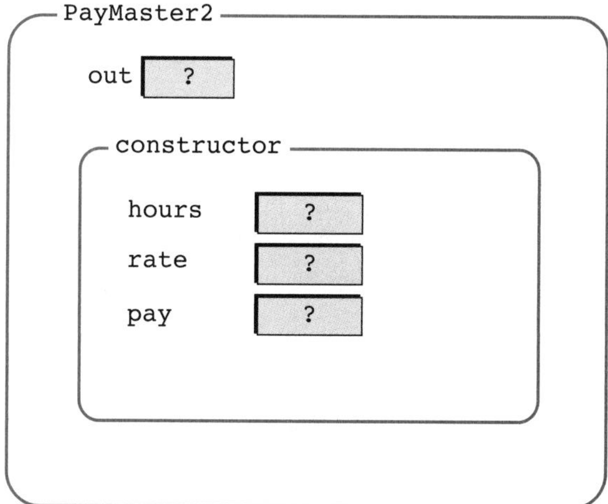

FIGURE 3.9 Memory model for PayMaster2 at beginning of constructor

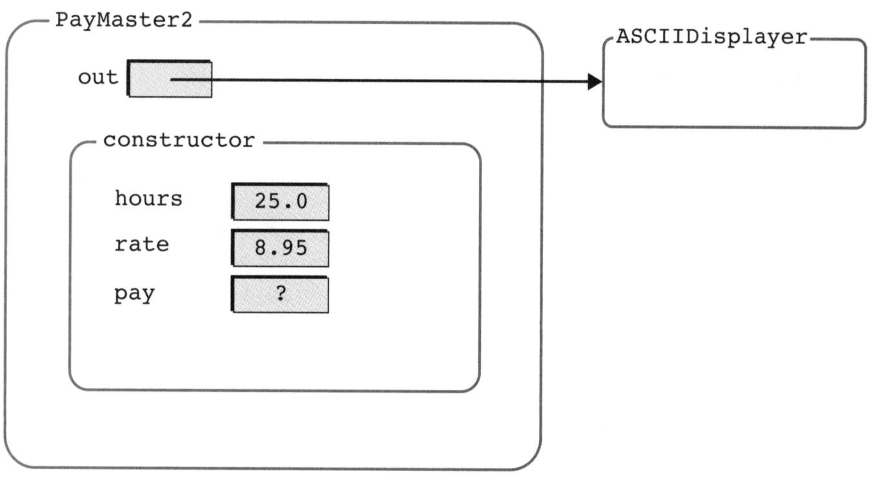

FIGURE 3.10 Memory model for PayMaster2 before the assignment to pay

CASE STUDY Plotting a Function

Problem

Many mathematical functions can be more readily understood if we can see a visual representation of them, such as a graph. To do this, we compute the function (say `f(x)`) over a number of values for `x` and plot the resulting points `(x,f(x))` on graph paper. Could we use a computer program to do this for us?

Analysis and Design

The Turtle Graphics library includes an additional `Turtle` method called `moveTo`:

`moveTo(x,y)` moves the turtle to coordinate position `(x,y)`

The turtle drawing area is arranged as a coordinate plane with the point `(0,0)` as the center. The method `moveTo` moves the turtle from its current position to the specified coordinates, drawing a line if the pen is down. The original turtle direction has no effect on the `moveTo` method and the method does not change the turtle direction.

To plot the function

$$0.0002x^3 - 0.02x^2 + 0.3x$$

we need to choose a range of values for `x`. Since the drawing area is `200×200`, a natural range would be `-100...100` (since `(0,0)` is the center). Next we need to decide on how many points we should draw, say, `21`. If we assume equal spacing, the `x` values will be:

```
-100, -90, -80 ... 80, 90, 100
```

Coding

We need to write the function as a Java expression, namely:

```
0.0002 * x * x * x - 0.02 * x * x + 0.3 * x
```

Note that since Java has no operator for exponentiation (raising a value to a power), we represent x^3 as `x * x * x` and x^2 as `x * x`. The *x*- and *y*-coordinates are represented by the variables *x* and *y*, respectively. After the first y-coordinate is computed, the turtle moved into position, and the pen put down, a loop running over the remaining 20 points can be written. The program is given in Figure 3.11 with the output in Figure 3.12.

There are a variety of different ways to create a `Turtle`, allowing, for example, the specification of the speed at which it draws or the drawing area size.

```
import TurtleGraphics.*;


/**  This program uses absolute positioning in Turtle Graphics
 **  to plot a function.
 **
 **  @author D. Hughes
 **
 **  @version    1.0 (May 2001)                              */
```

```
public class FunPlot {

    private Turtle   yertle;      // turtle for drawing


        /**  The constructor uses a Turtle to plot a function. */

        public FunPlot ( ) {

            double   x;         // x-coordinate
            double   y;         // y-coordinate (y = f(x))
            int      i;

            yertle = new Turtle(Turtle.MEDIUM);

            yertle.moveTo(-100,0);
            yertle.penDown();
            yertle.moveTo(100,0);
            yertle.penUp();
            yertle.moveTo(0,-100);
            yertle.penDown();
            yertle.moveTo(0,100);
            yertle.penUp();
            x = -100;
            y = 0.0002 * x * x * x - 0.02 * x * x + 0.3 * x;
            yertle.moveTo(x,y);
            yertle.penDown();
            for ( i=2 ; i<=21 ; i++ ) {
                x = x + 10;
                y = 0.0002 * x * x * x - 0.02 * x * x + 0.3 * x;
                yertle.moveTo(x,y);
            };
            yertle.penUp();

        };  // constructor


        public static void main ( String args[] ) { new FunPlot(); };


}// FunPlot
```

FIGURE 3.11 Example—Plot a function

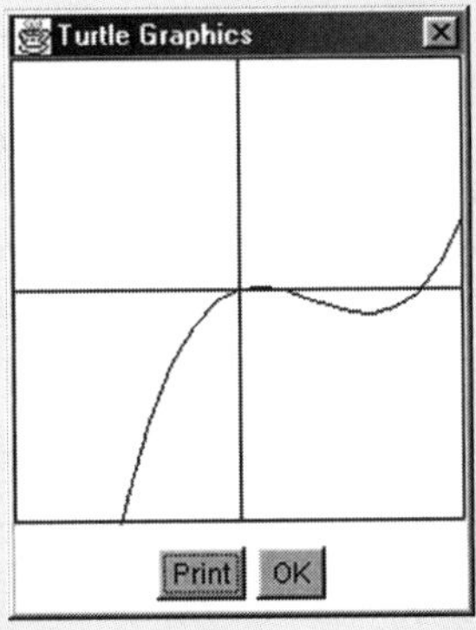

FIGURE 3.12 Function plotted

The complete specification of the `TurtleGraphics` package is given in Appendix D. So that the result can be seen in reasonable time, the program creates a `Turtle` that draws at medium speed. It then draws the axes by drawing a line from `(-100,0)` to `(100,0)` and another from `(0,-100)` to `(0,100)`. In preparation to plot the function, it moves the turtle to the first point `(-100,`*f*`(-100))` and then puts the pen down. Repeatedly, it draws the lines to the next 20 points (points 2 through 21), by increasing `x` by the increment (`10`) each time, recomputing the function value (`y`) and moving to the next point.

You might wonder about the statement:

```
x = x + 10;
```

The expression on the right-hand side is first computed as `x + 10` ⇒ `-100 + 10` ⇒ `-90` and then the current value of the variable on the left-hand side (that is, `x`) is replaced by the value computed (`-90`). Thus `x` is increased from `-100` to `-90`. This is a common form of an assignment statement; a variable's value is increased by a set amount (often 1), a process called **incrementation**. This statement also shows the difference between the use of a variable on the left-hand side, which represents a storage location, and its use on the right-hand side, which represents the value stored at the location.

> An **INCREMENT** is an operation in which a variable's value is increased by a set amount (often 1).

Testing and Debugging

This program only does one thing, so testing involves running it to see if the output is correct. How will we determine this? The only way would be to plot the function by hand and determine whether the graph produced by the program is the same as the one produced by hand. This is a general rule—when testing, it is necessary to know first what the correct output is supposed to be.

Of course, if we can plot the function by hand, why write the program? Once we have the program working for one function, we could consider modifying it for a different function. As long as the range of values `[-100,100]` is appropriate, all that is required is to change the function computation itself. In Chapter 4 we will see a technique—function methods—that makes this much easier to do.

3.5 MODIFYING EARLIER EXAMPLES

Now we will look back at some earlier examples and consider how they can be improved using the new ideas we have seen in Chapter 3.

Pay Calculation—One More Time

The pay calculation program in Figure 3.8 is not very exciting. It always uses the same pay rate of $8.95 per hour, and the same number of 25 hours. Thus it always produces the same result. In the real world, the user would want to be able to use the program for different pay rates and hours worked for different employees. What is needed is a way for the program to get input from the user. The `BasicIO` library supports input using an `ASCIIPrompter`. It presents a dialog box (Figure 3.13) into which a user can type the requested information and then click the `OK` button or press the Enter key on the keyboard.

Figure 3.14 is the pay calculation program rewritten using input. It declares an `ASCIIPrompter` variable called `in`, assigns a new `ASCIIPrompter` object to it, and then uses the `readDouble` method to obtain the `double` value that was entered. (The method `readDouble` is another function method that returns the value entered by the user in the dialog.) The value obtained is then assigned to the appropriate variable as before. Now when the program is run, the user can enter first, a number of hours, and second, a rate of pay. Then the program will compute and display the amount to be paid. The output is the same as in Figure 3.2 (assuming the user enters `8.95` as the rate and `25.0` as the number of hours).

Scaling the Hexagon

In Chapter 2, we wrote a program to draw a hexagon that had sides 40 pixels long and started at the turtle's current position. To make this code more useful, it would be better if the hexagon were centered on the turtle and if the size of the hexagon were specified in terms of the amount of space it occupies, rather than the length of its side.

If we consider the hexagon inscribed in a circle (as in Figure 3.15), the size of the hexagon can be specified by the radius of the circle (`r`) and the location of the hexagon as the center of the circle. To draw the hexagon, we must do the following: move the

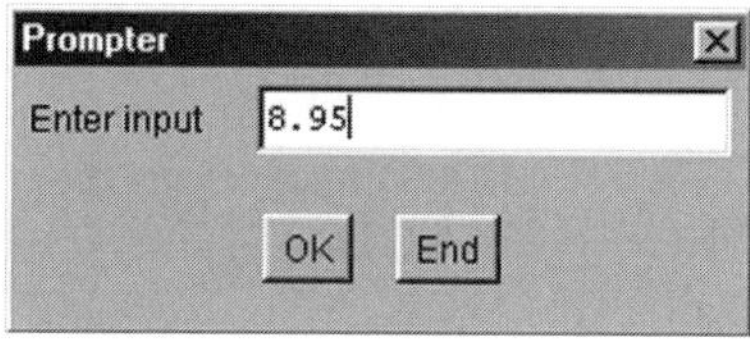

FIGURE 3.13 `ASCIIPrompter` dialog box

```
import BasicIO.*;


/** This program computes the pay for an employee paid at a
 ** particular rate per hour for a number of hours.
 **
 ** @author D. Hughes
 **
 ** @version    1.0 (May 2001)                                  */

public class PayMaster3 {


    private ASCIIPrompter       in;      // prompter for input
    private ASCIIDisplayer      out;     // displayer for output


    /** The constructor uses an ASCIIPrompter to input the pay rate
     ** and hours worked and an ASCIIDisplayer to display the pay
     ** for the employee.                                          */

    public PayMaster3 ( ) {

        double  hours;  // hours worked
        double  rate;   // hourly pay rate
        double  pay;    // amount paid out

        in = new ASCIIPrompter();
        out = new ASCIIDisplayer();

        rate = in.readDouble();
        hours = in.readDouble();
        pay = rate * hours;
        out.writeDouble(pay);
        out.writeEOL();

        in.close();
        out.close();

    };  // constructor


    public static void main ( String args[] ) { new PayMaster3(); };


}   // PayMaster3
```

FIGURE 3.14 Example—Pay calculation with input

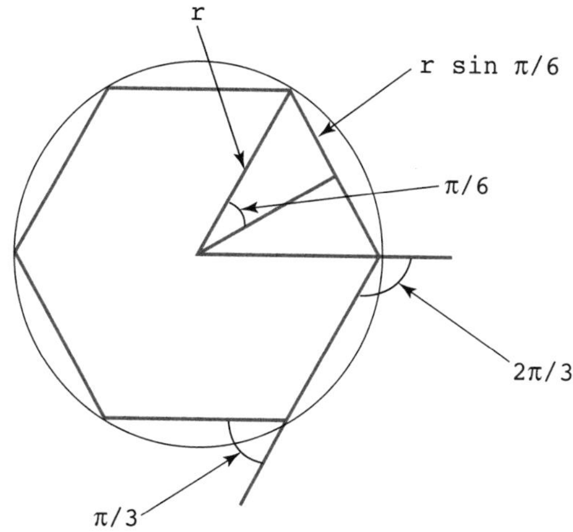

FIGURE 3.15 Geometry of a hexagon

turtle out from the center to the circumference (a distance equal to the radius), rotate it to face down the first side to be drawn (angle of 2π/3), and then draw the six sides (each of length `2 r sin π/6`) at an angle of π/3 from each other. When complete, we are back at the starting point of the drawing and can return the turtle to the center of the circle by reversing the original operations. The code is found in Figure 3.16. The output of the program is shown in Figure 3.17.

```
import TurtleGraphics.*;
import BasicIO.*;


/** This program uses TurtleGraphics to draw a hexagon
  ** with a particular radius, centered on the turtle's
  ** starting point. It leaves the turtle in its
  ** original position.
  **
  ** @version    1.0 (May 2001)
  **
  ** @author D. Hughes                                  */

public class ScaledHexagon {
```

(continued)

```
    private Turtle          yertle;     // turtle for drawing
    private ASCIIPrompter       in;         // prompter for input


    /**  The constructor draws a hexagon using TurtleGraphics.                   */

    public ScaledHexagon ( ) {

        double   radius;          // radius of hexagon
        double   angle;           // angle between sides of hexagon
        double   side;            // length of side of hexagon
        int i;

        yertle = new Turtle();
        in = new ASCIIPrompter();

        radius = in.readDouble();;
        angle = Math.PI / 3;
        side = 2 * radius * Math.sin(angle/2);
        yertle.forward(radius);
        yertle.right(2 * angle);
        yertle.penDown();
        for ( i=1 ; i<=6 ; i++) {
            yertle.forward(side);
            yertle.right(angle);
        };
        yertle.penUp();
        yertle.left(2 * angle);
        yertle.backward(radius);

    };   // constructor


    public static void main ( String args[] ) { new ScaledHexagon(); };


}   // ScaledHexagon
```

FIGURE 3.16 Example—Draw a scaled hexagon centered on the turtle

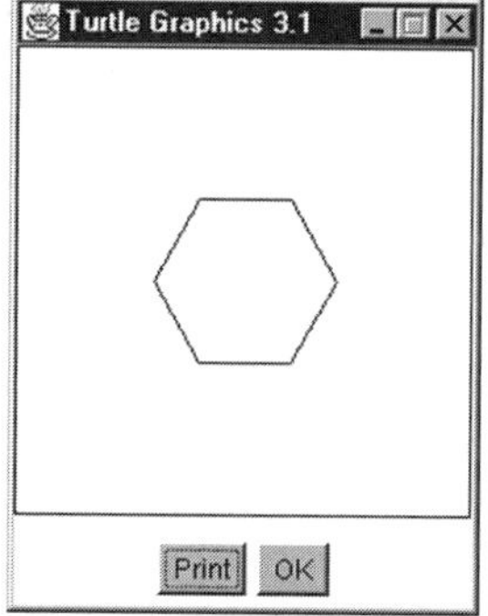

FIGURE 3.17 A scaled hexagon centered on the turtle

Note that the first point of the hexagon drawn is the one to which the turtle is originally pointing. In the code, we use variables to store (1) the radius of the figure, (2) the angle between the sides from which the other two angles can be computed, and (3) the length of the side, which is computed from the radius. To make the program more general, we input the size of the radius from the user. (Note that we import both `TurtleGraphics` and `BasicIO` so we can use both.)

By computing the angle and length of the side once and storing it in a variable, we avoid the repeated recomputations that would have occurred within the loop if we did the computations there. Although in this case the effect would be small (that is, only 10 extra computations), if we were to draw a lot of hexagons or we were drawing a figure with many more sides, this effect could become significant.

STYLE TIP

As a general rule, if we need the result of a computation a number of times as within a loop, it is better to compute it once, store the result in a variable and simply reference the variable as needed. This is a common use for local variables.

Note that we do compute the expression `2 * angle` twice. Here the saving of one computation hardly justifies an extra variable.

■ SUMMARY

Computers are designed primarily to process numeric information. In Java, this kind of information is represented by the numeric types. Although there are six numeric types in Java, we will primarily use just two: `int` and `double`. `int` is used when the information being represented is a count or a precise value without fraction. `double` is used when the information is a measurement (and thus imprecise) or has a fractional part.

The representation of numeric computations in Java is through expressions. Expressions involve values—represented by literals and variables—and operations—represented by operators. To precisely define the meaning of the expression (that is, the order in which the operations are performed), Java specifies operator precedence, with higher-precedence operators binding before lower-precedence ones and operators of equal precedence binding left to right. All expressions, including literals and variables, have a type. Conversion may occur in an expression to ensure that both operands of an operator are of the same type.

Information can be remembered by objects by using variables—either long-term, using instance variables, or short-term, using local variables. The assignment statement evaluates the expression on the right-hand side and stores the resulting value in the cell indicated by the variable on the left-hand side. Conversion may occur on assignment to ensure the value stored is of the type of the variable. When the variable is an object variable, the value stored is a reference to the object that was created by the `new` operator on the right-hand side.

REVIEW QUESTIONS

1. T F A fixed-point number is an exact value with a decimal fraction.
2. T F Division has higher precedence than subtraction.
3. T F In an expression, Java will automatically perform a narrowing conversion.
4. T F A mixed-mode expression involves operands of different types.
5. T F A cast can cause a widening conversion.
6. T F The following declaration declares an instance variable:

```
private  Turtle  yertle;
```

7. T F Retrieval of a value from a variable is destructive.
8. T F The sum of the exterior angles of a regular closed figure is 2π.
9. Which of the following is a constituent of an expression?
   a) operator b) variable
   c) literal d) all of the above
10. The expression:

$$\frac{2(x - y^2)}{2x^2 + y}$$

would be written in Java as:

a) `2x-yy/2xx+y`
b) `2*(x-y*y)/(2*x*x+y)`
c) `2*(x-y*y)/2*x*x+y`
d) `2*x-y*y/2*x*x+y`

11. The Java expression:

```
3.5 + 5 / 4
```

evaluates to:

a) `2.125`
b) `4`
c) `4.5`
d) `4.75`

12. Which of the following is a widening conversion:

a) `int` to `short`
b) `int` to `long`
c) `int` to `double`
d) `b` and `c`

13. A variable declared within a constructor is called a(n):

a) instance variable.
b) local variable.
c) object reference.
d) b and c.

14. If `a` is declared as `double`, which of the following expressions is assignment-compatible with `a`?

a) `7`
b) `1 / 3.7`
c) `new Turtle`
d) a and b

15. Which of the following is an example of incrementation?

a) `j = i + 1;`
b) `i = i * 10;`
c) `j = j + 10;`
d) none of the above

EXERCISES

1. Modify the program of Figure 3.11 to plot the function

$$0.0001x^4 - 0.005x^3 + 3x - 50$$

over the range `-100` to `100` using `41` points.

2. Write a program that will input a temperature given in °C (degrees Celsius) and display the equivalent temperature in °F (degrees Fahrenheit) using the formula:

$$F = \frac{9}{5}C + 32$$

3. Write a program that calculates the total price to carpet the floor of a room. The program should input the dimensions of the room in feet and the price of the carpet in dollars per *square meter* and display the cost in dollars. *Note*: `1` square meter equals `10.765` square feet.

4. Write a program that will input a principal (`p` in dollars), an interest rate (`r`, a decimal fraction, such as 0.05 = 5%), and a number of years (`n`), and then

displays the new value (a) of the investment after compounding the principal p at a rate of r for n years. The compound interest formula is:

$$a = p(1 + r)^n$$

The Math library provides a function `Math.pow(a,b)` that computes a^b.

5 Write a program to draw a pentagram (five-pointed star) of a specified radius, centered on the turtle. The geometry for the figure is shown below.

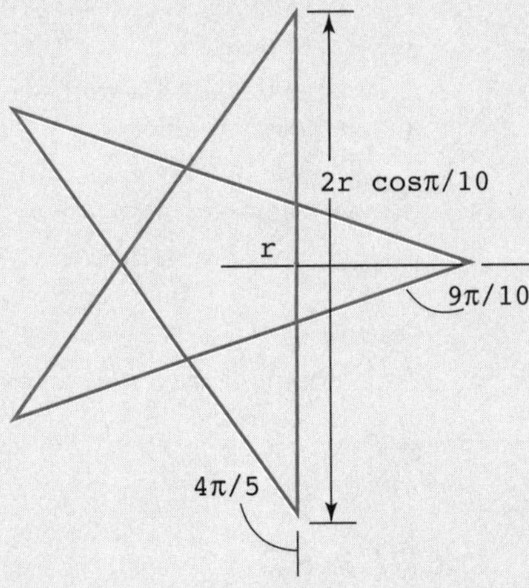

4

Methods

CHAPTER OBJECTIVES

- To understand the concept of procedural abstraction as represented by a method.
- To be able to use methods to represent cohesive sub-tasks in a program.
- To be able to differentiate between local and non-local methods.
- To recognize the main method and main class of a program.
- To know how and when to use parameters in writing methods.
- To be able to determine, in parameter passing, whether the actual parameter is compatible with the formal parameter.
- To be able to recognize and write function methods.
- To know how to use method stubs in testing and debugging methods.
- To understand the concepts of scope and visibility.
- To know, when a variable is used in a piece of code, which declaration is being referenced.
- To be able to decide where a declaration for a variable should be placed.

We have seen earlier, in Figure 2.16 when we nested the drawing of a square within a loop to repeat it eight times, that composition or nesting can be used to construct larger programs out of smaller pieces. This way of extending programs is effective as long as the resulting programs don't get too big. As programs get larger, the side effects of the compositions become more complex and eventually unmanageable. For example, what would happen if we used the same index variable in both loops? What would happen if we used composition 10 or 20 times; how would we keep track of the loop indices? Also, we often find that we need to do the same thing at a number of places within the program. For instance, in drawing a scene, we may need to draw a square at a number of different places. We need a mechanism to allow us to compose an operation like drawing a square, to give it a name, and then be able to refer to that operation by name at a variety of places in the program.

A **METHOD** (procedure) is a named sequence of instructions that can be referenced (invoked, called) in other places in the program through the use of a method (procedure) invocation statement.

The mechanism is called a method (also known as a **procedure** in other languages). A **method** is a named sequence of instructions that can be referenced in other places in the program through the use of a **method invocation statement**. In fact, we have already used methods and the method invocation statement in Chapter 2 when we used methods such as `forward` provided by the `Turtle` class. In this chapter, we will see how to write **method declarations** that specify the sequence of statements that make up the operation and give them a name. We will use a special form of the method invocation statement to then perform the method, sometimes called **invoking the method** or executing the method.

4.1 METHODS AND ABSTRACTION

Methods were the first and simplest of the mechanisms developed in computer science to deal with the complexity of large systems. The use of methods in designing large systems is called procedural abstraction. **Abstraction** is a way of dealing with complexity by ignoring the details; in **procedural abstraction**, we ignore the details of how something is done. For example, if we are drawing a scene, we may decide to draw a triangle at one place, a square at another place, and a pentagon at a third. We might express this sequence in **pseudocode**, an informal, English-like notation for algorithms, this way:

ABSTRACTION is a method of dealing with complexity by ignoring the details and differences and emphasizing similarities.

PROCEDURAL ABSTRACTION is the technique whereby we ignore the details of the procedure (i.e., the way it accomplishes its task) and emphasize the task itself.

PSEUDO-CODE is an informal, English-like notation for expressing algorithms.

```
move to position of triangle
draw a triangle
move to position of square
draw a square
move to position of pentagon
draw a pentagon
```

While we are designing the scene and figuring out how to move from one place to another, we can ignore the details about how to actually draw the figures. We are thus using abstraction. When we write the actual Java code we could, of course, simply write the statements that accomplish the drawing of the figures, but then we might lose any indication of how the program was designed. It could be quite useful to retain this knowledge if we want to change the program at a later date. So, to retain the original design, we make use of methods that contain the abstracted operations and write method invocations within our code. The resulting code might look like the code in Figure 4.1.

```
yertle.moveTo(-80,0);         // move to position of triangle
drawTriangle();
yertle.moveTo(-20,0);         // move to position of square
drawSquare();
yertle.moveTo(40,0);          // move to position of pentagon
drawPentagon();
```

FIGURE 4.1 Example—Drawing a scene

4.2 SIMPLE METHODS

Let us now consider the writing of a method declaration and its subsequent use in a program. The simplified syntax of a **method declaration** is found in Figure 4.2.

> A **METHOD DECLARATION** is the specification of the method, giving its result type, name, parameter list, and body.

You may notice that a method declaration is very similar to a constructor declaration (see Figure 2.7). This similarity is not accidental, since the constructor is the method that is to be used to start an object's life, and consists of a sequence of statements to be performed at that time. A method is a bit more general since it can be used at any time, not just when the object is created. It consists of a sequence of statements to be performed when required—in other words, when invoked. The method

SYNTAX

MethodDeclaration:
    MethodHeader MethodBody
MethodHeader:
    Modifiers$_{opt}$ void *MethodDeclarator*
    Modifiers$_{opt}$ *Type MethodDeclarator*
MethodDeclarator:
    Identifier (*FormalParameterList*$_{opt}$)
MethodBody:
    { *BlockStatements*$_{opt}$ }

FIGURE 4.2 Method declaration syntax

declaration consists of two parts: a method header and a method body. The **method header** specifies what the method defines (that is, the abstraction) and the **method body** supplies the details (that is, the statements to be performed). An example of a method declaration is found in Figure 4.3, which declares a method for drawing a square.

Here we have chosen the first alternative for a *`MethodHeader`* in Figure 4.2. The *`Modifier`* is the keyword `private`, which indicates that the method can be used only in this class. The name of the method is `drawSquare`; this *`Identifier`* has been chosen according to the same rules as variable identifiers (Section 3.3). This is the name that would be used elsewhere to refer to this method. There is no *`FormalParameterList`*. The *`MethodBody`* is the sequence of statements starting with the variable declaration for the index variable `i` and ending with the method invocation of `penUp`, enclosed in braces.

When the method is invoked, the method body is executed from beginning to end. In this case, an identifier `i` is declared to serve as a loop index and then, through a method invocation, the `Turtle` named `yertle` is requested to put the pen down. Then a loop drawing the sides is executed, followed by a request to put the pen up.

You will notice that the loop index `i` is declared within the method body, whereas the `Turtle` variable `yertle` is not. As we will see in Section 4.5, this means that the `Turtle` `yertle` must have been declared outside the method, in the class. The `drawSquare` method assumes that the declaration (and creation of the `Turtle` object) has already been done. Note that this assumption is checked both by the compiler and at execution time. If the `Turtle` `yertle` was not declared in the class, the compiler would have issued an error message saying there was an undeclared variable. If the variable was declared, but no object had been created before the `drawSquare` method was executed, an error would occur at execution time—a null reference.

Method declarations do not stand on their own—they are always part of a class. In fact, a class declaration is actually just a collection of declarations that include construc-

```
private void drawSquare ( ) {

    int i;

    yertle.penDown();
    for ( i=1 ; i<=4 ; i++) {
        yertle.forward(40);
        yertle.right(Math.PI / 2);
    };
    yertle.penUp();

};  // drawSquare
```

FIGURE 4.3 Example—Method for drawing a square

tor declarations, field declarations, and method declarations (see Figure 2.6). It is through method declarations that we specify what an object can do.

Eight Squares Revisited

In Figure 4.4, we rewrite the eight squares program of Figure 2.16 using a method. The method declaration for `square` has been written after the constructor. Actually, in Java, it doesn't really matter in what order the declarations are placed. We will always write the constructor first and the methods second. This way the first thing you see is how the object starts its life.

```
import TurtleGraphics.*;

/** This class uses the TurtleGraphics package to draw eight
 ** squares of side 40 using a method.
 **
 ** @author D. Hughes
 **
 ** @version    1.0 (June 2001)                              */

public class EightSquares2 {

    private Turtle  yertle;     // turtle for drawing

    /** The constructor uses a Turtle to draw eight squares.                    */

    public EightSquares2( ) {

        int i;

        yertle = new Turtle();
        for ( i=1 ; i<=8 ; i++) {
            drawSquare();
            yertle.right(Math.PI/4);
        };

    };  // constructor


    /** This method uses the TurtleGraphics package to draw a
     ** square of side 40. The first side of the square is drawn
     ** in the current turtle direction. The turtle is left in
     ** its original position and direction with the pen up.                 */
```

```
    private void drawSquare ( ) {

        int i;

        yertle.penDown();
        for ( i=1 ; i<=4 ; i++) {
            yertle.forward(40);
            yertle.right(Math.PI/2);
        };
        yertle.penUp();

    };  // drawSquare

    public static void main ( String args[] ) { new EightSquares2(); };

}   // EightSquares2
```

FIGURE 4.4 Example—Drawing eight squares using a method

STYLE TIP

Method headers, like constructor headers, are indented one tab from the left margin to show they are inside the class declaration. The local variable declarations and statements of the method body are indented one extra tab to show they are within the method. The close brace at the end of the method is indented one tab, to align with the method header. A comment with the method name is placed on this line to help pinpoint the end of the method.

Preceding the method header, a JavaDoc comment is used to describe the purpose of the method. As we will see later, there are special notations that are used in constructor and method comments like those used in class comments.

A method identifier is usually chosen as a verb or verb phrase since methods indicate some action. The identifier begins with a lowercase letter and subsequent words in the identifier begin with an uppercase letter.

Let us turn our attention to the constructor body in Figure 4.4. When an `EightSquares2` object is created, it declares an index variable `i`, creates a new `Turtle` object, assigning it to the instance variable `yertle`, and it then goes through a loop eight times. Within the loop body, it invokes (calls) the method `drawSquare` using a method invocation statement. This has a different form than the method invocations we have seen so far. The syntax for a method invocation is found in Figure 4.5.

Method invocations: Two versions. The first version of a **method invocation** is used when we are invoking a method of the same object, that is, a method whose decla-

SYNTAX

```
MethodInvocation:
    Name ( ArgumentList_opt )
    Primary . Identifier ( ArgumentList_opt )
```

FIGURE 4.5 Method invocation syntax

A **LOCAL METHOD** is a method of the same object (i.e., one whose declaration is in the same class as the code we are writing).

ration is in the same class as the code we are writing. Such a method is called a **local method**. Here we write only the method name, `drawSquare`. When we are not using a local method, as when we are asking the `Turtle` object `yertle` to do something, we use the second version. We write the object of which we are requesting the service before the period and the method name after the period. Actually, the first version is just a special case of the second where the object performing the action is this object itself. In Java we can also write it as `this.drawSquare()`, where `this` is a reserved word indicating this object itself. This explains the difference between the two method invocation statements in the body of the loop in Figure 4.4.

When the statements of a method are completed (or a return statement is executed), the method is said to **RETURN** to the place from which it was called (i.e., execution continues at the statement where the method was originally invoked).

Constructor execution. Within the constructor, after the creation of the `Turtle` object, the execution of the loop proceeds as follows. The method `drawSquare` is invoked. This causes the statements contained in the method body to be executed, in turn, as if they were written where the method invocation occurred. When the method body is completed, the method is said to **return** to the place from which it was called. Execution continues with the invocation of the `Turtle` method `right`. This process occurs eight times, drawing the eight squares.

An entity (class, method, or variable) that is declared is said to be **VISIBLE** at some point in the program if its use has meaning at that point in the program.

Memory model. There is one remaining thing to explain. Note that both the constructor and the method `drawSquare` declare a variable `i`, whereas there is only one declaration of the `Turtle` variable `yertle`. The declaration of a variable such as `yertle` within the class as an instance variable means that this variable is **visible**—can be referenced—within all constructors and methods of the class. The declaration of a variable such as `i` within a method as a local variable means that the variable is visible only within the method (or constructor) body in which it is declared. In fact, `i` is a different variable and has its own storage in memory, different from any variable with the same name in any other method (or constructor). This means that the constructor and the method `drawSquare` each have their own variable `i` that they use independently and without interference while sharing the use of the same `Turtle` object,

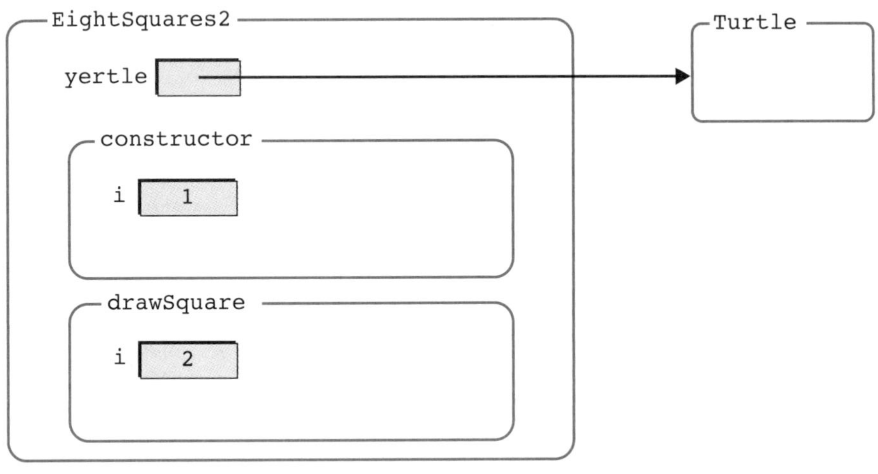

FIGURE 4.6 Memory model for `EightSquares2`

`yertle`. This indeed is one of the benefits we cited that are associated with using methods for procedural abstraction in the first place: reducing complexity in the use of variables.

The memory model in Figure 4.6 shows the status of memory at the second time through the loop in `drawSquare`, when the method is executed for the first time. There are two different memory locations for the variables `i` declared in the constructor and the method `drawSquare`. Each has its own value that changes independently. When code in `drawSquare` refers to `i`, it is referring the local variable `i` within the method. When code within the constructor refers to `i`, it is referring to the local variable `i` within the constructor. When code in either place refers to `yertle`, it is referring to the same instance variable `yertle`. In the memory model, we basically look from the inside out for variables. That is, within code for `square`, we look for a variable within the box for `square` first (for example, finding `i`) and then, if the variable isn't there, we look in the encompassing box (for example, we look in the box for `EightSquares2`, finding `yertle`). We will discuss the details of which variable is being referenced where in Section 4.5 in the discussion of scope.

> One class in each program (called the **MAIN CLASS**) must have a method called `main` (the **MAIN METHOD**) where execution begins.

The `main` method. In Figure 4.4, you may notice that the last line of code in the class beginning `public static void` is actually a method declaration of a method `main`, whose body consists solely of the creation of a new `EightSquares2` object. One class in each program, called the **main class**, must have a method called `main`, the **main method**, with these modifiers and parameters. The program actually begins with the execution of this method. In our case, the `main` method simply creates an `EightSquares2` object whose constructor does what we want. We will continue to include this trivial `main` method in the main class of all of our programs as a way of getting things started.

Drawing a Scene—An Example

Let's go back to our original problem of drawing a scene. We developed a partial solution in Figure 4.1 by using procedural abstraction and assuming the existence of methods for drawing a triangle, a square, and a pentagon. The complete program is found in Figure 4.7 as class `TriSqPent`, with output in Figure 4.8.

```
import TurtleGraphics.*;

/**
 ** This class uses the TurtleGraphics package to draw a
 ** triangle, square, and pentagon side by side using
 ** procedures.
 **
 ** @author D. Hughes
 **
 ** @version    1.0 (June 2001)                              */

public class TriSqPent {

    private Turtle  yertle;      // turtle for drawing

    /** The constructor initializes and draws the scene.        */

    public TriSqPent ( ) {

        yertle = new Turtle();
        draw();

    };  // constructor


    /** This method draws the scene consisting of a triangle,
     ** square, and pentagon.                                   */

     private void draw ( ) {

        yertle.moveTo(-80,0);
        drawTriangle();
        yertle.moveTo(-20,0);
        drawSquare();
```

(continued)

```
        yertle.moveTo(40,0);
        drawPentagon();
        yertle.moveTo(0,0);

    }; // draw


    /** This method uses the TurtleGraphics package to draw a
      ** triangle of side 40. The first side of the triangle is
      ** drawn in the current turtle direction. The turtle is
      ** left in its original position and direction with the pen
      ** up.                                                      */

    private void drawTriangle() {

        int i;

        yertle.penDown();
        for ( i=1 ; i<=3 ; i++) {
            yertle.forward(40);
            yertle.right(2*Math.PI/3);
        };
        yertle.penUp();

    };  // drawTriangle


    /** This method uses the TurtleGraphics package to draw a
      ** square of side 40. The first side of the square is drawn
      ** in the current turtle direction. The turtle is left in
      ** its original position and direction with the pen up.    */

    private void drawSquare() {

        int i;

        yertle.penDown();
        for ( i=1 ; i<=4 ; i++) {
            yertle.forward(40);
            yertle.right(2*Math.PI/4);
        };
        yertle.penUp();

    };  // drawSquare
```

(continued)

```
    /** This method uses the TurtleGraphics package to draw a
     ** pentagon of side 40. The first side of the pentagon is
     ** drawn in the current turtle direction. The turtle is
     ** left in its original position and direction with the pen
     ** up.                                                     */

    private void drawPentagon() {

        int i;

        yertle.penDown();
        for ( i=1 ; i<=5 ; i++) {
            yertle.forward(40);
            yertle.right(2*Math.PI/5);
        };
        yertle.penUp();

    };  // drawPentagon


    public static void main ( String args[] ) { new TriSqPent(); };


}   // TriSqPent
```

FIGURE 4.7 Example—Draw a scene with triangle, square, and pentagon

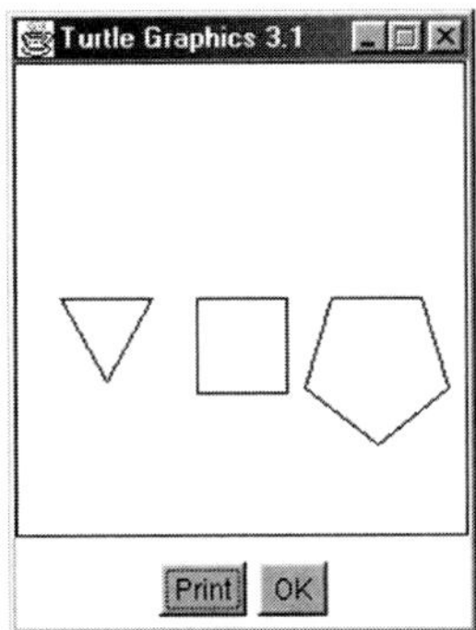

FIGURE 4.8 A scene with triangle, square, and pentagon

The constructor creates the `Turtle` object to draw the scene. It then uses the method `draw` to draw the scene. Constructors are meant to be as simple as possible, primarily initializing the object to its initial state—how it begins life. This involves setting the instance variables to appropriate values; in this case, creating the `Turtle` with which to draw. The constructor of the main class—that is, the one with the method `main`—also initiates the activity of the program, calling `draw`. Chapter 8 discusses state, behavior, and constructors in more detail.

The method `draw` uses `yertle` to perform the actions indicated in Figure 4.1, moving the `Turtle` to the position for the triangle, drawing it (using the method `drawTriangle`), moving to the position for the square, drawing it (using `drawSquare`), moving to the position for the pentagon, drawing it (using `drawPentagon`), and finally moving back to the original position, as any good `Turtle` program should. Note that a method may (and often does) call another method.

The methods `drawTriangle`, `drawSquare`, and `drawPentagon` are similar. They each put the pen down, and then, for the requisite number of sides, they draw a side and rotate to the next side, and finally put the pen up. Note the rotation is `2π/n` where `n` is the number of sides. This value is based on the idea that the `Turtle` must rotate a complete circle (2π) in drawing the figure. The methods leave the pen at the original position, making the transition code easier to figure out.

The method declarations for `draw`, `drawTriangle`, `drawSquare`, and `drawPentagon` are written after the constructor declaration within the class, as is our convention. The order in which they are written is irrelevant; however, they are often written in the order in which they are used.

As the memory model shows, each method has its own variable `i`, but shares the instance variable `yertle`. Figure 4.9 shows the memory model as the second side of the triangle is about to be drawn.

4.3 METHODS WITH PARAMETERS

Methods like those we wrote in Section 4.1 have their uses; however, they are not very versatile. For example, suppose we wished to draw a picture consisting of say, 10 squares of different size. We would have to write 10 methods, each to draw a square with a side of different length. In the example in Figure 4.10, if we were to compare two of these methods, we would see that, other than differing in their names, they differ in only one place: the length of the line to be drawn. It would be better if we could generalize the method code so that it would work for squares of different size much as the `Turtle` method `forward` can be used to draw lines of different lengths.

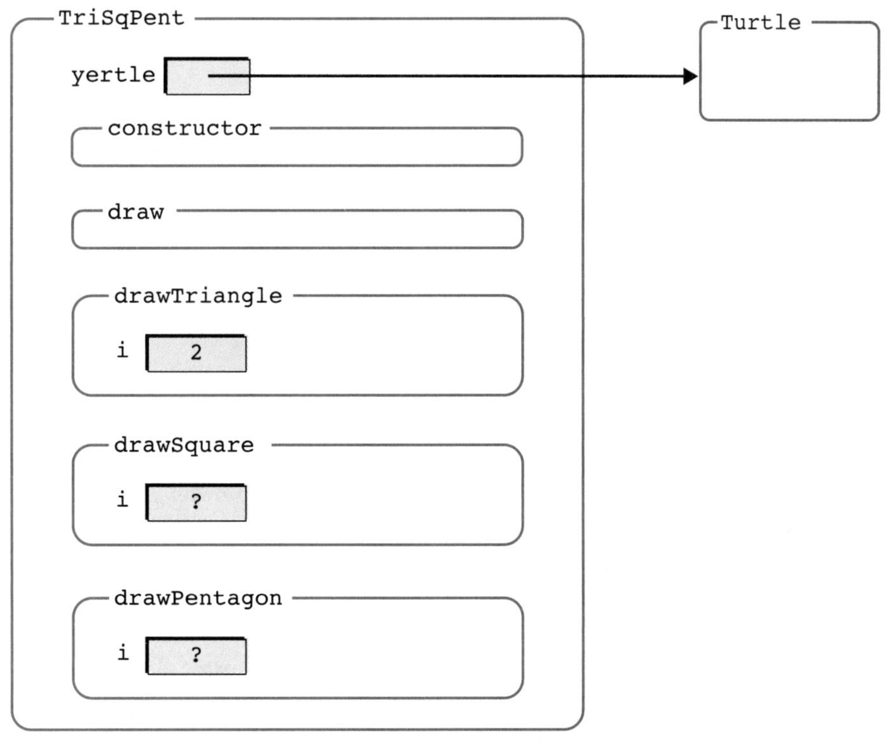

FIGURE 4.9 Memory model for TriSqPent

```
private void drawSquare40 ( ) {

    int i;

    yertle.penDown();
    for ( i=1 ; i<=4 ; i++) {
        yertle.forward(40);
        yertle.right(2*Math.PI/4);
    };
    yertle.penUp();

};  // drawSquare40
```

```
private void drawSquare80 ( ) {

    int i;

    yertle.penDown();
    for ( i=1 ; i<=4 ; i++) {
        yertle.forward(80);
        yertle.right(2*Math.PI/4);
        };
    yertle.penUp();

};  // drawSquare80
```

FIGURE 4.10 Example—Two methods for drawing a square

SYNTAX

```
FormalParameterList:
    FormalParameter
    FormalParameterList , FormalParameter
FormalParameter:
    Type Identifier
```

FIGURE 4.11 Formal parameter list syntax

Parameter Passing

If a single method is to be able to draw different-sized squares, it somehow needs to know how long the sides are to be. For the `Turtle` method `forward`, different length lines are drawn by providing values that indicate the different line lengths. This action is called **passing a parameter**. What we need is for our square method to use **parameters**.

PASSING A PARAMETER is the process, which occurs during a method call, by which actual parameter values are computed and assigned to formal parameters.

A **PARAMETER (FORMAL PARAMETER)** is a variable name declared in the method header that receives a value when a method is called.

The syntax of a method declaration (Figure 4.2) includes an optional *FormalParameterList* between the parentheses following the method name. This is where we specify that a method expects to be passed parameters. We say the method **accepts parameters.** The syntax for the formal parameter list is found in the syntax in Figure 4.11. Essentially, it is a list of one or more *formal parameter declarations* separated by commas. A formal parameter declaration looks essentially the same as a local variable declaration. That is, it is a type followed by an identifier.

To indicate that the method accepts a parameter, we would use the following header:

```
private void drawSquare ( double size )
```

This header indicates that the method `drawSquare` accepts as a parameter a `double` value that it calls `size`. Given the appropriate method body, we could use the method to draw a square with sides of length `80` using the method invocation:

```
drawSquare(80);
```

This passes the value `80` as a parameter. Note that `80` actually is an `int`, not a `double`. However, just as we can assign an `int` value to a `double` variable, we can pass an `int` value to a `double` parameter. Java will automatically convert the value to `double`. In general, any widening conversion—the same ones valid on assignment statements—can be used in passing a parameter.

Formal and Actual Parameters

Within the method body, the **formal parameter** `size` is used just as a local variable, except that it has a value as soon as the method starts, the value passed as the **actual**

```
private void drawSquare ( double size ) {

    int i;

    yertle.penDown();
    for ( i=1 ; i<=4 ; i++ ) {
        yertle.forward(size);
        yertle.right(Math.PI/2);
    };
    yertle.penUp();

};  // drawSquare
```

FIGURE 4.12 Example—Drawing a square using a method with a parameter

An argument (**ACTUAL PARAMETER**) is the expression in a method call that provides a value for a formal parameter.

parameter. We can view this as if an assignment statement occurs as the method is called, assigning the actual parameter value to the formal parameter. Whenever we need to refer to the length of the side and to tell the turtle how long a line to draw, we simply use the formal parameter `size`. The complete method would be written as in Figure 4.12.

Drawing Nested Squares—An Example

Figure 4.13 uses the `drawSquare` method to draw 10 nested squares of various sizes from `10` to `100` pixels, each sharing the same top-left corner, as shown in Figure 4.14. The method `draw` has two local variables: `side` to store the size of the square that is to be drawn next and `i` as a loop index. After creating and positioning the `Turtle`, `draw` initializes `side` to the size of the first square to be drawn (`10` pixels) and then goes through a loop 10 times to draw the 10 squares. Each time, after drawing a square of the specified size (the actual parameter `side`), it increments `side` by `10` in preparation for drawing the next square. The code for `drawSquare` is as given in Figure 4.12.

STYLE TIP

Note the extra comment line in front of the method declaration for `drawsquare`. When a method accepts a parameter, the comment specifies the requirement by a line starting with `@param`, then the parameter name followed by a description of the use of the parameter.

```
import TurtleGraphics.*;

/** This class uses the TurtleGraphics package to draw 10
 ** squares of different sizes with a common corner, making
 ** use of a method.
 **
 ** @author D. Hughes
 **
 ** @version    1.0 (June 2001)                          */

public class NestedSquares {

    private Turtle  yertle;     // turtle for drawing

    /** The constructor uses a Turtle to display ten squares.   */

    public NestedSquares ( ) {

        yertle = new Turtle();
        draw();

    };  // constructor


    /** This method draws 10 squares of different sizes sharing
     ** a common corner.                                     */

     private void draw ( ) {

        int side;       // the various side lengths
        int i;

        yertle.moveTo(-50,50);
        side = 10;
        for ( i=1 ; i<=10 ; i++ ) {
            drawSquare(side);
            side = side + 10;
        };
        yertle.moveTo(0,0);

     }; // draw
```

(continued)

```
    /** This method uses the TurtleGraphics package to draw a
     ** square with a specified side length. The first side of
     ** the square is drawn in the current turtle direction. The
     ** turtle is left in its original position and direction,
     ** with the pen up.
     **
     ** @param size length of side of the square.                  */

    private void drawSquare( double size ) {

        int i;

        yertle.penDown();
        for ( i=1 ; i<=4 ; i++ ) {
            yertle.forward(size);
            yertle.right(Math.PI/2);
        };
        yertle.penUp();

    };  // drawSquare


    public static void main ( String args[] ) { new NestedSquares(); };


}   // NestedSquares
```

FIGURE 4.13 Example—Drawing nested squares using a method with a parameter

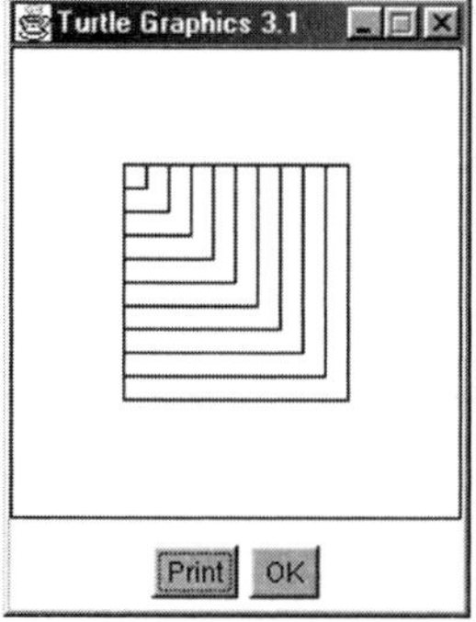

FIGURE 4.14 Nested squares

Parameter compatibility. Java requires that a method with no parameters be invoked with no parameters and a method with one parameter be invoked with one, and so on. In addition, the type of the actual parameter must be assignment-compatible with the formal parameter (see Section 3.4). In the program drawing nested squares, we passed an `int` value to a `double`. However, it would have been invalid to pass a `double` value if the formal parameter was of type `int`. When there are two or more parameters, the types of the corresponding actual and formal parameters must be assignment-compatible.

Parameters and the memory model. The memory model for a method with parameters includes the formal parameter as a cell in the box for the method, just as a local variable. Before the method is called, it has no value, indicated by `?`, just as the local variables have no value. However, when the method is called, and before the method body begins execution, the value of the actual parameter is copied into the storage for the formal parameter, just as if there were an assignment. This is shown in Figures 4.15 and 4.16, showing the model immediately before the first call to `drawSquare` and immediately before the method body is executed on that call, respectively.

One final note about the memory model. Once a method returns, the values of all of its local variables and of its formal parameters are lost. The next time the method is invoked, the formal parameter is initialized to the new actual parameter value and the local variables have indeterminate values. That means that the memory model looks like Figure 4.17 just before the method body is executed for the second time to draw the square `20` pixels wide.

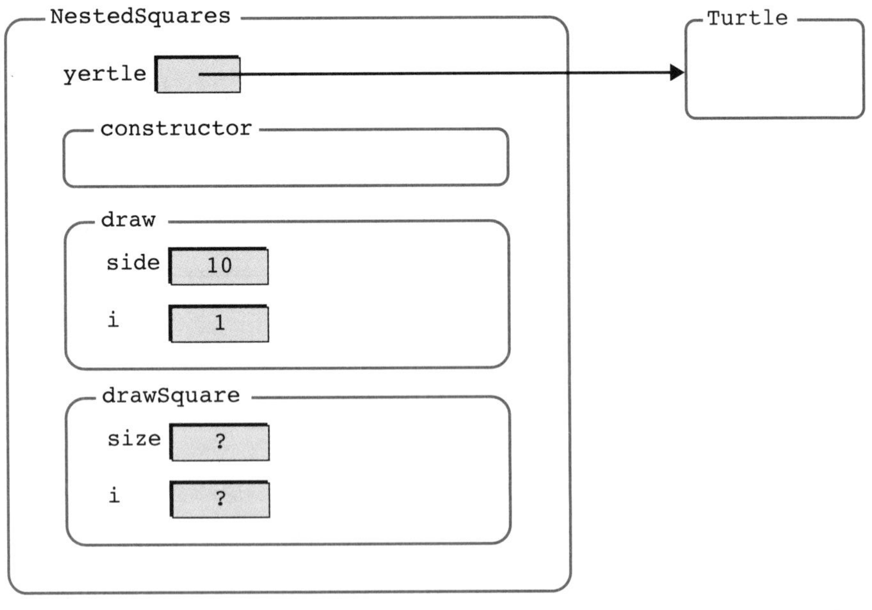

FIGURE 4.15 Memory model for `NestedSquares` (1)

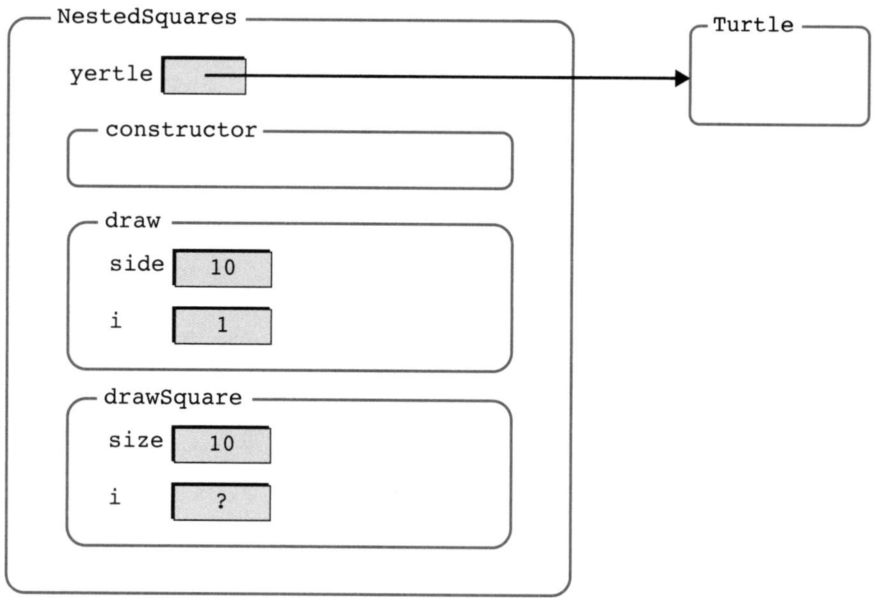

FIGURE 4.16 Memory model for `NestedSquares` (2)

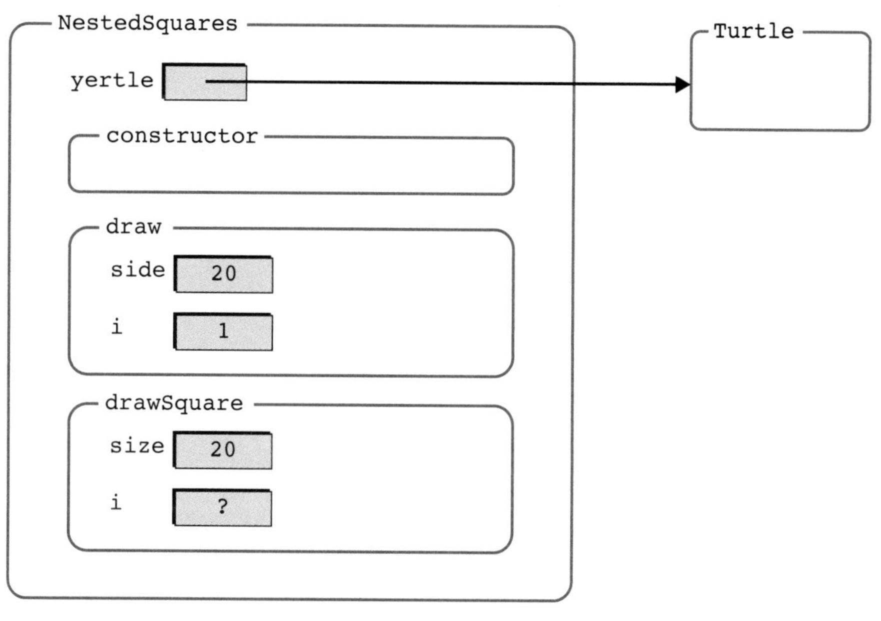

FIGURE 4.17 Memory model for `NestedSquares` (3)

Drawing a Beach Umbrella—An Example

As a second example in the use of parameters, we consider a method to draw a hexagon of specified size. By nesting the hexagons, we can draw a beach umbrella. As we saw in Section 3.5, the size of a hexagon, and in fact the size of any regular closed figure, can be specified by the radius of the circle in which it is inscribed. This means that the method would have one parameter: the radius of the hexagon (`double`). To make the method easier to use, we will have the method draw the hexagon centered on the current turtle position, with one point at the position indicated by the current turtle direction. It will also return the turtle to the original position and direction. The code for the method body is essentially that of the example in Figure 3.16.

The program to draw the beach umbrella is shown in Figure 4.18 and the result in Figure 4.19. The beach umbrella consists of 10 hexagons (centered on the same point) each with a radius from 10 to 100 pixels. The `draw` method is similar to the one that drew nested squares in Figure 4.13.

```
import TurtleGraphics.*;
import java.awt.*;

/** This class uses the TurtleGraphics package to draw a
 ** beach umbrella consisting of 10 concentric hexagons of
 ** radii from 10 to 100 pixels in red with a pen width of 4.
 **
 ** @author D. Hughes
 **
 ** @version    1.0 (June 2001)                          */

public class Umbrella {

    private Turtle  yertle;      // turtle for drawing

    /** The constructor uses a Turtle to display an umbrella.   */

    public Umbrella ( ) {

        yertle = new Turtle();
        draw();

    };  // constructor


    /** This method draws ten concentric hexagons of varying
     ** radius.                                               */
```

(continued)

```
    private void draw ( ) {

        double radius;        // radii for the hexagons
        int r;

        yertle.penColor(Color.red);
        yertle.penWidth(4);
        radius = 10;
        for ( r=1 ; r<=10 ; r++ ) {
            drawHexagon(radius);
            radius = radius + 10;
        };

    }; // draw

   /** This method uses the TurtleGraphics package to draw a
    ** hexagon with a specified radius centered at the current
    ** turtle position with one of the vertices in the position
    ** indicated by the current turtle direction. The turtle is
    ** left in its original position and direction, with the
    ** pen up.
    **
    ** @param radius   radius of the hexagon.                     */

   private void drawHexagon ( double radius ) {

        double side;     // length of a side
        int    i;

        side = 2 * radius * Math.sin(Math.PI/6);
        yertle.forward(radius);
        yertle.right(2*Math.PI/3);
        yertle.penDown();
        for ( i=1 ; i<=6 ; i++ ) {
            yertle.forward(side);
            yertle.right(Math.PI/3);
        };
        yertle.penUp();
        yertle.left(2*Math.PI/3);
        yertle.backward(radius);

   };  // drawHexagon

   public static void main ( String args[] ) { new Umbrella(); };

}  // Umbrella
```

FIGURE 4.18 Example—Draw a beach umbrella using a method with a parameter

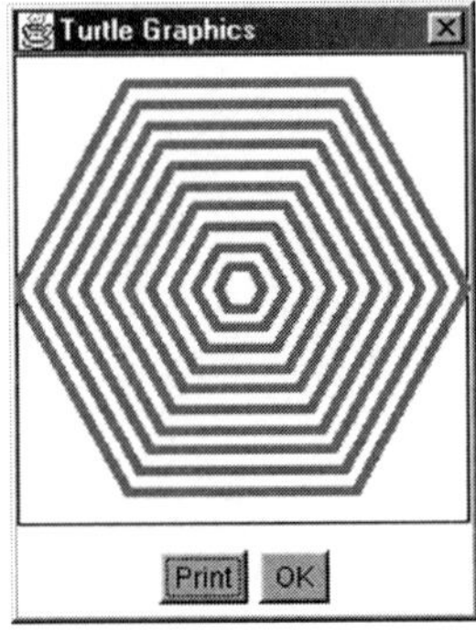

FIGURE 4.19 A beach umbrella

The program in Figure 4.18 demonstrates the use of two additional `Turtle` operations:

`penWidth(width)`	change the pen nib width to `width`
`penColor(color)`	change the pen color to `color`

Normally, the pen width is one pixel, but it can be set to any number of pixels. The usual pen color is black (`Color.black`), but it can also be set to any `Color` value. The package `java.awt` defines a class called `Color`, which provides a number of basic colors referred to as `Color.black`, `Color.red`, and so on.

Each of these methods affects subsequent drawing operations, such as turtle movement with the pen down, until the width or color is changed again. Note that we change the pen width and color before we call the `drawHexagon` method. Since the `drawHexagon` method shares the use of the `yertle` variable reference, these changes affect the drawing in the `drawHexagon` method. The `drawHexagon` method simply uses whatever pen width and color are in effect when it is called.

Drawing Rectangles—An Example

As a final example in the use of parameters, we will write a method to draw a rectangle. A rectangle has both a length and a width, and thus the method will have to take two parameters, both of type `double`. The header will be:

```
private void drawRectangle ( double width, double length )
```

We will need to decide the orientation of the rectangle. Orientation of a figure wasn't as big an issue earlier because we were working with squares, which are symmetric. Here the drawing will start with a width in the current `Turtle` direction and will proceed to draw the sides in a clockwise fashion. Other choices would do just as well, as long as we specify our choice so the user of the method knows what is happening. Figure 4.20 shows a program that uses such a `rectangle` method to draw three rectangles, one `80×20` across the page, one `80×20` down the page, and one `40×40` in blue with a border `6` pixels wide, as shown in Figure 4.21. Actually, the last rectangle is a square, since a square is just a special case of a rectangle.

```
import TurtleGraphics.*;
import java.awt.*;

/** This class uses the TurtleGraphics package to draw a
 ** number of rectangles of different sizes using a method.
 **
 ** @author D. Hughes
 **
 ** @version    1.0 (June 2001)                         */

public class Rectangles {

    private Turtle  yertle;      // turtle for drawing

    /** The constructor uses a Turtle to display rectangles.    */

    public Rectangles ( ) {

        yertle = new Turtle();
        draw();

    };  // constructor


    /** This method draws three different rectangles.           */

    private void draw ( ) {

        yertle.moveTo(-60,60);
        drawRectangle(80,20);
        yertle.moveTo(-20,20);
        yertle.right(Math.PI/2);
        drawRectangle(80,20);
        yertle.moveTo(20,-20);
        yertle.left(Math.PI/2);
        yertle.penWidth(6);
        yertle.penColor(Color.blue);
        drawRectangle(40,40);
        yertle.moveTo(0,0);

    };  // draw
```

(continued)

```
    /** This method uses the TurtleGraphics package to draw a
     ** rectangle of a specified width and length with a corner
     ** at the current turtle position, the first side being a
     ** width, proceeding clockwise from the current turtle
     ** direction. The turtle is left in its original position
     ** and direction, with the pen up.
     **
     ** @param width    width of the rectangle.
     ** @param length   length of the rectangle.              */

    private void drawRectangle ( double width, double length ) {

        int i;

        yertle.penDown();
        for ( i=1 ; i<=2 ; i++ ) {
            yertle.forward(width);
            yertle.right(Math.PI/2);
            yertle.forward(length);
            yertle.right(Math.PI/2);
        };
        yertle.penUp();

    };  // drawRectangle


    public static void main ( String args[] ) { new Rectangles(); };


}   // Rectangles
```

FIGURE 4.20 Example—Draw rectangles using a method with two parameters

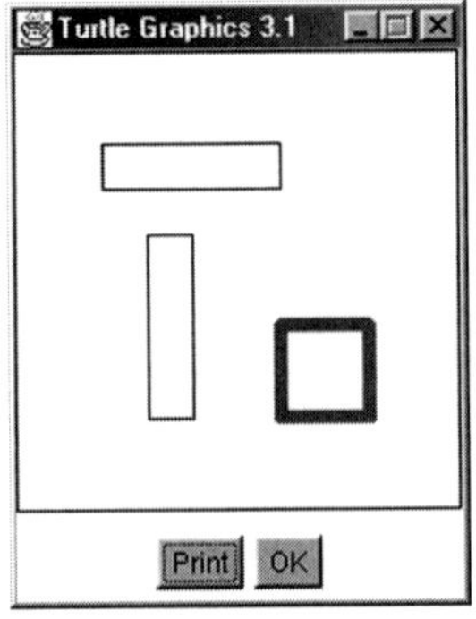

FIGURE 4.21 Rectangles

Since the sides of a rectangle are not the same size, we cannot use a loop to draw the four sides. However, since a rectangle is symmetric across its diagonal, we can use a loop that draws both a width and a length, repeating this action twice to draw the entire rectangle.

4.4 FUNCTION METHODS

A method that, like functions in Mathematics, computes a value is called a **FUNCTION METHOD** or simply a **FUNCTION**.

In addition to providing procedural abstraction, methods can be used to compute a value. These methods are like functions in mathematics and are called **function methods** or **functions**. Function methods are used when we wish to abstract a computation that would otherwise result in a complicated expression, or when the computation cannot be expressed as a simple expression. We will see another common use of function methods in Chapter 8 when we write accessor methods for classes.

Function Method Header

To indicate that we are writing a function method—a method produces a result—we use the second alternative for a *MethodHeader* in Figure 4.2 in which a *Type* is written instead of the keyword `void`. We write as the *Type* the kind of value that the function produces (for example, `int` or `double`). Consider the function method in Figure 4.22. The modifier is `private`; that is, the method can be used only in this class. The result type is `double`, indicating that the result of the computation the method is abstracting is a `double` value. There is one parameter of type `double` called `x`. The body of the method consists of a single statement: a `return` statement. A function method body may, of course, have more than one statement. In that case, the statements are executed in the order in which they are written.

The `return` Statement

The `return` statement is new to us. Its syntax is found in Figure 4.23. The statement begins with the keyword `return`, is (optionally) followed by an *Expression*, and ends with a semicolon. The `return` statement is just another statement; it can be placed anywhere within a method.

STYLE TIP

There can be more than one `return` statement in a method. However, use of more than one `return` statement in a method should be avoided as it leads to confusion. The return statement is usually written as the last statement.

```
private double f ( double x ) {

    return 0.0002 * x * x * x - 0.02 * x * x + 0.3 * x;

};  // f
```

FIGURE 4.22 Example—A function method

SYNTAX

ReturnStatement:
    return *Expression*$_{opt}$;

FIGURE 4.23 `return` statement syntax

The effect of the `return` statement is to compute the value of the expression and then terminate the method. Any statements following the return are not executed. The method produces the value computed in the `return` statement at the place at which the method was invoked.

This means that the function in Figure 4.22, when invoked, solely computes the value of the expression and returns it as its result. The value computed by the expression will be converted, if necessary, using only widening conversions, to the type indicated in the method header. If this cannot be done, the compiler will produce an error message. The version of the `return` without an expression is seldom used and may only be used in procedure methods. All returns in a function method must have an expression.

Function Plot Revisited

Figure 4.24 shows the function plot program of Figure 3.11 rewritten using a function method (from Figure 4.22) and a method `plot` to perform the program activity. In the method `plot`, the expression representing the function has been replaced by a function method invocation in both places that it originally occurred. This is one advantage of abstraction. By writing the code for the expression only once, we reduce the possibility of introducing a bug by mistyping the expression in one of the places in which it is used. It also makes the program easier to change, as we know exactly where—and the only place—to make a change if we wish to change the function we are plotting.

```
import TurtleGraphics.*;

/** This program uses absolute positioning in Turtle Graphics
 ** to plot a function using a function method.
 **
 ** @author D. Hughes
 **
 ** @version    1.0 (June 1999)                          */

public class FunPlot2 {

    private Turtle  yertle;     // turtle for drawing
```

(continued)

```
/** The constructor uses a Turtle plot a function.          */

public FunPlot2 ( ) {

    yertle = new Turtle(Turtle.MEDIUM);
    plot();

};  // constructor


/** This method plots the function over the range -100 to
 ** 100.                                                    */

 private void plot ( ) {

    double  x;      // x-coordinate
    double  y;      // y-coordinate (y = f(x))
    int     i;

    yertle.moveTo(-100,0);
    yertle.penDown();
    yertle.moveTo(100,0);
    yertle.penUp();
    yertle.moveTo(0,-100);
    yertle.penDown();
    yertle.moveTo(0,100);
    yertle.penUp();
    x = -100;
    y = f(x);
    yertle.moveTo(x,y);
    yertle.penDown();
    for ( i=2 ; i<=21 ; i++ ) {
        x = x + 10;
        y = f(x);
        yertle.moveTo(x,y);
    };
    yertle.penUp();

 }; // plot


/** This method computes the function value being plotted.
 **
 ** @param  x       point to compute the function
 **
 ** @return double  the function value at x                  */
```

(continued)

```
    private double f ( double x ) {

        return 0.0002 * x * x * x - 0.02 * x * x + 0.3 * x;

    };  // f

    public static void main ( String args[] ) { new FunPlot2(); };

}   // FunPlot2
```

FIGURE 4.24 Example—Plot a function using a function method

Invoking a function method. As we saw in Section 4.2, a procedure method is invoked using a method invocation as a statement (see the syntax in Figure 4.5). A function method, on the other hand, is invoked as part of an expression. A **function method invocation** is written in an expression as an operand, in the same context that we would write a variable or literal. The execution of the expression involves first evaluating the parameter(s), then invoking the function method, obtaining the value produced when the method returns, and, finally, using this value in the expression. For example, if we wished to compute the value twice that of `f(x)`, we could use the expression:

```
2*f(x)
```

Here, the value of the expression (`x`) is obtained and the function method `f` will be invoked. After it has computed the value of the function at `x`, it will return, producing that value as the operand. This value will then be multiplied by `2`, producing the desired result. You will note that function invocation occurs before arithmetic operators such as `*`. The reason is that function invocation has higher precedence than the arithmetic operators do.

Results from function methods can be converted to other types in the same way as other operand values. In this case, the `int` value `2` is converted to `double` before the multiplication, since the result of the function method is `double`.

Function methods with parameters. As for procedure methods, function methods may have any number of parameters, even none. The formal parameters are included between the parentheses. In Figure 4.22 there is a single parameter `x` of type `double`. Again, within the method, the formal parameter is used as a local variable that has been initialized to the value of the actual parameter.

Function methods can be written in any order. We choose to write them after the constructor and more significant methods.

STYLE TIP

Note the extra line in the comments for function methods. The result of a function method is specified using a comment line beginning with `@return` and giving the result type and the description of what the result is.

CASE STUDY Scaling the Plot to Fit the Window

Problem

In the case study in Chapter 3 that plotted a function (Figure 3.11), the plot only worked if the ranges on the *x*-coordinates and *y*-coordinates were equivalent to the window coordinates, that is, `(-100,-100)` to `(100,100)`. Can we write a program which will scale the plot so that it will fit within the Turtle Graphics window?

Analysis and Design

Basically, we have 200 possible values in each dimension because the window is 200 × 200. If we know the extent of the `x` values to be plotted (`xMin...xMax`), we can scale the values to the correct magnitude (200 values) by multiplying by `xScale = 200/(xMax - xMin)`. Similarly, if we know the extent of the resulting `y` values (`yMin...yMax`), we can scale the `y` values by multiplying by `yScale = 200/(yMax - yMin)`. Next we have to move the curve so that the lowest possible point is at `(-100,-100)`. If `xMin` were `0`, we could simply subtract `100`. When `xMin` is not zero, we have to subtract the number drawing units that `xMin` is from `0`. This results in an offset of `100 + xMin * xScale`, where `xScale` is the scale factor for the `x` dimension. A similar argument gives us an offset of `100 + yMin * yScale` for the `y` dimension.

Coding

If we are to plot `steps+1` points (i.e. `steps` lines in the graph), the `x` values start at `xMin` and are increased by `xInc = (xMax-xMin)/steps`. When drawing a point `(x,y)`, both the *x*- and *y*-coordinate must be scaled and offset appropriately as:

```
(xScale*x+xOffset,yScale*y+yOffset)
```

The program in Figure 4.25 uses these computations to plot a function scaled to the size of the drawing window. The method `plot` takes five parameters (four `double` and one `int`) that characterize the problem, namely, the range on the `x` values (`xMin` and `xMax`), the range on the `y` values (`yMin` and `yMax`) and the number of intervals to plot (`steps`). `steps` is one less than the number of points to be plotted. If the window is 200 units wide, we want to plot a point both at the left edge, at drawing position `-100`, and the right edge, at drawing position `100`. The method computes the scale factors and offsets. It then computes the first point to be plotted and moves the pen to the corresponding drawing position. It scales and offsets the point, then sets the pen down. It then repeatedly draws the remaining points, scaled and offset as appropriate.

The function to be plotted is represented by the function method `f`, which simply returns the value of the function at the point `x`. If we use parameters to set the ranges and number of points to plot and we use a function method to compute the function `f`, the method `plot` doesn't have to be modified in any way when we want to plot the function over a different range or to plot a different function. This is one of the advantages of abstraction—changes are localized to small regions of the program, making it easier to modify. Sample output for the program is shown in Figure 4.26

```
import TurtleGraphics.*;

/**  This program uses Turtle Graphics, methods, and functions
 **  to plot a function scaled to fit the Turtle Graphics
 **  window.
 **
 **  @author D. Hughes
 **
 **  @version`   1.0 (June 2001)                          */

public class ScaledPlot {

 private Turtle  yertle;

 /** The constructor plots the function scaled to the window.*/

 public ScaledPlot ( ) {

     yertle = new Turtle(Turtle.MEDIUM);
     plot(0,Math.PI,-2,1,100);

 };  // constructor

 /** This method plots the function f(x) over the specified
  ** range using the specified number of steps. The plot is
  ** scaled to fit a 200x200 window.
  **
  ** @param  xMin    minimum value on range of x
  ** @param  xMax    maximum value on range of x
  ** @param  yMin    minimum value on domain of f(x)
  ** @param  yMax    maximum value on domain of f(x)
  ** @param  steps   number of steps in plot (#points - 1)    */

 private void plot ( double xMin, double xMax,
                     double yMin, double yMax, int steps ) {

     double  xOffset;     // offset to left edge of window (x-coord)
     double  xScale;      // scale factor for x-coord
     double  xInc;        // increment in x-coord
     double  yOffset;     // offset to bottom edge of window (y-coord)
     double  yScale;      // scale factor for y-coord
     double  x;           // x-coordinate
```

(continued)

```
        double  y;            // y-coordinate
        int     i;

        xScale = 200/(xMax-xMin);
        xOffset = 100+xMin*xScale;
        xInc = (xMax-xMin)/steps;
        yScale = 200/(yMax-yMin);
        yOffset = 100+yMin*yScale;
        x = xMin;
        y = f(x);
        yertle.moveTo(xScale*x-xOffset,yScale*y-yOffset);
        yertle.penDown();
        for ( i=1 ; i<=steps ; i++ ) {
            x = x + xInc;
            y = f(x);
            yertle.moveTo(xScale*x-xOffset,yScale*y-yOffset);
        };

    };  // plot


    /** This function represents the function to be plotted.
      **
      ** @param  x        point to plot
      ** @return double   function value at x                      */

    private double f ( double x ) {

        return Math.cos(2*Math.PI*x) - 0.3*Math.cos(4*Math.PI*x) -
               0.06*Math.cos(6*Math.PI*x);

    };  // f


    public static void main ( String args[] ) { new ScaledPlot(); };


}// ScaledPlot
```

FIGURE 4.25 Example—Scaled function plot

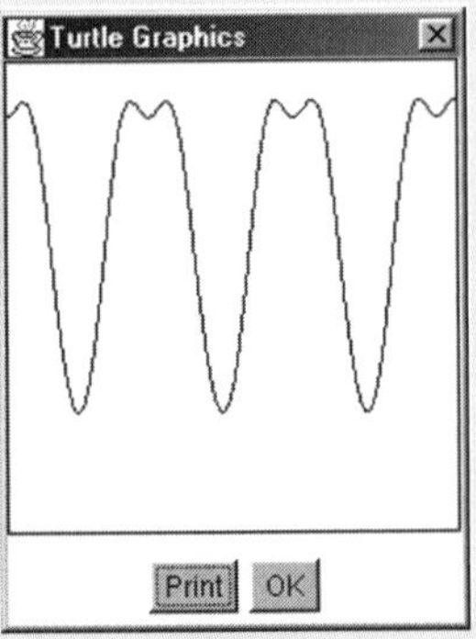

FIGURE 4.26 Scaled function plot

Testing and Debugging

This program also does only one thing, so it is simply necessary to plot the function by hand and compare the output produced by the program. Since the function being plotted is easy to change—just change the body of the function method `f`—different functions can easily be tried. For testing purposes, it is best to use an easily drawn function to see if everything is working correctly. One good test would be to use a straight line that should go from one corner to the other, as represented by the function:

```
f(x) = x
```

Different values of `steps`, `xMin` and `xMax`, and corresponding `yMin` and `yMax` can be used to test the plotting of this function. When all seems to be working, the original function can be plotted.

4.5 TESTING AND DEBUGGING WITH METHODS

As our programs get bigger, it is not always easy to see what has gone wrong when they do not work. As we discussed in Section 1.4, we must effectively test our software and then debug it to remove all errors. In this section, we will consider some techniques to help with the testing and debugging of programs containing methods.

First, consider that the entire program or class doesn't have to be written and tested all at once! Often it is much better to incrementally develop a class by writing the instance variable declarations and constructor first. Instead of the methods that the constructor calls, we write a method stub.

> A **METHOD STUB** is a replacement for a method not yet written that displays a message to the console for testing and debugging purposes.

A **method stub** is a substitute for a method for testing purposes. Instead of the actual method body, it simply contains a statement to display the fact that it was called and the values of its parameters. For example, if we were incrementally developing the `ScaledPlot` class shown in Figure 4.25, we could write a method stub for `plot` as follows:

```
private void plot ( double xMin, double xMax,
                    double yMin, double yMax, int steps ) {
    System.out.println("plot called with parameters:");
    System.out.println("     xMin: "+xMin+" xMax: "+xMax+
                       " yMin: "+yMin+" yMax: "+yMax+
                       " steps: "+steps);
}; // plot
```

The class `System` is a standard class, like `Math`, that provides access to certain system properties, including the system display console called `out`. The system console object has a method `println` that displays its parameter as a text string on the console, followed by a line feed, so that the next display begins on a new line. The parameter to `println` can be any number of values, separated by `+`. The operator `+`, used in this context, is actually string concatenation, as we will see in Chapter 10. The values can be variables, expressions, or sequences of text enclosed in quotes (`"`). These are actually string literals, as we will see also in Chapter 10.

The `ScaledPlot` class would simply contain the instance variable declarations, the constructor, and the method stub for `plot`. When run, the program would display the following to the system console and then quit:

```
plot called with parameters:
     xMin: 0 xMax: 3.141592653589793 yMin: -2 yMax: 1 steps: 100
```

This allows us to determine that the method `plot` is being called at the right point and with the correct parameters.

Continuing incremental development, we would now write the method body for `plot` and method stubs for any methods that `plot` calls, which, in our case, is the function method `f`. For a function method, the method stub also contains, as its last statement, a `return` statement with a literal return value; for example, `1.0`. This means that every call of the function returns the same value. However, for initial testing, this is sufficient as long as we know what value is being returned.

When we are convinced that `f` is being called the right number of times and with the appropriate parameters, we can replace the method stub with the complete body of `f`.

Such incremental development and testing allows us to build a program, knowing that certain parts are working correctly. When a bug is detected, we can concentrate our efforts on the untested portions to find the source of the problem. Often, the calls to `System.out.println` are left in the methods until testing is complete, even after replacing the method stub with an actual body, to allow further testing. The calls are removed when the class is considered complete and working.

 4.6 METHODS, SCOPE, AND VISIBILITY

> The rules that sort out the (unique) meaning of a name (e.g., a variable name) are called **SCOPE RULES**.
>
> The rules defining where a variable (or for that matter a method) declared in some declaration can be used (referenced) within the program are called the **VISIBILITY RULES** (essentially the converse of scope).

In our programs, we have sometimes used local variables and sometimes used instance variables. Sometimes variables in different methods have the same name and sometimes they have different names. Sometimes the formal parameter has the same name as the actual parameter and sometimes not. The rules that sort out the (unique) meaning of a variable, method or class name are called **scope rules**. The rules defining where a variable (or for that matter a method) declared in some declaration can be used (referenced) within the program are called the **visibility rules** (essentially the converse of scope).

Java Scope Rules

In Java the scope rules are quite simple. To determine which declaration of a name is being referenced within a piece of code, we follow the following steps:

1. Look for a declaration of the name in the method (or constructor) in which the code resides. If one exists, this is the defining declaration. This rule applies to both formal parameter declarations and local declarations.
2. If no such defining declaration exists, apply step 1 again, looking in the immediately enclosing code unit. In Java, this would be a class declaration. Continue until there is no enclosing unit. Usually in Java, there is only the method level and the class level to consider. In other languages, however, this could continue for a while, as procedures can be nested within other procedures.
3. If no such declaration exists, check the `public` declarations of `public` classes from imported packages. We'll consider this more completely later. However, this is how the names `Turtle`, `forward`, and `readInt` that are imported from the `TurtleGraphics` or `BasicIO` packages are resolved.
4. If no such declaration exists, the name is undeclared and the reference is in error.

Scope Rules Illustrated

We can see examples of the scope rules in Figure 4.13, in the line

```
yertle.forward(size);
```

of the method `drawSquare`, there are references to three names: `yertle`, `forward`, and `size`. Using the scope rules above, `size` is resolved to the declaration as a formal parameter referencing the length of the side for the square. `yertle` is resolved to the instance variable declaration in the `NestedSquares` class since there is no local or parameter declaration of a name `yertle`. `yertle` references the `Turtle` object that is created by the constructor. Finally, `forward` is resolved to the `public` method provided by the `Turtle` class in the `TurtleGraphics` package imported in the first line. This is the case since there is no local or class level declaration with this name. `forward` references the method to move the turtle forward.

Within the `drawSquare` method, a reference to `i` is resolved to the local declaration for `i`. Within the `draw` method, a reference to `i` is resolved to its local declaration for `i`. These are different declarations and hence different variables and thus different storage locations.

Figure 4.27 repeats the code for the nested squares program (Figure 4.13). The extents of the scope of the various declarations are indicated by the arrows. There are three different scope extents. All `public` classes, methods and variables of the `TurtleGraphics` class (indicated by `TurtleGraphics.*` in the figure), the `NestedSquares` class, the instance variable `yertle`, and the methods `draw` and `drawSquare` have scope including all of the `NestedSquares` class. The local variables `side` and `i` of `draw` have scope including all of the `draw` method. The formal parameter `size` and the local variable `i` of `drawSquare` have scope including all of the `drawSquare` method.

The memory model diagrams of Figures 4.15–4.17 help clarify the scope issues. We know that local variables and formal parameters are placed within the box for the method or constructor in which they are declared. We also know that constructors, methods, and instance variables of an object are placed within the box for that object. Therefore, we can simply trace from the appropriate box—the method in which the reference exists—outward through the enclosing boxes until we find the first occurrence of the name.

Java Visibility Rules

When coding, we must often make a decision as to where to place a declaration within the program. Here we are looking at the converse of scope: visibility. In general, it is desirable to give a variable the most restricted visibility possible that still provides what we need. That is, it is preferable for a variable to be local. We do this to make large programs easier to manage. The visibility rules are derived from the scope rules and, for Java, are:

1. A local variable or formal parameter is visible only within the method in which it is declared. For example, the local variable `i` and the formal parameter `size` are visible only in the method `drawSquare`.
2. An instance variable or method declared `private` within a class is visible within any constructor or method of that class, unless it is **hidden** by a local variable declared with the same name. For example, the instance variable `yertle` and the methods `draw` and `drawSquare` are visible in the `NestedSquares` class.

```
import TurtleGraphics.*;

/** This class uses the TurtleGraphics package to draw ten
 **   squares of different sizes with a common corner making
 **   use of a method.
 **
 **   @author    D. Hughes
 **
 **   @version   1.0 (May 1999)                              */

public class NestedSquares {

     private Turtle  yertle;

     /**   The constructor uses a Turtle to display ten squares.    */

     public NestedSquares ( ) {

          yertle = new Turtle();
          draw();

     };    // constructor

     /**   This method draws ten squares of different sizes sharing
      **   a common corner.                                              */

      private void draw ( ) {

          int side;       // the various side lengths
          int i;

          yertle.moveTo(-50,50);
          side = 10;
          for ( i=1 ; i<=10 ; i++ ) {
               drawSquare(side);
               side = side + 10;
          };
          yertle.moveTo(0,0);

      };  // draw


     /** This method uses the TurtleGraphics package to draw a
      **   square with a specified side length. The first side of
      **   the square is drawn in the current turtle direction. The
      **   turtle is left in its original position and direction,
      **   with the pen up.
      **
      ** @param size length of side of the square.              */

     private void drawSquare( double size ) {

          int i;

          yertle.penDown();
          for ( i=1 ; i<=4 ; i++ ) {
               yertle.forward(size);
               yertle.right(Math.PI/2);
          };
          yertle.penUp();

     };    // drawSquare


     public static void main ( String args[] ) { new NestedSquares(); };

}     // NestedSquares
```


FIGURE 4.27 Scope rules

3. An instance variable, method, or constructor declared `public` within a class is visible as in rule 2, and is also visible within any method or constructor of any class to which the declaring class is visible. For example, the method `forward` from the `Turtle` class is made visible because of the import of the `TurtleGraphics` package.

In deciding where to place the declarations, the declaration of `i` (the loop index for the loop within the `drawSquare` method) was made local to `square` since it was only of concern in that method and it did not need to be referenced anywhere else. The variable `yertle` was declared as an instance variable (but `private`) so that the constructor and the methods `draw` and `drawSquare` would refer to the same `Turtle` object, but no code outside the `NestedSquares` class need know about `yertle`. The method `drawSquare` was declared `private` since it was only to be used within the `NestedSquares` class, by the method `draw`.

STYLE TIP

Declaring Names—Rules of Thumb

There are a number of additional issues regarding scope and visibility that will be discussed in Chapter 8. For now, we will apply the following "rules of thumb," in order of importance, to guide us in declaring names.

1. A variable should be declared as a local variable if its value concerns only the single method or constructor. (See `i` within `drawSquare`.)
2. A variable should be declared as a formal parameter if the behavior of the method depends on the value of variable. (See `size` within `drawSquare`.)
3. A variable should be declared as a `private` instance variable if it serves to coordinate the activity of two or more methods or constructors. (See `yertle` in `NestedSquares`.)
4. A method should be declared as `private` unless it is to be used by code in other classes (See `drawSquare` in `NestedSquares`.)

■ SUMMARY

A method is a named sequence of code that can be invoked by referencing its name. A method may take parameters to modify its actions and may return a result. Methods provide for procedural abstraction; that is, they provide the ability to concentrate on the action to be performed without needing to be concerned with the details of how that action is accomplished. Abstraction is the primary mechanism for dealing with complexity in systems.

A method is executed by an object. There are two forms of method calls. One explicitly references the object and is used to ask the object to perform an action.

The other form of method call is without explicit object reference; it is used when the object performs the action itself, such as for invoking local methods.

Each method may have its own local, temporary storage for information it processes. Formal parameters behave as initialized local variables, with the initial value coming from the actual parameter in the method call. Methods may also reference instance variables.

The scope rules of the language match, with each use of a name, the declaration to which the name refers. The name might be a variable, a method name, or a class name. Visibility is the converse of scope; it indicates, for each declaration, where in the code the entity declared is visible. In general, entities should be declared as locally as possible.

REVIEW QUESTIONS

1. T F Abstraction is dealing with complexity by ignoring irrelevant details.
2. T F Implicit conversion can occur during parameter passing.
3. T F A function method is called in a method invocation statement.
4. T F The following is an example of a method header.

```
public void m ( int p ) { p = 10; };
```

5. T F A `private` instance variable is visible in all methods of the class.
6. T F The first thing executed in a program is always a constructor.
7. T F Method declarations can only be made inside a class.
8. T F Function methods must always be written after the constructor and other methods.
9. Pseudocode is:
   a) a second generation language.
   b) an informal notation for an algorithm.
   c) the machine language of the Z3.
   d) none of the above.
10. Variables may be declared:
    a) in a class.
    b) in a method.
    c) in a constructor.
    d) in all of the above.
11. In the following code:

```
public class Fred {
    int x;
    public Fred ( ) {
        int y;
        fredMeth(y,5);
    }; // constructor
```

```
    private fredMeth ( int p, int q ) {
        int r;
        r = p;
    }; // fredMeth
} // Fred
```

a) `x` is an instance variable and `p` is an actual parameter.
b) `5` is a formal parameter and `r` is a local variable.
c) `y` is an actual parameter and `q` is a formal parameter.
d) `5` is an actual parameter and `p` is a local variable.

12. In the following code:

```
public class Fred {

    public Fred() {
        int x;
        ...
        fredMethod(x);
    }; //constructor

    private void fredMethod(int f){
    ...
    }; //fredMethod
} //Fred
```

a) `x` and `f` are both formal parameters.
b) `x` is the actual parameter and `f` is the formal parameter.
c) `x` is the formal parameter and `f` is the actual parameter.
d) there is no formal parameter.

13. Consider the following method declaration:

```
private double abc(int x,int y){
    ...
}; //abc
```

If the method is invoked as follows:

```
double t;
...
t = abc(10.0);
```

then:

a) there is an error because of assignment incompatibility.
b) there is an error due to the wrong number of parameters.
c) `x = 10` and `y = 0`.
d) a and b are both true.

14. Consider the following method declaration:

```
private int pqr(double a,int b){
    . . .
}
```

If the method is invoked as follows:

```
double r;
. . .
r = pqr(5,3/2);
```

then:
a) there is an error because of assignment incompatibility.
b) there is an error due to the wrong parameter types.
c) `a = 5.0` and `b = 1`.
d) a and b are both true.

15. A `private` method declared in a class is visible:
a) in the constructor of the class.
b) in the methods of the class.
c) in methods of other classes where the class is visible.
d) a and b are both true.

EXERCISES

1. Modify the example in Figure 4.18 to draw 10 concentric pentagons using a method with header:

```
private void drawPentagon ( double radius )
```

The exterior angle for a pentagon is $2\pi/5$ and the length of a side is $2r\sin(\pi/5)$.

2. Write a method with header:

```
privare void drawPentagram ( double radius )
```

that draws a pentagram of specified radius centered on the `Turtle`. The geometry of a pentagram is found in Chapter 3, Exercise 5. Write a program that uses the method to draw a pentagram of radius 60 centered on the page.

3. As we have seen, the basic geometry and drawing process for regular closed figures (such as pentagon, hexagon, and so on—also known as regular polygons) is essentially the same. This indicates that a general method could be written to draw any polygon. Write a method with header:

```
private void drawPolygon ( int nSides, double radius )
```

that draws a regular polygon with `nSides` sides and radius of `radius` number of units, centered on the turtle. The geometry is:

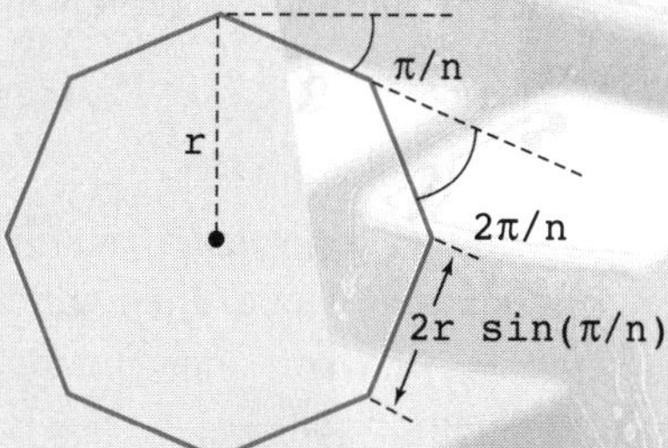

Write a program using this method to draw a triangle centered in the upper-left quadrant of the page, a square centered in the upper-right quadrant, a pentagon centered in the lower-right quadrant, and a hexagon centered in the lower-left quadrant. Each of the figures should have a radius of `40` units.

4. Use the `drawPolygon` method of Exercise 3 to draw the following picture:

The birdhouse consists of a triangle, square, and pentagon. The sun should be drawn using a method with header:

```
private void drawSun ( double radius, int nRays )
```

The sun itself is a 20-sided polygon (using `drawPolygon`) with radius of `radius` number of units. (Note that as the number of sides of a polygon increases, the figure looks more and more like a circle. This is the way circles are actually drawn in computer graphics.) The sun is surrounded by `nRays` rays, which are straight lines of length `radius`. The lines can be made bolder using the `penWidth` method. You can even add color using the `penColor` method.

5 A polyspiral is a spiral-shaped figure consisting of straight lines, each at a particular angle from the other and each line longer than the last by some amount (increment). Write a method with header:

```
private void drawPolyspiral ( double len, double angle,
                              double inc, int num )
```

that draws a polyspiral, starting at the current turtle position and direction, consisting of `num` lines, whose initial line is of length `len`, with `angle` radians between sides and the increment in line length of `inc`. For example, the method call:

```
drawPolyspiral(2,Math.PI/3,2,50);
```

would draw the following figure:

Write a program that will draw the figure above using `drawPolyspiral`. Modify the program to use the call:

```
drawPolyspiral(1,0.9*Math.PI,2,90);
```

Try some other sets of parameters.

6 An epitrochoid is a figure that results from one circle rotating about another circle with a pen attached to the outer circle. These figures are the kinds of figures drawn by the children's toy Spirograph™ where one disk (the outer circle) has a hole for a pen and rotates around the other disk (the inner circle). The figures are dependent on the radius of the inner circle (`a`), the radius of the outer circle (`b`), and the distance of the pen from the center of the outer circle (`k`). In Spirograph, `k` is always smaller than `b`.

Write a method with header:

```
private void drawEpitrochoid ( double a, double b,
                               double k, int num )
```

that draws an epitrochoid. The method will use the `Turtle` absolute drawing method `moveTo` (as in the `FunPlot2` Example in Figure 4.24) instead of the relative drawing method `forward`. The points `(x,y)` for the drawing are based on a variable `t` as follows:

```
x = (a + b)cos(2πt) - k cos(2π(a + b)t/b)
y = (a + b)sin(2πt) - k sin(2π(a + b)t/b)
```

The turtle must be moved to the first point (`t = 0`) with the pen up and then `num` (the last parameter) lines can be drawn (with the pen down) with `t` incremented by `1/num` each time. In other words, `t` runs in the interval `0..1`).

For example, the method call:

```
drawEpictrochoid(50,5,10,100);
```

would draw the following figure:

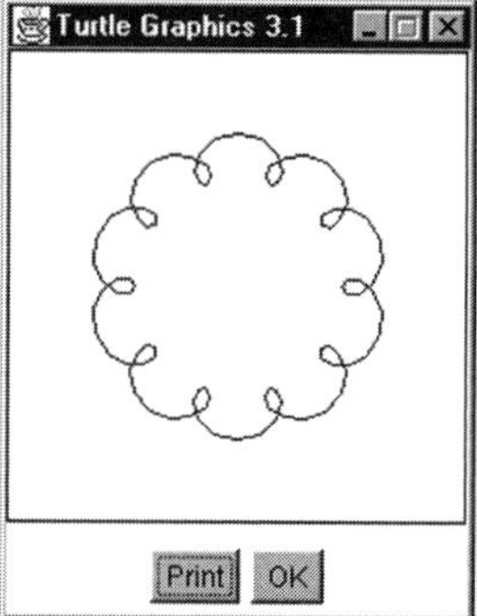

Write a program that uses the `drawEpitrochoid` method to draw the above figure. Modify the program to make the call:

```
drawEpitrochoid(20,10,40,100);
```

Try some other values of your own choice.

5 Input and Output

CHAPTER OBJECTIVES

- To understand the concept of a stream as an abstraction of I/O.
- To know the difference between a text and a binary stream.
- To be able to use the `BasicIO` library to read data from a variety of sources.
- To be able to use the `BasicIO` library to write information to a variety of destinations.
- To understand how to produce well-formatted output using the `BasicIO` library.
- To know the process for producing tables and reports.

Up to now, most of our programs have been self-contained and do precisely one thing. Most real-world computer programs, however, process data that comes from outside the program itself. To do this, a program must be able to access input and output devices such as the keyboard, hard disk, monitor, and printer, which were discussed in Chapter 1. A programming language must, therefore, provide facilities for doing **I/O** (input/output).

5.1 STREAMS

Different kinds of I/O hardware, such as keyboards, disks, and magnetic stripe readers, behave in different ways and even similar types of hardware behave differently from one manufacturer to another. Most programming languages standardize their view of the way I/O works using the concept of a stream. A **stream** is a sequence of information—either bytes for binary information or characters for text information—for input and output. A stream is connected to a source for input or a destination for output. The stream handles the details of the different types of hardware. Connecting a stream to a source or destination is called **opening** the stream, and disconnecting it, which is done when the source or destination is no longer being used, is called **closing** the stream. The act of obtaining information from an input stream is called **reading** and the act of appending information to an output stream is called **writing**.

> A **STREAM** is a sequence of information (either bytes for binary information or characters for text information) from/to which information (i.e., bytes/characters) may be obtained or appended.
>
> Connecting a stream to a source or destination is called **OPENING** the stream.
>
> Disconnecting a stream from a source or destination is called **CLOSING** the stream.
>
> The act of obtaining information from an input stream is called **READING**.
>
> The act of appending information to an output stream is called **WRITING**.
>
> On reading, since the amount of information contained in a stream is finite, there will be a situation when there are no more (or not enough) bytes or characters remaining in the stream. This situation is called reaching **END-OF-FILE** (**EOF**) since, traditionally, files have been the usual source for a stream.

On input, the information is read, starting with the first byte (or character), and each successive read performed by the program reads the next bytes or characters. Similarly, on output the stream starts as empty and each write appends to the end of the stream. On reading, since the amount of information contained in a stream is finite, there will be a situation when there are no more (or not enough) bytes or characters remaining in the stream. This situation is called reaching **end-of-file** (**EOF**) since, traditionally, files have been the usual source for a stream.

This leads to the stream I/O programming pattern shown in Figure 5.1, in which a stream is first opened, the information in it is processed (or generated), and finally the stream is closed. When a program processes several streams, this pattern can be used in a variety of ways. In some cases, the streams are opened at the beginning and closed at the end; essentially, the pattern is nested. Sometimes one stream is opened, processed, and closed, and then another is opened, processed, and closed, and so on. The pattern is sequentially applied. Sometimes both situations occur. It is also not

Programming Pattern

```
open stream
statements involving I/O to/from the stream
close stream
```

FIGURE 5.1 Stream I/O programming pattern

uncommon for a stream to be used to output information to some destination and, after the stream is closed, another stream is opened to input the information back from that destination. Here the destination is being used as temporary storage for information.

The `BasicIO` Package

The I/O facilities that are standard with Java, although based on the stream concept, are not easy to use and involve concepts beyond the scope of an introductory course. They deal with complicated **graphical user interfaces (GUIs)** and unreliable communications media such as the Internet. Instead, we will use a nonstandard library (the `BasicIO` package) that provides basic input/output without the complexity (or flexibility) of the standard Java facilities.

A **GUI (GRAPHICAL USER INTERFACE)** is an interface between the user and the computer that makes use of a graphical display on which symbols (called icons) can be displayed and a pointing device (e.g., mouse) that the user uses to point out actions to be performed.

As was briefly described in Chapter 3, the `BasicIO` package provides a mechanism for I/O. Since input may come from and output may go to a variety of I/O devices, a variety of kinds of streams can be created. Table 5.1 summarizes the facilities. The

TABLE 5.1 `BasicIO` classes

Class	I/O device	Description
`SimpleDataInput`		Input streams.
`ASCIIPrompter`	keyboard	Text input using a dialog box.
`ASCIIDataFile`	disk	Text input from a disk file.
`BinaryDataFile`	disk	Binary input from a disk file.
`SimpleDataOutput`		Output streams.
`ASCIIDisplayer`	monitor	Text output to scrolling window.
`ASCIIReportFile`	disk	Text output to disk file intended to be printed.
`ASCIIOutputFile`	disk	Text output to disk file intended to be input later.
`BinaryOutputFile`	disk	Binary output to disk file intended to be input later.

input streams are defined as SimpleDataInput and the output streams as SimpleDataOutput.

Human versus Computer Use

I/O can be used for two basic purposes: temporary or permanent storage of information by a program for later use by the same or another program, and acquisition or presentation of information from or to a human user. Since human users are more comfortable working with information represented by sequences of letters and digits, I/O intended for human consumption is presented as text. **Text** refers to sequences of characters that are typically represented according to the ASCII coding scheme (see Chapter 7). On the other hand, computers are more comfortable with the binary representation of information, so I/O intended for consumption by another computer program is presented in **binary** form, as a sequence of bytes. The classes BinaryDataFile and BinaryOutputFile are intended for computer program-to-computer program I/O. The classes ASCIIPrompter and ASCIIDisplayer are intended for immediate (and transient) computer-human interaction. The classes ASCIIDataFile and ASCIIReportFile are intended for situations where a human prepares information for a program ahead of time and the computer output is to be printed for later human consumption. Finally, the classes ASCIIDataFile and ASCIIOutputFile are for situations where computer program-to-computer program I/O is desired, but with human interpretation of the information.

> I/O intended for human consumption is presented as **TEXT** (sequences of characters typically represented according to the ASCII coding scheme).
>
> I/O intended for consumption by another computer program is presented in **BINARY** form (sequences of bytes).

All of these combinations could make things quite complicated. However, the BasicIO package has been designed so that all of the input classes work in the same way; that is, they have all the same methods. The output classes also work in the same way. Technically, we say that the input classes satisfy the SimpleDataInput interface, and the output classes satisfy the SimpleDataOutput interface. Although a complete discussion of interfaces is beyond the scope of this text, this means that the same methods are available for each set of input or output classes. To change a program to get input or output from or to a different source or destination, all that is necessary is to change the type in the declaration of the stream object and also in the corresponding object creation expression.

5.2 OUTPUT

SimpleDataOutput is the interface describing output streams in BasicIO. The four classes ASCIIDisplayer, ASCIIReportFile, ASCIIOutputFile, and Binary-

`OutputFile` represent two destinations for the stream: monitor via a window for `ASCIIDisplayer` and disk file for `ASCIIReportFile`, `ASCIIOutputFile`, and `BinaryOutputFile`. They also represent two kinds of information: characters for `ASCIIDisplayer`, `ASCIIReportFile`, and `ASCIIOutputFile`, and bytes for `BinaryOutputFile`. The methods provide for writing values of each of Java's basic types. This means that a single write operation might write one or more bytes or characters to the stream. For example, writing an integer involves writing four bytes in binary or from one to 11 characters in text.

When a stream is to be opened, a constructor for the appropriate class is used to create a new stream object. This object is then requested to perform the appropriate output operations by calling its `write` methods. Finally, the object's `close` method is called to close the stream, after which the object may no longer be used.

Example—Generating a Table of Squares

As an example, the program in Figure 5.2 produces a table of the integers from `1` to `10` and their corresponding squares.

This first line imports the `BasicIO` package so that we can use the I/O facilities. This is like importing the `TurtleGraphics` package, as we did previously. An `ASCIIDisplayer` variable (`out`) is declared as an instance variable to reference the output stream. In this program, we could have declared it as a local variable within the `display` method. However, in most cases, many methods of a class will share the same I/O stream, so we declare it at the class level. The body of the constructor is an example of the stream I/O pattern of Figure 5.1. Creating an `ASCIIDisplayer` object opens the stream, selecting text output to the monitor. The `display` method performs the processing, displaying the table, and the stream (`out`) is then closed via the `close` method.

The `display` method contains three calls to two of the `SimpleDataOutput` methods. The method `writeInt` writes the value of the expression passed as the parameter to the output stream as a sequence of characters (since this is a text stream). The method `writeEOL` writes an **end-of-line marker (EOL)** to the output stream. An end-of-line marker consists of characters that the display device treats as a signal to start the following text on a new line. The output from the program is found in Figure 5.3.

> An **END-OF-LINE (EOL)** marker is a character(s) that the display device treats as a signal to start the following text on a new line.

```
import BasicIO.*;

/**
 ** This program uses BasicIO to display the squares of the
 ** integers from 1 to 10.
 **
 ** @author D. Hughes
 **
 ** @version    1.0 (August 2001)                          */

public class Squares {

    private ASCIIDisplayer  out;    // displayer for output

    /** The constructor uses an ASCIIDisplayer to display the
     ** squares of the integers from 1 to 10.                          */

    public Squares ( ) {

        out = new ASCIIDisplayer();
        display();
        out.close();

    };  // constructor


    /** This method displays a table of squares.                       */

    private void display ( ) {

        int n;

        for ( n=1 ; n<=10 ; n++ ) {
            out.writeInt(n);
            out.writeInt(n*n);
            out.writeEOL();
        };


    };  // display


    public static void main ( String args[] ) { new Squares(); };


}   // Squares
```

FIGURE 5.2 Example—Generating a table of squares of integers from 1 to 10

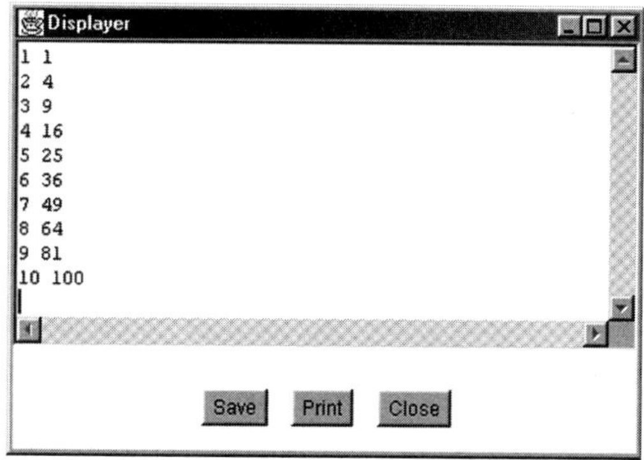

FIGURE 5.3 Squares program output

Example—Formatting the Table

Although this program produces the desired result, the layout of the table leaves a lot to be desired. It would be better if the table had a heading over each column and the columns lined up appropriately. `SimpleDataOutput` has facilities for creating this type of **formatted output**. The method `WriteLabel` writes out a sequence of characters, which serves as a heading within the output. A second version of `writeInt` takes two parameters, the first for the output value and the second for the number of characters to use in writing that value. The data output by a single call to a `write` method is called a **field**, and so the second parameter is called the **field width**. Figure 5.4 shows a second version of the squares program using these facilities.

> **FORMATTED OUTPUT** is a form of text output allowing control over layout of the information and insertion of headings, titles, etc.
>
> The data output by a single call to a write method is called a **FIELD**.
>
> The **FIELD WIDTH** is the number of characters the field is to occupy on output.

```
import BasicIO.*;

/**
 ** This program uses BasicIO to display a table of the squares
 ** of the integers from 1 to 10.
 **
 ** @author D. Hughes
 **
 ** @version    1.0 (August 2001)                             */

public class SquareTable {

    private ASCIIReportFile out;     // report file for output
```

(continued)

```
    /** The constructor uses an ASCIIReportFile to display the
     ** squares of the integers from 1 to 10.                                    */

    public SquareTable ( ) {

        out = new ASCIIReportFile();
        display();
        out.close();

    };  // constructor


    /** This method displays the table of squares.                               */

    private void display ( ) {

        int n;

        out.writeLabel(" n   n^2");
        out.writeEOL();
        for ( n=1 ; n<=10 ; n++ ) {
            out.writeInt(n,2);
            out.writeInt(n*n,5);
            out.writeEOL();
        };


    };  // display


    public static void main ( String args[] ) { new SquareTable(); };


}  // SquareTable
```

FIGURE 5.4 Example—Generating a formatted table of squares

In this example we use an `ASCIIReportFile` object for the stream since we expect that the purpose of the program is to produce a file suitable for printing. If we had wanted the output to be displayed on the monitor, we would have created an `ASCIIDisplayer` object instead, and the rest of the program would have remained the same. When the program runs, a dialog box is presented to allow the selection of a file for the output. The method `writeLabel` writes out the sequence of characters enclosed in the quotes ("). Technically, a sequence of characters enclosed in quotes is called a `String` in Java, as we

```
 n   n^2
 1     1
 2     4
 3     9
 4    16
 5    25
 6    36
 7    49
 8    64
 9    81
10   100
```

FIGURE 5.5 A formatted table of squares

shall see in Chapter 10. The following `writeEOL` makes this sequence one line of the output. The `writeInt` calls each have a second parameter, the field width, which indicates that the value of `n` should produce `2` characters to the output and the value of `n*n`, `5`. This version of `writeInt` also places commas every three digits, so room must be left for these. Since `ASCIIReportFile` and `ASCIIDisplayer` place one space between successive data values output, this means that each line will have the form:

XX_XXXXX

where `XX. . .` is a sequence of digits representing a single data value and _ represents a space character. When an integer is written in a field, if the number of digits making up that integer is smaller than the field width, the number is right justified with spaces filling the field to the left. If the number is too large for the field, a sequence of asterisks (*) is displayed in place of the field. The output of the program in Figure 5.4 is found in Figure 5.5.

Figure 5.4 also uses another programming pattern: table generation (see Figure 5.6). A table generally consists of a title, a heading, and a sequence of lines presenting the table information. Here we haven't bothered to produce a title but the heading is the line

```
 n   n^2
```

generated by the two method calls. A `for` loop is used to iterate over the lines. Unusually, a `for` loop is used in table generation; however, sometimes other types of loops may be used, as shown in Chapter 6.

Programming Pattern

```
generate title line(s)
generate heading line(s)
for each line of the table
    for each entry in the line
        generate entry
    mark end of line
```

FIGURE 5.6 Table generation programming pattern

Since the lines of the table are quite simple, two successive method calls are used to generate the table entries rather than the more general loop indicated by the pattern. Finally, the end of line is marked using `writeEOL`. Note that the table generation pattern has been nested in the stream I/O pattern, generating the table to a stream.

Example—Generating a Compound Interest Table

Integers are not the only kinds of values that can be written using `SimpleDataOutput`. Figure 5.7 shows a program to generate a compound interest table whose output is shown in Figure 5.8. In the program, the values for balance, rate, and interest are represented by `double` variables. Again, the program is an example of a table generation pattern. For the purposes of this example, the initial balance (principal), interest rate, and the number of years are initialized to `$1000`, `5%`, and `10` years, respectively. The title and heading are then generated by the `writeHeader` method. The information for the table entries is determined by computing the interest on the current balance and then increasing the balance by the interest amount. Finally, the line of the table is produced by the `writeDetail` method.

```
import BasicIO.*;

/**
 ** This program uses BasicIO to display a compound interest
 ** table for a principal of $1000 at a rate of 5% for 10 years.
 **
 ** @author D. Hughes
 **
 ** @version    1.0 (August 2001)                                  */

public class CompInt {

    private ASCIIDisplayer  out;     // displayer for output

    /** The constructor uses an ASCIIDisplayer to display the
     ** compound interest table.                                   */

    public CompInt ( ) {

        out = new ASCIIDisplayer();
        display();
        out.close();

    };  // constructor
```

(continued)

```
/** This method displays a compound interest table.                    */

private void display ( ) {

    double  b;      // balance
    double  r;      // rate
    double  i;      // interest
    int     n;      // number of years

    b = 1000;
    r = .05;
    writeHeader(b,r);
    for ( n=1 ; n<=10 ; n++ ) {
        i = b * r;
        b = b + i;
        writeDetail(n,i,b);
    };

};  // display


/** This method displays the table title and headings.
 **
 ** @param  b   the opening balance
 ** @param  r   the interest rate                                      */

private void writeHeader ( double b, double r ) {

    out.writeLabel("Principal: $");
    out.writeDouble(b,0,2);
    out.writeLabel(" Rate: ");
    out.writeDouble(r*100,0,0);
    out.writeLabel("%");
    out.writeEOL();
    out.writeEOL();
    out.writeLabel("Year  Interest   Balance");
    out.writeEOL();

};  // writeHeader
```

(continued)

```
    /** This method displays the detail line of the table.
     **
     ** @param  y   the year number
     ** @param  i   the interest
     ** @param  b   the balance                                        */

     private void writeDetail ( int y, double i, double b ) {

         out.writeInt(y,4);
         out.writeDouble(i,9,2);
         out.writeDouble(b,9,2);
         out.writeEOL();

     }; // writeDetail


    public static void main ( String args[] ) { new CompInt(); };


}   // CompInt
```

FIGURE 5.7 Example—Generating a compound interest table

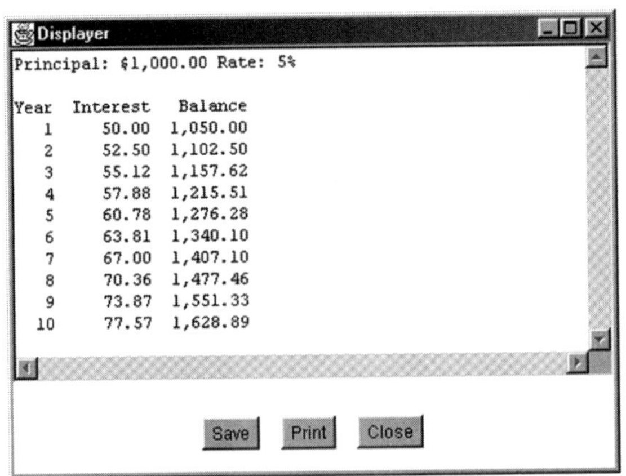

FIGURE 5.8 Compound interest table

STYLE TIP

Since the actual formatting of output information usually involves many method calls, it is common to place this code in a method and pass it the actual information to be printed as parameters. This makes the code easier to read and understand since the actual details of the output layout are abstracted into the methods. This is what is done in the `writeHeader` and `writeDetail` methods.

In the formatting methods (`writeHeader` and `writeDetail`), `writeDouble` is used to write the `double` values. `writeDouble` works similarly to `writeInt` except that it displays a `double` value. The second and third parameters are the field width and number of decimal places, respectively. The field width should be large enough to account for the decimal places, decimal point, and commas inserted every three digits. For example, `7654.321` written out with a field width of `10` and `2` decimal places would produce the field `__7,654.32`. If the field width is too small, a field of asterisks will be produced. There is also a version of `writeDouble` that has only one parameter, the value to be written, which writes the value using an appropriate number of characters.

Note the use of `0` for the field width in `writeHeader`. When a field width of `0` is specified, a width appropriate for the number of digits is used. That is, there are no leading spaces. This specification is useful when embedding a value in a sentence where no extra spaces are desired. Since no spaces are produced between label text that is written by `writeLabel` and data fields that have been written by `writeDouble`, spaces should be included in the label if desired. This technique also works when using `writeInt`. If the number of decimal places in `writeDouble` is `0`, the decimal point is not produced.

`SimpleDataOutput` Summary

Table 5.2 summarizes the constructors and Table 5.3 shows the methods available in the `SimpleDataOutput` interface. The method `successful` is used to determine whether the last method or constructor used on this stream completed successfully. A constructor does not successfully complete if it was unable to open the file or window. The method `close` completes unsuccessfully if it is unable to close the file. The other methods themselves do not normally fail; however, hardware problems and other errors can occasionally happen, which could cause them to fail. A secure program will check to see if a stream has successfully been opened before using it.

As can be seen from Table 5.3, there are a number of methods that we haven't discussed. Essentially, there is a method for output of any of the Java basic types. We have already seen the numeric types. The remaining primitive types (`boolean` and `char`) are discussed in Chapter 7, object types in Chapter 8, and strings in Chapter 10. Not all methods function for all types of streams. Essentially, methods that perform layout are functional only for formatted streams (see notes 1 and 2 of Table 5.3).

TABLE 5.2 `SimpleDataOutput` **constructors**

Constructor	Type	Description
`ASCIIDisplayer()`	Formatted text window	Constructs a window containing a scrollable text area to which values can be written.
`ASCIIReportFile()`	Formatted text file	Constructs a stream to access an ASCII text file for output. Displays the standard save dialog box.
`ASCIIOutputFile()`	Tab-delimited text file	Constructs a stream to access an ASCII text file for output. Displays the standard save dialog box.
`BinaryOutputFile()`	Binary file	Constructs a stream to access a binary data file for output. Displays the standard save dialog box.

TABLE 5.3 `SimpleDataOutput` **methods**

Method	Notes	Description
`close()`		Closes the output stream, releasing resources as necessary.
`successful()`		Indicates whether or not the previous operation was successful.
`writeBoolean(boolean v)`		Outputs a `boolean` value.
`writeBoolean(boolean v, int w)`	1	Outputs a `boolean` value left-justified in `w` positions.
`writeByte(byte v)`		Outputs a `byte` value.
`writeByte(byte v, int w)`	1	Outputs a `byte` value right-justified in `w` positions.
`writeC(char v)`	4	Outputs a `char` value without separators.
`writeChar(char v)`		Outputs a `char` value.
`writeChar(char v, int w)`	1	Outputs a `char` value left-justified in `w` positions.
`writeDouble(double v)`		Outputs a `double` value.
`writeDouble(double v, int w, int d)`	1	Outputs a `double` value right-justified in `w` positions with `d` decimal places.
`writeEOL()`	3	Writes an end-of-line marker.
`writeFloat(float v)`		Outputs a `float` value.
`writeFloat(float v, int w, int d)`	1	Outputs a `float` value right-justified in `w` positions with `d` decimal places.

TABLE 5.3 (Continued)

Method	Notes	Description
`writeInt(int v)`		Outputs an `int` value.
`writeInt(int v, int w)`	1	Outputs an `int` value right-justified in `w` positions.
`writeLabel(String v)`	2	Outputs a `String` as a label (nondata).
`writeLine(String v)`	4	Outputs a `String` as a line.
`writeLong(long v)`		Outputs a `long` value.
`writeLong(long v, int w)`	1	Outputs a `long` value right-justified in `w` positions.
`writeObject(Object v)`	5	Outputs an `Object`.
`writeObject(Object v, int w)`	1, 5	Outputs an `Object` left-justified in `w` positions.
`writeShort(short v)`		Outputs a `short` value.
`writeShort(short v, int w)`	1	Outputs a `short` value right-justified in `w` positions.
`writeString(String v)`		Outputs a `String`.
`writeString(String v, int w)`	1	Outputs a `String` left-justified in `w` positions.

Notes:
1. Effective only for formatted output streams; otherwise, same as unformatted version.
2. Effective only for formatted output streams; otherwise, no effect.
3. Effective only for text streams; otherwise, no effect.
4. Effective only for nonformatted text output streams; otherwise, same effect as `writeChar` or `writeString`.
5. Uses `v.toString()` for output to text streams. Only effective for binary streams if class is `Serializable`.

5.3 INPUT

To access information from outside the computer program—an input stream—we use the `SimpleDataInput` interface. There are three classes that define `SimpleDataInput` streams: `ASCIIPrompter`, `ASCIIDataFile`, and `BinaryDataFile`. These support keyboard (`ASCIIPrompter`) and disk (`ASCIIDataFile` and `BinaryDataFile`) streams in text mode (`ASCIIPrompter` and `ASCIIDataFile`) and binary mode (`BinaryDataFile`). The methods support the reading of the basic Java types, reading one or more bytes or characters per call.

Example—Compound Interest Table Revisited

The example in Figure 5.9 extends the compound interest table example of Figure 5.7. It allows the user to generate the table by entering a principal, a rate, and the number of years. For immediate response, it generates its output to an `ASCIIDisplayer` and gets its input from the user via an `ASCIIPrompter`. Since the program is going to do both input and output, it declares two stream variables (`in` and `out`) and then opens an `ASCIIPrompter` for input and an `ASCIIDisplayer` for output.

Instead of initializing the initial balance, rate, and number of years to fixed values, the program uses the `ASCIIPrompter` to prompt the user to enter these values. The methods `readInt` and `readDouble` are used to read `int` and `double` values, respectively, from an input stream. These are function methods taking no parameters. They return, as their result, the value read.

```
import BasicIO.*;

/**
 ** This program uses BasicIO to display a compound interest
 ** table for a given principal and rate for a given number of
 ** years.
 **
 ** @author D. Hughes
 **
 ** @version    1.0 (August 2001)                                */

public class CompInt2 {

    private ASCIIPrompter       in;          // prompter for input
    private ASCIIDisplayer      out;         // displayer for output

    /** The constructor uses an ASCIIPrompter to input the principal
     ** rate and number of years and an ASCIIDisplayer to display
     ** the compound interest table.                               */

    public CompInt2 ( ) {

        in = new ASCIIPrompter();
        out = new ASCIIDisplayer();
        display();
        in.close();
        out.close();

    };  // constructor
```

(continued)

```
/** This method displays the compound interest table.                    */

private void display ( ) {

    double  b;      // balance
    double  r;      // rate
    double  i;      // interest
    int     ny;     // number of years
    int     n;      // year number

    in.setLabel("Principal");
    b = in.readDouble();
    in.setLabel("Rate");
    r = in.readDouble();
    in.setLabel("Years");
    ny = in.readInt();
    writeHeader(b,r);
    for ( n=1 ; n<=ny ; n++ ) {
        i = b * r;
        b = b + i;
        writeDetail(n,i,b);
    };

};  // display


/** This method displays the table title and headings.
 **
 ** @param  b   the opening balance
 ** @param  r   the interest rate                                           */

private void writeHeader ( double b, double r ) {

    out.writeLabel("Principal: $");
    out.writeDouble(b,0,2);
    out.writeLabel(" Rate: ");
    out.writeDouble(r*100,0,0);
    out.writeLabel("%");
    out.writeEOL();
    out.writeEOL();
    out.writeLabel("Year  Interest   Balance");
    out.writeEOL();

};  // writeHeader
```

(continued)

```
    /** This method displays the detail line of the table.
     **
     ** @param  y   the year number
     ** @param  i   the interest
     ** @param  b   the balance                                          */

     private void writeDetail ( int y, double i, double b ) {

        out.writeInt(y,4);
        out.writeDouble(i,9,2);
        out.writeDouble(b,9,2);
        out.writeEOL();

     }; // writeDetail


    public static void main ( String args[] ) { new CompInt2(); };


}   // CompInt2
```

FIGURE 5.9 Example—Compound interest table with user input

When the input stream is an `ASCIIPrompter`, the `read` methods display a dialog box as shown in Figure 5.10. The dialog box contains a **prompt**, an area in which the program can indicate what input is desired. The method `setLabel` is used to set the prompt for the next dialog box that is displayed. The parameter is the prompt enclosed in quotes ("). This is a `String` literal, as we will see in Chapter 10. The user types the desired input and then either presses the `OK` button or hits the `return/enter` key. At this point, the method returns with the desired value. The rest of the program is the same as in the original example of Figure 5.7. When the program runs, the user is prompted first for a principal, then for a rate, and finally for a number of years. The program then displays the desired interest table to the displayer. The output is the same as in Figure 5.8.

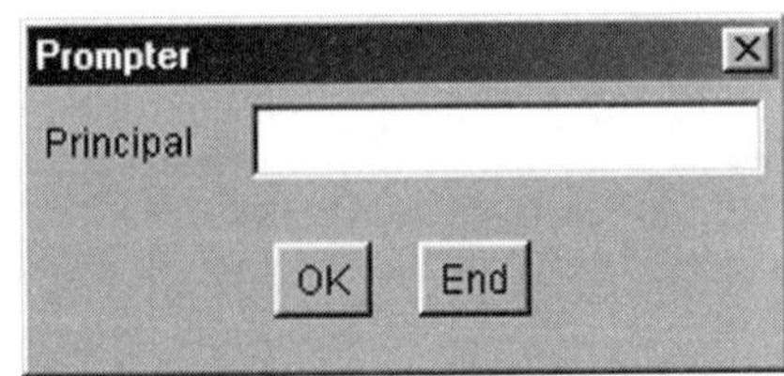

FIGURE 5.10 `ASCIIPrompter` dialog box

Example—Averaging Marks

To read from a text-oriented data file, an `ASCIIDataFile` stream is used. The data file is created ahead of time, either as a result of a Java program writing an `ASCIIOutputFile` or by an editor or other program. The text file can consist of a number of lines, each containing a number of fields that contain the data values. The fields are separated from each other by white space such as spaces and tabs. In preparing a file in an editor, it is probably easiest to separate the fields on the line by tabs and the lines by returns. This is how the file created by an `ASCIIOutputFile` is organized, and it is called **tab-delimited format.**

A file in **TAB-DELIMITED FORMAT** contains text fields separated by tabs or new lines.

Figure 5.11 shows a program that reads from a text data file containing student mark information and produces a report to a displayer giving the class average. A sample data file is given in Figure 5.12. Here, the first value is the number of students, and then each successive line contains a single student mark. The mark values are considered to be `double` since a student could get a fractional mark such as `75.5`. Note the blank line between the number of students and the first student's mark. This blank line is unnecessary and is there solely for the human reader; as white space, it will be ignored on input.

```
import BasicIO.*;

/**
 ** This program inputs a series of marks for students in a
 ** class and computes the class average.
 **
 ** @author D. Hughes
 **
 ** @version    1.0 (Aug. 2001)                          */

public class ClassAve {

    private ASCIIDataFile       in;          // file for data
    private ASCIIDisplayer      out;         // displayer for output
```

(continued)

```
/** The constructor uses an ASCIIDataFile to read a set of
 ** student mark data and then computes the class average,
 ** displaying it to an ASCIIDisplayer.                   */

public ClassAve ( ) {

    in = new ASCIIDataFile();
    out = new ASCIIDisplayer();
    display();
    in.close();
    out.close();

};  // constructor


/** This method computes and displays the class average.    */

private void display ( ) {

    int     numStd;      // number of students
    double  aMark;       // one student's mark
    double  totMark;     // total of marks
    double  aveMark;     // average mark
    int     i;

    numStd = in.readInt();
    totMark = 0;
    for ( i=1 ; i<=numStd ; i++ ) {
        aMark = in.readDouble();
        totMark = totMark + aMark;
    };
    aveMark = totMark / numStd;
    writeDetail(numStd,aveMark);

};  // display


/** This method writes the detail line.
 **
 ** @param  numStd  number of students
 ** @param  avemark average mark                             */
```

(continued)

```
    private void writeDetail ( int numStd, double aveMark ) {

        out.writeLabel("Number of students: ");
        out.writeInt(numStd);
        out.writeEOL();
        out.writeLabel("Average mark: ");
        out.writeDouble(aveMark,0,2);
        out.writeEOL();

    };  // writeDetail

    public static void main ( String args[] ) { new ClassAve(); };


}   // ClassAve
```

FIGURE 5.11 Example—Computing class average

The program reads the number of students (first field in the data file) and initializes the total of the students' marks (`totMark`) to zero. This makes sense as, so far, we haven't processed any marks, so the total of the marks processed so far is `0`. The program then loops for each student, reading the student's mark and adding it into the total. Remember, the statement:

```
totMark = totMark + aMark;
```

simply increases the value of `totMark` by `aMark`. Note that each time through the loop, the `readDouble` reads the next input field, assigning the value read to `aMark`, thus changing its value. We thus iterate through all the students in the file. When we are done, the program computes the average student mark as the sum (`totMark`) divided by the number of students (`numStd`). Note that `numStd` is converted to `double` before the division, since `totMark` is `double`. (What would have happened if `totMark` was `int`?) Finally, the number of students and average mark are displayed and the streams closed.

The program in Figure 5.11 also demonstrates another programming pattern: summation, shown in Figure 5.13. To compute a sum, we simply add up all the values in the set of data. By hand, we would add the first two values and then sequentially add the next value to the sum. To do this efficiently by computer, it is better to consider the sum as being initially zero (that is, the sum of zero values so far) and then add the first data value to it, then the second, and so on. After the first two additions, the computer version continues in the same manner as the manual one. The pattern reflects this order. It assumes that there is a variable into which the sum is being accumulated (*sum*). First, it initializes sum to zero and then, for each data value, obtains the next value and adds it to the sum.

Obtaining the next value may involve a computation, reading a value, or both. A variety of different loops could also be used, as we will see in Chapter 6.

```
10

57
85
29
68
87
92
45
75
89
78
```

FIGURE 5.12 Class average input file

Programming Pattern

```
sum = 0;
for all data values
    obtain next datavalue
    sum = sum + datavalue
```

FIGURE 5.13 Summation programming pattern

Figure 5.11 uses `totMark` as the sum, a `for` loop to iterate over the `numMark` values, and `readDouble` to obtain the next value (`aMark`).

CASE STUDY Generating a Marks Report

Problem

A system is required to allow an instructor to record marks for students at various times and to later be able to generate a marks report that lists, for each student, the student number and mark achieved. In the report, the average mark for the course should also be displayed.

Analysis and Design

This system really requires two programs, one to enter the marks and one to produce the report. We will assume that the first has been written and concentrate on the second of these. The marks entered by the first program will be stored in a file.

Binary data files are commonly used when the output of one program is to be used as the input to another, without human intervention. This process is more efficient since the data values are stored (in the file) in the computer's native representation and conversion to or from a text-based representation is avoided. Often the file is also considerably smaller.

The reporting program will read the number of students and then the mark data from the binary file. It must sum the marks so it can produce the average.

Implementation

Figure 5.14 is the program that produces the marks report by reading the binary file. It is assumed that the binary file contains, in order, the count of the number of students (`int`) followed by, for each student, the student number (`int`) and the student's mark (`double`). It is critical that the two programs agree on the layout of the binary file since the second program will read bytes, and, if they don't correspond to the data types originally written, the values read will appear to be garbage. The output is shown in Figure 5.15. Note the commas in the student numbers. These are undesirable; however, there is no facility for preventing this in `BasicIO`. We will see a method for dealing with this when we discuss strings in Chapter 10.

```
import BasicIO.*;

/**  This program inputs marks for students in a course and
 **  produces a report listing the student numbers and marks
 **  and the overall average.
 **
 **  @author D. Hughes
 **
 **  @version1.0 (Aug. 2001)                              */

public class MarkList {

 private BinaryDataFile      in;      // file for data
 private ASCIIReportFile     out;     // report for printer
 private ASCIIDisplayer      msg;     // displayer for messages

 /** The constructor uses a BinaryDataFile to read a set of
  ** student mark data and then produces a report to an
  ** ASCIIReportFile listing the marks and the overall average.
  **                                                          */

 public MarkList ( ) {

     in = new BinaryDataFile();
     out = new ASCIIReportFile();
     msg = new ASCIIDisplayer();
     display();
     in.close();
     out.close();
     msg.close();

 };  // constructor
```

(continued)

```
/** This method displays the mark list for the course.        */

private void display ( ) {


    int     numStd;       // number of students
    int     aStdNum;      // one student's student number
    double  aMark;        // one student's mark
    double  totMark;      // total of marks
    double  aveMark;      // average mark
    int     i;

    writeHeader();
    numStd = in.readInt();
    totMark = 0;
    msg.writeLabel("Processing students...");
    msg.writeEOL();
    for ( i=1 ; i<=numStd ; i++ ) {
        aStdNum = in.readInt();
        aMark = in.readDouble();
        writeDetail(aStdNum,aMark);
        totMark = totMark + aMark;
    };
    aveMark = totMark / numStd;
    writeSummary(aveMark);
    msg.writeInt(numStd);
    msg.writeLabel(" students processed.");
    msg.writeEOL();

};  // display


/** This method writes the header for the report.              */

private void writeHeader ( ) {

    out.writeLabel("Final Mark Report");
    out.writeEOL();
    out.writeLabel("    COSC 1P02");
    out.writeEOL();
    out.writeEOL();
    out.writeLabel("  St. #    Mark");
```

(continued)

```
        out.writeEOL();
        out.writeLabel("------------------");
        out.writeEOL();

    };  // writeHeader


    /** This method writes a detail line of the report.
     **
     ** @param  stdNum  the student number
     ** @param  mark    the mark                                    */

    private void writeDetail ( int stdNum, double mark ) {

        out.writeInt(stdNum,8);
        out.writeDouble(mark,6,2);
        out.writeEOL();

    };  // writeDetail


    /** This method writes the summary for the report.
     **
     ** @param  ave average mark                                    */

    private void writeSummary ( double ave ) {

        out.writeLabel("------------------");
        out.writeEOL();
        out.writeLabel(" Average ");
        out.writeDouble(ave,6,2);
        out.writeEOL();

    };  // writeSummary


    public static void main ( String args[] ) { new MarkList(); };


}   // MarkList
```

FIGURE 5.14 Example—Generating a marks report

```
         Final Mark Report
             COSC 1P02

          St. #     Mark
         -----------------
          111,111  67.00
          222,222  86.00
          333,333  67.00
          444,444  86.00
          555,555  34.00
          666,666  87.00
          777,777  97.00
          888,888  57.00
          999,999  85.00
          123,456  79.00
         -----------------
          Average  74.50
```

FIGURE 5.15 Marks report output

Using the report generation pattern. A report is very similar to a table, and programs that produce them come close to conforming to the table generation pattern (of Figure 5.6). In Figure 5.16 we define a new programming pattern for report generation, which is derived from the table generation pattern.

The program in Figure 5.14 uses the report generation pattern. Three data streams are opened, one for the binary data file (`in`), one for the report (`out`), and a third for messages (`msg`). The program produces the title and heading, inputs the number of students, and loops, producing the lines of the report. An entry of the report is the information for a single student. The report also contains a summary, in this case, the average mark of the students in the course, which is written by `writeSummary`.

To compute the average, the program also uses the summation pattern (of Figure 5.13). This pattern is not initially obvious here, as there is only one loop. However, the program is actually a merging of the patterns using the same loop to drive each pattern. The initialization

Programming Pattern

```
generate report title line(s)
generate report heading line(s)
for each line(entry) in the report
    obtain data for entry
    produce report line for entry
    mark end of line
produce report summary
```

FIGURE 5.16 Report generation programming pattern

of the sum (`totMark`) occurs before the report loop, and the code for summation occurs after the generation of the report line, within the loop. After the loop, at the point of generating the summary, the program computes the average from the sum (`totMark`) and number of students (`numStd`). Since this is a stream-processing application, the report generation and summation patterns, as represented by the `display` method, are embedded within stream I/O patterns.

Testing and Debugging

To test this program, a binary file must first be available. Since such a file cannot be simply entered via a text editor, we need a program to create a test file. If the mark entry program is not yet available, we can write a file creation program which simply reads a text file containing the test data and writes an equivalent binary file.

The test data should be a small, representative sample of values (student marks) for which the class average has already been determined.

STYLE TIP

The third stream (`msg`) in the program is used for immediate feedback to the user. When a program reads a file and writes another, the user cannot tell that anything is happening. The program can use a displayer to provide immediate feedback in what is called happiness messages. This informs the user that something is happening and tells the user when the program finishes correctly. Use of this kind of feedback is good technique in any file processing program.

A **HAPPINESS MESSAGE** is a message displayed by a program that informs the user that something is happening or lets the user know when the program finishes correctly.

`SimpleDataInput` Summary

Table 5.4 summarizes the constructors and Table 5.5 summarizes the methods of the `SimpleDataInput` interface. The second version of `ASCIIPrompter` allows the prompts displayed and the values entered to be logged to a text file for later consideration. This can sometimes be a useful debugging facility. The method `successful` (as in `SimpleDataOutput`) is used to determine whether the previous method or constructor used on the stream completed successfully. The constructor would fail if it were unable to open the file because, perhaps, the file wasn't on the disk. The constructor would also fail if it were unable to create the prompter. The read methods will fail in three circumstances: (1) if the input characters cannot be interpreted as a value of the indicated type (text streams only); (2) if end-of-file is reached because there is no more data (disk streams only); or (3) if the user hits the `End` button in a prompter, simulating end-of-file. These situations can be used in input processing, as we will see in Chapter 6. Sometimes, quite unusually, a read method may fail for other reasons such as disk error. We will usually ignore this possibility.

TABLE 5.4 `SimpleDataInput` **constructors**

Constructor	Type	Description
`ASCIIPrompter()`	prompted text dialog box	Constructs a dialog containing a prompt and text area in which values can be entered.
`ASCIIPrompter( boolean log )`	prompted text dialog box	Constructs a dialog containing a prompt and text area in which values can be entered. Logs prompts and entries to a text file if parameter is `true`.
`ASCIIDataFile()`	white space tab-delimited text file	Constructs a stream to access an ASCII text file for input. Displays the standard open dialog box.
`BinaryDataFile()`	binary file	Constructs a stream to access a binary data file for input. Displays the standard open dialog box.

TABLE 5.5 `SimpleDataInput` **methods**

Method	Notes	Description
`close()`		Closes the input stream, releasing resources as necessary.
`readBoolean()`	1	Inputs a `boolean` value.
`readByte()`	1	Inputs a `byte` value.
`readC()`	4	Inputs a `char` value (including separators).
`readChar()`	1	Inputs a `char` value.
`readDouble()`	1	Inputs a `double` value.
`readFloat()`	1	Inputs a `float` value.
`readInt()`	1	Inputs an `int` value.
`readLine()`	4	Inputs characters to end-of-line as `String`.
`readLong()`	1	Inputs a `long` value.
`readObject()`	1	Inputs an `Object`.
`readShort()`	1	Inputs a `short` value.
`readString()`	1	Inputs a `String`.
`setLabel(String)`	2	Sets the label for the next prompt.
`skipToEOL()`	3	Repositions the stream to the point after the next end-of-line marker.
`successful()`		Indicates whether or not the previous operation was successful.

Notes:
1. Returns a value of the indicated type.
2. Effective only for prompted input.
3. Effective only for text file streams.
4. Effective only for nonformatted text streams

Table 5.5 shows a number of methods we haven't discussed. There is one version of `read` for each of the basic types of Java, as well as strings and objects. These will be discussed more fully in Chapters 7, 8, and 10. `skipToEOL` skips over all characters and it is effective only for text file streams. It continues until it has skipped over the next end-of-line marker. This allows part of a line to be processed and the rest to be skipped before processing the first part of the next line. One difference exists between prompted input streams and text file streams. Each read for a prompter reads from a new dialog box. This means that if more than one data value is entered in response to a prompt, only the first will be processed by the program. Text input streams do not skip over any data values unless `skipToEOL` is called.

■ SUMMARY

Streams abstract the details of input, output, and storage devices as series of bytes or characters that can be read or written. The `BasicIO` library provides three input streams (`SimpleDataInput`) and four output streams (`SimpleDataOutput`). Processing a stream involves opening it by creating a stream object, performing I/O, and then closing it.

Output streams may be used to write to the monitor or disk in text mode, both formatted and unformatted, or in binary mode. Input streams can be used to read from the keyboard or disk in text or binary mode.

Table generation involves writing a title and header and then writing a number of table lines consisting of a number of entries. Report generation is similar to table generation except that a report usually has a summary at the end. Often a summary involves the calculation of a sum, which can be performed by adding each of the entries, in turn, to an accumulator, which has been initialized to zero.

Methods that receive data to be written and format (layout) the output appropriately are called formatting methods. They provide an effective technique for simplifying processing that involves output because they can abstract the details of the output formatting. Changes to output layout can be done by simply modifying these methods without risk of affecting the processing of the program.

REVIEW QUESTIONS

1. T F A stream is a standardized view of I/O.
2. T F A stream must be opened before data can be accessed.
2. T F A binary stream is a sequence of ASCII characters encoded as bytes.
4. T F EOL is the situation that occurs when there is no more data on the line.
5. T F The method `setLabel` is used to display a heading on a report.

6. T F It is not possible to have more than one output stream open at a time.
7. T F Binary files should only be used if a human user is able to interpret them.
8. T F The use of happiness messages is a good technique when writing a file processing program.
9. Obtaining data from a stream is called:
   a) fetching.
   b) reading.
   c) accessing.
   d) none of the above.
10. In the piece of code:
    `out.writeDouble(x,5,2);`
    a) `x` is a field and `5` is a number of decimal places.
    b) `out` is a stream and `2` is a field width.
    c) `x` is a field and `5` is a field width.
    d) `out` is a stream and `x` is a field width.
11. What output will the following code produce? (Spaces are represented by _.)
    `out.writeDouble(123456.789,0,1);`
    a) `123456.789`
    b) `123,456.789`
    c) `123,456.7`
    d) `__123,456.7`
12. What output will the following code produce? (Spaces are represented by _.)
    `out.writeDouble(123.456,7,0);`
    a) `123.456`
    b) `___123.`
    c) `__123.0`
    d) `____123`
13. What output will the following code produce? (Spaces are represented by _.)
    ```
    n = 100;
    out.writeInt(n*n, 6);
    ```
    a) `10,000`
    b) `_10000`
    c) `10000_`
    d) `******`
14. What output will the following code produce? (Spaces are represented by _.)
    `out.writeDouble(1.5, 0, 3);`
    a) `1.5`
    b) `__1`
    c) `1.50`
    d) `1.500`
15. What is wrong with the following program segment?
    ```
    private ASCIIDataFile in;
       ...
       int     i;
       ...
       in = new ASCIIDataFile();
       i = in.readInt();
    ```
    a) Nothing is wrong.
    b) `ASCIIDataFile` should be used for output, not input.
    c) `in` should be declared as `SimpleDataInput`.
    d) `in` should be `public`, not `private`.

EXERCISES

1. Write a program to generate a multiplication table for the integers from 1 to 10 (as shown below). The program would be based on the programming pattern in Figure 5.6 (table generation) and the example in Figure 5.4 (generating a formatted table of squares). Use formatted output to generate the table to an `ASCIIReport` file. Each line of the table would be generated by a nested `for` loop (explicitly following the pattern), preceded by the integer for the row.

```
*   1   2   3   4   5   6   7   8   9  10

1   1   2   3   4   5   6   7   8   9  10

2   2   4   6   8  10  12  14  16  18  20

3   3   6   9  12  15  18  21  24  27  30

4   4   8  12  16  20  24  28  32  36  40

5   5  10  15  20  25  30  35  40  45  50

6   6  12  18  24  30  36  42  48  54  60

7   7  14  21  28  35  42  49  56  63  70

8   8  16  24  32  40  48  56  64  72  80

9   9  18  27  36  45  54  63  72  81  90

10 10  20  30  40  50  60  70  80  90 100
```

2. Write a program to generate a standings table for the Niagara Hockey League. For each team, one line of data is stored in an `ASCIIDataFile` with the following information: team number (`int`), games won (`int`), games lost (`int`), and games tied (`int`). The table should display, for each team, the team number, games played, games won, games lost, games tied, and total points. Points are awarded based on `2` for a win, `0` for a loss, and `1` for a tie. The data file begins with an `int` representing the number of teams in the league. The input file might begin:

```
10
1111 3 2 1
2222 2 4 2
```

and the report might begin:

```
     NHL Standings

Team  GP  GW  GL  GT  TP
1111   6   3   2   1   7
2222   8   2   4   2   6
```

3. Widgets-R-Us has just completed an inventory of the items in its warehouse. Each kind of item is identified by an item number. They stock a quantity of each kind of item. Each kind of item also has a unit value—the value for one of the items. A file (`ASCIIDataFile`) has been created that gives, for each kind of item: the item number (`int`), the quantity on hand (`int`), and the unit value (`double`). A program is needed to produce a report (`ASCIIReportFile`) summarizing this information in a form similar to the following:

```
          Inventory Report

            Widgets-R-Us


Item #  Quantity  Unit Value  Gross Value

-----------------------------------------

12,524       214        2.75       588.50

17,823       123       10.95     1,346.85

83,731        13      127.36     1,655.68

73,562       212       27.95     5,925.40

-----------------------------------------

             Total Value         9,516.43
```

In the report, the item number, quantity, and unit value are the values from the file. The gross value is the product of the quantity on hand and the unit value. The total value is the sum of the gross values over all items. In other words, it is the total value of the inventory in the warehouse.

Write a Java program to produce this report from the data file. The program should, in addition to producing the report, produce happiness messages to an `ASCIIDisplayer`.

4. National Widgets desires to automate their payroll system. Each week, a timesheet is prepared for each employee giving the employee number (`integer`), number of hours worked (`double`), and rate of pay (`double`). The timesheets are entered into a data file, one timesheet per line. The first line of the timesheet file indicates the number of employees (`int`). A

program is needed to produce a payroll report giving the week's pay information for each employee in a form similar to the following:

```
                 National Widgets

                  Payroll Report


 Emp #   Hours   Rate    Gross       Tax        Net

-------------------------------------------------

111,111  40.0   9.50    380.00    133.00     247.00

222,222  24.0   8.75    210.00     73.50     136.50

333,333  10.0  10.95    109.50     38.32      71.18

444,444   5.0   6.75     33.75     11.81      21.94

555,555  35.0  15.50    542.50    189.88     352.62

-------------------------------------------------

               Total  1,275.75    446.51     829.24
```

In the report, the employee number, hours, and rate are the values from the timesheet file. The gross pay is the product of the hours and the rate. The tax is 35% of the gross, and the net pay is the gross pay minus the tax. The summary totals are the totals of the gross, tax, and net, respectively.

Write a Java program to produce this report. The program should read the timesheet information from an `ASCIIDataFile` and produce the report to an `ASCIIReportFile`. In addition to producing the report, the program should produce happiness messages to an `ASCIIDisplayer`.

In your program, you should use function methods to compute the gross pay, (given the hours worked and pay rate); and taxes, (given the gross pay). You should use procedure methods to: write the title and header lines; write a detail (report) line, given the employee number, hours, rate, gross, tax, and net; and write the summary line, given the total gross, tax, and net). Note: Using methods like these makes the program easier to modify. Consider what would have to be done to change the report layout. Consider where changes would be made to change the way pay is calculated, such as by paying time-and-a-half for overtime hours. These changes would be localized and wouldn't affect the rest of the program at all!

5 Every month, Sharkey's Loans produces a report that specifies the details of each loan. Sharkey has hired you to automate the production of this report. For each loan, the information concerning each month's activities is stored in a data file. The first line of the data file indicates the number of loans (`int`). After the first line, each line contains information about a different loan, and includes the following information: loan number (`int`), monthly interest rate (`double`), previous balance (`double`), amount borrowed by the customer this month ("debits", `double`), and amount paid by the customer this month ("credits", `double`). You are to write a program to produce a report in a form similar to the following:

```
                    Sharkey's Loans

                     Monthly Report

Loan #  IntRate PrevBal  Debits  Credits  NewBal  MinPaymt

----------------------------------------------------------

123       20.0   100.00   20.00   25.00   114.00    28.50

456       15.0   200.00    0.00  100.00   115.00    28.75

789       25.0   500.00  200.00  150.00   687.50   171.88

----------------------------------------------------------

Totals           800.00  220.00  275.00   916.50   229.13
```

In the report, the loan number, interest rate, previous balance, debits, and credits are the values from the monthly data file. The new balance is calculated as the previous balance, plus debits, minus credits plus interest, where the interest is computed on the previous balance plus debits, minus credits. The minimum payment is 25% of the new balance. The summary totals are the totals of the previous balance, debits, credits, new balance, and minimum payments, respectively.

Write a Java program to produce this report. The program should read the monthly data from an `ASCIIDataFile` and produce the report to an `ASCIIReportFile`. In addition to producing the report, the program should produce happiness messages to an `ASCIIDisplayer`.

In your program, you should use function methods to compute the new balance, given the previous balance, debits, and credits and interest rate; and compute the minimum payment, given the new balance. You should use procedure methods to: write the title and header lines; write a detail (report) line, given the loan number, interest rate, previous balance, debits, credits, new balance, and minimum payment; and write the totals line, given the total debits, credits, new balance, and minimum payments.

6

Control Structures

CHAPTER OBJECTIVES

- To understand how a program can adapt to input using control structures.
- To know the difference between a pre-test loop, an in-test loop, and a post-test loop, to be able to express each in Java, and to know which is the appropriate loop in each situation.
- To know the difference between an if-then, and if-then-else, and an if-then-elseif decision, to be able to express each in Java, and to know which is the appropriate decision in each situation.
- To be able to read data until end-of-file is reached.
- To understand the processes for producing a sum, for producing a count, and for determining the maximum or minimum.
- To know how and when to use a definite loop as opposed to an indefinite loop.
- To be able to apply the special techniques for testing and debugging with control structures.

When a Java program executes, execution begins with the first statement in the `main` method of the main class. In our examples, this has always been a call to the constructor of the main class; thus, execution appears to begin with the main class's constructor. Once execution begins within a method or constructor, it proceeds in order through the statements of the method until the end (or `return` statement). The method returns to the place from which it was called and execution continues in that sequence of statements, and so on, until execution reaches the end of the `main` method, at which point the program terminates. This process is called **sequential execution**. (There is another form of execution, parallel execution, that Java supports via threads. We will not, however, discuss threads in this book.)

> In **SEQUENTIAL EXECUTION**, execution begins at the start of the first method (main) and, as each method is called, the calling method is suspended. The called method executes and then returns to the place from which it was called and execution continues in the calling method, and so on, until execution reaches the end of the main method, at which point the program terminates.
>
> A **CONTROL STRUCTURE (STATEMENT)** is a statement that either controls a loop or makes a decision.

Often, we do not want execution simply to proceed from one statement to the next. Sometimes we wish to **loop**—execute a sequence of statements repeatedly—or to make a **decision**—a choice between executing a number of different statements. Java provides **control statements** (**control structures**) that allow us to perform loops and make decisions. We have already seen one such statement—the `for` statement.

6.1 THE `while` STATEMENT

> An **INDEFINITE LOOP** or **CONDITIONAL LOOP** is a loop that is repeated until (or as long as) some condition occurs.
>
> A **CONDITION** is a boolean expression that serves as the test in a loop or decision structure.

One of the most common kinds of loops is one in which we want to repeat an action as long as a particular situation exists. This situation is sometimes described as repeating an action until some other situation occurs. The `while` statement in Java supports this type of loop. It is called an **indefinite loop** or **conditional loop** since we cannot predict, ahead of time, how many times the repetition will occur. The common syntax of a `while` statement is found in Figure 6.1.

The statement is introduced by the reserved word `while`, which is followed by an *`Expression`*, in parentheses, called the **condition**. Next comes a sequence of statements

SYNTAX

```
WhileStatement:
    while ( Expression ) {
        BlockStatements_opt
    }
```

FIGURE 6.1 `while` statement syntax

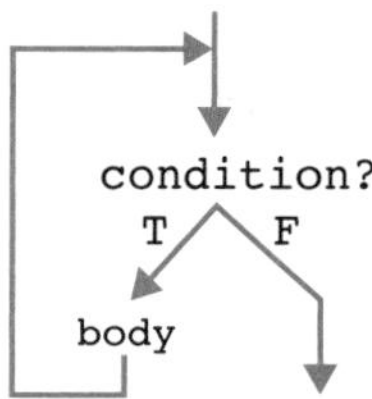

FIGURE 6.2 Execution of a while statement

> The **BODY** of a loop is the sequence of statements that is repeated as controlled by the loop statement.
>
> A **BOOLEAN EXPRESSION** is an expression that evaluates to a truth, or boolean, value: `true` or `false`.

called the **body** of the loop, enclosed in braces. The effect of the `while` statement is to repeat the sequence of statements within the braces some indefinite number of times—zero or more times.

It is the *`Expression`* that determines how long this repetition continues. The expression is a special kind of Java expression called a **boolean expression**. You will remember from Chapter 1 that the ALU of the computer is capable of performing arithmetic operations, such as addition and subtraction, as well as performing logical operations, such as comparing two values. In Java and most other programming languages, these logical operations are called boolean operations after the English mathematician George Boole. We will see more about boolean expressions in Chapter 7. Boolean expressions result, not in a numeric value, but in a truth (or logical, or boolean) value: `true` or `false`.

The execution of the `while` statement is shown in the flow diagram in Figure 6.2. Repeatedly, the condition is evaluated. If it evaluates to the truth value `true`, the body is executed and the condition evaluated again. If the condition evaluates to `false`, the `while` statement ends. If the expression is immediately `false`, the body of the loop is not executed. The body is always executed in its entirety—if one statement is executed, they all are.

Example—Filling a Packing Box

Let's write a program to simulate the activity of placing items into a box while packing to move. Basically, you keep putting items into the box, until it can hold no more, but we'll allow the last item to stick out of the box somewhat. The basic algorithm could be:

```
while ( box has some room left ) {
    put next item into box
}
```

Let's assume that the box has a capacity (say, `size`, an integer, as volume measured in cubic feet) and each item has a volume (say, between `1` and `10` cubic feet). We can represent an item simply by its volume (say, by item, an integer). We represent the current volume packed in the box as the sum of the volumes of the items packed (say, by amt, an integer). As long as the capacity of the box has not been exceeded, we can add another item. The code becomes:

```
while ( amt < size ) {
     determine volume of next item
     amt = amt + item;
}
```

The use of the < symbol in the condition:

```
amt < size
```

is new. As expected, this expression is a boolean expression, which compares the current value of the variable amt and the current value of the variable size, resulting in the value true if amt is less than size and false otherwise. The comparison is done by the ALU. When the result of the expression is true, the volume of the next item is determined and the total volume (amt) is increased appropriately. Note that, if we assume that amt is less than size initially and the volume of each item is positive, the value of amt will eventually equal or exceed the value of size, and the loop will terminate.

An **INFINITE LOOP** is a loop that doesn't terminate, in other words it runs forever. Usually this is a logic error or bug in a program.

It is a good thing that we can show that the loop will stop. A loop that doesn't terminate is called an **infinite loop** and means that the program will execute forever. When this happens, we have to force the program to stop some other way. Usually, the operating system or program development environment can help us here or we would have to shut the computer down. It is a good idea to convince yourself, as you write a loop, that it will always terminate.

To give the program a bit of interest, we'll simulate the packing activity by randomly creating items of various sizes to put into the box. The following statement

```
item = (int) (10 * Math.random() + 1 );
```

randomly computes a number between 1 and 10 and stores it in item. Math.random is a function in the Math package that randomly (in other words, without predictability) computes a double value in the interval [0.0,1.0). This means that the interval includes 0.0 but not 1.0. By multiplying by 10, we get the interval [0.0,10.0). Adding 1 gives us the interval [1.0,11.0). Since this is a double value, when we convert to int using the cast, the fractional part is truncated (dropped), leaving us a value in the interval [1,10]. This meets our requirements of items, randomly selected, in the range from 1 to 10 cubic feet.

Figure 6.3 shows the program. It starts by asking the user the size of box and then fills the box with randomly created items, displaying what is happening, until the box is full. Sample output is found in Figure 6.4.

```
import BasicIO.*;

/** This class simulates the packing of a box. It inputs the
 ** capacity of the box and then generates random items to
 ** pack until the last item packed exceeds the capacity of
 ** the box.
 **
 ** @author D. Hughes
 **
 ** @version    1.0 (June 2001)                          */

public class FillBox {

    private ASCIIPrompter      in;         // prompter for input
    private ASCIIDisplayer     out;        // displayer for output

    /** The constructor simulates the filling of a box.        */

    public FillBox ( ) {

        in = new ASCIIPrompter();
        out = new ASCIIDisplayer();
        fill();
        in.close();
        out.close();

    };  // constructor


    /** This method simulates the filling of a packing box.              */

    private void fill ( ) {

        int size;   // capacity of box
        int amt;    // amount in box
        int item;   // item item to pack

        in.setLabel("Enter box size");
        size = in.readInt();
        writeSize(size);
        amt = 0;
```

(continued)

```
        while ( amt < size ) {
            item = (int) (10 * Math.random() + 1);
            amt = amt + item;
            writeItem(item,amt);
        };
        writeResult(amt);

    };  // fill


    /** This method writes the box size.
     **
     ** @param size box size.                              */

    private void writeSize ( int size ) {

        out.writeLabel("With a box of size ");
        out.writeInt(size);
        out.writeEOL();
        out.writeEOL();

    };  // writeSize


    /** This method writes the item added.
     **
     ** @param  item    size of item added
     ** @param  amt     total amount in box.                   */

    private void writeItem ( int item, int amt ) {

        out.writeLabel("added ");
        out.writeInt(item);
        out.writeLabel(" for a total of ");
        out.writeInt(amt);
        out.writeEOL();

    };  // writeItem


    /** This method writes the amount in the box.
     **
     ** @param  amt     total amount in box.                   */
```

(continued)

```
    private void writeResult ( int amt ) {

        out.writeEOL();
        out.writeLabel("Amount in box is ");
        out.writeInt(amt);
        out.writeEOL();

    };  // writeResult


    public static void main ( String args[] ) { new FillBox(); };


}   // FillBox
```

FIGURE 6.3 Example—Filling a box

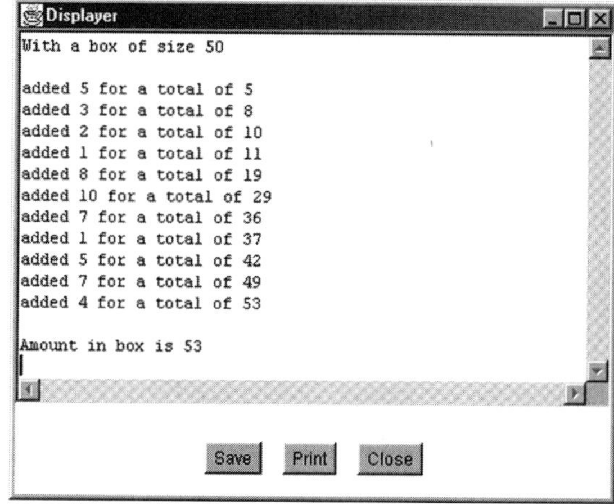

FIGURE 6.4 Filling a box

The amount in the box (`amt`) is initially set to zero because the box is empty and, each time through the loop, it increases (to values `5`, `8`, `10`, ..., `42`, `49`) until, on the last time through the loop, it is increased to `53`. At this point, the value of `amt` (`53`) is not less than `size` (`50`), which means that the value of the condition `amt < size` is `false`. The loop terminates.

Note that the loop is an alternate representation of the summation pattern of Figure 5.13, using a `while` loop to process overall values.

STYLE TIP

In Figure 6.3 you will notice that the statements that comprise the body of the loop are indented one tab position from the `while` itself. The close brace marking the end of the loop body is aligned with the `while`. This convention makes it obvious which statements are controlled by the loop and which is the statement that follows the loop. You will notice that the syntax specifications for control structures are written so as to suggest such an arrangement.

Example—Finding Roots of an Equation

In mathematics, it is often important to be able to find the roots of a function $f(x)$. The roots of an equation are the values of x that satisfy the equation $f(x) = 0$. An equation may have zero or more roots; however, often it is necessary to find only one. Although there are mathematical methods to find roots for some types of equations, for other equations it is very difficult, if not impossible. In these cases, determining an approximation to the root may be necessary. Computer programs are often used in cases where mathematical methods are difficult to use or nonexistent. This is a branch of computer science called **numerical analysis** or **numerical methods**—the numerical but approximate solutions of mathematical problems that are analytically intractable.

The secant method. There are a variety of methods for numerical solution for roots of an equation and we will look at one of the simplest, the so-called **secant method**. Here, to start, two approximations (call them a and b) reasonably close to the root are needed. The method computes another approximation (c) by taking the point where the line joining $f(a)$ and $f(b)$ crosses the x-axis (see Figure 6.5). If this approximation is not close enough to the actual root, the process can be repeated using a and c, and so on

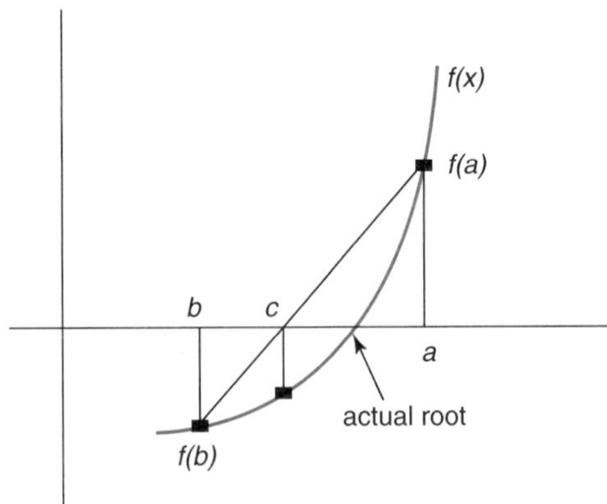

FIGURE 6.5 Secant method

until an approximation close enough to the root is found. The goal is to find one for which $f(c)$ is close to zero. The equation for the new approximation (c) is:

$$\frac{af(b)-bf(a)}{f(b)-f(a)}$$

To turn this into a computer program, we need to input two approximations to the root. To get these, we could graph the function and choose two values close to the point where the graph crosses the x-axis. We can then repeat the approximation process as long as the next approximation is not close enough to the root:

```
while ( approximation is not close enough ) {
    compute next approximation
}
```

Approximations and convergence. Figure 6.6 shows such a program, with sample output in Figure 6.7. Here `a` and `b` are the two approximations. A new approximation replacing the old `b` is computed according to the formula given previously. The loop uses the condition:

```
Math.abs(f(b)) > 0.0001
```

to continue the process until the approximation (`b`) yields a value `f(b)` close enough to zero to be considered a root. The functional value of the root is to within four decimal places of zero. The function `abs` from the `Math` package returns the absolute value (`double`) of its parameter (`f(b)`). As long as this is more than `0.0001`, the value `b` isn't a good enough approximation.

```
import BasicIO.*;

/** This program uses the secant method to find a root
 ** of an equation represented by a function.
 **
 ** @author D. Hughes
 **
 ** @version    1.0 (June 2001)                               */

public class Roots {

    private ASCIIPrompter       in;         // prompter for input
    private ASCIIDisplayer      out;        // displayer for output
```

(continued)

```
/** The constructor uses the secant method to find a root of
 ** the equation represented by the function f.              */

public Roots ( ) {

    in = new ASCIIPrompter();
    out = new ASCIIDisplayer();
    find();
    in.close();
    out.close();

};  // constructor


/** This method finds a root of the equation f.              */

private void find ( ) {

    double  a;       // first bound for root
    double  b;       // second bound for root
    int     nIter;   // number of iterations

    in.setLabel("Enter first approximation");
    a = in.readDouble();
    in.setLabel("Enter second approximation");
    b = in.readDouble();
    nIter = 0;
    while ( Math.abs(f(b)) > 0.0001) {
        b = (a * f(b) - b * f(a)) / (f(b) - f(a));
        nIter = nIter + 1;
    };
    writeRoot(b,f(b),nIter);

};  // find


/** This function represents the equation for which the root
 ** is being sought.
 **
 ** @param  x        the point on the function
 ** @return double   the value of the function at x          */

private double f ( double x ) {

    return 2 * x * x + 3 * x - 2;

}; // f
```

(continued)

```
    /** This method writes the root found.
     **
     ** @param  root    the root
     ** @param  value   value of f at root
     ** @param  nIter   number of iterations                    */

     private void writeRoot ( double root, double value, int nIter ) {

        out.writeLabel("f(");
        out.writeDouble(root);
        out.writeLabel(") = ");
        out.writeDouble(value);
        out.writeEOL();
        out.writeLabel("Approximation found in ");
        out.writeInt(nIter);
        out.writeLabel(" iterations");
        out.writeEOL();

    };  // writeRoot


    public static void main ( String args[] ) { new Roots(); };


}   // Roots
```

FIGURE 6.6 Example—Finding roots of an equation

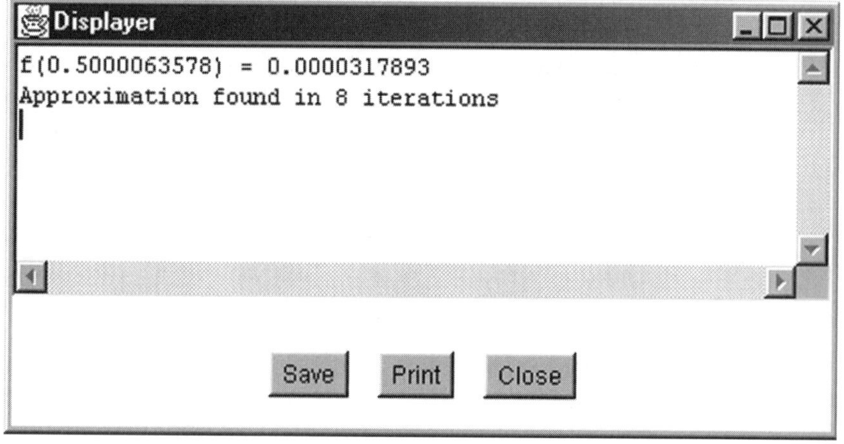

FIGURE 6.7 Finding roots of an equation

Programming Pattern

```
compute initial state
while ( state hasn't converged ) {
    compute next state
}
```

FIGURE 6.8 Convergence programming pattern

The **TOLERANCE** is a specification of how close an approximation should be in finding an algorithmic solution to a numerical problem.

The value `0.0001` is called the **tolerance**; it indicates how good we want the approximation to be. The smaller this value, the better the approximation, but it will take the program more iterations (steps) to find it. Note that we didn't use

```
f(b) == 0.0
```

since `double` values are approximations and it is unlikely that the value would ever be exactly zero.

The program inputs two approximations, then loops until the approximation is close enough. It counts the number of times through the loop (`iter`), and then outputs the approximation (`b`), its functional value (`f(b)`), which should be close to zero, and the number of iterations required to find the approximation (`nIter`). The number of iterations is a function of how close the original approximations are to the root, the tolerance, and the shape of the curve in the local area. In fact, the method does not guarantee termination if the guesses bound a discontinuity—a point for which there is no defined value of $f(x)$.

Comparing the programs. Both Figures 6.3 and 6.6 demonstrate another programming pattern: convergence, as shown in the programming pattern of Figure 6.8. This pattern is used whenever there is the need to make successive approximations to a value, under the assumption that these guesses will converge to the desired value because each guess is better than the last.

In the program for filling the box, we were trying to "guess" the number of items we could put into the box, each guess filling the box a bit more until there was no more space. The initial guess was that the box would hold no items (`amt = 0`). The test for convergence was to see if there was any more space in the box (`amt < size`). The next state computation added the size of the next item to the total (`amt = amt + item`). In the program using the secant method, we were trying to guess the root of the equation (the value b, such that $f(b) = 0$). The initial guess was supplied by the user, the test for convergence was to see if `f(b)` was within a particular tolerance of zero, and the next state was the next approximation as a function of the other two values `a` and `b`.

6.2 THE BREAK STATEMENT

The `while` statement works well as long as we always want to execute all of the statements in the body before testing for loop termination. Oftentimes, it is necessary to execute some or all of the statements before it is possible to determine whether the loop should continue.

Kinds of loops. The `while` loop is what is called a **pre-test loop** because the test for loop termination (or continuation) occurs *before* the body is executed. There are two other kinds of loops: a **post-test loop**, in which the test for termination occurs *after* the body is executed, and an **in-test loop**, in which the test for termination occurs in the *middle* of the body. Since, in the pre-test loop, the test is first, the loop executes the body zero or more times. Since, in the post-test loop, the test is last, the loop executes the body one or more times. In the in-test loop, the test is in the middle of the body, so the first part of the body is executed one or more times and the second part of the body is executed zero or more times. The first part is always executed one more time than the second part. As we will see in a later section of this chapter, the `do` statement is a post-test loop; however, there is no in-test loop in Java.

A **PRE-TEST LOOP** is a loop in which the test for loop termination (or continuation) occurs before the first statement of the loop body. This is represented by the `while` statement in Java.

A **POST-TEST LOOP** is a loop in which the test for loop termination (or continuation) occurs after the last statement of the loop body. This is represented by the `do` statement in Java.

An **IN-TEST LOOP** is a loop in which the test for loop termination (or continuation) occurs within the loop body. There is no in-test loop in Java although one can be manufactured using a `while` statement, an `if` statement, and a `break` statement.

Use of the `break` statement. The `break` statement, although not technically a control structure, allows us to construct an in-test loop out of a `while` statement. The syntax of the `break` statement is shown in Figure 6.9. The optional identifier is used in special cases; however, we will omit it here. When executed, the `break` statement causes immediate termination of the encompassing loop regardless of the continuation condition. The encompassing loop may be any loop statement. To write an in-test loop, we need a `while` loop in which the continuation condition is always `true` and the loop will always continue. The in-test loop contains a `break` statement that is executed when we wish the loop to terminate. This statement "breaks out of" the `while` loop. The in-test loop would look like the following:

```
while ( true ) {
    first part of body
if ( Expression ) break;
    second part of body
}
```

SYNTAX

```
BreakStatement:
    break Identifier_opt ;
```

FIGURE 6.9 `break` statement syntax

Note that the `while` condition is just the word `true`. As described in Chapter 7, the reserved word `true` is a boolean literal representing the truth value `true`. That is, it is an expression that always evaluates to `true`. This means that the `while` loop is an infinite loop. After we complete the first part of the body, we determine whether we wish to terminate. We evaluate the termination expression and execute the `break` statement if so. If not, we execute the second part of the body, and make the continuation test (`true`, so continue). We execute the first part of the body, and so forth. The statement in the middle of the loop controlling the exit is actually a form of `if` statement. Basically, if the expression is `true`, the `break` is executed and the loop terminates; if the expression is `false`, the `break` is not executed. The execution of an in-test loop is shown in the flow diagram of Figure 6.10.

Example—Class Average Revisited

Chapter 5, Figure 5.11, presented a program to compute the class average for the marks in a test. It required that the number of student marks in the file be known ahead of time and included in the file. Although it is possible to know this information in advance, it puts the burden of counting the number of marks on the user, when the program could easily do it. Let's consider writing a version of the class average program that doesn't have this requirement.

Counting the marks. The count of the number of students (`numStd`) was used in two places in computing the class average (Figure 5.11). First, it was used to determine the number of values to read in the `for` loop, and second, it was used to compute the average. If we could determine when there are no more marks to read (that is, when we have reached the end of the file), we wouldn't need to know the number of students ahead of time. We could simply read until we run out of data, counting the students as

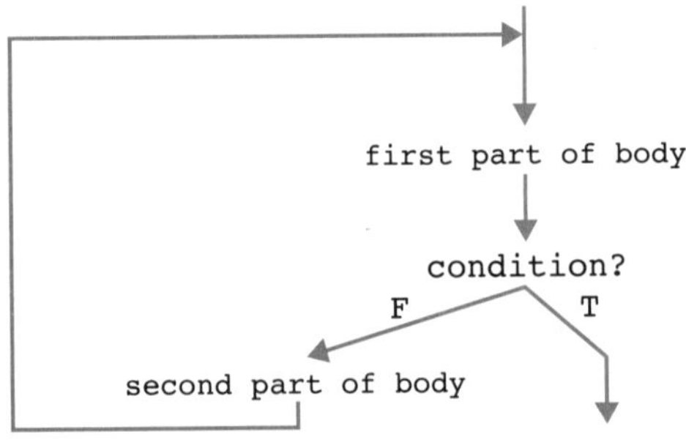

FIGURE 6.10 Execution of an in-test loop

Programming Pattern

```
while ( true ) {
    try to read data
if ( at end of file ) break;
    process the data
}
```

FIGURE 6.11 Processing until EOF programming pattern

we go. This leads to the programming pattern shown in Figure 6.11 for processing an indefinite amount of data until end of file.

The `BasicIO` package provides the method `successful`, which, for an input stream, returns `true` if the last operation was successful. For example, it would return `true` if an attempt to read was successful. Usually, being unable to read means we are at the end of the file. There are other situations, such as hardware errors or bad data format, but we will ignore these possibilities to simplify things. For a loop termination condition, we want to compute the inverse of this, that is, *not* being able to read. In Java, there is a boolean operator (`!`, called **not**) for the inverse of a boolean expression. It yields `false` when the expression is `true` and `true` when the expression is `false`. This allows us to write the pattern as:

```
while ( true ) {
    aMark = in.readDouble();
if ( ! in.successful() ) break;
    process the data
}
```

The `readDouble` either successfully reads a value, returning the next mark read, or fails, in which case the value returned is indeterminate. If it fails, `in.successful` will return `false` and `! in.successful()` will evaluate to `true`, terminating the loop. Otherwise, the value that was read can be processed and an attempt made to read the next value, and so on. Since all files are finite, the `readDouble` must ultimately fail at EOF, when there is no more data, and it ends the loop.

We still need to know how many marks there were in order to compute the average. We must count the student marks as we successfully read them. Counting is simply incrementing from zero by 1s, so the loop, with counting, will be:

```
numStd = 0;
while ( true ) {
    aMark = in.readDouble();
if ( ! in.successful() ) break;
    numStd = numStd + 1;
    process the data
}
```

Initially, no student marks have been read, so the count (`numStd`) is zero. Each time we successfully read a mark, we increment the count by `1`. At the end of the loop, the count will be the number of marks successfully read.

This gives us the program in Figure 6.12. The data file will be exactly the same as for our earlier class average program in Figure 5.12, except that the count of the number of students will not be included. That is, the first data item will be the mark of the first student. The number of students is not read, the process to EOF pattern is used instead of the countable repetition pattern, and the marks are counted on the fly (as they are encountered).

```
import BasicIO.*;

/** This program inputs an unknown number of marks for
  ** students in a class and computes the class average.
  **
  ** @author D. Hughes
  **
  ** @version    1.0 (June 2001)                            */

public class ClassAve2 {

    private ASCIIDataFile       in;     // file for data
    private ASCIIDisplayer      out;    // statistics display


    /** The constructor uses an ASCIIDataFile to read a set of
      ** student mark data and then computes the class average.   */

    public ClassAve2 ( ) {

        in = new ASCIIDataFile();
        out = new ASCIIDisplayer();
        display();
        in.close();
        out.close();

    };  // constructor
```

(continued)

```
    /** This method computes and displays the class average.                    */

    private void display ( ) {

        int     numStd;      // number of students
        double  aMark;       // one student's mark
        double  totMark;     // total of marks
        double  aveMark;     // average mark

        numStd = 0;
        totMark = 0;
        while ( true ) {
            aMark = in.readDouble();
        if ( ! in.successful() ) break;
            numStd = numStd + 1;
            totMark = totMark + aMark;
        };
        aveMark = totMark / numStd;
        writeDetail(numStd,aveMark);

    };  // display


    /** This method writes the detail line.
     **
     ** @param  numStd  number of students
     ** @param  avemark average mark                              */

     private void writeDetail ( int numStd, double aveMark ) {

        out.writeLabel("Number of students: ");
        out.writeInt(numStd);
        out.writeEOL();
        out.writeLabel("Average mark: ");
        out.writeDouble(aveMark,0,2);
        out.writeEOL();

    };  // writeDetail

    public static void main ( String args[] ) { new ClassAve2(); };


}   // ClassAve2
```

FIGURE 6.12 Example—Computing class average

Note that this program, and the one in Figure 5.11, both suffer from one flaw. If the data file is empty and the number of students is zero, the program will report the average as `NaN` (not a number) since `n/0` is not defined mathematically. This could be remedied using an `if` statement, which is described in Section 6.3.

STYLE TIP

Note that in Figure 6.12, the statements in the body of the `while` are indented, with the exception of the `if` statement. It is aligned with the `while`. Unlike a pre-test loop where the condition is always at the beginning, or a post-test loop where the condition is always at the end, the condition in an in-test loop may occur anywhere. By aligning the `if` with the `while`, it is easy to pick out the loop exit condition.

6.3 THE `if` STATEMENT

Computer programs, to be useful, must react to user needs. The user must be able to indicate what s/he wishes to do, and the program must respond. This means that, as a result of user input or input from a file, the program must make a decision about what steps to follow next. **Decision structures** are the control structures that allow this to happen.

The **IF-THEN STATEMENT** is a decision structure in which the nested sequence of statements is executed or not. It is represented by the `if-then` form of the `if` statement in Java.

The **IF-THEN-ELSE STATEMENT** is a decision structure in which one of a pair of nested sequences of statements is executed. It is represented by the `if-then-else` form of the `if` statement in Java.

The **THEN-PART** is the first of the nested sequences of statements in an `if` statement and is executed when the condition is `true`.

The **ELSE-PART** is the second of the nested sequences of statements in an `if` statement and is executed when the condition is `false`.

The most common kind of a decision structure (or decision for short) is the `if` statement. It has two forms; one (sometimes called the **if-then statement**) allows selective execution of a block of statements. It allows the program to do the block of statements one time or not at all. A second form (often called the **if-then-else statement**) allows a choice between execution of two blocks of statements. It allows the program to choose to do one block of statements once, and the other not at all. The common syntax of the two forms of `if` statements is found in the syntax in Figure 6.13.

In both cases, the expression in parentheses is, as in the `while` statement, a boolean expression (or condition) and thus evaluates to either `true` or `false`. In the `if-then` statement, if the condition evaluates to `true`, the sequence of statements *in* the braces (called the **then-part**) is executed. On the other hand, if the condition is `false`, the then-part is not executed. In either case, the statement following the `if` statement—*after* the close brace—is executed next as usual. This is shown in the flow diagram of Figure 6.14.

In the `if-then-else` statement, if the condition is `true`, the statements in the braces following the condition—the then-part—are executed. If the condition is `false`, the statements in the braces after the keyword `else` are executed. This group of statements is called the **else-part**. In any event, after the execution of either the then-part or the else-part, the statement after the `if` statement is executed. This is shown in Figure 6.15.

SYNTAX

```
IfThenStatement:
    if ( Expression ) {
        BlockStatements_opt
    }
IfThenElseStatement:
    if ( Expression ) {
        BlockStatements_opt
    }
    else {
        BlockStatements_opt
    }
```

FIGURE 6.13 if statement syntax

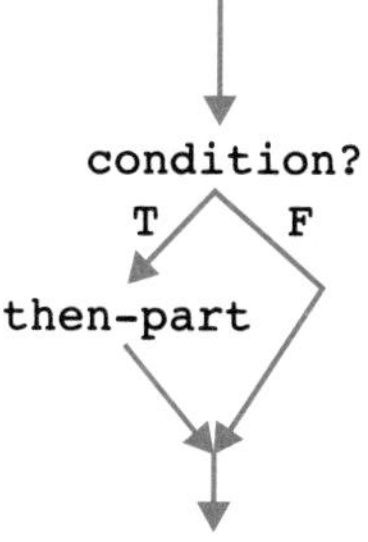

FIGURE 6.14 Execution of if-then statement

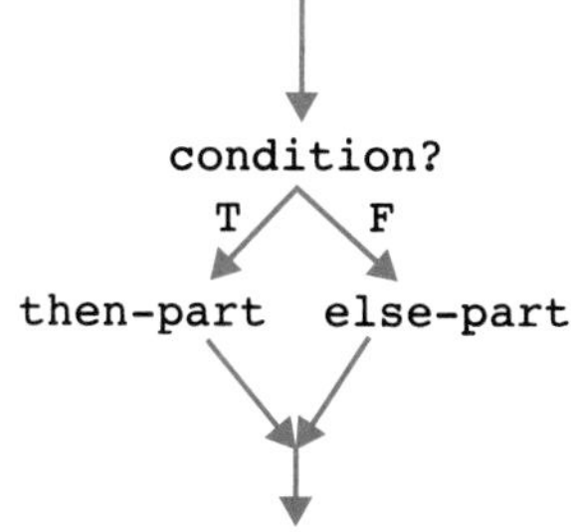

FIGURE 6.15 Execution of if-then-else statement

Actually, the syntax allows, in special cases, a single statement to be written instead of the sequence of statements, without the braces. We used this form for an `if-then` statement in Section 6.2 to write the exit from a loop, and we will use this form in the `if-then-elseif` statement in a later section of this chapter. It is not a good idea to use this form except in these special cases, as it tends to lead to errors when used otherwise.

Example—The Dean's List

Suppose we wished to produce a mark report similar to that produced by the program in Figure 5.14. We want to list only the students who achieved the Dean's List; which we define as 80% or higher. This time, however, instead of a binary file, we will use an ASCII text file, and we will also process the input to EOF instead of requiring the user to count the number of students. As in the program in Figure 5.14, the file will contain, for each student, the student number (`int`) and the student's mark (`double`). A sample data file is shown in Figure 6.16.

To produce a report listing only these students, we will have to read the information for each student in turn and list the information only when the student has a mark of 80% or higher. This clearly calls for an `if-then` statement because we are deciding to do something or not. The statement will look like:

```
if ( student is on the Dean's List ) {
    produce report line
}
```

This statement will produce a report line only when the student is on the Dean's List. Since being on the list implies that the student has a mark of no less than 80, the condition will be:

```
aMark >= 80
```

Note that the boolean operator for greater than or equal to ($\geq$ in mathematics) is written as >= in Java with no space between the symbols and the > always written first.

The program is found as the example in Figure 6.17 with sample output in Figure 6.18. The program will report Dean's List of students and summary information that

```
111111  57
222222  85
333333  29
444444  68
555555  87
666666  92
777777  45
888888  75
999999  89
123456  78
```

FIGURE 6.16 Sample data file for Dean's List

includes the total number of students processed and the number on the list (numStd and numList, respectively). Since a file is being read, and output is also to a file, happiness messages are generated to a displayer. As an instance of the report generation pattern (programming pattern of Figure 5.16), the report title and heading are first produced, and then a loop processing all students to EOF is entered. Here the report line is selectively generated when the student is on the list.

```
import BasicIO.*;

/** This program lists only the students on the Dean's List.
  **
  ** @author D. Hughes
  **
  ** @version    1.0 (June 2001)                          */

public class List {

    private ASCIIDataFile       in;     // file for student data
    private ASCIIReportFile     out;    // file for report
    private ASCIIDisplayer      msg;    // displayer for messages

    /** The constructor lists the students on the list.       */

    public List ( ) {

        in = new ASCIIDataFile();
        out = new ASCIIReportFile();
        msg = new ASCIIDisplayer();
        display();
        in.close();
        out.close();
        msg.close();

    };  // constructor
```

(continued)

```
/** This method generates the report.                                */

private void display ( ) {

    int     numStd;      // number of students
    int     numList;     // number on the list
    int     aStdNum;     // one student's student number
    double  aMark;       // one student's mark

    msg.writeLabel("Processing students...");
    msg.writeEOL();
    numStd = 0;
    numList = 0;
    writeHeader();
    while ( true ) {
        aStdNum = in.readInt();
    if ( ! in.successful() ) break;
        aMark = in.readDouble();
        if ( aMark >= 80 ) {
            numList = numList + 1;
            writeDetail(aStdNum,aMark);
        };
        numStd = numStd + 1;
    };
    writeSummary(numList);
    msg.writeInt(numStd);
    msg.writeLabel(" students processed.");
    msg.writeEOL();

};  // display


/** This method writes the report header.                            */

private void writeHeader ( ) {

    out.writeLabel("   Dean's List");
    out.writeEOL();
    out.writeEOL();
    out.writeLabel("  St. #    Mark");
    out.writeEOL();
    out.writeLabel("-----------------");
    out.writeEOL();

};  // writeHeader
```

(continued)

```
    /** This method writes a report detail line.
     **
     ** @param  stdNum  the student number
     ** @param  mark    the mark                              */

    private void writeDetail ( int stdNum, double mark ) {

        out.writeInt(stdNum,8);
        out.writeDouble(mark,6,2);
        out.writeEOL();

    };  // writeDetail


    /** This method writes the report summary
     **
     ** @param  numHons number of students on the list.                  */

    private void writeSummary ( int numHons ) {

        out.writeLabel("-----------------");
        out.writeEOL();
        out.writeEOL();
        out.writeLabel("Number of students: ");
        out.writeDouble(numHons);
        out.writeEOL();

    };  // writeSummary


    public static void main ( String args[] ) { new List(); };

}   // List
```

FIGURE 6.17 Example—Producing the Dean's List

```
   Dean's List

  St. #    Mark
-----------------
 222,222  85.00
 555,555  87.00
 666,666  92.00
 999,999  89.00
-----------------

Number of students: 4
```

FIGURE 6.18 The Dean's List

Programming Pattern

```
while ( true ) {
    try to read first data field
if ( at end of file ) break;
    read remaining fields
    process the record
}
```

FIGURE 6.19 Processing records to EOF programming pattern

STYLE TIP

When writing an `if` statement (as in Figure 6.18), the statements of the then-part are indented one tab beyond the `if`. The close brace for the then-part is aligned with the `if`. When there is an else-part (see Figure 6.22), the `else` is written aligned with the `if`, the statements in the else-part indented one tab, and the close brace aligned with the `else`. This arrangement makes it obvious which statements are included in each part.

Note also that when one control structure (for example an `if`) is nested within another (for example a `while`) the nested statement, and hence its body, are indented one extra tab, marking them as contained in the outer statement. The close braces are appropriately aligned to mark the end of each statement.

Note that the read for the student number, which always comes first, occurs before the test for loop exit, and the read for the mark, which occurs second, occurs after the test. This makes sense if we consider that there is a mark for a student only if the student number was there first. Thus, if there is no student number, there is no mark. We shouldn't try to read the mark unless we are successfully able to read a student number.

A **RECORD** is a set of related pieces of information or fields about a single entity stored in a file.

This technique is commonly used when we are reading **fields** (information) of **records** (collections of information about a single entity) until EOF is reached. In fact, it represents another programming pattern, or at least a variation on the programming pattern of Figure 6.11. This programming pattern, processing records to EOF, is shown in Figure 6.19.

Example—Determining Highest and Lowest Mark

What if we wanted to determine, in addition to the class average, the highest and lowest marks in the class? How would we do this manually? Basically, we could scan down the list of marks and, at each mark, determine whether this mark was higher (or lower) than the highest (or lowest) mark we had seen so far. If it were, we would remember this as the highest (or lowest) mark so far. When we reached the end of the list, we would know the highest (or lowest) mark. The algorithm for finding the highest mark would look something like:

```
for all the marks in the course
    if the mark is greater than the highest so far
        remember this as highest so far
```

If we assume that the variable `highMark` contains our most recent guess as the highest mark and `aMark` is the current mark we are processing, we could express the test as:

```
for all the marks in the course
    if ( aMark > highMark ) {
        highMark = aMark;
    };
```

That is, when the mark we are processing (`aMark`) is greater than the highest we have seen so far (`highMark`), update the highest to the mark we are processing.

How can this process begin? If we haven't seen any marks so far, what value should `highMark` be? We want it to have a value such that, when we process the very first mark, the test in the `if` statement will be successful, and we will set `highMark` to the first mark we process. This means that we want the initial value of `highMark` to be as small as possible so any other value will be greater. Although, in this case, we could use the value `-1` (since no real mark would be below `0`), this wouldn't work where negative values would be valid data.

Java provides some assistance through a special helper class called `Double`. The class `Double` provides a constant `Double.MAX_VALUE`, similar to `Math.PI`, that specifies the largest value of the `double` type. We want the smallest possible value, and so we initialize `highMark` to the negative of `Double.MAX_VALUE` since, upon consulting Table 3.1, we see that the smallest `double` value is just the negative of the largest value. This gives us the following code:

```
highMark = - Double.MAX_VALUE;
for all the marks in the course
    if ( aMark > highMark ) {
        highMark = aMark;
    };
```

A similar argument can be applied to finding the lowest mark (`lowMark`).

The complete program is presented in Figure 6.20. It is a modification of the program in Figure 6.12, but adds code to determine and list the highest and lowest marks. As in Figure 6.16, the data consists of, for each student, the student number and mark. A single loop is used to determine the total of the marks as well as the highest and lowest marks. We need to process the data only once to determine all three statistics. Prior to the loop, `totMark`, `highMark`, and `lowMark` are appropriately initialized. In the loop, the processing of the current mark (`aMark`) involves counting it, adding it into the total, and then determining if it is the highest (or lowest) mark so far. Note that this is represented by two consecutive, and hence independent, `if` statements. After the loop, the statistics are displayed.

```
import BasicIO.*;

/** This program inputs an unknown number of marks for
 ** students in a class and computes the class statistics.
 **
 ** @author D. Hughes
 **
 ** @version    1.0 (Jan. 2001)                              */

public class HighLow {

    private ASCIIDataFile       in;     // file for data
    private ASCIIDisplayer      out;    // statistics display

    /** The constructor uses an ASCIIDataFile to read a set of
     ** student mark data and then computes the class average,
     ** highest mark, and lowest marks.
     **                                                          */

    public HighLow ( ) {

        in = new ASCIIDataFile();
        out = new ASCIIDisplayer();
        display();
        in.close();
        out.close();

    };  // constructor


    /** This method displays the average, highest, and lowest marks
     ** in the course.                                           */

    private void display ( ) {

        int     numStd;     // number of students
        double  totMark;    // total of marks
        double  aveMark;    // average mark
        double  highMark;   // highest mark
        double  lowMark;    // lowest mark
        int     aStdNum;    // one student's student number
        double  aMark;      // one student's mark
```

(continued)

```
        numStd = 0;
        totMark = 0;
        highMark = - Double.MAX_VALUE;
        lowMark = Double.MAX_VALUE;
        while ( true ) {
            aStdNum = in.readInt();
        if ( ! in.successful() ) break;
            aMark = in.readDouble();
            numStd = numStd + 1;
            totMark = totMark + aMark;
            if ( aMark > highMark ) {
                highMark = aMark;
            };
            if ( aMark < lowMark ) {
                lowMark = aMark;
            };
        };
        aveMark = totMark / numStd;
        writeDetail(numStd,aveMark,highMark,lowMark);

    };  // display


    /** This method writes the statistics to the output stream.
     **
     ** @param  numStd  number of students
     ** @param  ave     average mark
     ** @param  high    highest mark
     ** @param  low     lowest mark                              */

    private void writeDetail ( int numStd, double ave,
                               double high, double low ) {

        out.writeLabel("Number of students: ");
        out.writeInt(numStd);
        out.writeEOL();
        out.writeLabel("Average mark: ");
        out.writeDouble(ave,0,2);
        out.writeEOL();
        out.writeLabel("Highest mark: ");
        out.writeDouble(high,0,2);
        out.writeEOL();
        out.writeLabel("Lowest mark: ");
```

(continued)

```
        out.writeDouble(low,0,2);
        out.writeEOL();

    };  // writeDetail


    public static void main ( String args[] ) { new HighLow(); };


}   // HighLow
```

FIGURE 6.20 Example—Determining class statistics

Finding the maximum or minimum. The process described here represents another programming pattern: finding the maximum (or minimum) value. This pattern is shown in Figure 6.21. The maximum is initialized to the smallest value for the data type and then, over all the values, each is compared to the current maximum and the maximum is updated if the data value is larger. To use the pattern for minimum, the initial value for the minimum is the largest possible value and the test in the `if` statement is reversed, using <.

In the example in Figure 6.20, four patterns are merged: process records to end of file, summation, find maximum, and find minimum. The first of these is used as the loop for the other three. The maximum is represented by `highMark` and the minimum by `lowMark`. The data value is `aMark`. Note that, although the student number is read each time, it is never used. It is not uncommon for a program to process only some fields of a record. This happens because different programs often process the same data file, but need different fields. For example, the mark report program needed student number and student mark, while the statistics program needed only the marks themselves. However, each program must still read all the fields of the record or the data will be misinterpreted and student numbers read as marks.

Example—Counting Pass and Fail

In addition to the statistics we have already computed for student marks, other statistics that might be of interest would be the number who passed the course and the number who failed. Let's write a program to produce these five statistics: average mark, highest

Programming Pattern

```
maximum = smallest possible value;
for all data values
    if ( datavalue > maximum ) {
        maximum = datavalue;
    };
```

FIGURE 6.21 Finding the maximum (minimum) value programming pattern

mark, lowest mark, number of students who passed, and number of students who failed. Each student's mark contributes to the average and that mark may be either the highest or the lowest. On the other hand, for the passes and failures, we have two possibilities for each student. If the student passed, we count one more pass; if not, we count one more fail. This can be done using an `if-then-else` of the following form:

```
if ( student passed ) {
    process as passed
}
else {
    process as failed
}
```

The program of Figure 6.22 is a modification of that of Figure 6.20. It produces a report of these five statistics. As in the other examples, it uses a data file similar to Figure 6.16. In addition to the processing for total, highest, and lowest marks, if the student passed (`aMark >= 60`), the number of passing students (`numPass`) is incremented; otherwise, the number of failing students (`numFail`) is incremented. When all the records have been processed, the results are displayed.

```
import BasicIO.*;

/** This program computes a variety of statistics about a class.
 **
 ** @author D. Hughes
 **
 ** @version    1.0 (June 2001)                              */

public class PassFail {

    private ASCIIDataFile       in;     // file for data
    private ASCIIDisplayer      out;    // statistics display

    /** The constructor reads the student records, computes the
     ** average, highest and lowest marks, and counts the passes and
     ** failures.
     **                                                          */

    public PassFail ( ) {

        in = new ASCIIDataFile();
        out = new ASCIIDisplayer();
        display();
        in.close();
```

(continued)

```
        out.close();

    };  // constructor


    /** This method displays the mark statistics.                           */

    private void display ( ) {

        int     numStd;      // number of students
        double  totMark;     // total of marks
        double  aveMark;     // average mark
        double  highMark;    // highest mark
        double  lowMark;     // lowest mark
        int     numPass;     // number who passed
        int     numFail;     // number who failed
        int     aStdNum;     // one student's student number
        double  aMark;       // one student's mark

        numStd = 0;
        totMark = 0;
        highMark = - Double.MAX_VALUE;
        lowMark = Double.MAX_VALUE;
        numPass = 0;
        numFail = 0;
        while ( true ) {
            aStdNum = in.readInt();
        if ( ! in.successful() ) break;
            aMark = in.readDouble();
            numStd = numStd + 1;
            totMark = totMark + aMark;
            if ( aMark > highMark ) {
                highMark = aMark;
            };
            if ( aMark < lowMark ) {
                lowMark = aMark;
            };
            if ( aMark >= 60 ) {
                numPass = numPass + 1;
            }
            else {
                numFail = numFail + 1;
            };
        };
```

(continued)

```
        aveMark = totMark / numStd;
        writeDetail(numStd,aveMark,highMark,lowMark,numPass,numFail);

    };  // display


    /** This method writes the statistics details to the output stream.
     **
     ** @param  numStd  number of students
     ** @param  ave     average mark
     ** @param  high    high mark
     ** @param  low     low mark
     ** @param  pass    number of passes
     ** @param  fail    number of failures.                          */

    private void writeDetail ( int numStd, double ave, double high,
                               double low, int pass, int fail ) {

        out.writeLabel("Number of students: ");
        out.writeInt(numStd);
        out.writeEOL();
        out.writeLabel("Average mark: ");
        out.writeDouble(ave,0,2);
        out.writeEOL();
        out.writeLabel("Highest mark: ");
        out.writeDouble(high,0,2);
        out.writeEOL();
        out.writeLabel("Lowest mark: ");
        out.writeDouble(low,0,2);
        out.writeEOL();
        out.writeLabel("Number of passes: ");
        out.writeInt(pass);
        out.writeEOL();
        out.writeLabel("Number of failures: ");
        out.writeInt(fail);
        out.writeEOL();

    };  // writeDetail

    public static void main ( String args[] ) { new PassFail(); };

}   // PassFail
```

FIGURE 6.22 Example—Counting passes and failures

Example—Tallying Grades

What if we wanted to know not only how many passes and failures we had, but also the exact breakdown by letter grade (where A is 90–100%, B is 80–90%, C is 70–80%, D is 60–70% and F is under 60%)? Here we need to choose between five alternatives! It appears that an `if` statement won't help because it allows only two alternatives; however, there is a way of doing it. Consider the following. If a student has at least 90% he or she has an A; otherwise, the student doesn't have an A. If the student doesn't have an A, then if he or she has at least 80% the grade is a B; otherwise, the grade is not a B, and so on. Here we have replaced a choice between five alternatives with nested choices between two alternatives. We could write it as:

```
if ( aMark >= 90 ) {
    process as an A                                          ≥90
}
else {
    if ( aMark >= 80 ) {
        process as a B                                 ≥80  }
    }                                                       }
    else {                                                  }
        if ( aMark >= 70 ) {                          }     }
            process as a C                     ≥70    }     }
        }                                             }     } <90
        else {                                        }     }
            if ( aMark >= 60 ) {       }              } <80 }
                process as a D   ≥60   }              }     }
            }                          } <70          }     }
            else {                     }              }     }
                process as an F  <60   }              }     }
            }
        }
    }
}
```

Note that the `if` statements are nested within each other. That is, the `if` testing for B is within the else-part of the `if` testing for A, and so on. This means that the test for B only occurs when the mark is *not* an A (`aMark<90`). The braces on the right show the values of the conditions that hold over each part of the construct. The first `if` statement divides the construct into two parts, one where the condition is `true` (when `aMark≥90`), and one where the condition is `false` (where `aMark<90`). The second `if` subdivides the else-part (`aMark<90` part) into two alternatives (`≥80`, `<80`), and so on. This means that, for example, the code processing a C only occurs only when `aMark<90` and `aMark<80` and `aMark≥70` (when the mark is between 70 and 80). Similarly, the code for processing an F occurs only when `aMark<90` and `aMark<80` and `aMark<70` and `aMark<60` (when the mark is less than 60).

An `if` construct of this form occurs often enough that some languages have a special construct for it as a third form of `if` statement, sometimes called an **if-then-elseif**. Java doesn't have this construct, but there is a way to get something close to it that is shorter than the example above. It looks like the following:

```
if      ( aMark >= 90 ) {
    process as A
}
else if ( aMark >= 80 ) {
    process as B
}
else if ( aMark >= 70 ) {
    process as C
}
else if ( aMark >= 60 ) {
    process as D
}
else {
    process as F
}
```

Here, if we consult the syntax of the `if` statement in Figure 6.13, we see that, in each case, the nested `if` is written in place of the *`BlockStatements`* within the braces in the else-part. This form is allowed by the complete Java syntax and, as mentioned earlier in this section, is one of two cases for which we will use it.

The complete program for tallying the letter grades is found in Figure 6.23. Like the previous examples, it processes the file of student records (Figure 6.16). To simplify the program, it counts only the number of students in each grade category. It doesn't determine the other statistics, although this would be a simple extension. The counters for the number of each grade (`numA`, `numB`, etc.) are initialized to zero before the loop, and then, when we know that the student's mark represents a particular grade, the appropriate counter is incremented. The total number of students and the average grade are computed as before. When the data is exhausted, the results are displayed.

```
import BasicIO.*;

/** This program summarizes the grades for students in a class.
 **
 ** @author D. Hughes
 **
 ** @version    1.0 (June 2001)                               */

public class Grades {
```

(continued)

```
    private ASCIIDataFile       in;      // stream for student file
    private ASCIIDisplayer      out;     // stream for grade display

    /** The constructor summarizes the grades for students.          */

    public Grades ( ) {

        in = new ASCIIDataFile();
        out = new ASCIIDisplayer();
        display();
        in.close();
        out.close();

    };  // constructor


    /** This method displays the summary of grades.                  */

    private void display ( ) {

        int     numStd;     // number of students
        int     numA;       // number of As
        int     numB;       // number of Bs
        int     numC;       // number of Cs
        int     numD;       // number of Ds
        int     numF;       // number of Fs
        int     aStdNum;    // one student's student number
        double  aMark;      // one student's mark

        numStd = 0;
        numA = 0;
        numB = 0;
        numC = 0;
        numD = 0;
        numF = 0;
        while ( true ) {
            aStdNum = in.readInt();
        if ( ! in.successful() ) break;
            aMark = in.readDouble();
            numStd = numStd + 1;
            if      ( aMark >= 90 ) {
                numA = numA + 1;
            }
```

(continued)

```
        else if ( aMark >= 80 ) {
            numB = numB + 1;
        }
        else if ( aMark >= 70 ) {
            numC = numC + 1;
        }
        else if ( aMark >= 60 ) {
            numD = numD + 1;
        }
        else {
            numF = numF + 1;
        };
    };
    writeDetail(numStd,numA,numB,numC,numD,numF);

};  // display


/** This method writes the grade summary to the output stream.
 **
 ** @param  numStd  number of students
 ** @param  numA    number of As
 ** @param  numB    number of Bs
 ** @param  numC    number of Cs
 ** @param  numD    number of Ds
 ** @param  numF    number of Fs                             */

private void writeDetail ( int numStd, int numA, int numB,
                           int numC, int numD, int numF ) {

    out.writeLabel("Number of students: ");
    out.writeDouble(numStd);
    out.writeEOL();
    out.writeLabel("Number of As: ");
    out.writeDouble(numA);
    out.writeEOL();
    out.writeLabel("Number of Bs: ");
    out.writeDouble(numB);
    out.writeEOL();
    out.writeLabel("Number of Cs: ");
    out.writeDouble(numC);
    out.writeEOL();
    out.writeLabel("Number of Ds: ");
```

(continued)

```
        out.writeDouble(numD);
        out.writeEOL();
        out.writeLabel("Number of Fs: ");
        out.writeDouble(numF);
        out.writeEOL();

    };  // writeDetail


    public static void main ( String args[] ) { new Grades(); };


}   // Grades
```

FIGURE 6.23 Example—Tallying grades

6.4 THE for STATEMENT

We have seen the `for` statement in Chapter 2 and have made significant use of it already. The `for` statement provides a **definite loop**. This is one for which the number of loop iterations can be computed before the loop is executed. The common syntax for the `for` statement is shown in Figure 6.24.

> A **DEFINITE LOOP** is one in which the number of times the loop body will be repeated is computable before the execution of the loop is begun.

As in other loops, the *`BlockStatements`* part in the braces is called the body of the loop. The loop repeats the body some computable number of times as controlled by the *`ForInit`*, *`Expression`*, and *`ForUpdate`* parts.

Actually, in Java, unlike in most languages, the `for` statement is just a `while` loop in disguise. The `for` statement of the syntax above is defined to be equivalent in execution to the following `while` loop:

```
    ForInit;
    while ( Expression ) {
        BlockStatements;
        ForUpdate;
    }
```

```
ForStatement:
for ( ForInit_opt ; Expression_opt ; ForUpdate_opt ) {
    BlockStatements_opt
}
```

FIGURE 6.24 `for` statement syntax

That is, in execution of the `for` statement, first the *`ForInit`* is executed to initialize the loop. Then, as long as the *`Expression`* is `true`, the *`BlockStatements`* are executed, followed by the *`ForUpdate`*.

The *`ForInit`* is actually a statement (recall that we have often used something like `i=1`). The *`Expression`* is a condition, such as `i<=10`. The *`ForUpdate`* is also a statement. We have used `i++`, which is a Java shorthand for `i = i + 1`.

STYLE TIP

Because of the equivalence of the `for` and `while`, many programmers—especially those raised on C—use a `for` as a shorthand for a `while`. Unless the loop is clearly a definite loop, this practice should be avoided and a `while` loop written instead; it is misleading to see the keyword `for`, which implies a definite loop. A `for` loop should always have a loop index variable (called an **index** for short; for example, `i`). The index should be initialized in the *`ForInit`*, tested in the *`Expression`*, and updated in the *`ForInit`*. The index should *not* be modified within the body.

A LOOP INDEX VARIABLE, or index for short, is the variable used within a `for` loop to count through the repeated executions of the loop.

Since the *`ForInit`* and *`ForUpdate`* are general statements, the `for` statement has greater flexibility than we have used so far. The initial value of the loop index may be determined in any way, and the index updated as appropriate. It may be incremented or decremented, possibly by a value (often called an **increment**) other than `1`.

Example—Compound Interest, One More Time

As an example, let's rewrite the compound interest table program of Figure 5.7 one more time. In addition to the principal and rate, this time the user will supply an initial number of years, an increment of a specific number of years, and the final number of years for the table. Thus we may start the table at year `5` and display it in increments of `5` years up to year `50`. The program is shown in Figure 6.25; the output of the program is shown in Figure 6.26.

```
import BasicIO.*;

/** This program displays a compound interest table for a given
 ** principal and rate for a given number of years with entries
 ** starting at a particular year and incrementing by a specified
 ** number of years.
 **
 ** @author D. Hughes
 **
 ** @version    1.0 (June 2001)                                  */

public class CompInt3 {
```

```
    private ASCIIPrompter      in;          // prompter for user input
    private ASCIIDisplayer     out;         // displayer for output

    /** The constructor displays a compound interest table.                */

    public CompInt3 ( ) {

        in = new ASCIIPrompter();
        out = new ASCIIDisplayer();
        display();
        in.close();
        out.close();

    };  // constructor


    /** This method displays the compound interest table.                  */

    private void display ( ) {

        double  p;      // principal
        double  r;      // rate
        double  a;      // amount
        int     n;      // year number
        int     iy;     // initial year
        int     fy;     // final year
        int     inc;    // increment number of years

        in.setLabel("Principal");
        p = in.readDouble();
        in.setLabel("Rate");
        r = in.readDouble();
        in.setLabel("Initial year");
        iy = in.readInt();
        in.setLabel("Final year");
        fy = in.readInt();
        in.setLabel("Increment");
        inc = in.readInt();
        writeHeader(p,r);
        for ( n=iy ; n<=fy ; n=n+inc ) {
            a = p * Math.pow(1+r,n);
            writeDetail(n,a);
        };
```

(continued)

```
    };  // display


    /** This method writes the table header.
     **
     ** @param  prin    principal
     ** @param  rate    interest rate                               */

    private void writeHeader ( double prin, double rate ) {

        out.writeLabel("Principal: $");
        out.writeDouble(prin,0,2);
        out.writeEOL();
        out.writeLabel("Rate:       ");
        out.writeDouble(rate*100,0,0);
        out.writeLabel("%");
        out.writeEOL();
        out.writeEOL();
        out.writeLabel("Year    Balance");
        out.writeEOL();

    };  // writeHeader


    /** This method writes the table detail line.
     **
     ** @param  year    the year number
     ** @param  bal     the balance.                                */

    private void writeDetail ( int year, double bal ) {

        out.writeInt(year,4);
        out.writeDouble(bal,10,2);
        out.writeEOL();

    }; // writeDetail


    public static void main ( String args[] ) { new CompInt3(); };


}   // CompInt3
```

FIGURE 6.25 Example—Compound interest table with user input

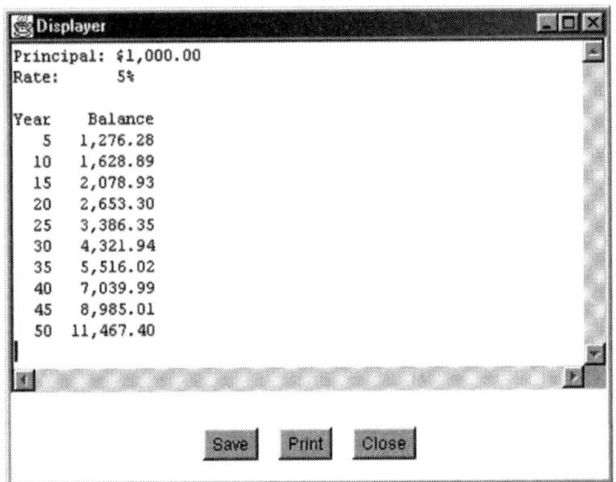

FIGURE 6.26 Compound interest table

The compound interest formula (see Chapter 3, Exercise 4) is used instead of the recurrence relation (of Figure 5.7) because the years are not consecutive. The initial year (`iy`), final year (`fy`), and year increment (`inc`) are input and used to initialize, test, and update the loop index variable (`n`, year number), respectively. Since the increment isn't `1`, the statement `n=n+inc` is used instead of `n++` for the update. The table itself is produced as before.

6.5 OTHER CONTROL STRUCTURES

There are three other control structure statements in Java: `continue`, `do`, and `switch`. These are used much less frequently than the other statements and are described here for completeness.

The `continue` Statement

The `continue` statement is almost never used; indeed, we will not use it in this book. It has the syntax given in Figure 6.27. The identifier is almost always omitted.

```
ContinueStatement:
    continue Identifier_opt ;
```

FIGURE 6.27 `continue` statement syntax

The continue is related to a break statement except that, instead of exiting the loop, the program simply omits the rest of the loop body and continues execution with the next iteration. A loop of this type might look like the following:

```
for ( i=1 ; i<=10 ; i++ ) {
     if ( i % 2 == 0 ) continue;
     out.writeInt(i);
     out.writeEOL();
};
```

The expression:

```
i % 2 == 0
```

evaluates to true whenever i is even. That is, i%2 is the remainder on division by 2, which is 0 for even numbers and 1 for odd numbers. The boolean operator == tests for equality. It asks if the result of i%2 is equal to 0—is i even? Thus, every second time through the loop, when i=2, 4, 6, 8, 10, the expression evaluates to true and the continue statement is executed. The program omits the rest of the loop body—the output statements—and continues with the *ForUpdate* and test. The result is the output:

```
1
3
5
7
9
```

The do Statement

The do statement is Java's post-test loop, in which the test for loop termination is after the body. It guarantees that the loop body is executed at least once and so is used whenever it is necessary to execute a sequence of statements one or more times. The common syntax of the do statement is found in Figure 6.28.

As in a while statement, the *BlockStatements* are called the body and the *Expression* is a boolean expression called the condition. The do statement executes the body and then tests the condition. If the condition is true, the body is executed again, as is the test, and so on, until the condition is false, at which time the next

```
DoStatement:
    do {
        BlockStatements_opt
    } while ( Expression ) ;
```

FIGURE 6.28 do statement syntax

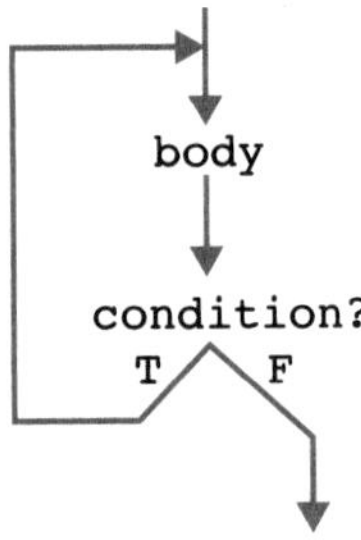

FIGURE 6.29 Execution of a do statement

statement—the one following the *Expression*—is executed. This is shown in Figure 6.29.

Consider the `while` loop used in the filling-the-box example in Figure 6.3. It would probably be reasonable to assume that the size of the box would never be zero or smaller. Under this reasoning, the loop will always execute at least once. In other words, `amt<size` will be `true` initially since `amt` is initially zero, and we can assume `size` is greater than zero. This means that under these assumptions, the `while` loop could be replaced by the following `do` loop:

```
amt = 0;
do {
    item = (int) (10 * Math.random() + 1);
    amt = amt + item;
    writeItem(item,amt);
} while ( amt < size );
```

The original `while` loop is probably still better since we don't have to make the assumption about the box size. If the box size is zero or negative, the loop executes zero times, as appropriate. There are cases, however, in which it is perfectly reasonable, and sometimes absolutely required, that the loop execute at least once. Generally, the `while` is used much more frequently than the `do` loop.

The `switch` Statement

The `switch` statement is a decision structure (like the `if` statement), except that it chooses between any number of alternatives. Since the number of alternatives is both finite and discrete, the choice is based on an integer expression as opposed to a boolean expression, which has only two possible values.

We will not show the formal syntax of the switch statement here (since it is very confusing), but will rather show a template for its use:

```
switch ( Expression ) {
     case Literal1 :
          BlockStatements1;
          break;
     case Literal2 :
          BlockStatements2;
          break;
     :
     :
     default :
          BlockStatementsn
}
```

The statement executes as follows. The `Expression` is evaluated and its value is compared, in turn, to each of the constant integral values—the `Literals` that follow the keyword `case`. When the expression is found equal to the literal, the corresponding `BlockStatements` are executed. This is followed by a `break` statement, which breaks out of the `switch`, causing the statement immediately following the close brace (`}`) to be executed. If none of the `Literals` is found equal to the value of the `Expression`, the `BlockStatements` after the keyword `default` are executed and the switch ends. The execution continues with the statement after the `switch`. When written this way, the `switch` statement is equivalent to a case statement in other languages. Note that this isn't the only form of the `switch` allowed in Java; however, it is the form most commonly used.

As an example, consider the set of nested `if` statements in Figure 6.23. It is possible to use a `switch` statement to cause the same effect. First, we need an integral expression that separates the student averages into the five cases we want. Unfortunately, this is not immediately obvious. Consider, however, the following expression:

```
(int) aMark / 10
```

The value of `aMark` is converted to `int` and the fractional part is dropped. The resulting `int` value is divided by `10` using integer division, yielding a value between `0` and `10`. Here we assume that the original mark values were between `0.0` and `100.0`. This gives us `11` cases. Two of them are grade A (`10` and `9`) and six are grade F (`5`, `4`, `3`, `2`, `1`, `0`). Each of the rest represents one of the other letter grades. We can write the `switch` statement as follows:

```
switch ( (int) aMark / 10 ) {
     case 10 : case 9 :
          numAs = numAs + 1;
          break;
     case 8 :
          numBs = numBs + 1;
          break;
```

```
        case 7 :
            numCs = numCs + 1;
            break;
        case 6 :
            numDs = numDs + 1;
            break;
        default :
            numFs = numFs + 1;
    };
```

Note that it is possible to associate more than one literal with the same set of statements by simply repeating the `case` *`Literal`* `:` part a number of times, as we did for the A grades. Note also that, if the expression were not equal to any of the values `10`, `9`, `8`, `7`, or `6`, (that is, if it were `5`, `4`, `3`, `2`, `1`, or `0`), the default case would be executed for the F grades.

A case statement is not used very often in object-oriented languages such as Java but has a significant role in many other languages. Its most common use is in user interfaces, to handle choices made by a user that are limited to a small, finite, predetermined set such as menu item selections. We will not use it very often in this book since we do not discuss user interfaces.

6.6 TESTING AND DEBUGGING WITH CONTROL STRUCTURES

Before we introduced control structures, there was only one path through a method, or program. To ensure that a method was tested, all we had to do was to make sure it was executed. Control structures introduce alternative paths. Now it is possible that executing a method will not completely test it, if one of the alternative paths is not followed.

This introduces a new complication in testing. All paths through a program must be tested. When designing the test data for a method, we must consider all conditions, including loop conditions, `if` conditions, and switch cases, and ensure that the data we choose for testing guarantees that each path is executed.

Consider, for example, the grade-tallying program shown in Figure 6.23. The `display` method involves a loop whose condition is `! successful()` and an `if-then-elseif` statement whose conditions are: `aMark>=90`, `aMark>=80`, `aMark>=70`, and `aMark>=60`. To fully test this method, we must ensure that the data includes values that will lead to both `true` and `false` results for each of these conditions.

Processing any file of at least one data record will ensure that both values of the loop condition are tested. To test all possibilities of the `if` conditions, we need a mark ≥`90` (say, `95`), one in the range `90`>mark≥`80` (say, `85`), one in the range `80`>mark≥`70` (say, `75`), one in the range `70>mark≥60` (say, `65`), and finally one in the range `60`>mark (say, `25`). Thus five test values would suffice.

```
111111  95.0
222222  90.0
333333  85.0
444444  80.0
555555  75.0
666666  70.0
777777  65.0
888888  60.0
999999  25.0
```

FIGURE 6.30 Test data for the grade tallying program

One common error in programming is making an error at the boundary of a condition; for example, using > instead of >=. For this reason, it is desirable to include a test value that is right on the boundary of each condition. In the grade-tallying program, this would be marks of `90`, `80`, `70`, and `60`. This requires four more test values.

One final test is needed for loops—that the program works when immediate exit occurs. In a pre-test loop this means zero executions, in an in-test loop it means one-half execution where the first part executed but not the second, and in a post-test loops it means one execution. In the grade-tallying program, testing this would require an empty data file.

Thus, to test the `display` method we need two data files. One would be empty and the program should indicate that there are zero students. The second would have nine data values for marks and would report 2 As, 2 Bs, 2 Cs, 2 Ds, and 1 F. Figure 6.30 shows such a test file.

In debugging a program with control structures, we usually have to determine which path is being taken erroneously. If we cannot deduce the problem simply from looking at the test results, we must try another technique. One technique is to put a debugging output statement using `System.out.println` that uniquely identifies the path, on each path. The program can then be run with the data values that fail, and it is possible to determine where the program went wrong by seeing which incorrect path was taken. Now the program can be corrected.

Be careful to rerun the complete test suite (all test sets) after any change is made to the program, in case the change causes a new bug. Of course, once all tests work successfully, the debugging statements may be removed.

■ SUMMARY

Control structures allow a program to adapt to the data presented or to respond to user requests. There are two kinds of control structures: loops and decision structures. Loops repeat a sequence of code—the loop body—some number of times. Decision structures choose between some number of alternative sections of code, executing one of them at most.

There are four kinds of loops. The pre-test loop, represented by the `while` statement in Java, tests the continuation condition before executing the loop body. This leads to zero or more executions of the loop body. The post-test loop, represented by the `do` statement in Java, tests the continuation condition after executing the body. This leads to one or more executions of the body. The in-test loop is not represented by a statement in Java, but can be manufactured from a `while` loop, an `if` statement, and a `break` statement. It tests the termination condition in the middle of the loop body, executing the first half one more time than the second half. The iterative loop, represented by the `for` statement in Java, executes the loop body, counting through a sequence of values of the loop index. The number of times the loop body is executed is computable before the loop is executed.

The decision structures include two forms of the `if` statement. The `if-then` chooses to perform a sequence of statements or not. The `if-then-else` chooses between two alternative sequences of statements. Although Java has no `if-then-elseif`, one can be developed from nested `if-then-else` statements. In the `if-then-elseif`, a series of conditions are tested until one of them is found `true`. Then the corresponding sequence of statements is executed. The case statement, which is created from `switch` and `break` statements in Java, allows the choice between a number of alternative sequences of statements based on the value of an integral expression.

Common processing patterns include processing all data in a file. Here, an in-test loop is used, attempting to read a value in the first half of the loop, with the termination condition of encountering EOF. The second half of the loop processes the data read. A variation—processing records to EOF—involves reading groups of related data, such as all the information about one student. Similar to the process-to-EOF pattern, the first half reads the first piece of data about the entity, the condition tests for EOF and the second half reads the rest of the data for the entity and then processes it.

Finding the maximum (or minimum) value from a set of data involves a trial maximum (or minimum), which is initially set to the smallest (or largest) possible value. Then, over all data values, the data value is compared to the trial maximum (or minimum) and, if larger (or smaller), the trial maximum (or minimum) is updated.

REVIEW QUESTIONS

1. T F A boolean expression is an expression that results in a truth value.
2. T F The `while` statement in Java is an in-test loop.

3. T F The tolerance in a convergence pattern is how close the approximation should be to the desired result.
4. T F The then-part of an `if` statement is executed when the condition is `true`.
5. T F Java does not have an `if-then-elseif` statement.
6. T F The following is an example of the summation pattern:

```
candy = 0;
    while ( candy < bucketSize ) {
    treat = getNewTreat();
    candy = candy + treat;
}
```

7. T F The statement:

```
for( j=start; j<=end; j++ ) {
    boo();
}
```

is equivalent to:

```
j = start;
while( j <= end ) {
    boo();
}
j++;
```

8. T F In Java, a pre-test loop is written using the `do` statement.
9. In the code:

```
a = 10;
while ( a < 10 ) {
    some statements
    a = a - 1;
};
```

some statements is executed:

a) 0 times. b) 1 time.
c) 10 times. d) This is an infinite loop.

10. In the code:

```
a = 1;
if ( a <= 10 ) {
    some statements
    a = a + 1;
};
```

some statements is executed:

a) 0 times. b) 1 time.
c) 10 times. d) This is an infinite loop.

11. In the code:

```
for ( a=1; a<=10; a=a+10 ) {
    some statements
    a = a - 9;
};
```

some statements is executed:

a) 0 times.
b) 1 time.
c) 10 times.
d) This is an infinite loop.

12. The code:

```
out.writeDouble(6.5/0.0);
```

will:

a) print 6.5.
b) print 0.0.
c) print NaN.
d) crash the program.

13. What is the range of the numbers generated by the following?

```
boo = (int)(7*Math.random()+1);
```

a) [1, 7)
b) [1, 7]
c) [2, 8)
d) [2, 8]

14. If pumpkin = 1, what is the value of spooks after executing the following?

```
spooks = 0;
if      (pumpkin < 1) {
    spooks = spooks + 3;
}
else if (pumpkin < 2) {
    spooks = spooks + 2;
}
else if (pumpkin < 3) {
    spooks = spooks + 1;
}
```

a) 1
b) 2
c) 3
d) 6

15. What is the effect of the following?

```
choice = 0;
while ( true ) {
    choice = choice + 1;
if( choice == 13 ) break;
    treat();
};
trick();
```

a) There is an infinite loop.
b) 13 treats and 1 trick.
c) 13 treats and 13 tricks.
d) 12 treats and 1 trick.

EXERCISES

1. Write a program that inputs a one-digit odd number and prints a series of lines, each repeating the digit one more time up to the input number, and then each with one less digit back to one, making a triangular pattern. For example, with an input of `5`, the program would print:

```
5
5 5
5 5 5
5 5 5 5
5 5 5 5 5
5 5 5 5
5 5 5
5 5
5
```

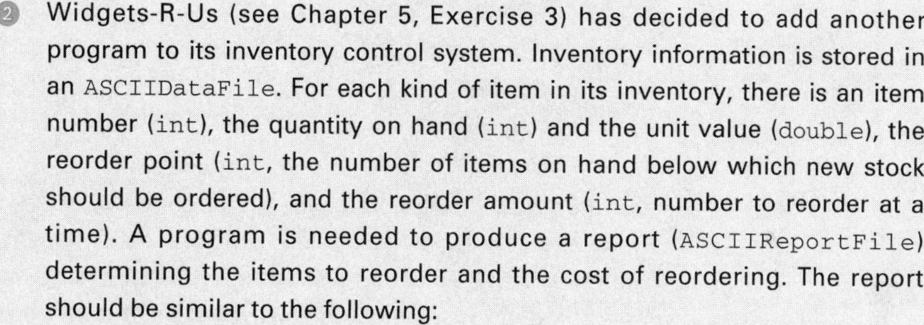

2. Widgets-R-Us (see Chapter 5, Exercise 3) has decided to add another program to its inventory control system. Inventory information is stored in an `ASCIIDataFile`. For each kind of item in its inventory, there is an item number (`int`), the quantity on hand (`int`) and the unit value (`double`), the reorder point (`int`, the number of items on hand below which new stock should be ordered), and the reorder amount (`int`, number to reorder at a time). A program is needed to produce a report (`ASCIIReportFile`) determining the items to reorder and the cost of reordering. The report should be similar to the following:

```
          Inventory Reorder Report
                Widgets-R-Us

Item #  Reorder  Unit Value  Reorder Cost
-----------------------------------------
12,524       50        2.75        137.50
17,823      100       10.95      1,095.00
83,731       25      127.36      3,184.00
73,562      200       27.95      5,590.00
-----------------------------------------
          Total Reorder Cost    10,006.50
```

3. Write a program that inputs a number (`double`) and a tolerance (`double`) and computes the square root of the number to within the degree of accuracy indicated by the tolerance. A recurrence relation for the square root of *a* is:

$$x_{n+1} = \frac{1}{2}\left(x_n + \frac{a}{x_n}\right)$$

That is, the next approximation (x_{n+1}) is computed from the last approximation (x_n) according to the formula. Starting with a first approximation of $\frac{a}{2}$, apply the formula until the square of the new approximation is within the specified tolerance of *a*.

4 Broccoli University maintains records about each student in an `ASCIIDataFile`. For each student, the student number (`int`), major department number (`int`), and average (`double`) are recorded. There are four departments: computer science (department number `1`), mathematics (department `2`), philosophy (department `3`), and business (department `4`). Write a program that reads the student file and produces a report giving the number of majors in each department and the average mark of the majors in the department, similar to:

```
Department  # Majors  Average
------------------------------
     1          125     82.75
     2           50     85.25
     3           10     78.50
     4          250     81.65
```

5 In the game "High-Low," one player chooses a number between 1 and 50 and the other tries to guess it. After each guess, the chooser tells the guesser whether or not s/he is correct and, if not, whether the last guess was high or low. The game ends when the guesser guesses correctly.

Write a program to play the game. The computer will take the part of the chooser, and the player will take the part of the guesser. The program will play a number of games and display the number of games played and the average number of guesses per game. The player should be prompted each time to see if he or she wishes to play another game. (Use `0` to stop and anything else to continue.) If so, the computer chooses a random number between 1 and 50 and the player begins guessing. Play of one game ends when the player guesses the number correctly. When the player quits, the statistics about the games are presented and the program terminates.

The user input should be done using an `ASCIIPrompter` and the results displayed to an `ASCIIDisplayer`. The user's guess should be displayed on the displayer. Finally, after all games are played, the statistics should be displayed. Output from the program might look like the following:

```
Guess: 25  High
Guess: 13  High
Guess:  7  Low
Guess: 10  Correct in 4 guesses.
       ⋮
Games played: 5
Average guesses: 6.0
```

Make some use of methods to break the program down into manageable parts. A method that handles the play of a single game would probably be useful. Be careful as you decide where variables are declared. (Try to keep variables as local as possible.)

7

Primitive Types

CHAPTER OBJECTIVES

- To understand the difference between reference variables and value variables, and between reference equality and value equality.
- To be familiar with Java's primitive types and when to use each.
- To be able to construct boolean expressions involving boolean and relational operators.
- To understand the effects of operator precedence on expression evaluation.
- To know and be able to use de Morgan's laws.
- To be able to process text files at the character-by-character level.
- To be able to read and understand a state transition diagram.

> An **OBJECT REFERENCE VARIABLE** (or **REFERENCE VARIABLE**) is a variable that references an object and is declared using a class name as the type.
>
> A **VALUE VARIABLE** is a variable that stores a value and is declared using a primitive type name as the type.
>
> A **PRIMITIVE TYPE** is a type that is fundamental to the programming language. It is not represented in terms of other types. In Java the primitive types are `byte`, `short`, `int`, `long`, `float`, `double`, `char`, and `boolean`.

As discussed in Chapter 3, variables can either reference an object or store a numeric value. Variables referencing an object are called **object reference variables** (or simply **reference variables**) and are declared using a class name, such as `Turtle`, as the type name. Variables storing values are called **value variables** and are declared using a numeric type such as `int` as the type name. Actually, value variables can be declared to store any of Java's so-called **primitive types** as opposed to referencing an object or class. The six numeric types (`byte`, `short`, `int`, `long`, `float`, and `double`) are primitive types. In addition, there are two other primitive types: `boolean` (representing truth values) and `char` (representing single text characters). In this chapter we will examine these two additional primitive types.

7.1 THE boolean TYPE

As we saw in Chapter 6, there are expressions in Java called boolean expressions that compute truth values as their result. Since we know that every expression has a type, there must be a truth value type in Java. This type is called `boolean` (after George Boole, an English mathematician).

Boolean values are limited to the two possible truth values: `true` and `false`; hence boolean values require only one bit for representation. The words `true` and `false` are reserved words in Java and are **boolean literals**. That is, they are the literal representations of the truth values, just as `1` and `2` are literal representations of integer values. A variable (called a **boolean variable**) can be declared to store a boolean value in the usual way:

> A **BOOLEAN VARIABLE** is a value variable that stores one of the two boolean values, `true` or `false`.

```
boolean tryAgain;
```

This declaration indicates that the variable `tryAgain` will be used to store a boolean (single-bit, truth) value. In an assignment statement, only a boolean value—as represented by a boolean literal or computed by a boolean expression—may be assigned to a boolean variable. Nothing else is assignment-compatible with `boolean`. For example:

```
tryAgain = true;
```

assigns the truth value `true` to `tryAgain` and:

```
tryAgain = i <= 0;
```

assigns `true` to `tryAgain` when `i` is less than or equal to zero, and assigns `false` otherwise.

Boolean Expressions

A boolean expression is any expression that evaluates to a boolean value, just as an `int` expression is one that evaluates to an `int` value. Boolean literals and boolean variables are the simplest forms of a boolean expression. However, as we have seen, there are more complex expressions involving special operators, which evaluate to boolean results. One such set of operators called the **relational operators** can be used to compare two values. The relational operators are enumerated in Table 7.1.

A **RELATIONAL OPERATOR** is one of six operators (in Java: `<`, `<=`, `==`, `>=`, `>`, `!=`) that can be used to compare values, producing a `boolean` result.

Numeric values can be compared for any of the six possible relationships between ordered values. As for arithmetic operations, conversion is done as necessary (widening only) to put the two operands into the same type before the comparison is performed. Note the form of the operators. They must always be written as shown, with no extra spaces; that is, <= is written, not => or < =. Note also the unusual notation for equality (==). This is to distinguish it from assignment (=). The use of the `!` in the not-equal-to operator is consistent within Java with `!` meaning *not*. We saw this already in Section 6.2.

Note that the equality and nonequality operators can be used with any type of operands. This means that we can compare not only numeric values for equality but also `boolean` values, where equality means both `true` or both `false`. We can also compare `char` values, as we will see in Section 7.2, where equality means the same text character. It is also possible to compare object values for equality, where equality means referencing the same object.

Value versus reference equality. It is important to understand the difference between the comparison of values of primitive types (numeric, `boolean`, and `char`) and the comparison of object references (that is, references of any other type, indicated by a class

TABLE 7.1 Relational operators

Operator	Meaning	Operand
<	less than	numeric
<=	less than or equal to	numeric
>	greater than	numeric
>=	greater than or equal to	numeric
==	equal to	any
!=	not equal to	any

The equality operators (`==` and `!=`), when used on values of a primitive type, indicate equality if the values are equivalent. This is called **VALUE EQUALITY**.

The equality operators (`==` and `!=`), when used on reference variables, indicate equality if the variables reference the *same* object. This is called **REFERENCE EQUALITY**.

name). Comparison of primitive types compares the actual values; this is called **value equality**. Comparison of object types, on the other hand, compares the references. It sees if the two reference variables refer (point to) the same object; this is called **reference equality**. In considering comparison of objects, think of identical twins. They may look identical, but they are different people. The same is true for objects. Two different `Turtles` or `ASCIIDisplayers` may appear identical; however, they are different objects. The object comparisons are consistent with this idea. The two `Turtles` or two `ASCIIDisplayers` would not be considered as equal by the equality operators.

Our memory model helps us understand the difference. Primitive type values are stored within the cell for the variable. More than one variable may contain the same value. Object type values are not stored in the cell for the variable. Rather, a reference to the object (a pointer, an address) is stored. Two different variables might reference the same object, in which case they are equal, or they might reference different objects, in which case they are not equal.

Consider Figure 7.1. Value variables `i` and `j` both store the same value (`1`) and hence are equal (`i==j` ⇒ `true`). Variables `i` and `k` store different values (`1` and `2`) and hence are not equal (`i==k` ⇒`false`). Reference variables `p` and `q` refer to the same object (the upper `Turtle`) and hence are equal (`p==q` ⇒`true`). Variables `p` and `r` reference differ-

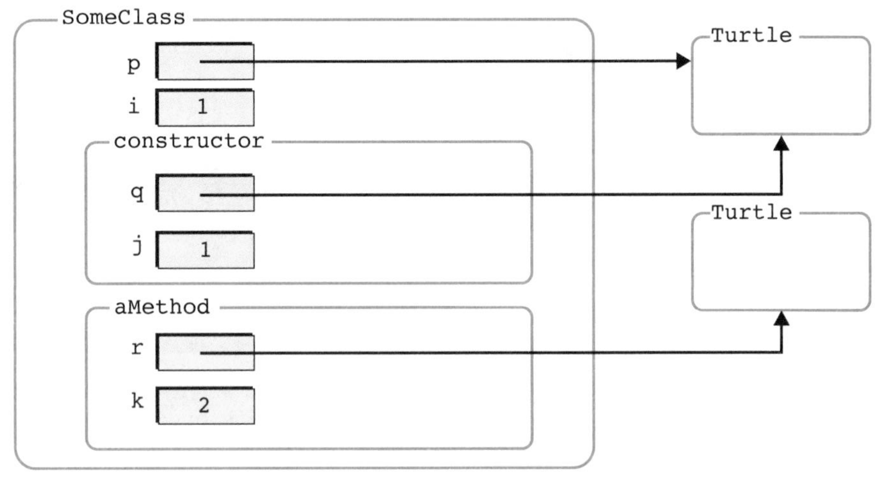

FIGURE 7.1 Value versus reference equality

TABLE 7.2	Boolean operators
Operator	**Meaning**
!	*not*
&	*and*
|	*or*
&&	*and then* (short circuit *and*)
||	*or else* (short circuit *or*)

ent `Turtle` objects (although they may look the same, like identical twins) and hence are not equal (`p==r` ⇒`false`). The consistency is that it is the value *within* the cell that is compared when the equality operators are used. For example, the number `1` is compared to the number `1`, or the address of the upper `Turtle` is compared to the address of the lower `Turtle`.

A **BOOLEAN OPERATOR** is one of the three operations *and* (`&` or `&&` in Java), *or* (`|` or `||` in Java), and *not* (`!` in Java). These operators take boolean operands and produce a boolean result.

A **TRUTH TABLE** is a table, similar to an addition table, that shows the results of a boolean operation or expression for each operand value.

In addition to the relational operators that apply to numeric and other operands to produce a boolean result, there are also **boolean operators** that apply to boolean operands—literals, variables and other expressions that produce boolean results. The boolean operators are listed in Table 7.2.

Truth tables. We have already seen the *not* operator (`!`), but there are four other boolean operators, two for logical conjunction (*and*) and two for logical disjunction (*or*). The easiest way to understand the boolean operators is to use a **truth table**. A truth table is like an addition or multiplication table—it shows the possible values of the operands and gives the result of the expression. Since boolean variables have only two possible values, it is possible to write the complete table. This is not true of the table for addition, which would contain an infinite number of integer values, making it impossible to write the complete table. Table 7.3 gives the truth table for *not* (`!`).

TABLE 7.3	not
b	! b
T	F
F	T

TABLE 7.4	and	
a	b	a & b
T	T	T
T	F	F
F	T	F
F	F	F

TABLE 7.5	or	
a	b	a | b
T	T	T
T	F	T
F	T	T
F	F	F

The first column is the value of the operand, here represented by the boolean variable `b`. The second column is the result of the operation `! b`, using `T` for `true` and `F` for `false`. As can be seen, *not* inverts the value of its operand so that when `b` is `true`, `! b` is `false` and vice versa.

Table 7.4 gives the truth table for *and* (`&`). The first two columns give the values of the operands represented by the boolean variables `a` and `b`. Note that `&` takes two operands (like `*`) but `!` takes only one operand. Operators that take two operands are called **binary operators**, whereas operators that take only one operand are called **unary operators**. The last column gives the result of the operation `a & b`. Note that *and* yields `true` only when both of its operands are `true`, and it yields `false` otherwise. This is consistent with the usual meaning of "and" in English, meaning that both statements are true. "He is rich and famous" is a true statement in English only if the person being referred to is both rich and famous.

Table 7.5 gives the truth table for *or* (`|`). Note that *or* yields `true` when either of its operands is `true`, and it yields `false` otherwise. This is consistent with the usual meaning of "or" in English: that one or the other statement is true. "He is rich or famous" is a true statement if the person being referred to is either rich or famous, or both rich and famous.

A SHORT-CIRCUIT (or McCarthy) OPERATOR is an operator which does not always evaluate both of its operands to produce a result. The short-circuit operators in Java include `&&` (*and-then*) and `||` (*or-else*). They are used in special cases in place of the usual *and* (`&`) and *or* (`|`) operators.

LAZY EVALUATION is a process by which operands in an expression are evaluated only as needed. It was first used in the language LISP. The short-circuit operators in Java use lazy evaluation.

Short-circuit operators. The two other boolean operators are special forms of *and* and *or*, called **short-circuit** or McCarthy **operators**, after the designer of LISP, the first language in which so-called **lazy evaluation** was used. Usually the way an expression is computed is that the two operands are first evaluated by simply obtaining their values if they are literals or variables, or by evaluating the subexpressions if they are expressions. Then the operation, such as addition or subtraction, is performed. For *and* and *or*, however, this sequence isn't always necessary. Look at the last two lines of the truth table for *and*. When `a`, the left operand, is `false`, the value of `b`, the right operand, doesn't matter; the result is always

TABLE 7.6		Short-circuit and
a	b	a && b
T	T	T
T	F	F
F	–	F

false. Similarly, the first two lines of the truth table for *or* reveal that when the left operand is true, it doesn't matter what the value of the right operand is; the result is always true. This means that for *and*, when the left operand if false (true for *or*), it is not necessary to evaluate the right operand at all because the result is already known. The so called short-circuit operators take this approach. Having evaluated the left operand, they only evaluate the right operand when necessary, hence the term lazy evaluation.

Table 7.6 shows the short-circuit *and* (&&, again no spaces) and Table 7.7 shows the short-circuit *or* (||). The use of – in the b column indicates a "don't care" condition; in other words, the operand is not evaluated. Otherwise, the tables are the same as those for the usual *and* and *or*.

Normally we will use the usual form (& and |). However, there are some situations in which there could be a problem if the right operand were evaluated, causing the program to crash. Often a properly written short-circuit expression can provide a good solution.

Operator precedence. We have introduced a number of new operators, so it would be instructive to reconsider operator precedence as previously described in Section 3.2. The operator precedence levels, including the relational and boolean operators, are shown in Table 7.8. There are still more operators and additional levels of precedence in Java, but we will not discuss them in this book.

As usual, parentheses can be used for grouping to effect any evaluation order desired. However, the precedence levels have been carefully chosen so that most common expressions do not require extra parentheses. Some examples and their evaluation order using complete parenthesization are given in Table 7.9.

TABLE 7.7		Short-circuit or
a	b	a || b
T	–	T
F	T	T
F	F	F

TABLE 7.8 Operator precedence

Operator	Meaning	Precedence
`-, !, (type)`	numeric and boolean negation, cast	highest
`*, /, %`	numeric multiplying operators	
`+, -`	numeric adding operators	
`<, <=, >, >=`	numeric relational operators	
`==, !=`	quality operators	
`&`	boolean *and*	
`|`	boolean *or*	
`&&`	short-circuit *and*	
`||`	short-circuit *or*	lowest

In the first example, to negate the subexpression `a<b`, the subexpression must be in parentheses since the precedence level of `!` is higher than `<`. Of course, this could also be written as `a>=b`. Since the arithmetic operators have higher precedence than the relational operators, arithmetic expressions can be compared without resorting to the use of parentheses. Similarly, since the boolean operators have lower precedence than the relational operators, it is not necessary to use parentheses when combining relational and logical operators (with the exception of `!`). Note the use of the short-circuit *and* in the fourth example. Here, when `a` is zero, the value of `b/a` is undefined; the program would crash if `b/0` were evaluated. The short-circuit operator prevents the evaluation of `b/a` exactly in the case where it would be a problem, and it still produces the desired result. In the last example (assuming `d` is `double`), the value of `d` is converted to `int` because of the cast. The conversion occurs before the division, resulting in integer division. Thus, when the whole part of `d` is even, the arithmetic subexpression yields `0` (or `1` if the whole part of `d` is odd). Hence, the entire expression tests to see if the whole part of `d` is even.

TABLE 7.9 Example expressions

Expression	Fully parenthesized equivalent
`!(a<b)`	`(!(a<b))`
`a+5<b-3`	`((a+5)<(b-3))`
`a<b&c<d`	`((a<b)&(c<d))`
`a!=0&&b/a>1`	`((a!=0)&&((b/a)>1))`
`(int)d/2==0`	`((((int)d)/2)==0)`

STYLE TIP

Parentheses may always be added within an expression to help make the meaning clear, even if they are not strictly required by the precedence rules. For example, the expression

```
a < b & b < c
```

could be written as

```
(a < b) & (b < c)
```

to emphasize that the comparisons are done first. The meaning of the two expressions is the same in Java.

de Morgan's laws. Before we leave boolean operators, there is one last issue to discuss: **de Morgan's laws**, named after the logician de Morgan who first described them. These define the interpretation of complex expressions involving the boolean operators *and* and *or* with *not.* de Morgan's law for *and* (stated as a Java expression) states:

```
! ( a & b ) == (! a | ! b)
```

and de Morgan's law for *or* states:

```
! ( a | b ) == (! a & ! b)
```

Table 7.10 demonstrates de Morgan's law for *and* using a truth table, and Table 7.11 shows de Morgan's law for *or* using a truth table.

See that, in both cases, the right-hand two columns are equivalent. de Morgan's laws define the correct way to negate the expressions `a&b` and `a|b`. When expanding the expression and distributing the `!` through the expression, `&` changes to `|` and `|` to `&`.

TABLE 7.10 de Morgan's law for and

a	b	a&b	!a	!b	!(a&b)	!a | !b
T	T	T	F	F	F	F
T	F	F	F	T	T	T
F	T	F	T	F	T	T
F	F	F	T	T	T	T

TABLE 7.11 de Morgan's law for or

a	b	a|b	!a	!b	!(a|b)	!a & !b
T	T	T	F	F	F	F
T	F	T	F	T	F	F
F	T	T	T	F	F	F
F	F	F	T	T	T	T

de Morgan's laws often become important when writing `while` loops. Sometimes the thing that is evident is the termination condition for the loop—the condition that is `true` when the loop is to terminate. However, the `while` statement requires a continuation condition. Recall that this is the condition under which the loop is to continue, and is the opposite or logical negation of the termination condition. When the termination condition is complex, for example, involving `&` or `|`, it is important that we know the correct way to negate it to write the continuation condition.

CASE STUDY Playing Evens-Odds

Problem

Consider a program that plays the game Evens-Odds, in which two players simultaneously expose some number of fingers on one hand, and one player wins if the total number of fingers from both players' hands is even, and the other player wins if the total number is odd. As a simulation of the game, the program takes the part of one player and the user takes the part of the other. To make things a bit more interesting, the program plays several games, totaling the number of wins and losses for the player. The player is asked if he or she wishes to play again or quit. If the user enters `1`, the game continues; if not, or if the user clicks the `End` button on the displayer, the game ends.

Analysis and Design

To simulate choosing the number of fingers, the program can generate a random number between 0 and 5. It then asks the player for a number between 0 and 5, and determines whether the sum is even or odd, with the player winning if it is even. Prior to each game, it prompts the user to determine whether he or she wishes to play again, with a negative response producing the summary statistics and ending the program.

Implementation

The example in Figure 7.2 is an implementation of the game.

```
import BasicIO.*;

/** This program plays the game Evens-Odds with the user.
  ** Both the computer and the player choose a number between
  ** 0 and 5 (representing some number of fingers displayed).
  ** If the sum of the two numbers is even, the player wins;
  ** if it is odd, the computer wins.
  **
  ** @author D. Hughes
  **
  ** @version    1.0 (July 2001)                                  */
```

(continued)

```
public class EvensOdds {

    private ASCIIPrompter       in;      // prompter for input
    private ASCIIDisplayer      out;     // displayer for output

    /** The constructor plays the game Evens - Odds with the
     ** user.                                                          */

    public EvensOdds ( ) {

        in = new ASCIIPrompter();
        out = new ASCIIDisplayer();
        play();
        in.close();
        out.close();

    }; // constructor


    /** This method plays the Even-Odds game.                          */

    private void play ( ) {

        int     resp;        // player's respones (play/quit)
        int     computer;    // computer's play (0-5)
        int     player;      // player's play (0-5)
        int     numGames;    // number of games played
        int     numWins;     // number of times player won
        int     numLosses;   // number of times player lost

        numGames = 0;
        numWins = 0;
        numLosses = 0;
        in.setLabel("Enter 1 to play, 0 to quit");
        while ( true ) {
            resp = in.readInt();
        if ( ! in.successful() || resp != 1 ) break;
            computer = (int) (6 * Math.random());
            in.setLabel("Enter number of fingers");
            player = in.readInt();
            writePlay(player,computer);
            if ( (player + computer) % 2 == 0 ) {
                out.writeString(" WIN");
                numWins = numWins + 1;
                in.setLabel("Yow win!. play(1) or quit(0)");
            }
```

(continued)

```
            else {
                out.writeString("LOSE");
                numLosses = numLosses + 1;
                in.setLabel("You lose! play(1) or quit(0)");
            };
            numGames = numGames + 1;
            out.writeEOL();
        };
        writeResults(numGames,numWins,numLosses);

    };  // play


    /** This method writes the play by the player and computer
      ** without an EOL.
      **
      ** @param  player          player's play
      ** @param  computer        computer's play.                    */

    private void writePlay ( int player, int computer ) {

        out.writeString("player: ");
        out.writeInt(player);
        out.writeString(" computer: ");
        out.writeInt(computer);

    };  // writePlay


    /** This method displays the results to the output stream.
      **
      ** @param  games   number of games played
      ** @param  wins    number of games won
      ** @param  losses  number of games lost.                       */

    private void writeResults ( int games, int wins, int losses ) {

        out.writeString("Number of games: ");
        out.writeInt(games);
        out.writeEOL();
        out.writeString("Number of wins: ");
        out.writeInt(wins);
```

(continued)

```
            out.writeEOL();
            out.writeString("Number of losses: ");
            out.writeInt(losses);
            out.writeEOL();

        };  // writeResults


        public static void main ( String args[] ) { new EvensOdds(); };


}   // EvensOdds
```

FIGURE 7.2 Example—Playing Evens-Odds

The boolean expression:

```
! in.successful() || resp != 1
```

handles the decision to quit the program. If the user clicks `End`, `in.successful()` returns `false`. We want to break the loop when this happens so we need the expression `! in.successful()`. We also need to break the loop when the user enters any value other than `1` (`resp != 1`). Since, when the user clicks `End`, the value read (`resp`) has an unknown value, we should not test it. Hence the use of the short-circuit *or*. Note that `in.successful` is a **boolean function**, a function that returns a boolean value.

To determine who won, the program sums the number of fingers of the computer and player and determines whether the sum is even. This is handled by the boolean expression:

```
(player + computer) % 2 == 0
```

Remember, remainder on division by `2` is zero for an even number and is `1` for an odd number, and testing for the remainder being equal to zero tests for evenness.

The code:

```
(int) (6 * Math.Random())
```

generates the computer's play. Remember that `Math.random` (see Section 6.1) returns a number between `0` and less than `1`. Multiplying by `6` gives us a range between `0` and less than `6`. Casting to `int` truncates the fraction, giving us a number between `0` and `5` as desired.

Finally, the uses of `in.setLabel` should be considered. Remember, the method sets the prompt for the display of the prompter at the next input operation. By setting it before the loop, the message:

```
Enter 1 to play, 0 to quit
```

occurs only the first time. Subsequently, the prompt is set to either:

```
You win! play (1) or quit (0)
```

or:

```
You lose! play (1) or quit (0)
```

This allows the program to give feedback to the player. In any event, the message is not actually displayed until the prompter is presented in response to the call `in.readInt()`.

Testing and Debugging
Testing an interactive program presents a new problem. There is no data file that can be stored for future testing when necessary. The solution is to develop a test script which indicates, for each prompt by the program, what the tester should enter and how the program should respond. In this case, the problem is even worse. The program is meant to be unpredictable! The best that can be done is to play a number of games, expecting to win and lose in relatively equal numbers, and determine whether the statistics are correct each time.

7.2 THE char TYPE

Although the ALU of a computer is designed primarily to process numeric data, a great deal of computer processing involves text, such as word processing programs, compilers, and web browsers. Java has two types: `char` and `String` (see Chapter 10) that support text processing. The `char` type represents a text character—letter, punctuation, tab, space, etc. A variable declared using the `char` type, for example:

```
    char    c;
```

stores a single text character and may be assigned a value represented by a character expression. As we will see later in this section, there are few operations that can be performed on text characters; however, these are sufficient to handle all requirements.

Coding Schemes

Remember that everything operated on by the ALU and stored in memory must be represented by bit strings. To represent text data, a **coding scheme** is used. Basically, a coding scheme is a convention that associates each character from a **character set** (a chosen set of characters) with a unique bit pattern—a binary representation of the integers from 0. The most common coding schemes are **ASCII** (American Standard Code for Information Interchange) and **EBCDIC** (Extended Binary Coded Decimal Interchange Code). ASCII is an ISO standard and used by microcomputers and the Internet while EBCDIC is used primarily on mainframes.

ASCII associates each of 128 different characters with a seven-bit representation using the integers from 0 to 127. ASCII–8 is an eight-bit version (1 byte per character), which is the ASCII representation with an additional leading `0` bit. It allows the possibility of an additional 128 characters, a set sometimes called extended ASCII, where the leading bit is `1`. It might seem that this is more than enough. However, when you consider that 33 of these are **control characters** (nonprinting characters like tabs and line feeds that control various devices), and that we need both lower- and

> A **CODING SCHEME** is a convention that associates each character from a character set with a unique bit pattern—a binary representation of the integers from 0. The common coding schemes are ASCII, EBCDIC and Unicode.
>
> **ASCII** (American Standard Code for Information Interchange) is a coding scheme that is the current standard for text storage and transmission on computer networks.
>
> **EBCDIC** (Extended Binary Coded Decimal Interchange Code) is a coding scheme used primarily on mainframe (especially IBM) computers.
>
> A **CONTROL CHARACTER** is a nongraphic character from a character set that is used to control a display, printer, or network connection.

uppercase versions of the Latin alphabet (52 in total), the digits (10), and punctuation characters (periods etc.), the set is really quite limited.

Java was developed along with the World Wide Web. Since the web is international, the Latin alphabet is not sufficient. In standard ASCII, not even all languages that use the Latin alphabet can be supported since diacritical marks (accents, cedillas, umlauts, and so forth) are not available. However, there is another ISO standard that supports the alphabets of most of the world's languages: **Unicode** (UNIversal CODEing scheme). Unicode uses 16 bits per character, allowing 65,536 different characters (plenty of room!). Java, naturally, uses the Unicode standard, and `char` values occupy two bytes of storage.

> **UNICODE** (UNIversal CODE) is a coding scheme that is the new ANSI standard. It supports most of the world's languages and is becoming the Internet standard. Java uses the Unicode coding scheme for `char` values.

This represents a potential problem. Microcomputers, their operating systems, and the Internet all use ASCII, while Java programs process Unicode. Luckily, the Java I/O system and the Java virtual machine handle the difference automatically, and the compilers allow us to use the standard ASCII when writing program text. This means that, except where we wish to develop internationalized programs (beyond the scope of this book), we do not have to worry about the differences between ASCII and Unicode. We should remember, however, that within a Java program, `char` values really occupy two bytes.

We often talk about alphabetic order as when we describe a telephone book or ask for a report such as a class list. This implies that there is an ordering to the letters of the alphabet from A to Z. This ordering is preserved in the various coding schemes, including ASCII and Unicode; thus the letter `A` is less than (comes before) the letter `Z`. There is a problem with this, however. Since the uppercase and lowercase letters are distinct characters, the relationship holds only for letters of the same case. That is, `a < z` and `A < Z`; however, `a > Z`. To allow ordering by digits, the digit characters are also ordered from `0` to `9`. Actually, the entire character set is ordered. This order is imposed by the coding scheme based on the order of the underlying bit patterns. Usually it isn't necessary to know the complete ordering.

char Expressions

Since `char` is a type, we can reasonably expect that there is a notation for generating `char` values; that is, a `char` expression. Actually, `char` expressions are limited to character literals and character variables. A character literal is any **graphic** (noncontrol) ASCII character enclosed in single quotes (`'`). Actually, there is a notation allowing any Unicode character, but we will not discuss this. Thus the statement:

```
c = 'a';
```

assigns the Unicode representation for the Latin letter `a` to the `char` variable `c`. To allow the representation (as a `char` literal) of certain nongraphic characters, **escape sequences** are used. An

> An **ESCAPE SEQUENCE** is a representation of a character (usually a nongraphic character) by a sequence of graphic characters. In Java, escape sequences begin with a `\`.

TABLE 7.12 Escape sequences

Escape	Meaning
`\b`	backspace
`\n`	newline
`\r`	return
`\t`	tab
`\'`	single quote
`\"`	double quote
`\\`	backslash

escape sequence is a sequence of two or more graphic ASCII characters, beginning with a backslash (\) and representing a single, nongraphic Unicode character. The common escape sequences are listed in Table 7.12.

Thus the statement:

```
c = '\t';
```

assigns the Unicode tab character to the variable `c`.

Interestingly, in Java, the `char` type is considered to be a numeric type. This means that arithmetic operations (especially numeric comparisons) can be performed on `char` values. Specifically, `char` is considered to be a numeric type narrower than `int`. Whenever a `char` value is used in an expression with numeric operators, it is widened to `int` by simply taking the bit pattern (according to the Unicode coding scheme) as a 16-bit binary number and extending it with 16 zero bits to the left. The value is always positive, between 0 and 65,535.

Since the alphabetic characters are ordered in the Unicode coding scheme, their `int` representations are likewise ordered, and so `'a'<'z'`⇒`true` and `'x'<'d'`⇒`false`, as expected. This means that we can use the relational operators to produce alphabetic ordering as long as we know the values are in the same case. Of course, the equality operators work for any type and so work equally for `char` values.

The classification as numeric types makes it possible to do arithmetic on `char` values (actually, on their corresponding `int` equivalents). For example, the statements:

```
c = 'd';
i = c - 'a';
```

assign the value `3` to the `int` variable `i`. The lowercase Latin letters are ordered and consecutive, and so, since `d` comes three letters after `a`, `'d'-'a'`⇒`3`. Similarly, `'D'-'A'`⇒`3` and `'8'-'5'`⇒`3`. Using a cast, we can produce new `char` values from old ones, as in the second statement following:

```
c = 'a';
c = (char) (c + 3);
```

which assigns the Latin letter d (three letters after the letter a) to the variable c. The value of c is converted to int, that value is increased by 3, and the result is converted back to char, yielding the letter d. Arithmetic operators other than the relational and adding operators can be used with char values, but they do not have much practical use.

Example—Converting Uppercase to Lowercase

Let's consider a problem in text processing. Suppose we have a file that has already been typed, except that the typist typed it all in uppercase and what we really wanted was lowercase. What we need is a program that can read the text file and produce a new file containing all the same characters, with the uppercase letters replaced by their lowercase equivalents.

ASCII text files. First of all, let us consider what an ASCII text file looks like. A text file is just a long sequence of ASCII characters. It is a linear, one-dimensional sequence, one character after another. We usually think of text as being two-dimensional, with a page consisting of a number of lines, each of which is a sequence of characters. The transformation from a one-dimensional file to a two-dimensional page is handled by some program that allows us to view or print the text. This might be a text editor like the one we use to edit Java programs, or it might be a word processor. To provide for the transformation from a one-dimensional file to a two-dimensional page, a line separator—a sequence of one or more ASCII control characters—is placed at the end of the characters for each line. Whenever the program detects this separator, it knows the end of a line has been reached.

Processing a line-oriented text file. This is the scheme we will adopt: we assume that the text file has been prepared by a standard text editor that placed line separators at the end of each line. We will process the text, one line at a time, reading the characters from the original file, transforming the uppercase letters into lowercase, and writing the characters to the new file. At the end of each line we have processed, we will write a line separator. This corresponds to a new programming pattern (Figure 7.3) for processing a

Programming Pattern

```
while ( true ) {
    get next character
if ( end-of-file ) break;
    if ( end-of-line ) {
        handle end-of-line
    }
    else {
        handle other characters
    };
};
```

FIGURE 7.3 Processing line-oriented text file programming pattern

line-oriented text file. Essentially, until end-of-file, the characters are processed one at a time. When the end-of-line is detected, special processing for end-of-line is performed.

The code for the program is given in Figure 7.4. Since we are doing text processing, and we wish to process every character in the file, we use the unformatted text I/O classes `ASCIIDataFile` and `ASCIIOutputFile` for I/O and the two methods that process every character of the file (including any control characters): `readC` and `writeC`.

```
import BasicIO.*;

/** This class is an application to convert a text file from
 ** uppercase to lowercase.
 **
 ** @author D. Hughes
 **
 ** @version    1.0 (July 2001)                                 */

public class ToLower {

    private ASCIIDataFile       in;      // text file for input
    private ASCIIOutputFile     out;     // text file for output
    private ASCIIDisplayer      msg;     // displayer for messages

    /** The constructor reads a text file character-by-character
     ** and converts the uppercase characters to lowercase.      */

    public ToLower ( ) {

        in = new ASCIIDataFile();
        out = new ASCIIOutputFile();
        msg = new ASCIIDisplayer();
        convert();
        in.close();
        out.close();
        msg.close();

    };  // constructor
```

(continued)

```
    /** This method converts the text from upper- to lowercase. */

    private void convert ( ) {

        int     numLines;        // number of lines of text
        int     numChars;        // number of characters in text
        char    c;               // a text character

        numLines = 0;
        numChars = 0;
        while ( true ) {
            c = in.readC();
        if ( ! in.successful() ) break;
            if ( c == '\n' ) {
                numLines = numLines + 1;
                out.writeEOL();
            }
            else {
                numChars = numChars + 1;
                if ( 'A' <= c & c <= 'Z' ) {
                    out.writeC((char) (c - 'A' + 'a'));
                }
                else {
                    out.writeC(c);
                };
            };
        };
        msg.writeLabel("Number of lines: ");
        msg.writeInt(numLines);
        msg.writeEOL();
        msg.writeLabel("Number of characters: ");
        msg.writeInt(numChars);
        msg.writeEOL();

    };  // convert


    public static void main ( String args[] ) { new ToLower(); };


}   // ToLower
```

FIGURE 7.4 Example—Conversion to lowercase

The main text processing loop is an instance of the line-oriented text file pattern. End-of-file is detected using `! in.successful()`. Since `readC` returns the newline

('\n') character when it reads a line separator, we compare the character read to newline to detect end-of-line. The processing for end-of-line simply involves writing a line separator. Note that we use `out.writeEOL()` instead of simply writing the newline character. This is because, on different systems, the characters used for line separators differ. `writeEOL` handles this problem.

Since the program is processing a file, it generates happiness messages indicating the number of lines read, which is the same as the number of line separators, and then it indicates the number of other characters processed. These counts are initialized before the loop and incremented when we know what character we are dealing with.

Once we know we have an uppercase letter between 'A' and 'Z',[1] the actual conversion from uppercase to lowercase is done using arithmetic manipulation of the characters themselves. We know that the letters in each case are consecutive and in alphabetic order. This means that, regardless of the actual `int` equivalent values, the distance (numeric difference) between the uppercase letter and 'A' is the same as the distance between the equivalent lowercase letter and 'a'. Subtracting 'A' from the uppercase letter gives us that distance, and then adding 'a' gives us the equivalent lowercase letter. Note that, at the end of the computation, the result is `int`. We must cast it to `char` before we write it out.

Although this method works in this case, it is not the desirable way to perform case conversion. This program only works for the Latin alphabet. The Unicode coding scheme, however, allows for a variety of languages with differing alphabets. Some of these have multiple cases; some do not. To internationalize the program, we need to use the facilities of the `Character` class, which we will discuss in the next subsection.

The `Character` Class

Checking to see if a character is lower- or uppercase and converting to one or the other case is quite commonly done in text processing. The standard Java library includes a special class, like the `Math` class for numerics, that provides methods for working with characters. This class is called `Character`. A partial list of the methods from the class is given in Table 7.13.

The first five methods are so-called **predicates**, that is, boolean methods that tell something about the character. White-space characters are any of the characters that Java considers to be white space—the separators: space, tab, newline, and so on. The last two methods return the lower (upper) case equivalent of the character if the character is an alphabetic character, or return the character itself if it is not alphabetic (for example, `Character.toLowercase('C')('c'`, `Character.toLowercase('c')('c'`, and `Character.toLowercase('!')('!')`. These methods make working with characters much easier. They also have a side benefit: internationalization (the

[1] Note that we cannot use the expression `'A' <= c <= 'Z'` since this would evaluate as `(('A' <= c) <= 'Z')`, the first part of which evaluates to a boolean. The result is a syntax error because boolean values cannot be compared with character values.

TABLE 7.13 Methods of the `Character` class

Method	Result	Meaning
`isWhitespace(c)`	`boolean`	white space character?
`isDigit(c)`	`boolean`	digit character?
`isLetter(c)`	`boolean`	letter character (either case)?
`isLowerCase(c)`	`boolean`	lowercase letter?
`isUpperCase(c)`	`boolean`	uppercase letter?
`toLowerCase(c)`	`char`	lowercase equivalent
`toUpperCase(c)`	`char`	uppercase equivalent

ability for a program to operate correctly when used in different locales where different languages are used). Where appropriate, they return the meaningful result for alphabets other than the Latin alphabet. If the alphabet has different cases, then `isUpperCase` and `toUpperCase` have appropriate meanings; similarly, if the alphabet has digit characters, `isDigit` has the appropriate meaning.

It is advisable to use these methods instead of writing the code yourself. The code doing the actual conversion from uppercase to lowercase in Figure 7.4 could be rewritten as:

```
numChars = numChars + 1;
if ( Character.isUpperCase(c) ) {
    out.writeC(Character.toLowerCase(c));
}
else {
    out.writeC(c);
};
```

or even more simply as:

```
numChars = numChars + 1;
out.writeC(Character.toLowerCase(c));
```

CASE STUDY Counting Words

Problem

Let's look at another example of text processing: a program for counting the number of words in a text file. For the purposes of the program, we need a working definition of "word." We will consider a word to be a sequence of consecutive alphabetic characters separated by sequences of nonalphabetic characters. This definition is not really complete because it doesn't consider contractions or hyphenated words, for example, but it is sufficient for our purposes.

Analysis and Design

There is a bit of a problem here. To count words, we will have to determine where a word begins and where it ends, since words can consist of one or more characters. We input the characters one at a time. When we see an alphabetic character, we won't know if it is the first, the last, or a middle character in a word. How can we count the words?

The solution requires that the program remember something about the state of the processing so it can decide what the next character implies. For example, if the program has been processing nonalphabetic characters and it sees an alphabetic character, it knows it is at the start of a word. Similarly, if it has been processing alphabetic characters, and it encounters a nonalphabetic character, it knows it is at the end of a word. This situation is described by Figure 7.5.

> A **STATE TRANSITION DIAGRAM** is a diagram that represents the possible changes of state in a finite state machine. It consists of ovals representing states and arcs representing transitions. A version of state transition diagrams, called state charts or state diagrams, can be used to represent the possible states and transitions of an object in an object-oriented program.

State transition diagrams. Figure 7.5 is what is called a **state transition diagram**. It represents a process that has two possible states (the ovals) with transitions between them (the arcs). The arrow that doesn't start anywhere marks initial state, the state when processing begins. The two states are labeled, indicating that they represent being within a word, or not, respectively. The transitions are labeled by the condition under which the transition occurs, such as reading an alphabetic character or a nonalphabetic character.

The diagram describes what in mathematics is called a **finite state machine**. The operation of such a machine is to repeatedly input a symbol

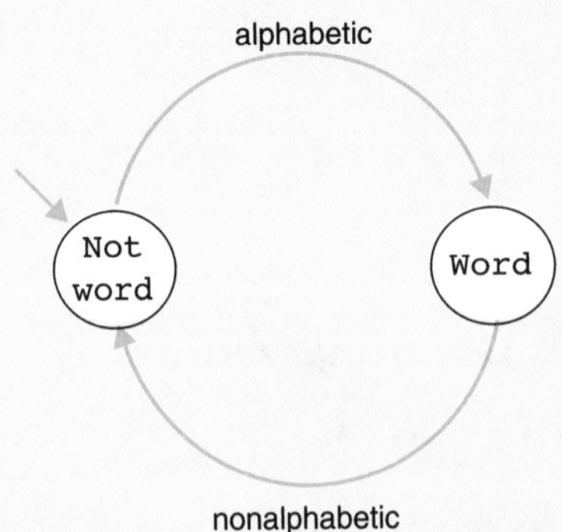

FIGURE 7.5 State transitions

(a character, in our case) and then, depending on the symbol and the current state, to make a transition to another state. If there is no transition for the particular symbol, implicitly the machine stays in the same state. In our case, the top arc means "when in the `Not word` state and an alphabetic character is read, transfer to the `Word` state" and the bottom arc means "when in the `Word` state and a nonalphabetic character is read, transfer to the `Not word` state."

Recording the state of the program. To use this description in our program, we need a way of recording which state the program is in. There are a variety of ways to do this, but since there are only two states, and they have opposing meanings, we will use a boolean variable `inWord`, which is `true` when the program is in the `Word` state and `false` when in the `not word` state. The program will begin in the `Not word` state. Characters will be read repeatedly and appropriate transitions made depending on the character read and the current state.

Now we only have to decide how to count the words. The easiest time to do this is when a transition is occurring. That is, we can count a new word either as we encounter its first letter (the transition from `Not word` to `Word` state) or when we have found its end (the transition from `Word` to `Not word`). Since the program starts in the `Not word` state, there would be a transition for a word, beginning with the very first character in the input. However, since it is possible that the last character in the input is alphabetic and that there is no line separator after the last line, there might not be a transition after the last word. Thus we are safest to do the count on the transition from `Not word` to `Word` state.

Implementation

The program is given in Figure 7.6. It produces a number of statistics: number of characters, number of words, and number of lines. It essentially uses the line-oriented text processing pattern, except that, since a word could end a line and the next line begin immediately with another word, the line separator must be processed as a character to separate the words. Thus the "character processing" is done after the `if` statement, not in the else-part as indicated in the pattern. Each time a character, including the line separator, is read, the current state (`inWord`) is checked. If a transition is required, as indicated in the state transition diagram, the transition is made by changing the value of `inWord`. Then any processing required during the transition is performed, such as counting the words upon leaving the `Not word` state.

```
import BasicIO.*;

/** This program counts the number of characters, lines and
 ** words in a text file.
 **
 ** @author D. Hughes
 **
 ** @version    1.0 (Aug. 2001)                                    */
```

```
public class WordCount {

    private ASCIIDataFile      in;      // text file stream
    private ASCIIDisplayer     out;     // displayer for output

    /** The constructor counts the lines, words and characters
     ** in the text file.                                                  */

    public WordCount ( ) {

        in = new ASCIIDataFile();
        out = new ASCIIDisplayer();
        count();
        in.close();
        out.close();

    };  // constructor


    /** This method counts the number of words in the text.               */

    private void count ( ) {

        int     numChars;         // number of characters
        int     numWords;         // number of words
        int     numLines;         // number of lines
        boolean inWord;           // currently in word?
        char    c;                // the next character

        numChars = 0;
        numWords = 0;
        numLines = 0;
        inWord = false;
        while ( true ) {
            c = in.readC();
        if ( ! in.successful() ) break;
            if ( c == '\n' ) {
                numLines = numLines + 1;
            }
            else {
                numChars = numChars + 1;
            };
```

(continued)

```
            if ( inWord ) {
                if ( ! Character.isLetter(c) ) {
                    inWord = false;
                };
            }
            else {  // not inWord
                if ( Character.isLetter(c) ) {
                    numWords = numWords + 1;
                    inWord = true;
                };
            };
        };
        writeResults(numChars,numWords,numLines);

    };  // count


    /** This method displays the results to the output stream.
     **
     ** @param  chars   number of characters
     ** @param  words   number of words
     ** @param  lines   number of lines.                                     */

    private void writeResults ( int chars, int words, int lines ) {

        out.writeLabel("Total number of characters: ");
        out.writeInt(chars);
        out.writeEOL();
        out.writeLabel("Total number of words: ");
        out.writeInt(words);
        out.writeEOL();
        out.writeLabel("Total number of lines: ");
        out.writeInt(lines);
        out.writeEOL();

    };  // writeResults


    public static void main ( String args[] ) { new WordCount(); };


}   // WordCount
```

FIGURE 7.6 Example—Counting words

Testing and Debugging

To test the program, a number of test data files must be produced to test the various situations. At least one empty file and one non-empty file should be included. In the non-empty file, there should be words that begin at the beginning of a line and some space from the beginning of the line. Similarly, there should be words that end at the end of the line and, on other lines, some space after the last word. There should be at least one line with exactly one word and one line with no words.

■ SUMMARY

The primitive types of Java include the numeric types (`byte`, `short`, `int`, `long`, `float`, and `double`), as well as the character type (`char`) and the logical or boolean type (`boolean`). Unlike reference variables (variables declared using a class name), which store a reference to an object, variables declared of a primitive type (called value variables) store the actual value.

Java provides operators for boolean values, including conjunction (*and*), disjunction (*or*), and negation (*not*). Boolean expressions, which include boolean literals, variables, operators, and/or relational operators, produce a boolean result: `true` or `false`. Boolean expressions are most commonly used as conditions in control structures (see Chapter 6).

There are no operators for character values. However, since Java considers `char` to be a numeric type, arithmetic operators can be used with character values. This is useful in limited situations. The helper class `Character` provides a number of additional methods for manipulation of character values.

Character values are defined by a coding scheme. Java uses the Unicode coding scheme, including 65,536 possible character values and providing support for most of the world's languages. Currently, most operating systems' file systems and I/O facilities use an older coding scheme: ASCII. Java's I/O facilities automatically convert between ASCII and Unicode.

Much of computing involves text processing, for example, in compilers, word processors, and editors. Text refers to a sequence of characters organized into lines; one line is separated from another by an end-of-line marker. Processing such a line-oriented text file involves a pattern shown in Figure 7.3.

In some situations, the program (or object, as we will see in Chapter 8), must keep track of what has happened so far and perform different operations in different situations. A finite state machine models such a program. The program's state gives some indication of what has happened so far. The state is recorded in an instance variable(s). The program's behavior, that is, what it does next, depends on its current state. We saw a simple example of this kind of processing in Figure 7.6 when we used character processing to count words.

REVIEW QUESTIONS

1. T F "Lazy evaluation" occurs when not all of the subexpressions of an expression are evaluated.
2. T F In Java the boolean operators not (`!`) and or (`|`) are called unary operators because they consist of one symbol.
3. T F The ASCII–8 coding scheme can represent over 60,000 characters.
4. T F A predicate is another name for a function that returns a boolean value.
5. T F A reference variable contains a reference to a primitive type value.
6. After the following statements, which of the boolean expressions is `true`?

```
Turtle   t, u;
int      i, j;
t = new Turtle();
u = t;
i = 3;
j = 5;
i = i + 2;
```

   a) `t == u & i != j` b) `t != u | i == j`
   c) `t == u & i == j` d) b and c

7. The inverse (boolean negative) of the expression:

```
i<j & j<k
```

   is:
   a) `i>j & k<j` b) `j<=i | j>=k`
   c) `i>j | j>k` d) `j>i & k>j`

8. Which values of `i` make the following expression true?

```
(5 < i) | (i < 7)
```

   a) none b) 6
   c) 5, 6, 7 d) all

9. Which of the following is a common character coding scheme?
   a) ASCII b) EBCDIC
   c) Unicode d) all of the above

10. What is the value of c after the following statements?

```
char      c;
c = 'n';
c = (char) (c - 'q' + 'D');
```

a) 'a' b) 'G'
c) 'A' d) none of the above

EXERCISES

1 Write a program to play a simple guessing game. In the game, the computer chooses a number between 1 and some upper limit. The player must then guess this number. After each guess, the computer will give feedback: "getting colder" (new guess is farther from correct than last), "getting warmer" (new guess is closer to correct than last), "getting hot" (new guess is closer to correct than last and is within 5 of correct), "getting hotter" (new guess is closer to correct than last and last guess was already within 5 of correct), and "same" (new guess and last are the same distance from correct).

The program should play a number of games with the user, asking the user each time if s/he wishes to play again. (Use 0 for stop and anything else for continue.) For each game it should prompt for the upper limit (guessing will be between 1 and this limit), choose a number, and then begin the guessing. Then, until the user guesses correctly, it should prompt for a guess and then report on the guess: "getting hotter," "getting colder," etc.

In choosing the number to be guessed, a random number should be used. A random number between 1 and n can be generated with the following code:

```
(int) (n * Math.random() + 1)
```

2 In the dice game Craps, the player rolls a pair of dice. If the result of this first roll adds up to 7 or 11, the player wins immediately. If it adds up to 2 or 12, the player loses immediately. If not, the sum of the two dice is called the point. The player now rolls the dice again. If the dice add up to the point, the player wins. If they add up to 7 or 11, the player loses. If the player has neither won nor lost, s/he rolls again, and so on.

Write a Java program to allow a user to play the game of Craps. The user should repeatedly be prompted, asking if s/he wishes to play a game. (Use 0 to quit, and anything else to continue.) If s/he does, the program should roll the two dice, determine the point and then, until the player either wins or loses, roll the dice subsequent times. At each roll, the program should display to the `ASCIIDisplayer` the result of the roll. When the player has won or lost, the program should indicate which happened and then prompt for another game. When the player decides not to play any more games, the program should display the number of games won and lost. The output to the displayer for a series of games might look like the following:

```
Game 1

Initial roll: 2, 2, point: 4

roll 2: 1, 5, count: 6

roll 3: 4, 3, count: 7

You lost


Game 2

Initial roll: 1, 5, point: 6

roll 2: 4, 2, count: 6

You won!!!

      ⋮


You won 1 games

You lost 4 games
```

In writing the program, use an `ASCIIPrompter` to ask if the user wishes to play a game, and use an `ASCIIDisplayer` to display the results. To simulate the roll of a die (singular of dice), generate a random integer between `1` and `6`.

3. Over/Under is a gambling game often available at casinos. The player places a bet on either over 7, under 7, or 7. A pair of dice is rolled and the player wins if the sum of the dice is either over 7, under 7, or equal to 7, respectively. The payout is even (1-to-1) for over or under and is 3-to-1 for 7. The player has an initial stake of money with which s/he starts the game, and can continue betting until either s/he wishes to quit or has nothing more to bet with and the stake has reduced to zero.

   Write a Java program to simulate the game Over/Under. The program will take the part of the casino game operator and the user the part of the player. The player will begin with a stake of $100 and can bet any number of dollars up to the stake. First, the player is asked whether s/he wishes to play a(nother) game. (Use 0 for no and anything else for yes.) If not (or if the player's remaining stake is 0), the program terminates after displaying the player's remaining stake. If so, the player is asked to choose to bet on over, under, or 7 by entering a positive number for over, a negative number for under, or 0 for 7. The player then enters his/her bet amount in dollars. The computer displays the bet, rolls the dice, decides whether the player wins or loses, informs the player of the result, and adjusts the stake appropriately. The player may then choose whether or not to play another game. A sample session of play might look like:

```
Current stake: $100
Your bet is $10 on Over 7
Roll is 4
You lose

Current stake: $90
Your bet is $10 on 7
Roll is 9
You lose

Current stake: $80
Your bet is $10 on Over 7
Roll is 7
You lose

Game over.
Your remaining stake is: $70
```

The program will use an `ASCIIPrompter` to get information from the player and display the results of the games to an `ASCIIDisplayer`.

4. Write a program to encode a message into a secret code. The process involves replacing each alphabetic character with another as specified by a key. The key (integer) specifies the number of characters the replacement character is to the right in the alphabet. For example, if the key is 3, then the letter 'a' would be replaced by 'd', the letter 'b' by 'e', etc. The process is cyclic, so the letter 'x' would be replaced by 'a', the letter 'y' by 'b', and the letter 'z' by 'c'. Punctuation, spaces, and other nonalphabetic characters would be left untouched and case would be maintained. For example, with key 3, the message:

```
This is a message
to be encoded with key 3.
```

would be encoded as:

```
Wklv lv d phvvdjh
wr eh hqfrghg zlwk nhb 3.
```

The scheme used can be similar to the first program for converting upper- to lowercase (Figure 7.4). If the alphabetic character is converted to an integer between `0` and `25` (for `'a'` to `'z'`), the key added, and the remainder on division by `26` computed (`% 26`), the result will be between `0` and `25`, being a cyclic shift by the key. This can be converted back into an alphabetic character and the result is the shifted character. (Note that each case would likely be handled separately.)

Read the key from an `ASCIIPrompter` and then read the message as an `ASCIIDataFile`, producing the result as an `ASCIIOutputFile`.

5 On the World Wide Web (WWW), pages must be presented on a variety of different hardware from text-based terminals to large full graphics screens, from microcomputers to mainframes. To enable this, the pages are stored in a special format called HTML (Hypertext Markup Language). HTML is a representation of the pages using plain ASCII text as simple text characters with the inclusion of mark-up to describe the special kinds of formatting (headings, paragraphs, table, and so on) that must be provided by the browser. The browser—Netscape Navigator or Internet Explorer—is a program that receives HTML pages and presents them appropriately on the hardware being used. The markup consists of tags that surround pieces of text, describing their form. When the browser is presenting the page, it reads the text, determines what tags are present, and presents the text accordingly.

Write a browser (presenter) for a simple markup language (PTML: Plain Text Markup Language). Each of the tags is a single character, and the tags (with the exception of the list element tag) are paired into an opening and closing tag, which surround the text affected. The tags are described below:

{ (begin heading) and } (end heading)	The text enclosed is a heading and should be presented in all uppercase characters. There should be one blank line before the heading and one blank line after the heading.
> (begin paragraph) and < (end paragraph)	The text enclosed is a paragraph and the first line should be indented 5 spaces. There should be a blank line after the paragraph.

[(begin list) and] (end list)	The text enclosed is a numbered list, that is, a number of list items each with a consecutive number starting at `1`. There should be a blank line at the end of the list.
# (list item)	The text following (up to the next `#` or `]`) is a new item within a list. Each list item should start on a new line with the list item number (up to two digits, one greater than the last item of this list) followed by a period, followed by two spaces, followed by the list item text.
^ (begin emphasis) and ~ (end emphasis)	The text enclosed is to be emphasized by presenting it in all uppercase characters.

Since the text must be presented on screens of different size, the number of characters presented on a line must depend on the presentation device, not on the text itself. This means that end-of-line (EOL) characters in the text do not automatically represent ends of lines in the output text. In our presenter, the lines are filled up with characters until they are approximately `40` characters long and the last word begins no later than position `40` on the line. The next word begins at the beginning of a new line. This means that EOLs and spaces must be treated the same and, when they occur after position `40`, are treated as a new line and otherwise as a space.

As an example, the following PTML text:

```
{This is a heading}
>This is a paragraph consisting
of a number
of lines which are ^arbitrary lengths~
but
are wrapped after column 40.<
>Now a list<
[#item one
#item two
#item three]
{Another heading}
>Another list<
[#item 1
#item 2]
>That's it<
```

would be presented (by our presenter) in the following way:

```
THIS IS A HEADING

     This is a paragraph consisting of a
number of lines which are ARBITRARY LENGTHS
but are wrapped after column 40.

     Now a list

 1.  item one
 2.  item two
 3.  item three

ANOTHER HEADING

     Another list

 1.  item 1
 2.  item 2

     That's it
```

You may assume that the text is valid PTML and all the opening tags are matched with closing tags, list items only occur in lists, and lists are not nested. Your program should read the PTML text from an `ASCIIDataFile` and display the formatted text in an `ASCIIDisplayer`.

8

Classes

CHAPTER OBJECTIVES

- To be able to use multiple classes in developing a program.
- To recognize the relationship between class state and behavior.
- To understand, and be able to use, data abstraction in the design of a class.
- To know the principles of information hiding and how to design a class to capitalize on this principle.
- To recognize the need for reuse in system development and to be able to develop a class with reuse in mind.

So far all of our examples have involved writing one class (the main class) and making use of library classes such as `Turtle` and `SimpleDataInput`. Real-world projects usually involve hundreds or thousands of classes, some written explicitly for the project and some from libraries that have been custom-written or purchased. In this chapter, we will look at how programs with multiple classes are written and how the classes—actually, objects as instances of those classes—interact.

8.1 CLASSES REVISITED

We first encountered classes in Chapter 2. There we saw that the class is the major building block of Java programs. Everything that we write is a part of a class and a program is a collection of classes. When a program executes, we create instances (objects) of one or more classes and these objects interact to produce the desired results. In Section 2.1, we wrote one class: `Square`. The one instance of the class `Square`, created in the **main method**, interacted with the one instance of the class `Turtle` (a library class) created in the constructor of `Square` and called `yertle` to draw a square on the screen. Later programs used more classes; for example, we used a number of input and output streams. However, we still wrote only one of them.

> One class in each program (called the main class) must have a method called `main` (the **MAIN METHOD**) where execution begins.

The syntax in Figure 2.6 shows that a class is a collection of declarations that includes constructors, fields, and methods. The constructors are "methods" that are executed when an instance of the class is created. We used this idea to achieve the goal of our program; the main method simply created an instance of our class. Fields, which we also called instance variables, allow information to be remembered by the object, and methods allow the object to perform some actions.

Any object can have instance variables that serve as the object's memory. For example, we used an instance variable to remember which `Turtle` object we were using. Clearly, the `Turtle` object itself must remember where it is on the page and in which direction it is traveling, so the `Turtle` class must define some instance variables as well.

We used methods in two different ways. When we were using methods of the object itself—those defined in the class—we used the simple method call syntax:

```
methodName(parameterList)
```

When we were using methods of another object—those defined in a different class such as `Turtle`—we used the method call syntax:

```
objectName.methodName(parameterList)
```

where *`objectName`* is a reference to the object we are asking to do the task. In the first case, we consider that the object itself is doing the task, so it is not named. In fact, there is a reserved word `this` that always represents the object itself, and so the first case is really a shorthand for:

```
this.methodName(parameterList)
```

Thus a method is always performed by some object. It may be this object itself or some other referenced by a reference variable.

An object, which is an instance of a class, can have a memory. In other words, its memory is retained in the instance variables defined for the class. An object can perform actions, the methods defined for the class. So we can think of the objects as sentient entities having an intelligence of their own. When we write large-scale programs, we consider the execution to be a result achieved by the cooperation of a number of such sentient entities, much like any human endeavor. By analogy, in the real world we interact with other people to achieve some goal: We might interact with a teller in a bank to withdraw some money. Writing large programs involves writing a number of classes and, in the main class, creating instances of a number of these classes, which cooperate to produce the result. In this chapter we will look at object interaction, and in Chapter 9 we will look at the software development process, in which we decide which classes to include in a project.

8.2 CLASS BEHAVIOR

As we have seen, a class declaration consists of constructor declarations, field (instance variable) declarations, and method declarations. When a new object is created, the constructor is first executed. While the object exists, it has memory represented by its instance variables and can perform actions, which are its methods.

> The **STATE** of an object is represented by the set of values stored in each of its instance variables. The effect of a method call to an object can depend on its state.
>
> The **BEHAVIOR** of an object is the effect of its methods. The behavior can depend on the state of the object.

Since the methods of the class can refer to the instance variables of the class, what they do can depend on the current values of the instance variables. The method could do different things at different times. For example, the line drawn by `forward` goes in a different direction, depending on the current direction the `Turtle` is facing. We say that objects have a **state**, which is the accumulation of the values of all instance variables. And the objects have a **behavior**, which is what the methods of the object do. The behavior depends on the state. In this respect, an object is like a complex finite-state machine in that what it does in response to an input (method call) depends on its current state (values of its instance variables). (See Section 7.2.) In fact, a version of a finite-state transition diagram called a state diagram is often used in object-oriented software engineering to describe the behavior of a class.

Since behavior depends on state, an object must be in a well-defined state when it begins its life if it is to have well-defined behavior. This is the role of a constructor: to put the object into a well-defined initial state consisting of appropriate initial values for the instance variables. For example, the constructor for a `Turtle` object sets the initial direction to east and the initial position to the center of the drawing page.

8.3 DATA ABSTRACTION

As we have seen with procedural abstraction, as a system gets more complex, it is necessary to abstract details to allow an understanding and make it possible to write a program. Unfortunately, procedural abstraction is not powerful enough, on its own, to allow us to handle large programs. A second kind of abstraction, **data abstraction**, is also needed.

> **DATA ABSTRACTION** is a technique for dealing with complexity in which a set of data values and the operations upon them are abstracted, as a class in an object-oriented language, defining a type. The abstraction can then be used without concern for the representation of the values or implementation of the operations.

Classes allow us to abstract details concerning a certain kind of entity, perhaps the employees in a company or the students in a university. Within the class, we can use information hiding (described in Section 8.4) and hide the details of what an object will remember via instance variables and how it achieves its behavior via method bodies. In a program with many classes, only the class representing the particular entity needs to concern itself with what is remembered and how the behavior is achieved; all other classes (objects) need worry only about what the entity can do. This is exactly how we have used `Turtle` objects since Chapter 2. We used `Turtle` objects, knowing only what they could do for us; for example, move `forward` or turn `right`. We didn't have to know how they knew where they were on the page or how a line was drawn from one place to another on the screen.

CASE STUDY Payroll System

Problem

A small company named National Widgets Inc. needs a program to handle its weekly payroll. Each employee is paid according to a particular rate of pay in dollars per hour. The payroll system is to inquire of the user (paymaster) how many hours each employee worked in the past week, and it will produce a report indicating the net pay for each employee, such as seen in Figure 8.1.

Analysis and Design

This problem lends itself to the use of multiple classes: one to represent an employee within the company and one for the payroll problem itself. The `Employee` class can encapsulate all the details about individual employees, and the main (`Payroll`) class can treat an employee as a sentient entity and concentrate on the report generation.

```
    National Widgets Inc.
       Payroll Report

 Emp #   Hours   Rate    Pay
 ----------------------------
 1,111   40.0  12.50   385.00
 2,222   40.0   5.50   220.00
 3,333   20.0   7.50   150.00
 4,444   40.0  45.00 1,386.00
```

FIGURE 8.1 Payroll report

We can see how the program might be written as a merger of the process records to EOF and the report generation patterns:

```
generate report header
while ( true ) {
    get information about next employee
if ( at EOF ) break;
    read hours for employee
    compute pay for employee
    generate report detail line
};
```

Using Data Abstraction. Although we could probably use procedural abstraction in this small problem, let's consider using data abstraction. Within a class called `Employee`, we can encapsulate all the details about an employee, including the rate of pay and the technique used to calculate the employee's net pay. If we had a variable `anEmployee` that was a reference to an `Employee` object, we could do something like the following:

```
generate report header
while ( true ) {
    get information about next employee
if ( at EOF ) break;
    hours = in.readDouble();
    pay = anEmployee.calculatePay(hours);
    generate report detail line
};
```

This assumes that the `Employee` class defines a function method `calculatePay` that computes the net pay the particular employee should receive if s/he worked a specified number of hours, the actual parameter.

Note that we can write this code without worrying about details such as how the employee knows his or her rate of pay or how the pay is calculated. We can neglect concerns such as overtime hours and taxes. This is the power and beauty of abstraction.

Employee information. Of course, eventually we must figure out the details and someone must write the `Employee` class. For this company, the details include the fact that each employee is identified by an employee number. Employees are paid according to their own particular rate of pay. If an employee works in excess of 40 hours in the week, s/he is paid for the additional hours at a rate of time-and-a-half for overtime. Taxes must also be deducted for each employee. If the employee earns in excess of $250.00 in the week, s/he is taxed at the rate of 23% for that week's earnings. For accounting purposes, the paymaster must keep track of the employee's year-to-date earnings, including gross earnings (before taxes), taxes withheld, and (by inference from the previous two) net earnings.

The data file containing the employee information contains, for each employee: the employee number (`int`), pay rate (`double`), year-to-date gross earnings (`double`), and year-to-date taxes withheld (`double`). So that this information is accurate from week to week, the program must create a new file with the updated year-to-date information, suitable for input next week. Since the paymaster must be able to read the data file, it is maintained as an `ASCIIDataFIle`. Figure 8.2 shows a sample data file.

The `Employee` Class The `Employee` class will not be a main class, but just another class within a program. The syntax for a class is the same (see Figure 2.6) whether or not it is a main class. The primary difference is whether the class has the special method `main`. Another difference between a main class and any other class is that execution begins within the main class, specifically in the method `main`. Execution occurs in other classes only when an object is created (when the constructor is executed) or the object is called upon to perform some action (when a method is executed). For example, in our early drawing programs, the `Turtle` constructor was executed, creating the window and placing the turtle in the middle. This occurred when our main class explicitly created a `Turtle` object (`yertle = new Turtle()`). Once created, the `Turtle` object sat idly by until it was asked to do something, as in the statement `yertle.forward(40)`.

Figure 8.3 shows the `Employee` class. Since the class is going to do I/O to read the employee data, it imports the `BasicIO` package. The class body consists of four instance variable declarations, which serve as the memory of the employee. These are the things that

```
1111        12.50       10000.00  2300.00
2222        5.50        4400.00   0.00
3333        7.50        3000.00   0.00
4444        45.00       36000.00  8280.00
```

FIGURE 8.2 Sample payroll data file

make one employee different from another and allow the `Employee` object to do its job. Following these is a constructor and a number of methods, the actions that an `Employee` object can perform.

Consider the method `calculatePay`. This method would be called (by the main class in our case) via a statement such as:

```
pay = anEmployee.calculatePay(hours);
```

assuming that an `Employee` object has been created and referenced by `anEmployee` and a `double` value has been obtained and remembered in the variable `hours`. The `Employee` object would perform its `calculatePay` method using its remembered information, such as rate of pay and the supplied information from the parameter describing the number of hours worked. The `calculatePay` method has three local variables and begins by computing the gross pay using the local method `computeGross`. We know that `computeGross` is a local method because it is called without an object reference, implying that this `Employee` object itself will execute the method. After computing the gross pay, it uses another local method, `computeTax`, to compute the taxes to be withheld. It then updates its knowledge of the year-to-date gross pay and taxes withheld in the instance variables and it returns the net pay as the result of the method.

```
import BasicIO.*;

/**  This class represents an employee in the company. An
 **  employee has an employee number and is paid according to a
 **  rate of pay. The year-to-date gross pay and taxes withheld
 **  are also stored.
 **
 **  @author    D. Hughes
 **
 **  @version    1.0 (Jan. 2001)                               */

public class Employee {

    private int     empNum;     // employee number
    private double  rate;       // pay rate
    private double  ytdGross;   // year-to-date gross pay
    private double  ytdTax;     // year-to-date taxes paid

    /** The constructor creates a new employee reading the employee
     ** data from a file.
     **
     ** @param  fromdata file for employee data.               */

    public Employee ( ASCIIDataFile from ) {
```

(Continued)

```
        empNum = from.readInt();
        if ( from.successful() ) {
            rate = from.readDouble();
            ytdGross = from.readDouble();
            ytdTax = from.readDouble();
        };

    };  // constructor

    /** This method returns the employee number.
     **
     ** @return int employee number.                               */

    public int getEmpNum ( ) {

        return empNum;

    };  // getEmpNum

    /** This method returns the employee's pay rate.
     **
     ** @return double  pay rate.                                  */

    public double getRate ( ) {

        return rate;

    };  // getRate

    /** This method changes the employee's rate of pay.
     **
     ** @param  newRate new pay rate.                              */

    public void setRate ( double newRate ) {

        rate = newRate;

    };  // setRate

    /** This method returns the employee's year-to-date gross pay.
     **
     ** @return double  year-to-date gross pay.                    */
```

(Continued)

```
public double getYtdGross ( ) {

    return ytdGross;

};  // getYtdGross

/** This method returns the employee's year-to-date taxes paid.
 **
 ** @return double  year-to-date taxes paid.                    */

public double getYtdTax ( ) {

    return ytdTax;

};  // getYtdTax

/** This method returns the employee's year-to-date net pay.
 **
 ** @return double  year-to-date net pay.                       */

public double getYtdNetPay ( ) {

    return ytdGross - ytdTax;

};  // getYtdNetPay

/** This method returns the employee's net pay for the pay period
 ** based on hours worked.
 **
 ** @param  hours   hours worked
 **
 ** @return double  net pay amount                              */

public double calculatePay ( double hours ) {

    double  gross;  // gross pay
    double  tax;    // taxes paid
    double  net;    // net pay

    gross = computeGross(hours);
    tax = computeTax(gross);
    ytdGross = ytdGross + gross;
```

(Continued)

```
        ytdTax = ytdTax + tax;
        return gross - tax;

    };  // calculatePay

    /** This method writes the employee information as a line to an
     ** output file.
     **
     ** @param  to  file to write to.                              */

    public void write ( ASCIIOutputFile to ) {

        to.writeInt(empNum);
        to.writeDouble(rate);
        to.writeDouble(ytdGross);
        to.writeDouble(ytdTax);
        to.writeEOL();

    };  // write

    /** This method computes the gross pay for the employee.
     **
     ** @param  hours   hours worked
     **
     ** @return double  gross pay                                  */

    private double computeGross ( double hours ) {

        double  gross;      // gross pay

        if ( hours > 40.0 ) {
            gross = ((hours - 40.0) * 1.5 + 40.0) * rate;
        }
        else {
            gross = hours * rate;
        };
        return gross;

    };  // computeGross
```

(Continued)

```
    /** This method computes the taxes due for a given gross pay.
     **
     ** @param  gross   gross pay
     **
     ** @return double  taxes due.                                  */

    private double computeTax ( double gross ) {

        double  tax;

        if ( gross > 250.00 ) {
            tax = gross * 0.23;
        }
        else {
            tax = 0.00;
        };
        return tax;

    };  // computeTax

}// Employee
```

FIGURE 8.3 Example—The `Employee` class

Memory model. Figure 8.4 shows the memory model at the point of the call to `computePay` for the first employee within the main class. (Note that only the relevant methods and variables have been shown.) The main class, `Payroll`, has, within the `runPayroll` method, a reference to an employee (`anEmployee`), the number of hours worked (`hours`), and storage for the computed net pay (`pay`). The `Employee` object was previously created via the constructor. The object has instance variables `empNum`, `rate`, `ytdGross`, and `ytdTax`, which contain the values of the employee number, rate of pay, and year-to-date gross pay and taxes withheld, for the particular employee. Within the called method (`calculatePay`), the formal parameter `hours` has been passed the value of the actual parameter (`hours` in `Payroll`). When execution begins within `calculatePay`, the code may reference the rate of pay (instance variable `rate`) for the employee and the hours worked (formal parameter `hours`) to compute the gross pay (local variable `gross`). Although the values of local variables become undefined each time a method is called, the values of the instance variables are retained as long as the object exists, providing the object's long-term memory.

Constructor in the `Employee` class. Let's turn our attention to the constructor for the `Employee` class. The purpose of a constructor is to place the object into its initial state. For this program, when an `Employee` object is created, it must come into existence knowing about itself—its employee number, rate of pay, previous year-to-date gross pay, and taxes withheld.

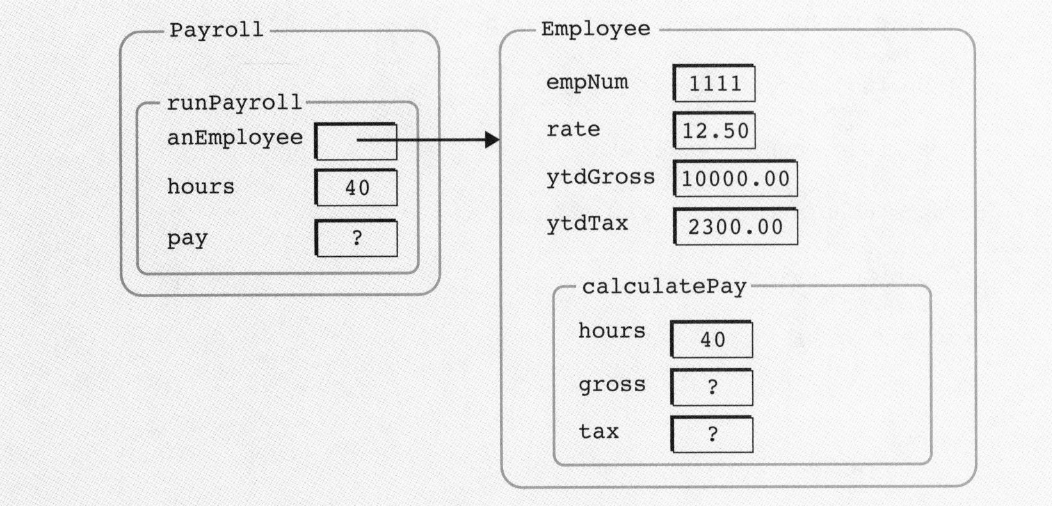

FIGURE 8.4 Memory model for `Payroll` program

Since this information is present in a file, the constructor must read from the file. Since all the employee information is in one file, each time an `Employee` object is created, the same file must be read. This means that the `Employee` constructor cannot open the data file (or different files would be used each time). The solution is to pass the file object as a parameter to the constructor. Remember, just like methods, constructors may have parameters.

We know that a file is not infinite—at some point there will be no further data to read. In this program, the data file should be read, one employee (line) at a time, until there is no more data, which is the signal to end processing. The data is read by calls to the `Employee` constructor. This means the constructor must be able to handle the possibility that there is no data left in the file. Basically, the constructor implements the body of the process-records-to-EOF pattern without the loop, attempting to read the employee number and, only if successful, to read the rest of the fields. After the constructor returns, the calling method can check the status of the input stream object to see if the last read operation within the constructor was successful and, if it was unsuccessful, terminate the loop. The code would thus be as follows:

```
generate report header
while ( true ) {
    anEmployee = new Employee(empFile);
if ( ! empFile.successful() ) break;
    hours = in.readDouble();
    pay = anEmployee.calculatePay(hours);
    generate report detail line
};
```

Note that the call to the constructor is being used as if it were a read operation.

Garbage collection. The code reading the Employee records demonstrates an important concept. Each time through the loop, a new Employee object is created, one for each record of input data. Over the complete execution, a potentially large number of objects will be created. Since each object uses up some computer memory, it is possible that the program could run out of memory.

Note, however, that there is only one Employee variable in the code. Since a variable can store only one value because storing another replaces the first, only one Employee object is referenced at any time. All of the previously created Employee objects are not referenced by any variable. When an object is not referenced by a variable, it can never be used. That's because the only way to use an object is via a variable. An unreferenced object is said to be garbage. The Java runtime—the program code that supports the execution of every Java program—contains a process called garbage collection. This code periodically looks through memory for objects that cannot be accessed (garbage) and recovers the memory previously allocated to them. Through this process, the program will not run out of memory.

> In Java, objects that have been created but are no longer accessible, not being referenced by any variable, are termed GARBAGE. The storage representing such objects can be recovered and reused in a process called GARBAGE COLLECTION.

Writing Employee records. As a final consideration for the Employee class, we must remember that one of the responsibilities of the program was to write to a new ASCIIOutputFile an updated version of the input data file. This was to be one record per employee with the employee number, rate of pay, and updated year-to-date gross pay and taxes withheld. Since this information forms the long-term memory of the Employee object and is stored as instance variables of the object, it makes sense that the object itself should write out the information. There is also a symmetry here; if the object reads the data, it should also write it.

The method write of the Employee class serves this purpose. It is passed an ASCIIOutputFile object and uses this object to write out the data values from its instance variables, being careful to write them in the same order that the constructor reads them. Remember that this file will be used next week by the program to get the employee data. The write method also writes an EOL marker, so each employee record is on a different line.

With this method available, the code for payroll processing becomes:

```
generate report header
while ( true ) {
    anEmployee = new Employee(empFile);
if ( ! empFile.successful() ) break;
    hours = in.readDouble();
    pay = anEmployee.calculatePay(hours);
    generate report detail line
    anEmployee.write(newEmpFile);
};
```

assuming that `newEmpFile` is the desired `ASCIIOutputFile` and that it has been previously opened. Note that the data is written out before the value of `anEmployee` is changed the next time though the loop. The writing happens before the object is garbage collected, and information is not lost.

The `Payroll` Class The second class in our system for the payroll application is the main class: `Payroll`, found in Figure 8.5. The constructor opens the five streams representing the original and new employee data files, the report file, a prompter to obtain hours worked from the user, and a displayer for user feedback. The method `runPayroll` performs the payroll report generation, essentially using the process developed in the previous section. The local method `writeHeader` is used to write the report header, and the method `writeDetail` is used to write the report detail line.

```
import BasicIO.*;

/**  This class performs a simple weekly payroll for a small
 **  company.
 **
 **  @see Employee
 **
 **  @author D. Hughes
 **
 **  @version   1.0 (Jan. 2001)                                  */

public class Payroll {

    private ASCIIDataFile   empFile;     // employee data file
    private ASCIIPrompter   in;          // prompter for hours
    private ASCIIReportFile payroll;     // payroll report file
    private ASCIIOutputFile newEmpFile;  // new employee data file
    private ASCIIDisplayer  msg;         // displayer for messages

    /** The constructor performs a simple weekly payroll
     ** generating a report and updated employee file.           */

    public Payroll ( ) {

        empFile = new ASCIIDataFile();
        in  = new ASCIIPrompter();
        payroll = new ASCIIReportFile();
```

(Continued)

```
        newEmpFile = new ASCIIOutputFile();
        msg = new ASCIIDisplayer();
        runPayroll();
        empFile.close();
        in.close();
        payroll.close();
        newEmpFile.close();
        msg.close();

    };  // constructor

    /** This method does the payroll calculations reading employee
      ** data and producing a payroll report and updated employee
      ** data file.                                                */

    private void runPayroll ( ) {

        int         numEmp;      // number of employees
        Employee    anEmployee;  // current employee
        double      hours;       // hours worked
        double      pay;         // weekly pay

        msg.writeLabel("Processing...");
        msg.writeEOL();
        writeHeader();
        numEmp = 0;
        while ( true ) {
            anEmployee = new Employee(empFile);
        if ( ! empFile.successful() ) break;
            in.setLabel("Employee: "+anEmployee.getEmpNum());
            hours = in.readDouble();
            pay = anEmployee.calculatePay(hours);
            writeDetail(anEmployee.getEmpNum(),
                        hours,anEmployee.getRate(),pay);
            anEmployee.write(newEmpFile);
            numEmp = numEmp + 1;
        };
        msg.writeInt(numEmp);
        msg.writeLabel(" employees processed");
        msg.writeEOL();

    };  // runPayroll
```

(Continued)

```
    /** This method writes the report header.                         */

    private void writeHeader ( ) {

        payroll.writeLabel("   National Widgets Inc.");
        payroll.writeEOL();
        payroll.writeLabel("       Payroll Report");
        payroll.writeEOL();
        payroll.writeEOL();
        payroll.writeLabel("Emp #  Hours   Rate    Pay");
        payroll.writeEOL();
        payroll.writeLabel("----------------------------");
        payroll.writeEOL();

    };  // writeHeader

    /** This method writes the report detail line.
     **
     ** @param  empNum  employee number
     ** @param  hours   hours worked
     ** @param  ratepay rate
     ** @param  pay net pay.                                          */

    private void writeDetail ( int empNum, double hours,
                               double rate, double pay ) {

        payroll.writeInt(empNum,5);
        payroll.writeDouble(hours,6,1);
        payroll.writeDouble(rate,6,2);
        payroll.writeDouble(pay,8,2);
        payroll.writeEOL();

    };  // writeDetail

    public static void main ( String args[] ) { new Payroll(); };

}// Payroll
```

FIGURE 8.5 Example—Payroll system main class

After the employee record is read using the `Employee` constructor, the user is to enter the hours worked for the employee. So that the user knows the employee for which to enter the data, the employee number is displayed in the prompter box using `in.setLabel`. The method `getEmpNum` of the `Employee` class returns the employee's employee number. As we saw in Section 4.4, +, when used with a string, represents string concatenation. The `int` returned by `getEmpNum` is converted to text, joined on the end of the string `"Employee:  "`, and used as the prompt, as seen in Figure 8.6.

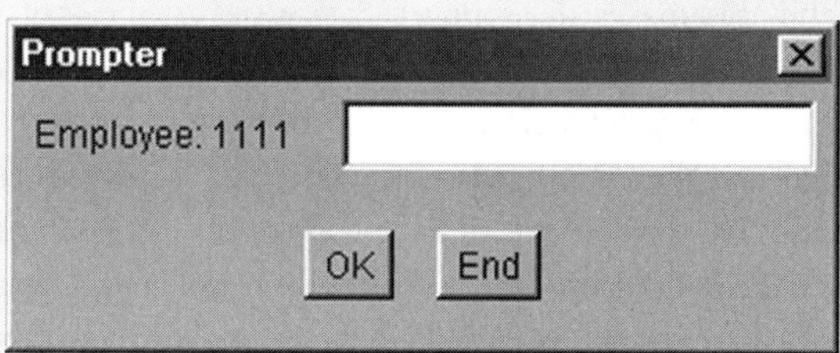

FIGURE 8.6 Prompter in payroll system

The detail line is to contain information remembered in the `runPayroll` method (`hours` and `pay`) as well as from the `Employee` object (employee number and rate of pay). The `Employee` methods `getEmpNum` and `getRate` return, respectively, the employee number and the rate of pay for the employee. The results of the method calls are passed as actual parameters to the `writeDetail` method.

Testing and Debugging

To test the system, a number of different employee records are needed. Since the program is interactive, test scripts are needed to correspond to the data files used. The `Payroll` class is tested by having both an empty and a non-empty employee data file. The `Employee` class is tested by having the test script include employees that worked overtime and those that did not, as well as one on the boundary line. The report output and new data file contents must be predicted to allow validation of the results.

Testing of programs that involve a number of classes can be a major undertaking. The process and special techniques are discussed in Section 9.2.

STYLE TIP

Note the new feature in the class comments for the `Payroll` class beginning `@see`. When a class is a client of another class, other than a library class, a reference to that class should be added as `@see`. The JavaDoc processor will create a link to that class definition in the generated HTML documentation. Since Payroll is a client of Employee, we include `@see Employee`.

8.4 INFORMATION HIDING

A class is COHESIVE if its instance variables represent information logically associated with the entity that the class represents and the methods represent operations the entity would logically perform.

To achieve the reduction of complexity afforded by the use of classes for data abstraction, care is needed in the design of a class. First, a class should be **cohesive**. This means that the instance variables represent information logically associated with the entity that the class represents and that the methods represent operations the entity would logically perform.

Second, a class should use selective disclosure; it should present to other classes in the system only those things that other classes need to know about. The class should not expose its inner workings. If other classes cannot see the inner workings, they cannot make use of them, and this makes the supplier class easier to use. For example, when we used the `Turtle` class, we didn't have to know how the position of the turtle was stored or how a line was actually drawn on the screen. This made the turtle easier to use. Additionally, it afforded the designer of the `Turtle` class a wide choice of representations and even the ability to change the class without affecting the users of the class. Information hiding is the choice to hide the details of the representation of information and the implementation of the methods within a class, selectively exposing only those details necessary for the use of the class.

Accessor and Updater Methods

The first concern in information hiding is visibility of the attributes of the object as represented by the instance variables. Clearly, some of the attributes are of concern to outside classes. For example, the employee number is needed by the `Payroll` class for the detail line in the report. Some of these attributes should be modifiable from outside the class. For instance, giving the employee a raise involves changing the rate of pay. Other attributes should not be changed at all; an employee number is permanent. Still others should change, but only because of an operation performed by the object. Thus, year-to-date gross pay should change only when the employee is paid via a call to `calculatePay`.

`private` versus `public`. The best way to control the access to attributes is to declare all instance variables `private`. That way they are visible only within the class itself; see Section 4.5. You should use methods to permit controlled access. A method such as `getEmpNum` that simply returns the value of an attribute is called an **accessor method**. It allows other objects to access the information without running the risk that they may change it. Accessor methods are declared `public` so other objects may use them. In the `Employee` class, `getEmpNum`, `getRate`, `getYtdGross`, and `getYtdTax` are all accessor methods. Although it is not necessary to make all attributes accessible, in this case it makes sense.

> An **ACCESSOR METHOD** is a method that serves to return the value of an attribute, usually an instance variable, of an object.

STYLE TIP

The Java convention is that accessor methods are named `get` followed by the attribute (instance variable) name such as `getEmpNum`.

Methods that allow other objects to modify the value of an attribute are called **updater** or **mutator methods**. These methods take the new value for the attribute as a parameter and update the instance variable accordingly. Again, updater methods are declared `public`. Only those attributes that should be updatable have updater methods. In this case, only `setRate` is provided to update the `rate` instance variable, to give the employee a raise. This means the other attributes cannot be updated, except by the object itself. In addition to selective updating, updater methods can check that the update is appropriate. This

> An **UPDATER** (or **MUTATOR**) **METHOD** is a method that serves to modify the value of an attribute, usually an instance variable, of an object.

check can prevent inappropriate updates and allows the object to ensure that its state (as represented by its instance variables) is maintained as valid.

STYLE TIP

The Java convention is that updater methods are named `set` followed by the attribute (instance variable) name such as `setRate`.

Of course, a class does not have to expose all of its methods. Methods that are intended to be used only by other methods of the class are declared `private`. These methods are called **local methods**. In Figure 8.5, this includes `computeGross` and `computeTax`, which abstract the gross pay calculation and tax calculation, respectively. They are only intended to be used as helper methods for the `calculatePay` method.

The remaining method in the `Employee` class, `getYtdNetPay`, is a bit different. By its name it appears to be an accessor method; however, there is no `ytdNetPay` instance variable. If we consider an employee, one reasonable attribute might be the year-to-date net pay. Thus it makes sense to have an accessor method for this attribute. However, in terms of representation of this information, it is not necessary to have an additional instance variable, since it can be computed from the `ytdGross` and `ytdTax`. This approach is what has been taken here. To the outside world, it looks like an attribute, but the representation is hidden; it is a calculation, not an instance variable. Note that, should we decide that it would be more efficient to represent this as an instance variable, we could make the change, being sure to change the constructor and `calculatePay` method appropriately. Nothing would change from the point of view of the outside world. The effect of the change would be limited to the `Employee` class. This is one prime advantage of information hiding.

*8.5 DESIGNING FOR REUSE

CODE REUSE is one of the major advantages of object-oriented programming. It involves the use of the same code in a variety of locations in a project or in multiple projects, without the need to duplicate the code.

You will note that there are a number of methods provided in the `Employee` class that are not used in the payroll application. One of the advantages of object-oriented programming is the possibility for code reuse.

Code Reuse

In the development of a system, it is advantageous to reuse code that was developed for a system that was previously written and is likely to be still in use. This code has already been written and tested, both during testing and during continuous use in the existing system. We have already seen reuse in one form, using prewritten classes that are stored in a library.

The unit for code reuse in an object-oriented language is the class. Classes can be placed in a library, or the code can simply be borrowed, although the former is preferable.

When a class is first written, it is a good idea to think ahead and consider how the same class might fit into other systems. For example, the company might need to do weekly payroll now, but it also has to provide income statements to the government for tax purposes. The company might therefore want to keep track of pension and benefit information. In all these systems, there is the presence of an employee, so some `Employee` class would likely be used. It makes good sense to develop the `Employee` class once, for the first system, and then reuse it in subsequent systems. Thus additional methods have been added to the employee class to support systems yet unwritten.

Generalization of I/O Streams

There is another consideration in generalizing a class for reuse. The data for the system might come from a variety of sources or be written to a variety of destinations. When a class is being written, it is not always possible to decide what source or destination will be used. If a class is to be reused, the sources and destinations may differ for different uses. How can we accommodate these situations?

The `BasicIO` library and the standard Java I/O library were written to help address this scenario. As was described in Chapter 5, the input classes all provide the same set of methods as defined by the interface `SimpleDataInput` and the output classes by `SimpleDataOutput`. Although we won't describe interfaces fully in this text, it is important to know that an interface, like a class, defines a type, and an interface name can be used to declare variables. For example, the following declaration is valid:

```
SimpleDataInput in; // input stream for data
```

This declares that `in` is a `SimpleDataInput` stream. Since `SimpleDataInput` is an interface, not a class, it is not possible to create objects of the `SimpleDataInput` type; however, any class that satisfies the `SimpleDataInput` interface specification (called *implementing the interface* in Java), may be used to create an object that may be assigned to `in`. Classes that implement an interface are called **subtypes** of the interface type. For example, `ASCIIPrompter` is a subtype of `SimpleDataInput`. The definition of assignment compatibility (see Section 3.4) indicates that a subtype is assignment-compatible with the supertype. Think of the **supertype** as the set of all possible objects that can do certain things as defined by the interface. The subtype is a subset of these that are particular in some way. For instance, a subtype might use a dialog box for input. If all we are interested in is that we can do the specific things (the supertype), then any of the particular implementations (the subtypes) will suffice.

We can make use of this feature by declaring all streams using the interface types `SimpleDataInput` and `SimpleDataOutput` and then choosing the particular implementation when we create the stream object. For example, we could chose an ASCIIPrompter implementation for the input stream using

```
in = new ASCIIPrompter()
```

When streams are passed as parameters, the formal parameter is declared with the interface type, allowing any of the particular stream objects to be passed. Remember that parameter passing uses the assignment-compatibility rules. This allows a class to be written without specifying the particular stream type, and thus aids code reuse.

If this technique is to be used effectively, the class does require a bit of extra work. The code that uses the stream must handle to the most general stream. For example, if an input stream is used, it is possible that it is a prompted input stream, and prompts should be generated. If the actual input stream is not a prompted stream (for example, if it is a file stream), the prompts are simply ignored in the BasicIO implementation. Therefore, having a nonprompted stream does not present a problem.

As an example, the constructor for the Employee class could be rewritten for generality as shown in Figure 8.7.

```
/** The constructor creates a new employee reading the employee
 ** data from a file.
 **
 ** @param  fromdata stream for employee data.                 */

public Employee ( SimpleDataInput from ) {

    from.setLabel("Employee number");
    empNum = from.readInt();
    if ( from.successful() ) {
        from.setLabel("Pay rate");
        rate = from.readDouble();
        from.setLabel("YTD gross pay");
        ytdGross = from.readDouble();
        from.setLabel("YTD taxes");
        ytdTax = from.readDouble();
    };

};  // constructor
```

FIGURE 8.7 Example—Generalized Employee constructor

Disadvantages of Code Reuse

There is a downside to reusing code. If a class has to be modified for one system, there are two possible approaches: (1) either make a copy of the class, modify the copy, and use the copy in the new system, or (2) change the original class, necessitating, at the very least, recompilation of all existing systems that use the class. The first approach has the problem that there are now really two different classes and maintenance has to be done on both of them. The problem with the second is that a change in the class for use in one system may make it fail to work for the other system. A technique using inheritance addresses these problems. However, the topic of inheritance is beyond the scope of this book.

SUMMARY

Classes are the basic building block of programs in object-oriented languages, including Java. Most real-world programs consist of tens, hundreds, or even thousands of classes, some written for the project, some reused from libraries. A class consists of a set of declarations, including instance variables (fields), constructors, and methods. Instances of a class (objects) are created and interact to produce the effect of the program. Each object has its own instance variables (as long-term memory) and each shares the same method code with other objects of the same class. A method is always executed by some object.

Classes provide a powerful abstraction mechanism: data abstraction by which large, complex systems may be built. Information hiding within classes allows reduction of complexity by allowing the client programmer to concentrate on what an object can do, rather than on what data it stores and how it performs its operations.

A class can control visibility by using the visibility modifiers `public` and `private` for instance variables and methods. To provide the most control, instance variables are declared `private` and accessor or updater methods are made available as desired. An accessor method allows access to the value of an instance variable, and an updater method allows controlled update of the value of an instance variable. Methods are declared `public` if they are intended to be used by a client class or declared `private` if they are intended to be used only by methods within the class (local methods).

REVIEW QUESTIONS

1. T F An object's behavior depends on its state.
2. T F An accessor method is a method of a class whose sole purpose is to return the value of one of the instance variables of the class.

3. T F The constructor should ensure well-defined behavior by putting the object into a well-defined state.
4. T F A constructor must have at least one parameter.
5. T F Accessor and updater methods should be written for every variable.
6. T F A method call always has a target object.
7. T F Information hiding is hiding the representation (instance variables) of a class while exposing its operations (methods).
8. A constructor:
   a) is called when an object is used.
   b) must not have parameters.
   c) puts the object into valid state.
   d) all of the above
9. The reuse of memory previously allocated to an object that is no longer being referenced is called:
   a) storage deallocation.
   b) memory reclamation.
   c) object destruction.
   d) garbage collection.
10. Which of the following is false?
    a) Java provides automatic garbage collection.
    b) Objects become garbage when they are no longer referenced by a variable.
    c) If no garbage collection is performed, then a program may eventually use all of the main memory.
    d) Garbage collection occurs immediately after an object becomes inaccessible.
11. Data abstraction is:
    a) using classes to represent data objects.
    b) using information hiding to hide the details of an object.
    c) using methods in a class to implement the operations on an object.
    d) all of the above.
12. Accessor methods:
    a) are function methods.
    b) return the value of an instance variable.
    c) may return a value computed from instance variables.
    d) are all of the above.
13. A class is cohesive if:
    a) the instance variables are `private`.
    b) the methods are `public`.
    c) the methods represent operations logically associated with the class.
    d) All of the above are true.
14. An updater method:
    a) computes a new value for an instance variable.
    b) may validate the value to be stored in an instance variable.
    c) should be declared `private`.
    d) All of the above are true.

15. A local method:
    a) may only reference parameter values.
    b) is declared `private`.
    c) must not return a value.
    d) Both a and b are true.

EXERCISES

1. Rewrite Exercise 3 from Chapter 5 using two classes, one describing inventory items and one, the main class, to generate the report. The gross value should be computed from the quantity and unit value attributes by the `Inventory` class.

2. Rewrite Exercise 2 from Chapter 6 using two classes, one describing inventory items and one, the main class, to produce the report. The `Inventory` class should provide a method that indicates whether an item needs to be reordered and a method that returns the cost of ordering a particular number of an item as computed from the unit value.

3. The Registrar's Office at Broccoli University keeps track of students' registration in courses. For each registration of a student in a course, a record (line) is entered in an `ASCIIDataFile` recording: student number (`int`), department number (`int`), course number (`int`), and date of registration (`int` as `yymmdd`). Write a Java class called `Registration` that encapsulates this information.

   Periodically, the Registrar's Office must produce class lists for faculty. Write a main class that uses the `Registration` class and the data file to produce a class list for a course. The program should read, from an `ASCIIPrompter`, the department number and course number and then print a report to an `ASCIIReportFile` that displays, under an appropriate header, the student number and date of registration for all students registered in the course. As a report summary, it should print the number of students currently registered in the course.

4. Peach Computers Inc. requires a program to process its payroll. Employees in the company are paid each week and are either hourly employees whose gross pay is determined by the number of hours worked and the pay rate, or they are salaried employees whose pay for the week is a fixed amount. Hourly employees are paid straight-time for the first 40 hours of work in the week and time-and-a-half for overtime (any hours worked in excess of 40). Salaried employees are not paid overtime, and so the number of hours they

have worked is irrelevant. The federal and state governments require that the company withhold tax, each at a particular taxation rate that may be subject to change.

An `ASCIIDataFile` of timesheet information is created each week containing information for each employee that is to be paid. The first two values in the file are the federal taxation rate (`double`) and the state taxation rate (`double`). Following that is information for each employee consisting of (1) employee number (`int`), (2) pay class (`char`, `h` for hourly, and `s` for salaried), (3) pay rate (`double`, the hourly rate for hourly employees and the weekly rate for salaried employees), and (4) hours worked (`double`, irrelevant for salaried employees).

The program is to input the employee information and compute and display the employees' gross pay, federal tax withheld, state tax withheld, and net pay. Since the company must remit the federal and state taxes withheld to the respective governments, the program must also display the total taxes withheld. In addition, so that the auditors can audit the payroll records, the total gross and total net pay paid out must be computed and displayed.

If the timesheet file contained the following information:

```
0.2 0.1

1111       h      25.00  20.0

2222       h      15.00  40.0

3333       h      10.00  50.0

4444       s      600.00 40.0
```

the report generated by the program should look similar to the following:

```
          Peach Computers Inc.


Emp#    Gross     Fed       State     Net

--------------------------------------------

1111    500.00   100.00    50.00    350.00

2222    600.00   120.00    60.00    420.00

3333    550.00   110.00    55.00    385.00

4444    600.00   120.00    60.00    420.00

--------------------------------------------

Total 2250.00   450.00   225.00   1575.00
```

9 Software Development

CHAPTER OBJECTIVES

- To understand the phases of a software development project.
- To recognize the roles of the members of a software development team.
- To be able to identify the classes that make up a system.
- To know how to use CRC cards to perform responsibility-based design.
- To be able to develop class specifications.
- To know how to code a class from its specification.
- To recognize the need for a process for testing a system of multiple classes.

Large software systems can involve hundreds or thousands of classes and are developed and maintained over many years by possibly a hundred people. Systems of this complexity cannot be built unless a careful and well-thought-out development plan exists. Smaller systems developed by a single developer also benefit from such a process, even if it is done informally.

In this chapter we will consider the software development process. Many methodologies for development have been proposed and used and new ones proposed and used for object-oriented development. Here we will consider the common features of these processes and go through a development exercise from start to finish. As you proceed in your career, you will study this process in more detail.

9.1 THE DEVELOPMENT PROCESS

Large-scale software development is a complicated exercise often involving a large staff and many person-years. For software development to succeed, it is imperative that there be some overlying structure or methodology to the process. There are many different software development methodologies in use; however, they all share a number of similar phases that are performed more or less in order. You will see much more of this in your future study of software engineering. The common phases of software development are:

1. analysis
2. design
3. coding
4. testing
5. debugging
6. production
7. maintenance

> In software development, **ANALYSIS** is the process of determining what is actually required of a proposed software system.
>
> A **SOFTWARE SYSTEM** is a set of programs and related files that provides support for some user activity.
>
> A **PROBLEM STATEMENT** is a loose specification of the requirements for a software system, and is usually written by a user (or user group). It serves as the starting point for analysis.
>
> A **REQUIREMENTS SPECIFICATION** is a formal specification of the requirements of a software system and is one of the products of the analysis phase of software development.

Analysis is the process of determining what is actually required of the proposed **software system**. We say system, since, in general, it may consist of a number of programs that work together. Usually, when a system is first proposed, all that is available is a general statement of what is desired; this is sometimes called a **problem statement**. This may have been written by a customer or by someone in a noncomputing division of the organization, and typically is not complete or unambiguous, or necessarily even feasible! Analysis is just that: analysis of what is proposed, to ensure that what is to be done is well-defined and feasible. The result of analysis is a clear specification of what is to be done, often called a **requirements specification**. When the development is being done on contract for another organization, the requirements specification may be part of the legal contract.

Analysis involves interaction between the computer scientist and the expected user group. In a large software development company, there are specialists, usually senior computer scientists called **software** or **systems analysts**, who perform this task. In smaller organizations, the task may be done by people who also write program code; they are often called **programmer/analysts**.

A **SOFTWARE** (or **SYSTEM**) **ANALYST** is a senior computer scientist who performs the analysis phase of software development.

A **PROGRAMMER/ANALYST** is a computer scientist who is involved in analysis, design, and coding.

DESIGN is the phase in software development in which decisions are made about how the software system will be implemented in a programming language.

A **CLASS SPECIFICATION** is a semi-formal specification of a class, as a part of the implementation of a software system, that defines the responsibilities of the class.

An **ARCHITECTURAL PLAN** is the specification of how the classes in the implementation of a system work together to produce the desired result.

A **SYSTEM DESIGNER** is a senior computer scientist who performs the design phase of software development.

A **SENIOR PROGRAMMER** is a more experienced programmer who may be called upon to do design, or to lead a programming team.

CODING is the phase of software development in which the classes defined in the design phase are implemented in a programming language.

A **PROGRAMMER** is a computer scientist whose primary responsibility is to develop code according to specifications laid out in the design phase.

Since programs are information processing systems, one of the tasks of analysis is to determine what data the system needs and what information the system is to produce—the inputs and outputs. It is necessary to determine where the input will come from and what form it is in, as well as where the output will go and its format.

Another task is to develop a model of the system. This can be based on the existing system, or it could be a model of a hypothetical system. Since real-world manual systems involve cooperation between a number of people, the model should reflect this cooperation. Here is an advantage of the object-oriented approach since object-oriented programs involve interacting objects. The model will be a description of a number of entities (objects) that interact in particular ways.

Design is the step in which we come to some decisions about how the system will be implemented in a programming language. Basically, we take the analysis model, refine it, add classes for implementation purposes, and come up with a detailed description of the classes that will make up the software system we are building and the relationships among those classes. The result of the design stage is, for each class of the system, a **class specification** that completely defines the responsibilities of the class and an **architectural plan** that shows how the classes work together.

Again, in a large organization, design will be done by senior staff often called **system designers** or sometimes analyst/designers. They must know programming well, as well as have design experience. Design makes or breaks a project. In smaller organizations, design is performed by **senior programmers** or programmer/analysts.

Analysis and design can be done in a language-independent way, but in the **coding** phase, code for the system is written in a particular programming language. Basically, each of the classes identified in the design phase is coded as a class in a target language such as Java. In a large project, there may be many **programmers** performing this task, each working on a different class. It is important that the class specifications are clear so that each programmer can know what his/her class is responsible for and what s/he can rely on other classes for. In large systems, no single individual can comprehend the details of all parts of the system at one time. Clear specifications allow a programmer to concentrate only on the details of his/her class, without having to understand the details of other classes. Remember, we were able to write a program to draw a square without having to understand the details of how the `Turtle` produces the particular sequence of dots to draw a line and how those are actually placed on the screen.

TESTING is the phase of software development in which the implemented classes are executed, individually and in groups, to determine whether they meet the specifications.

SYSTEM TESTING is the part of testing that involves the complete set of classes that makes up the system. It is the last phase of testing.

A **TESTER** is a computer scientist that caries out testing of system components, usually groups of classes that must work together.

When a class or program doesn't perform according to specification, it is said to contain a bug. **DEBUGGING** is the phase of software development in which it is determined why the class(es) fail and the problem is corrected.

PRODUCTION is the phase of software development in which the developed system has been tested and debugged and is made available to the user community.

A **TRAINER** is a computer scientist whose role is to train users in the use of the developed software system.

TECHNICAL SUPPORT staff provide assistance to users when they are encountering problems with a software system.

Once a class has been written, it is necessary to determine if it, in fact, lives up to its specification. This is called **testing**. Testing involves putting a class (object) through its paces, to see that it works correctly in all cases. Usually, the number of cases is large or even infinite, so it is not possible to do exhaustive testing. Rather, representative sets of tests are used that cover the possible conditions that may occur. Test sets are part of the design specification of a class and should include an indication of the expected results, against which the actual results of the test are compared. Test sets and outputs should be saved for future use in the maintenance phase.

Once individual classes are tested, and found working, it is necessary to determine if they work together—**system testing**. Usually, the programmer is responsible for class-level testing; however, in a large organization, some (or all) of the rest of the testing could be done by **testers**.

Typically, a class or set of classes doesn't work as required right from the start. This means that the class(es) must be **debugged**. Debugging involves determining which class or part of the class is not performing as required and changing the code to correct the problem. The classes are then tested again on their own and in integration with other classes, until all classes and the system itself pass all tests. Sometimes the error is not in the coding of the class but in the design or in the analysis. In these cases, it is necessary to return to these earlier phases and correct the problem. This can be very costly, and this is why analysis and design are very important and are done by the most experienced staff. Note that testing can never *prove* that a system works, it can only provide a high level of confidence that the system works.

Once the system has passed all tests, it can be released to the actual users to use in a **production** environment. At this time, the programming staff is not involved, although **trainers** and **technical support** staff are often necessary to assist the users.

MAINTENANCE is the phase of software development in which bugs detected in the field are corrected and new features are analyzed and implemented.

A **RELEASE** of a software system is a minor upgrade to the system, primarily to fix bugs. It does not usually involve a change in functionality.

A **VERSION** of a software system is a major upgrade of the system, usually to provide new functionality.

DOCUMENTATION is a collection of descriptions and other information about a software system to support training and use by users (user documentation) or to support the maintenance phase (technical documentation).

TECHNICAL DOCUMENTATION includes specifications, architectural plans, implementation notes and other documentation to support the maintenance phase.

USER DOCUMENTATION includes user guides, tutorials, reference manuals, and help systems that support user training and use of a software system.

A **TECHNICAL WRITER** is a computer scientist whose role in software development is to write documentation, primarily user documentation.

Software is seldom static. Since testing cannot prove that the system works, errors are sometimes found during production. As users are using the system, they see additional things that the system could do for them. The environment (operating system, hardware) in which the system is used often changes. Sometimes the task that the system is to perform itself is changed. All of these lead to the next phase: **maintenance** of the system. Basically, maintenance involves returning to earlier phases to fix bugs or enhance the system. Bug fixes usually involve returning to the coding phase and the ultimate **release** of a fixed version of the system. The release number is indicated by a number to the right of the decimal point, such as in PaySys v1.1. Significant enhancements or major modifications usually mean starting again at analysis; and they lead to a new **version** of the software. This is indicated by a new version number to the left of the decimal point, such as in PaySys v2.

There is one more (not insignificant) part of software development—**documentation**. Documentation consists of **technical documentation** and **user documentation**. Technical documentation includes the requirements specification, class specifications, test specifications, and so forth, as produced by the analysts and designers, class-level documentation produced by programmers, and test results documented by testers. This documentation is produced to track the project and to assist subsequent maintenance. User documentation consists of user manuals, guides, tutorials, online help, and other support documentation for user groups. Often this material is prepared by **technical writers**.

CASE STUDY A Grade Report System

As usual, it is easiest to describe the process by going through an example. We will consider a system used to produce a report of final grades for a course based on the marks students have achieved in different assignments, tests, exams, and so on. We will call each of these *pieces of*

A program is needed to compute the final marks in a course. Students in the course are awarded a final mark based on their marks in each of four pieces of work (two assignments, a test, and a final exam), according to a marking scheme. A report is to be generated that gives, for each student, the student number and final mark, as well as the average final mark over all students in the course.

FIGURE 9.1 Problem statement

work. Figure 9.1 is a possible problem statement. Actually, although this statement may be incomplete, it is probably more detailed than many initial problem statements that analysts must deal with!

Analysis

There are basically three parts to the analysis: refining the problem statement, determining inputs and outputs, and developing the model. Our problem statement is almost complete; however, it does not describe what a marking scheme is. The refined problem statement is shown in Figure 9.2.

The inputs to the system must include the actual bases and weights that make up the marking scheme, since these may change from year to year, and, for each student, it must include the student number and marks in each piece of work. If a student didn't complete a piece of work, the mark will be zero. The inputs will have been collected into a file by another program. (For our purposes we will assume an `ASCIIDataFile` since we can prepare it using any text editor. However, in the real-world system, the file would probably be a `BinaryDataFile` created by a special mark-entry program.)

The output consists of the final mark report. It contains, for each student, the student number and final grade, as well as the course average. Since the report may consist of several pages, it should be properly paginated and have the appropriate title and headings on each page. The format of the report is shown in Figure 9.3

A program is needed to compute the final marks in a course. Students in the course are awarded a final mark based on their marks in each of four pieces of work (two assignments, a test, and a final exam), according to a marking scheme. *The marking scheme defines, for each piece of work, its base mark and weight towards the final mark.* A report is to be generated that gives, for each student, the student number and final mark, as well as the average final mark over all students in the course.

FIGURE 9.2 Refined problem statement

```
Final Mark Report    page:  1

          COSC 1P02

         ST #   Mark
      -----------------

        1,111  100.0
        2,222   50.0
        3,333    0.0
        4,444   74.7

      -----------------

         Ave:   56.1
```

FIGURE 9.3 Grade report format

Determining the candidate objects. To construct the model, it is necessary to determine what entities (objects) are present in the system. The easiest way to start this process is to underline all the nouns or noun phrases in the refined problem statement (Figure 9.4). These nouns represent candidate objects (Figure 9.5). The next step is to examine each candidate to determine if it represents an actual entity. A candidate may be eliminated if it simply represents a value, if it is just another name for an entity, or if it is not part of the actual system being developed.

Identified objects. We can eliminate final mark, mark, base mark, weight, student number, and average final mark since they are simply values. Program is not part of the system (what we are writing is the program). Assignment, test, and final exam are the pieces of work, so they can be eliminated. Finally, a piece of work will be represented within the system as sim-

> A program is needed to compute the final marks in a course. Students in the course are awarded a final mark based on their marks in each of four pieces of work (two assignments, a test and a final exam), according to a marking scheme. The marking scheme defines, for each piece of work, its base mark and weight towards the final mark. A report is to be generated giving, for each student, the student number and final mark, as well as the average final mark over all students in the course.

FIGURE 9.4 Selecting candidate objects

program	final mark	course	student
mark	piece of work	assignment	test
final exam	marking scheme	base mark	weight
report	student number	average final mark	

FIGURE 9.5 Candidate objects

course	student	marking scheme	report

FIGURE 9.6 Identified objects

ply the mark for that piece of work, so it too can be eliminated. This leaves the objects listed in Figure 9.6.

Analysis model. There are a variety of notations for describing the model. We will use a simplified version here. Essentially, what is desired is to show the relationships between the objects. In the diagram (Figure 9.7), the boxes identify the objects and the lines indicate relationships. The labels on the lines describe the relationships. The ranges on a line indicate the number of entities at that end that are associated with each entity at the other end. For example, there are zero or more students in each course. Where no ranges are given, it is a one-to-one association.

Since this is not a software engineering course, we won't write a formal requirements specification. However, this document would include the specification of inputs and outputs and the analysis model, as well as a detailed version of the problem statement indicating all the relevant formulas for computing such values as the final marks.

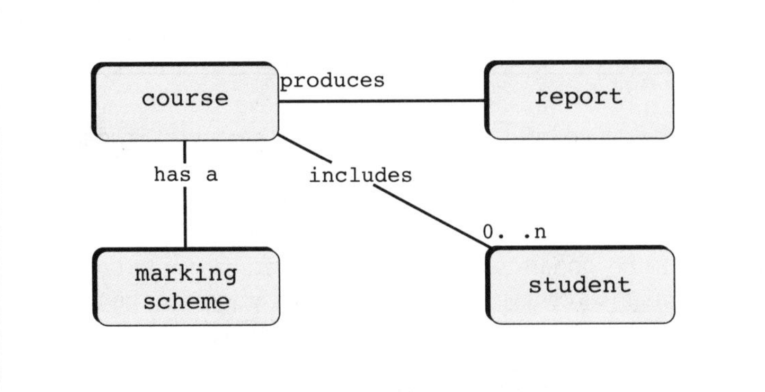

FIGURE 9.7 Analysis model

Design

Since this system is quite simple, we won't need to add much in the way of implementation objects. Clearly, we will have a few additional classes (`ASCIIDataFile` for input and `ASCIIReportFile` for output), but to keep things simple we won't add these to our diagram. There is also the issue of a main class, but we will address this later.

CRC cards. What we are interested in is a detailed description of each class. This description must include the responsibilities of the class and how the classes cooperate. By responsibilities we mean a statement of what information and what operations it takes care of. One technique is to use **CRC** (Class Responsibilities Collaborators) **cards**, a simple design methodology described by Beck and Cunningham[1] and refined by Wirfs-Brock and Wilkerson.[2] In this methodology, a standard index card is used to describe each class. The card is divided into three areas: class, responsibilities, and collaborators, as shown in Figure 9.8. In the class area of the card you fill in the class name, in the responsibilities area you fill in the things that the class is responsible for, and finally, in the collaborators area you fill in the other classes with which the class collaborates.

> A **CRC** (Class Responsibilities Collaborators) **CARD** is a device used during design to help flesh out the classes discovered during analysis by assigning responsibilities to each class. Each class is represented by an index card and the responsibilities of the class and the classes with which it collaborates in fulfilling its responsibilities are recorded.

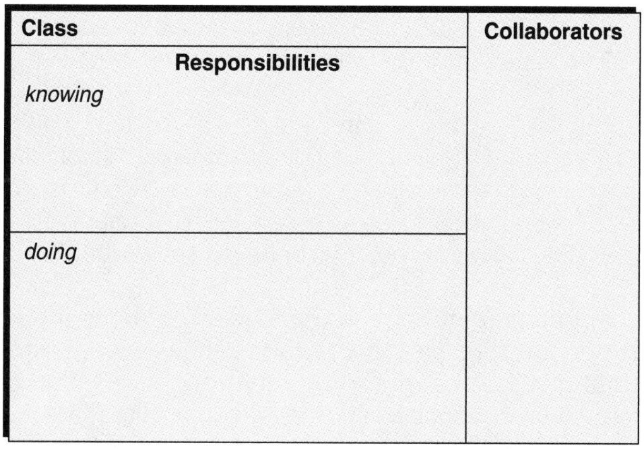

Class	**Collaborators**
Responsibilities	
knowing	
doing	

FIGURE 9.8 CRC card

[1] Beck, K. & Cunningham, W. "A Laboratory for Teaching Object-Oriented Thinking," Proc. OOPSLA '89 (New Orleans, LA Oct. 1989). SIGPLAN Notices v24, n10 (Oct. 1989) pp. 1–6; ACM Press (1989).

[2] Wirfs-Brock, R. & Wilkerson, B. "Object-Oriented Design: A Responsibility Approach," Proc. OOPSLA '89 (New Orleans, LA Oct. 1989). SIGPLAN Notices v24, n10 (Oct. 1989), pp. 71–76; ACM Press (1989).

final mark	assignment (mark)	test (mark)	final exam (mark)
base mark	weight	student number	average final mark

FIGURE 9.9 Field values

We start with four cards, one for each of `Course`, `Student`, `MarkingScheme`, and `Report`, and we fill those names in the class entry of each card. The next step is to decide which class has responsibility for knowing what information. First, we have to consider the information we might have to store. The list of nouns from the problem statement (Figure 9.5) is a good place to start. Those that were rejected as being values probably represent information we need to store. Eliminating the classes already selected, the duplicates, and items not really part of the model, we get the fields shown in Figure 9.9. We may discover others as we continue with design; however, this is a start.

Responsibility for knowing. Now we want to allocate these values to the classes. When we decide, we write the field on the CRC card under the ***knowing*** heading. We might want to do this in pencil in case we change our mind. This process is a bit of an art; however, we can often consider the situation in the real world and ask who would know the piece of information. We can also develop an argument as to why a particular class should know the information. Normally, we do not wish to duplicate values in different classes since this uses extra storage and we have an update problem—we must update the value in every place it is stored when the value changes.

Let's try this distribution. The two assignment marks, the test mark, and the final exam mark are products of a particular student's work in the course. Although in the real world we would probably record these somewhere, they logically belong to the student. Thus it makes sense for the `Student` class to take responsibility. Remember, we are in control of the model and of defining how the objects behave, so we don't have to worry about cheating.

Similarly, the student number belongs to the student, as does the final mark. The base marks and weights for the four pieces of work define—along with the algorithm for computing the final mark—the marking scheme, so it makes sense for the `MarkingScheme` class to take responsibility for these. Finally, the average final mark is a property of the course—the result of students taking the course—so the `Course` class should take responsibility. That takes care of the fields we know about so far.

Responsibility for doing. Now let's look at distributing the tasks among the classes. Again, the problem statement is a starting point. We select the verb phrases and examine each to see if it is part of the model and represents a task we must achieve. The tasks discovered are shown in Figure 9.10. The last one (compute average mark) was implicit in the statement, since the value had to be reported.

compute the final mark	report is to be generated	compute average mark

FIGURE 9.10 Identified tasks

In general, it is best for the object that knows the required information to perform a task involving that information, so we can often use the responsibilities for knowing as a guide. Unfortunately, this isn't that much help here. Computing the final mark for a student requires information from both `Student` and `MarkingScheme`. Clearly, they will have to collaborate. However, it seems clear that the algorithm for computing the mark is part of the marking scheme. (What if the instructor decided to take the better of the two assignments? This would be a change in the marking scheme, not the student.) Thus the `MarkingScheme` should do the actual computation with information from the `Student`. Similarly, the generation of the report will be a collaboration between the `Course`, which knows about the students (see the analysis model, Figure 9.7) and the `Report`, which will take responsibility for the report layout. Computing the average requires a total of the students' marks and a count of the number of students. `Student` cannot do this since it represents only one student, so it is most reasonable for `Course` to do it in collaboration with `Student`.

We should finally address the issue of the main class, which is the class in which computation will start. Since the project is to generate a report of marks for a course, we could think of either `Course` or `Report` as the starting point. However, if we consider the bigger picture, courses are involved in a number of systems within the University, and there is the possibility that we might like to generate a number of different reports about a course. Making either of these two classes the main class would make it harder to reuse the same class in another system without considerable rewriting. Instead, we will add one more class (call it `GradeReport`), which will serve as the main class and simply get the process going. It is fairly typical of object-oriented programs, especially those using a graphical user interface, that the main class is very simple, serving to simply get things started.

Collaboration among classes. In each case of collaboration, we still have the issue of which class will drive the process and which will simply provide services or data. In the case of generating the report, `Course` will drive the process, using appropriate services of `Report` as needed and supplying required information. A report consists of header information, detail lines, and summary information. The header information must be produced at the top of each page and so must be completely under the control of `Report`. The decision to produce a detail line must lie with `Course` since it alone knows about the students; however, `Report` must be in control of formatting and pagination. Thus `Report` will provide a method to write a detail line based on student information supplied by `Course`. Since `Course` computes the average that must be formatted for the report, `Report` provides a method to generate the summary based on the average supplied by `Course`.

Since `Student` must record the final mark, which is the result of the final mark calculation, it seems reasonable that `Student` must drive the final mark calculation process.

`MarkingScheme` will provide a method to apply the marking scheme to mark information supplied by `Student`. `Student` will be requested to perform the calculation when `Course` needs the final mark before generating the detail line of the report.

In the ***Collaborators*** section we list the classes with which the controlling class collaborates, not the inverse. The completed CRC cards for the four classes are found in Figure 9.11.

Architectural plan. The architectural plan is the overall approach that the program will take to solving the problem. In our case we will use a **sequential file processing architecture**, in which we input one record of student information at a time, producing a detail line to the report. This architecture will govern our implementation of the classes.

> In the **SEQUENTIAL FILE PROCESSING ARCHITECTURE**, each entity for which processing is to be performed is represented by a record on a sequential file. The records are read and processed, one at a time, to produce the result.
>
> **DETAILED DESIGN** is the second subphase of design in which detailed class specifications are produced. A detailed class specification includes all public variables and methods with their types and parameters.

Class specifications. The class specifications can now be drawn from the CRC diagrams. This is often called **detailed design**. The responsibilities for knowing become instance variables and the responsibilities for doing become methods. The detailed design involves determining the types for each instance variable and the result types and parameters for each method.

There are a variety of notations for class specifications. Here we will use a simplified form of a Java class declaration since we will be writing in Java anyway. An alternative is to use Java interfaces or a language-independent notation. These are beyond the scope of this text.

When doing class specifications, we need to specify all the instance variables, constructors, and methods that other classes may wish to use. Private variables and local methods need not be specified; they can be left up to the programmer. As described in Section 8.4, it is not a good idea to make instance variables public, so instead we will provide accessor and updater methods as appropriate. We should also spend some time considering possible uses of the class in future systems and perhaps add features now to make it easier to reuse the class later, as described in Section 8.5. (We will not do this here to keep the example simple and emphasize the development process.) Finally, the specification should include comments describing the class and each method, as we have done so far in our code. These comments help define what the classes and methods do for both the user of the class and the programmer writing the class, and so are very important.

`Course` class specification. For the class `Course`, we get the specification in Figure 9.12. Note that we have written it in a syntax similar to a Java class except that we have omitted the method bodies. This is *not* Java code, just a notation. However, it would be easy for the programmer to take the specification and edit it, adding the instance variables, method bodies, and so forth.

The constructor takes an `ASCIIDataFile` parameter to allow course information to be read from a file. The number of students and the average final mark are not made available via accessor methods. The method `doReport` is the method that does the bulk of the work for this

Class Course	**Collaborators**
Responsibilities	
knowing	Report
number of students	Student
average final mark	MarkScheme
doing	
generate report	

Class Student	**Collaborators**
Responsibilities	
knowing	MarkScheme
student number	
marks in pieces of work	
final mark	
doing	
calculate final mark	

Class MarkingScheme	**Collaborators**
Responsibilities	
knowing	
base marks for work	
weights for work	
doing	
calculate final mark	

Class Report	**Collaborators**
Responsibilities	
knowing	Student
doing	
write detail line	
write summary	

FIGURE 9.11 Grade report class design

system. It takes a `Report` object as a parameter to use to produce the report. This gives us the flexibility to eventually use different `Report` objects at different times to do special reports. The `doReport` method returns the number of students in the course to allow feedback to the user.

```
/** This class represents a course offering with the
 ** associated students. A course has a marking scheme and
 ** a mark report can be generated.
 **
 ** @see    Student
 ** @see    MarkingScheme
 ** @see    Report                                                    */

public class Course {

    /** The constructor reads the course information from the
     ** specified file and creates the marking scheme.
     **
     ** @param  from    file from which to read course data.            */

    public Course ( ASCIIDataFile from ) ;

    /** This method produces a mark report using the specified
     ** report generator.
     **
     ** @param  theReport   report generator for the report
     **
     ** @return int number of students processed.                       */

    public int doReport ( Report theReport ) ;

}   // Course
```

FIGURE 9.12 Example—`Course` class specification

Student class specification. The class specification for `Student` is found in Figure 9.13. The constructor allows student information to be input from a file. Only an accessor method is provided for the student number because the student number shouldn't change once the student object has been created. Accessor methods have been provided for the piece-of-work fields since they may need to be accessed by a more detailed mark report. If we were generalizing for reuse, we might decide to provide updater methods to support, say, a mark entry system that might use this class. Calculation of the final mark is provided by the method `calcFinalMark`, which is provided with the `MarkingScheme` to be used. This allows the collaboration. To allow access to the final mark, an accessor method is provided. Since the final mark is only available after it has been calculated by `calcFinalMark`, the `getFinalMark` method returns a recognizable value (`-1`) to signal that the final mark has not yet been calculated. This may happen, for example, in the middle of a term.

```
/** This class represents a student in a course. A
 ** student has a student number, marks in a number of
 ** pieces of work (2 assignments, a test, and an exam)
 ** from which a final mark can be computed according
 ** to a marking scheme.
 **
 ** @see    MarkingScheme                                      */

public class Student {

    /** This constructor creates a new student reading the
     ** student number and marks from a specified file.
     **
     ** @param from the file to read from                      */

    public Student ( ASCIIDataFile from ) ;

    /** This method returns the student number of the
     ** student.
     **
     ** @return int the student number                         */

    public int getStNum ( ) ;

    /** This method returns the student's mark in
     ** assignment 1.
     **
     ** @return double  the student's assignment 1 mark        */

    public double getAssign1 ( ) ;

    /** This method returns the student's mark in
     ** assignment 2.
     **
     ** @return double  the student's assignment 2 mark        */

    public double getAssign2 ( ) ;
```

(Continued)

```
    /** This method returns the student's mark in the
     ** test.
     **
     ** @return double  the student's test mark                              */

    public double getTest ( ) ;

    /** This method returns the student's mark in the
     ** exam.
     **
     ** @return double  the student's exam mark                              */

    public double getExam ( ) ;

    /** This method returns the final mark for the
     ** student. If the final mark has not yet been
     ** calculated, it returns -1.
     **
     ** @return double  the student's final mark                             */

    public double getFinalMark ( ) ;

    /** This method calculates the final mark for the
     ** student by applying the supplied marking scheme
     ** to the pieces of work.
     **
     ** @param  ms  the marking scheme                                       */

    public void calcFinalMark( MarkingScheme ms ) ;

}   // Student
```

FIGURE 9.13 Example—`Student` class specification

`MarkingScheme` class specification. The specification for `MarkingScheme` is found in Figure 9.14. The constructor reads the marking scheme information from a file. The method `apply` is used to apply a marking scheme to a particular student's work. The `Student` provides (via parameters) the marks received in each piece of work, and the method returns the final mark as computed according to the scheme.

```
/** This class represents the marking scheme for a
 ** course with 2 assignments, a test, and a final exam.
 ** Each piece of work has a base mark and a weight.                      */

public class MarkingScheme {

    /** This constructor creates the marking scheme reading
     ** the bases and weights from a specified file.
     **
     ** @param from the file to read from                                 */

    public MarkingScheme ( ASCIIDataFile from ) ;

    /** This method applies the marking scheme to marks for
     ** the pieces of work, producing a final mark. The final
     ** mark is the sum of the scaled, weighted marks for
     ** the pieces of work.
     **
     ** @param a1    assignment 1 mark
     ** @param a2    assignment 2 mark
     ** @param test  test mark
     ** @param exam  exam mark
     **
     ** @return double  the final mark                                    */

    public double apply ( double a1, double a2, double test, double exam ) ;

}   // MarkingScheme
```

FIGURE 9.14 Example—`MarkingScheme` class specification

`Report` class specification. Finally, the class specification for `Report` is shown in Figure 9.15. The constructor is passed the report file to which the report is to be written, and the page size of the printer (in number of lines) is also passed, so the `Report` can do pagination. The method `writeDetailLine` writes the details about the `Student` that is passed as the parameter. It can use the accessor methods of `Student` to get the information it needs. `writeSummary` closes off the report, writing the average student mark provided as the parameter. Note that there is no method to write the header lines. This has to be handled completely by `Report` since it could happen at any time during the writing of a detail line. Of course, the first header lines have to be written at the start by the constructor.

```
/** This class represents the final mark report for a
 ** course. The report consists of a header followed by
 ** a number of student information lines followed by
 ** summary statistics. The report is targeted to a
 ** specific output stream.
 **
 ** @see Student                                              */

public class Report {

    /** This constructor initializes the report, setting the
     ** output stream, initializing the counts, and writing
     ** the header.
     **
     ** @param  to  stream to write to                        */

    public Report ( ASCIIReportFile to, int ps ) ;

    /** This method writes a report line for the student
     ** including the student number and the final mark to
     ** the report.
     **
     ** @param  std the student.                              */

    public void writeDetailLine ( Student std ) ;

    /** This method ends the report by displaying the summary
     ** statistics, i.e., the average mark in the course.     */

    public void writeSummary ( double ave ) ;

}   // Report
```

FIGURE 9.15 Example—`Report` class specification

> A **CLIENT CLASS** is a class that makes use of services provided by another class and thus depends on the supplier class's specification.

Between the class design, architectural plan, and class specifications we now have enough information to allow the classes to be written. One programmer can write a specific class, such as `Student`. At the same time, another programmer may write a **client class** that uses the `Student` class. This second class can be written since the class specification for `Student` details all that must be provided and all that can be expected from the `Student` class.

Coding

In the coding phase, one or more programmers goes about writing the actual Java classes defined in the detailed design. Other implementation classes might also be designed and written in support of these. Basically, the programmer has a contract to fulfill—the class specification—but is free to implement it in any reasonable manner. The programmer must think of this class as the ultimate goal and not be concerned about the system as a whole. The advantage of object-oriented programming is that components can be developed separately and assembled later. The system as a whole is generally far too large to be comprehended at any single instant, and a programmer would easily get lost in the details.

The `MarkingScheme` class. The class `MarkingScheme` is the easiest, so let's do it first. Remember, the order of development is really irrelevant since development would probably be done in parallel by a number of programmers. According to the model (Figure 9.7), class design (Figure 9.11), and class specification (Figure 9.14), there will be one marking scheme for a course. It remembers the bases and weights for the pieces of work and performs the final mark calculation, given the actual marks. The code is found in Figure 9.16.

```
import BasicIO.*;

/** This class represents the marking scheme for a
 ** course with 2 assignments, a test, and a final exam.
 ** Each piece of work has a base mark and a weight.
 **
 ** @author D. Hughes
 **
 ** @version1.0 (Jan. 2001)                                          */

public class MarkingScheme {

    private double  a1Base, a1Weight;      // base & weight for assignment 1
    private double  a2Base, a2Weight;      // base & weight for assignment 2
    private double  testBase, testWeight;  // base & weight for test
    private double  examBase, examWeight;  // base & weight for exam
```

(Continued)

```
    /** This constructor creates the marking scheme reading
     ** the bases and weights from a specified file.
     **
     ** @param  fromthe file to read from                              */

    public MarkingScheme ( ASCIIDataFile from ) {

        a1Base = from.readDouble();
        a1Weight = from.readDouble();
        a2Base = from.readDouble();
        a2Weight = from.readDouble();
        testBase = from.readDouble();
        testWeight = from.readDouble();
        examBase = from.readDouble();
        examWeight = from.readDouble();

    };  // constructor

    /** This method applies the marking scheme to marks for
     ** the pieces of work, producing a final mark. The final
     ** mark is the sum of the scaled, weighted marks for
     ** the pieces of work.
     **
     ** @param  a1    assignment 1 mark
     ** @param  a2    assignment 2 mark
     ** @param  test  test mark
     ** @param  exam  exam mark
     **
     ** @return double  the final mark                                 */

    public double apply ( double a1, double a2, double test, double exam ) {

        return a1 / a1Base * a1Weight +
               a2 / a2Base * a2Weight +
               test / testBase * testWeight +
               exam / examBase * examWeight;

    };  // apply

}  // MarkingScheme
```

FIGURE 9.16 Example—MarkingScheme class

The bases and weights are instance variables since they exist from the creation of the marking scheme throughout processing of all students. The constructor inputs the bases and weights from the supplied file.

The method `apply` must compute the final mark, given the marks for the pieces of work that are passed as parameters and the bases and weights that are remembered by the `MarkingScheme` itself. The final mark is just the weighted sum of the marks on the pieces of work. We divide the actual mark by the base mark and multiply by the weight. We assume that the weights add to 100%. This computation was determined during the analysis phase.

The `Student` class. Figure 9.17 shows the `Student` class. The class remembers all information concerning a *single* student. During execution there will be multiple instances (objects) of the class, one for each student (see Figure 9.7). Thus the instance variables represent the information about one student. The constructor inputs the `Student` information from the input file. It then sets the final mark to `-1` because the final mark has not yet been computed.

```
import BasicIO.*;

/** This class represents a student in a course. A
 ** student has a student number, marks in a number of
 ** pieces of work (2 assignments, a test, and an exam)
 ** from which a final mark can be computed according
 ** to a marking scheme.
 **
 ** @see    MarkingScheme
 **
 ** @author D. Hughes
 **
 ** @version    1.0 (Jan. 2001)                                */

public class Student {

    private int     stNum;                  // student number
    private double  a1, a2, test, exam; // marks
    private double  finalMark;              // final mark

    /** This constructor creates a new student reading the
     ** student number and marks from a specified file.
     **
     ** @param  from   the file to read from                   */
```

(Continued)

```
    public Student ( ASCIIDataFile from ) {

        stNum = from.readInt();
        if ( from.successful() ) {
            a1 = from.readDouble();
            a2 = from.readDouble();
            test = from.readDouble();
            exam = from.readDouble();
            finalMark = -1;
        };

    };  // constructor

    /** This method returns the student number of the
     ** student.
     **
     ** @return int the student number                                    */

    public int getStNum ( ) {

        return stNum;

    };  // getStNum

    /** This method returns the student's mark in
     ** assignment 1.
     **
     ** @return double  the student's assignment 1 mark                   */

    public double getAssign1 ( ) {

        return a1;

    };  // getAssign1

    /** This method returns the student's mark in
     ** assignment 2.
     **
     ** @return double  the student's assignment 2 mark                   */

    public double getAssign2 ( ) {

        return a2;
```

(Continued)

```
};  // getAssign2

/** This method returns the student's mark in the
 ** test.
 **
 ** @return double  the student's test mark                              */

public double getTest ( ) {

    return test;

};  // getTest

/** This method returns the student's mark in the
 ** exam.
 **
 ** @return double  the student's exam mark                              */

public double getExam ( ) {

    return exam;

};  // getExam

/** This method returns the final mark for the
 ** student. If the final mark has not yet been
 ** calculated it returns -1.
 **
 ** @return double  the student's final mark                             */

public double getFinalMark ( ) {

    return finalMark;

};  // getFinalmark


/** This method calculates the final mark for the
 ** student by applying the supplied marking scheme
 ** to the pieces of work.
 **
 ** @param  ms  the marking scheme                                       */
```

(Continued)

```
    public void calcFinalMark ( MarkingScheme ms ) {

        finalMark = ms.apply(a1,a2,test,exam);

    };  // calcFinalMark

}   // Student
```

FIGURE 9.17 Example—`Student` class

The accessor methods are written as required. They simply return the instance variable value. This task is so common and tedious that some other languages provide these methods automatically. Note the comment on `getFinalMark`. Since the final mark is calculated only on demand by a call to `calcFinalMark`, the method returns `-1` unless there has been a prior call to `calcFinalMark`. This is ensured by the constructor setting `finalMark` to `-1`. The `calcFinalMark` method takes the `MarkingScheme` as a parameter and simply calls its `apply` method, passing the actual marks and saving the result in the `finalMark` variable.

The `Course` class. The `Course` class is found in Figure 9.18. As indicated in the model (Figure 9.7), the `Course` class acts to hold things together. Each course has a `MarkingScheme` and a number of `Students`. When a report is being generated by a call to `doReport`, a `Report` is used by the `Course`. The architectural plan calls for sequential processing of the students. This means that each student will be read, processed, and the report line written, before the next student is read. Thus, the `Course` object will deal with only one `Student` object at any time.

```
import BasicIO.*;

/** This class represents a course offering with the
 ** associated students. A course has a marking scheme and
 ** a mark report can be generated.
 **
 ** @see     Student
 ** @see     MarkingScheme
 ** @see     Report
 **
 ** @author D. Hughes
 **
 ** @version    1.0 (Jan. 2001)                                  */

public class Course {
```

(Continued)

```
    private ASCIIDataFile   courseData; // file for course data
    private MarkingScheme   scheme;     // marking scheme for course

    /** The constructor reads the course information from the
      ** specified file and creates the marking scheme.
      **
      ** @param  from   file from which to read course data.          */

    public Course ( ASCIIDataFile from ) {

        courseData = from;
        scheme = new MarkingScheme(courseData);

    };  // constructor

    /** This method produces a mark report using the specified
      ** report generator.
      **
      ** @param  theReport   report generator for the report
      **
      ** @return int number of students processed.                      */

    public int doReport ( Report theReport ) {

        Student aStudent;    // one student
        double  totMark;     // total of students' marks
        int     numStd;      // number of students in course

        numStd = 0;
        totMark = 0;
        while ( true ) {
            aStudent = new Student(courseData);
        if ( ! courseData.successful() ) break;
            numStd = numStd + 1;
            aStudent.calcFinalMark(scheme);
            totMark = totMark + aStudent.getFinalMark();
            theReport.writeDetailLine(aStudent);
        };
        theReport.writeSummary(totMark/numStd);
        return numStd;

    };  // doReport

}  // Course
```

FIGURE 9.18 Example—Course class

The Course has an instance variable to remember the MarkingScheme since this exists for the entire processing. That is, it is *the* marking scheme for the course. Course doesn't have an instance variable for a Student since different students will be processed at different times. If we were using a different architectural model such as random processing (see Chapter 11), we might have the Course remember all the students by using a special kind of instance variable called an array. Since Course will have to read the marking scheme and the student information from the same input stream, but at different times, it remembers the stream in another instance variable (courseData).

The constructor remembers the file and then uses the MarkingScheme constructor to read and create the marking scheme for the course.

The method doReport does the actual processing we set out to accomplish. It is passed a Report, which will take responsibility for report formatting. The method body is basically an instance of the process-to-EOF pattern (Figure 6.11), using the Student constructor to do the input. Having successfully read the information about one Student, it asks the Student to compute the final mark using the MarkingScheme for the course. It then requests the Report to generate the detail line about the Student. When the loop is complete, it generates the report summary by the call to the writeSummary method of the Report. The author of the Course class doesn't have to worry about how the report is formatted or how a final mark is calculated. These details are left to the appropriate objects.

To be able to generate the class average, the Course must count the number of students and total the students' final marks. This is done in the usual manner. The method returns this count as a check that the processing has been done correctly. The client object can use this value to inform the user in happiness messages or as a check against other information.

The Report class. The code for the last of the designed classes, the Report class, is found in Figure 9.19. The class is responsible for handling the layout and pagination for the report. Each time the writeDetailLine method is called, Report must write to the same stream, so it makes sense to save this in an instance variable (report) for the entire report. To handle pagination, we need to know the number of lines per page (hence pageSize), the current line number (lineNum), and the current page number (pageNum). These will be modified as we write lines to the page.

```
import BasicIO.*;

/** This class represents the final mark report for a
 ** course. The report consists of a header, followed by
 ** a number of student information lines, followed by
 ** summary statistics. The report is targeted to a
 ** specific output stream.
 **
 ** @see Student
 **
```

(Continued)

```
 ** @author D. Hughes
 **
 ** @version    1.0 (Jan. 2001)                                    */

public class Report {

    private ASCIIReportFile report;     // printer file for report
    private int             pageNum;    // current page number
    private int             lineNum;    // current line number
    private int             pageSize;   // page size (in lines)

    /** This constructor initializes the report, setting the
      ** output stream, initializing the counts, and writing
      ** the header.
      **
      ** @param  to  stream to write to                                */

    public Report ( ASCIIReportFile to, int ps ) {

        report = to;
        pageSize = ps;
        pageNum = 0;
        lineNum = 1;
        writeHeader();

    }; // constructor

    /** This method writes a report line for the student,
      ** including the student number and the final mark to
      ** the report.
      **
      ** @param  std the student.                                      */

    public void writeDetailLine ( Student std ) {

        if ( lineNum >= pageSize-2 ) {
            writeFooter();
            writeHeader();
        };
        report.writeInt(std.getStNum(),13);
        report.writeDouble(std.getFinalMark(),6,1);
        report.writeEOL();
        lineNum = lineNum + 1;
```

(Continued)

```
    };  // writeDetailLine

    /** This method ends the report by displaying the summary
      ** statistics, i.e., the average mark in the course.              */

    public void writeSummary ( double ave ) {

        if ( lineNum >= pageSize-3 ) {
            writeFooter();
            writeHeader();
        };
        report.writeEOL();
        report.writeLabel("       -----------------");
        report.writeEOL();
        report.writeEOL();
        report.writeLabel("           Ave: ");
        report.writeDouble(ave,6,1);
        report.writeEOL();

    };  // writeSummary

    /** This method writes the page header.                             */

    private void writeHeader ( ) {

        pageNum = pageNum + 1;
        report.writeLabel("Final Mark Report    page: ");
        report.writeInt(pageNum,2);
        report.writeEOL();
        report.writeEOL();
        report.writeLabel("            COSC 1P02");
        report.writeEOL();
        report.writeEOL();
        report.writeLabel("          ST #   Mark");
        report.writeEOL();
        report.writeLabel("       -----------------");
        report.writeEOL();
        report.writeEOL();
        lineNum = 7;

    };  // writeHeader

    /** This method writes the page footer.                             */
```

(Continued)

```
    private void writeFooter ( ) {

        while ( lineNum < pageSize ) {
            report.writeEOL();
            lineNum = lineNum + 1;
        };

    };  // writeFooter

}   // Report
```

FIGURE 9.19 Example—`Report` class

The constructor remembers the stream to which the report is to be written and the size of the page. It then sets the current page number to zero because we haven't yet started the first page. It sets the line number to `1` for the first line of the page. Finally, it calls the method `writeHeader`, which writes out a header for a new page. As we discussed previously, `Report` must be in control of writing the headers since they might come at any detail line. Thus the client class, `Course`, cannot make the call to write the first header. To ensure that the header is written before any calls to `writeDetailLine`, we must do this in the constructor.

The method `writeDetailLine` writes out one detail line about the specified `Student`. It first checks to see if there is enough room left on the page for this line and two blank lines at the bottom of the page. If not, it calls `writeFooter` to write a page footer and `writeHeader` to write the page header for the next page. It then writes the detail line, using the accessor methods from `Student` to access the specific information required. Note how easily the content of the report could be changed. This method could be made to access other fields of `Student` to print a more detailed report, without any changes to the `Course` or `Student` classes.

The `writeSummary` method generates the report summary given the class average. It first checks to see if there is enough room on the page for four lines and, if not, writes out a footer and a header for the next page. It then writes out the summary lines.

The report generation programming pattern (Figure 5.15) is hidden in this code. If we look at the pattern, the `Report` constructor (using `writeHeader`) handles the generation of the report title and header lines at the beginning of the report. The loop over all lines in the report actually occurs in the `doReport` method of the `Course` class, where it also serves as the process-to-EOF pattern. The call by `doReport` to `writeDetailLine` accomplishes the loop body, and the call to `writeSummary` accomplishes the report summary.

The methods `writeHeader` and `writeFooter` are written as `private` methods. This means that they cannot be called by any client class such as `Course`, but only by other methods of the `Report` class itself. If other classes were to call these methods, it would disturb the pattern of the report processing, so this must be prevented. `writeHeader` increments the page number, writes the header lines, and then sets the line number to `7` since it wrote six lines at the top of the new page. The method `writeFooter` writes out enough blank lines to get to the bottom of the page, incrementing the line number appropriately.

The main class. The only thing left to do is to code the main class that we will call `GradeReport` (Figure 9.20). Typically, in object-oriented programming, the main class simply creates the permanent objects of the model (Figure 9.7) and the I/O objects, and then sets them to work, cleaning up when things are done. This is what our `GradeReport` class does. It creates the I/O objects as usual—one for the course data, one for the report and one for happiness messages. It then creates the `Course` object and the `Report` object. The `Course` object creates its own `MarkingScheme` object. After writing out some happiness messages, it gets things started by calling the `doReport` method of the `Course` object, passing the `Report` object. Finally, `GradeReport` displays a happiness message indicating the number of students processed, and then closes the files. The other objects do everything else.

```
import BasicIO.*;

/** This class is an implementation of a grade reporting
 ** program for a university course.
 **
 ** @see    Student
 ** @see    MarkingScheme
 ** @see    Report
 **
 ** @author D. Hughes
 **
 ** @version    1.0 (Jan. 2001)                                    */

public class GradeReport {

    private ASCIIDataFile   courseData; // file for course data
    private ASCIIReportFile reportFile; // printer file for report
    private ASCIIDisplayer  msg;        // displayer for messages

    /** The constructor opens the course data file and report
     **  file, creates the course and report, and generates the
     **  report.                                                    */

    public GradeReport ( ) {

        courseData = new ASCIIDataFile();
        reportFile = new ASCIIReportFile();
        msg = new ASCIIDisplayer();
        runReport();
        courseData.close();
        reportFile.close();
        msg.close();
```

(Continued)

```
    }; // constructor

    /** This method generates the course grade report.          */

    private void runReport ( ) {

        Course  aCourse;     // course being processed
        Report  aReport;     // report generator
        int     numStd;      // number of students processed

        aCourse = new Course(courseData);
        aReport = new Report(reportFile,12);
        msg.writeLabel("Processing ...");
        msg.writeEOL();
        numStd = aCourse.doReport(aReport);
        msg.writeLabel("Processing complete");
        msg.writeEOL();
        msg.writeLabel("Students processed:");
        msg.writeInt(numStd);
        msg.writeEOL();

    }; // runReport

    public static void main ( String args[] ) { new GradeReport(); };

}   // GradeReport
```

FIGURE 9.20 Example—`GradeReport` (main) class

Note that the `MarkingScheme` object is created by the `Course` while the main class creates the `Report` object. A course always has a marking scheme—it is an integral part of the way a course works. Thus it makes sense for the `Course` to be responsible for creating it. On the other hand, only when we are producing some type of report will a `Report` object exist, and different kinds of reports could be created by different `Report` objects. It thus makes sense to de-couple this from the `Course` class and give responsibility to the main class.

Testing

Once the code has been written, it must be tested. Tests are designed during the analysis and design phases, and they are performed during this phase. First, each class must be tested on its own, and later with classes with which it collaborates, until the complete system is assembled and system tests are performed. We will not describe the complete testing here, but rather look at some examples.

Let's consider first the class-level testing of the `Student` class. We have a bit of a problem. First, there is no main class to use for the test. Second, the class `MarkingScheme` isn't available for testing, at least not until integration testing; in fact, it might not even be written yet.

A class stub. We solve the problem of the missing `MarkingScheme` class by writing what is called a **class stub**. A class stub is a class that provides all of the methods defined by the class specification, but does not include the actual code, rather just method stubs, which we encountered in Section 4.4. Method stubs are just simple versions of the methods that receive the parameters and indicate (usually by doing I/O) what is going on, and if necessary they return some well-defined value. An example class stub for the `MarkingScheme` class is found in Figure 9.21.

> A **CLASS STUB** is a substitute for a supplier class used in the testing of a client class. It contains method stubs for each of the public methods of the real supplier class.

```
import BasicIO.*;

/** This class serves as a class stub for MarkingScheme to
  ** test the Student class.
  **
  ** @seeStudent
  **
  ** @author D. Hughes
  **
  ** @version1.0 (Jan. 2001)                                      */

public class MarkingScheme {

    public MarkingScheme ( SimpleDataInput from ) {

        System.out.println("Constructor called");

    };  // constructor

    public double apply ( double a1, double a2, double test, double exam ) {

        System.out.print("apply called with parameters: (");
        System.out.print(a1);
        System.out.print(",");
        System.out.print(a2);
        System.out.print(",");
        System.out.print(test);
        System.out.print(",");
        System.out.print(exam);
```

(Continued)

```
        System.out.println(")");
        return 75;

    };  // apply

}   // MarkingScheme
```

FIGURE 9.21 Example—MarkingScheme stub class

In the class stub there are no instance variables, and the constructor doesn't do anything; it simply displays a message to the console, indicating that it was called. The apply method simply displays the parameters it was passed. Since it is a function method, it must return a value. For testing, an arbitrary but known value is returned. We are not supposed to be writing the actual MarkingScheme class.

A **TEST HARNESS** is a substitute main class used to drive the testing of a class or set of classes.

A test harness. To test the Student class, we also need a main class. A specialized main class for testing a class is called a **test harness**. The test harness should perform all the desired tests of the class by calling the appropriate methods and displaying the results. What the test harness does will depend on the test specifications developed in the analysis and design phases. Tests should be repeatable; if the test harness is doing I/O, it should be from a file so the file can be saved along with the test harness for future use.

A test harness for the Student class is found in Figure 9.22. It must test the constructor and all methods of Student in all appropriate cases. Since the Student object doesn't do much besides read information from a file and calculate a final mark, there are not a lot of cases to test. We must test that the EOF processing is working correctly, so we need a process-to-EOF loop. We must also test all accessor methods and we need to see if the data was read, so we use them in the loop to dump out the student information to the console. We test calcFinalMark to see if it calls apply appropriately. Note that we should run this test at least twice, once with a file of a few sets of student information and once with an empty file, to cover all cases of files we might encounter. The console output from a sample test run is found in Figure 9.23.

```
import BasicIO.*;

/** This class serves as a test harness for testing the Student
 ** class.
 **
 ** @see    Student
 **
```

(Continued)

```
 ** @author D. Hughes
 **
 ** @version    1.0 (Jan. 2001)                                              */

public class TestStudent {

    private ASCIIDataFile   in; // file for course data

    public TestStudent ( ) {

        MarkingScheme   ms;             // marking scheme for course
        Student         aStudent;       // one student

        in = new ASCIIDataFile();
        ms = new MarkingScheme(in);

        while ( true ) {
            aStudent = new Student(in);
        if ( !in.successful() ) break;
            System.out.println("Student read");
            System.out.print("     ");
            System.out.print(aStudent.getStNum());
            System.out.print(",");
            System.out.print(aStudent.getAssign1());
            System.out.print(",");
            System.out.print(aStudent.getAssign2());
            System.out.print(",");
            System.out.print(aStudent.getTest());
            System.out.print(",");
            System.out.println(aStudent.getExam());
            aStudent.calcFinalMark(ms);
            System.out.print("     ");
            System.out.println(aStudent.getFinalMark());
            System.out.println();
        };

        in.close();

    };  // constructor

    public static void main ( String args[] ) { new TestStudent(); };

}   // TestStudent
```

FIGURE 9.22 Example—Student class test harness

```
Constructor called
Student read
    1111,10.0,10.0,50.0,100.0
apply called with parameters: (10.0,10.0,50.0,100.0)
    75.0

Student read
    2222,5.0,5.0,25.0,50.0
apply called with parameters: (5.0,5.0,25.0,50.0)
    75.0

Student read
    3333,0.0,0.0,0.0,0.0
apply called with parameters: (0.0,0.0,0.0,0.0)
    75.0

Student read
    4444,8.0,7.0,37.0,75.0
apply called with parameters: (8.0,7.0,37.0,75.0)
    75.0
```

FIGURE 9.23 `TestStudent` console output

Each of the other classes would be tested with appropriate harnesses and stubs until each is determined to be working. Then integration testing would be done with complete classes tested together (possibly with stubs for other classes) using a harness. Finally, all classes would be grouped for the system test, this time using the real main class. In all the testing, care should be taken to test all cases. This means that a number of different values should be tested for each piece of data, including values at the beginning and end of any data ranges. For example, both 0 and full marks should be tested, as well as at least one value in between. In addition, any error situations that the program should be able to handle should be tested. For files, at least a case with an empty file and one containing a number of records should be tested.

Debugging, Production, and Maintenance

When, during any phase of testing, the program crashes, or works but produces unexpected results, debugging must be done. Often the test harness and class stubs give enough information to pinpoint the source of the error and it can be corrected. Sometimes, the source of the error is a bit harder to detect. In these cases, it is often useful to place calls to `System.out.println` at appropriate points in the code to trace what is happening to the values of variables, in an attempt to track down the error (see Section 6.6).

When the error is corrected, the class-level testing must be reapplied, continuing up to integration testing, and finally to system testing. This continues until no further bugs are detected and the system is considered complete.

The system would now be released to the users as we enter the production phase. Maintenance now begins. Records are kept of any problems (bugs) encountered by users, and the bugs are fixed on a not-yet-released copy of the system. At some point it is determined that it is time to issue a new release, so this copy is moved into production. Over time, new features requested by users are analyzed. The development cycle for the next version is started, and we're back to the start.

■ SUMMARY

Large-scale software development is often done by teams of developers over an extended period of time. To ensure that such projects successfully come to completion, a well-defined process must be followed. This process is usually defined to have seven phases: analysis, design, coding, testing, debugging, production, and maintenance. Even if the project is relatively small and involves only one developer, the development can benefit form the use of the process, even if it is only done informally.

The analysis phase involves determination of what the proposed system is supposed to do through the development of a requirements specification, and the development of a model of the system. During design, the classes to be used in the system are chosen and the responsibilities are divided amongst the classes. A common tool for this part of design is the CRC card. During detailed design, complete specifications of the primary classes of the system are produced. Coding involves the realization of the classes in a programming language. Testing involves running the classes individually and in groups to determine if the classes and ultimately the system perform as required. Debugging is recoding, redesigning, or possibly reanalysis of the system to address errors detected during testing. Finally, when the system is felt to be free of problems, it is released to the user community (production phase). At this point maintenance begins, during which further errors are corrected and new features are added to the existing system.

REVIEW QUESTIONS

1. T F Candidate objects are identified by underlining nouns in the problem statement.
2. T F "Responsibility for doing" should be determined before "responsibility for knowing" in designing classes.

3. T F A class stub is used as the main class when testing another class.
4. T F The main purpose of analysis is to write the problem statement.
5. T F We do not wish to duplicate values in different classes because duplication causes an update problem.
6. T F "Responsibilities for knowing" become methods.
7. T F A client class is a class written for a client of the software development company.
8. Which of the following is *not* a phase in software development?
   a) debugging b) compiling
   c) designing d) testing
9. What is the output from the analysis phase of software development?
   a) requirements specification b) inputs and outputs
   c) system model d) all of the above
10. Trainers and technical support personnel are involved in which phase of software development?
    a) analysis b) testing
    c) production d) maintenance
11. Which of the following is part of the design phase?
    a) determining the inputs and outputs of the system
    b) writing a class specification for each class
    c) developing a model of the system
    d) writing a requirements specification
12. Which of the following is not a valid reason for eliminating a candidate object?
    a) It represents a value.
    b) It is just another name for an existing entity.
    c) There could be more than one object of that type.
    d) It is not part of the system being developed.
13. A specialized main class for testing a class is called a:
    a) class stub. b) method stub.
    c) test harness. d) test stub.
14. System testing:
    a) is usually done by testers.
    b) is done on a class-by-class basis.
    c) is done by programmers.
    d) should be avoided.
15. A CRC card
    a) is a Cyclic Redundancy Check card.
    b) should always be used in analysis.
    c) helps in distributing responsibilities to objects.
    d) None of the above is true.

EXERCISES

1. Modifying the classes already written for the grade reporting system described in this chapter, produce a new application that allows the instructor to produce a mark summary report. This report should display the student mark information for each piece of work and indicate the average mark over all students for each piece of work. The report might look like:

```
Progress Report              page:  1


            COSC 1P02


 ST #  Asgn 1  Asgn 2  Test   Exam
 ---------------------------------


1,111   10.0    10.0   50.0  100.0

2,222    5.0     5.0   25.0   50.0

3,333    0.0     0.0    0.0    0.0

4,444    8.0     7.0   37.0   75.0


 ---------------------------------


 Ave:    5.8     5.5   28.0   56.0
```

Try to modify the classes as little as possible. Clearly, the `Report` class will require considerable modification. However, the modification to the others should be minimal. Consider the design decisions made in the original system and how they helped or hindered code reuse.

2. ACME Widgets, Inc. requires a program to process its payroll. Employees in the company are paid weekly, and their salary is based on their hours worked and rate of pay. The federal and state governments require that the company withhold tax based on a formula provided by the governments and subject to change annually.

Employees are paid straight time for the first 40 hours worked and time-and-a-half for overtime hours (hours in excess of 40). Federal tax is based on a three-tier system. Zero tax is paid on the amount less than or equal to the first tier amount, a lower tax rate on the amount greater than the first tier amount and less than or equal to the second tier amount, and finally a higher tax rate on the amount exceeding the second tier amount. For example, the system might be that $0 is paid on the first $13,000 (first tier), 30% (low rate) on the amount between $13,000 and $52,000 (second tier), and 50% on the remaining. If the employee earned $62,000, the tax would be $16,700 [$0 + (39,000*0.3) + (10,000*0.5)]. State tax is computed as a percentage of federal tax.

A file of timesheet information is created each week as an `ASCIIDataFile` containing information about the employees. The file contains, for each employee: (1) the employee number (`int`), (2) pay rate (`double`), and (3) hours worked (`double`). Another file (a second `ASCIIDataFile`) of taxation information is also available, containing: (1) first tier amount (`double`), (2) low rate (`double`), (3) second tier amount (`double`), (4) high rate (`double`), and (5) state rate (`double`). The tier amounts are provided based on weekly pay, which is annual rate / 52.

The program is to input the employee information, compute pay and taxes, and generate a report (`ASCIIReportFile`) indicating the employees' gross pay, federal tax withheld, state tax withheld, and net pay. Since the company must remit the federal and state taxes withheld to the respective governments, the program must also display the total taxes withheld. In addition, so that the auditors may audit the payroll records, the total gross and total net pay paid out must be computed and displayed. Appropriate happiness messages should be generated to an `ASCIIDisplayer` stream.

The report generated by the program might look similar to the following, properly paginated using 12 lines per page with two blank lines at the bottom of all but the last page:

```
                  ACME WIDGETS                page  1


Emp#   Gross Pay   Fed Tax   State Tax    Net Pay

-----  ----------  ---------  ---------  ----------

1,111   $  500.00    $ 75.00    $ 33.75   $  391.25

2,222  $2,400.00    $925.00    $416.25  $1,058.75

-----  ----------  ---------  ---------  ----------

Total  $ 2,900.00  $1,000.00  $  450.00  $ 1,450.00
```

3. The Hydro-Electric Commission requires a program to do its monthly billing. For each customer, a record (line) is entered in an `ASCIIDataFile` recording: customer number (`int`), customer type (`char`, `c` for commercial and `r` for residential), previous reading (`double`), and current reading (`double`). The program should produce a report that gives, for each customer, the customer number, consumption, and amount billed, in a paginated report with appropriate headers. The report summary should indicate the total amount billed. The report should look something like:

```
Hydro-Electric Commission    page  1

          Billing Report


     Customer   Consumption   Amount

     ------------------------------

     1,111         1215.0      92.90

       :             :           :

     ------------------------------

          Total Billed:    23,259.70
```

There is a fee schedule that determines the amount to be billed based on customer type and consumption. For residential customers, there are two billing levels. Consumption up to the specified limit is billed at the first (higher) rate, and consumption in excess of the limit is billed at the second (lower) rate. Commercial customers are billed at a single rate for all consumption. A file (`ASCIIDataFile`) is prepared that contains the fee schedule amounts for the month. The information is recorded in order: first residential rate (`double`), limit (`double`), second residential rate (`double`) and commercial rate (`double`). Readings are in kilowatt-hours and rates are in dollars per kilowatt-hour.

4. Sharkey's Loans loans money to individuals and each month collects a payment with (considerable) interest. Every month, Sharkey's Loans produces a report that specifies the details of each loan.

Sharkey is a member of a business consortium that enforces the prompt payment of the minimum balance each month for each loan customer. Due to changing market conditions, the business people in the consortium frequently change the interest rates applied to the loans.

The business people have noticed that loans with a high outstanding balance tend to require enforcement of payment. For this reason, the interest rate for the next month is calculated using a three-tier system based on the new balance from the current month. A low interest rate is used on the first tier amount, a middle interest rate on the second tier amount, and a high interest rate on the third tier amount.

Interest is paid on the previous balance, plus debits, minus credits. For example, suppose that the consortium has decided to charge 10% monthly interest on the first $1,000 (first tier = $1,000), 20% interest on the amount between $1,000 and $6,000 (second tier = $6,000), and 30% interest on the remaining amount. Then the interest this month for a loan with a previous balance of $9,000, debits this month of $3,500 and credits this month of $2,500 would be $2,300, computed as:

```
0.10*1000 + 0.20*(6000-1000) + 0.30*(10000-6000)
```

This gives a new balance of $12,300 ($10,000 + $2,300). The minimum payment each month can also vary, but is calculated as a straight percentage of the new balance.

For each loan, the information concerning each month's activities is stored in an `ASCIIDataFile`. Each line concerns a separate loan, and includes the following information: loan number (`int`), previous balance (`double`), amount borrowed by the customer this month ("debits": `double`), and amount paid by the customer this month ("credits": `double`). Another `ASCIIDataFile` of rate information is also available containing: low rate (`double`), first tier amount (`double`), middle rate (`double`), second tier amount (`double`), high rate (`double`), and minimum payment rate (`double`). Note that all rates are given as monthly percentages.

The monthly report might look similar to the following, properly paginated using 12 lines per page with two blank lines at the bottom of all but the last page. Page numbers are not required.

```
                    Sharkey's Loans
                     Monthly Report

Loan#   PrevBal    Debits   Credits   Interest   NewBal   MinPaymt
-------------------------------------------------------------------
123    $1,000.00 $  200.00 $  400.00 $   80.00 $  880.00 $  220.00
456    $2,000.00 $    0.00 $  500.00 $  200.00 $1,700.00 $  425.00
789    $5,000.00 $3,000.00 $2,000.00 $1,100.00 $7,100.00 $1,775.00
-------------------------------------------------------------------
Totals $8,000.00 $3,200.00 $2,900.00 $1,380.00 $9,680.00 $2,420.00
```

In the report, the loan number, previous balance, and debits and credits are the values from the monthly data file. The interest is calculated as described above, and the new balance is calculated as the previous balance, plus debits, minus credits, plus interest. The minimum balance is calculated as the specified percentage of the new balance. The summary totals are the totals of the previous balance, debits, credits, interest, new balance, and minimum payments, respectively.

Write a Java program to produce this report. The program should read the loan data from an `ASCIIDataFile`, read the rate data from another `ASCIIDataFile`, and produce the report to an `ASCIIReportFile`. In addition to producing the report, the program should produce happiness messages to an `ASCIIDisplayer`.

10

Strings

CHAPTER OBJECTIVES

- To be able to manipulate text sequences as objects of the `String` class.
- To understand the difference between a mutable and an immutable object.
- To know how to perform `String` I/O.
- To be familiar with the use of the primary methods of the `String` class.
- To understand `String` comparison.

As we saw in Chapter 1, the hardware of a computer is primarily designed to do arithmetic, but in actuality, much of what computers are used for is manipulation of textual information. For example, a word processor is a program in which text is edited, cut/copied/pasted, spell-checked, and so on. Similarly, the editor in an interactive development environment is a text manipulation program, as is the compiler that translates text in one language, such as Java, into text in another language—machine language.

To do text manipulation, it is necessary to have a way to represent pieces of text within a program. The Java `char` type allows us to represent single text characters; however, we need something more powerful if we want to work with words, sentences, and so on. The standard library (`java.lang`) includes a class designed for text manipulation: `String` (see Section 10.3). Note that `String` is not a primitive type such as `char`, but is a reference type that is always available because it comes from the standard library.

10.1 `String` OBJECTS

A string (that is, an object of type `String`) is a sequence of zero or more characters from the Unicode character set. The sequence consisting of zero characters is called the **null string**. A **string literal** is written as a sequence of zero or more graphic ASCII characters or escapes (see Section 7.2) enclosed in double quotation marks ("). As we can see, the text we have been using in calls to methods like `writeLabel` are actually string literals. Table 10.1 shows some examples.

> A string consisting of zero characters is called the **NULL STRING**.
>
> A **STRING LITERAL** is a representation for a string value within the program text. In Java a string literal is a sequence of zero or more graphic characters from the Unicode character set or escape sequences, enclosed in double-quotes (").

The `String` class provides methods for string manipulation. However, there are a few operators that apply to strings. The operator + between two strings is interpreted as concatenation, joining strings end-to-end. The operators `==` and `!=` are defined for strings (as they are for any object type). However, remember (see Section 7.1) that object equality is interpreted as "referencing the same object," *not* as "the two strings have the same sequence of characters," so the `equals` and `compareTo` methods of the `String` class are most frequently used.

TABLE 10.1 `String` **literals**

String Literal	Meaning
`""`	The empty or null string consisting of zero characters
`"a"`	The string consisting of the one character `a` (not the same as `'a'`, which is the `char` literal `a`)
`"some text\tand more"`	Spaces and escapes can occur in the string and each represents one character. (This string is 18 characters long.)

```
String  s, t;
s = new String("a string");
t = new String("a string"); // point 1
s = s + t                   // point 2
```

FIGURE 10.1 Example—`String` assignment

A string, once created, does not change; rather, methods produce new strings from old ones. When an object cannot be changed, it is called **immutable**. Most objects like `Students` or `Employees` are **mutable**; that is, their state (the values of their instance variables) changes when methods are executed. `int` values, `double` values, and other primitive type values are immutable—five is always five, never six. Value variables can change when a different value is stored there by assignment, replacing the original value. The same is true for `String` variables. Remember, reference variables *reference* the actual string object; they do not contain it. If we assign a new string reference to a `String` variable, the variable now refers to a different string. For example, the code of Figure 10.1 produces the memory model of Figure 10.2. (In the diagram, an underscore (_) is used to show space characters in the string objects; the actual character is a space.)

Objects of a class are **IMMUTABLE** if their state (value) cannot be changed. String objects are immutable in Java.

Objects of a class are **MUTABLE** if their state (value) can be changed. Most objects are mutable.

`s` and `t` are reference variables; they contain the address on the object to which they refer. In the assignment to `s`, a new string value is created and `s` is modified to refer to this new object. Similarly, the assignment to `t` causes `t` to refer to a new object. Note

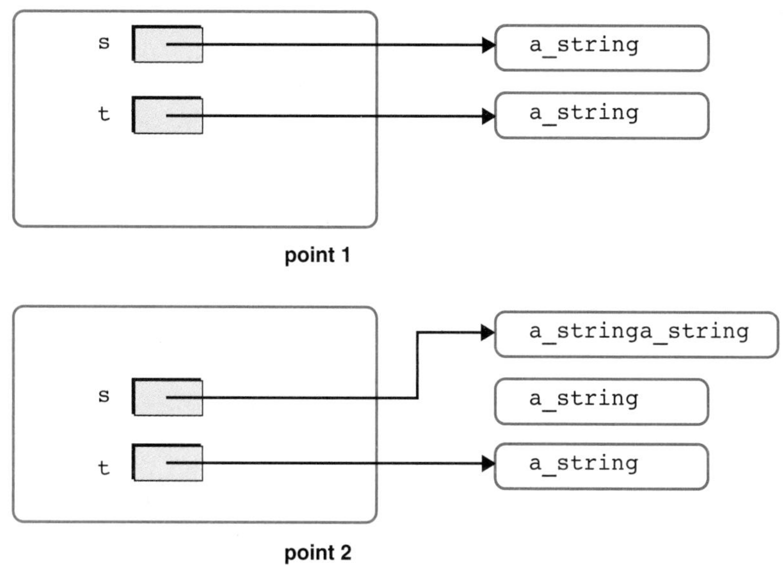

FIGURE 10.2 `String` assignment

that s and t refer to *different* strings, which happen to be composed of the same characters (s == t ⇒ false). At point 2, s is assigned a new String object created by the **concatenation** (joining end-to-end) of the strings referenced by s and t. The string objects are not changed; rather, a new string object is created. s now refers to this new object, and the original object is unchanged and is now unreferenced. It will eventually be garbage collected. This same situation is true if the object assigned to s is a literal or the result of a String method (Section 10.3).

String literals behave essentially as string constructors. There is one difference, however. To conserve space, the Java compiler checks to see if an identical String object has been created as another string literal. If so, it uses the exact same object. This means that if the following statements were used to create s and t in Figure 10.1:

```
s = "a string";
t = "a string"; // point 1
```

the result would be only one string object being created by point 1 to which both s and t refer. However, since String objects are immutable, the code would behave the same in all respects, except that s == t would be true for literals and false for constructors. This is a subtle point; it does not really matter much in String processing. If the String methods (see Section 10.3) are used for string comparison as opposed to using the equality operator, the correct results are assured.

10.2 String I/O

The BasicIO library provides methods for doing I/O of strings from and to streams (see Tables 5.3 and 5.5). The method out.writeString(s) writes the characters of s to the stream out. The number of characters written is the number of characters in s (zero or more). The method out.writeString(s,w) writes s in a field of width w characters. If s is shorter than w, the appropriate number of blanks are written *after* s. (In other words, s is left justified.) If s is longer than w, only the first w characters of s are written. (In other words, s is truncated.)

On input, there are special considerations. Strings can logically contain white space; for example, the first and last name of a person's name would be separated by a space. Therefore, string input must allow for input of white space, whereas other input methods skip over white space. At the same time, there must be some way of separating strings in input. The rule used by BasicIO is that tabs and line markers separate strings, while all other white space can be part of a string. The effect is that, through the use of s = in.readString(), s can contain any white space characters *except* tabs and line markers. This also means that tabs can be used to separate string fields on input. If it is necessary to allow the string to contain all white space characters and we wish to process the tabs as characters within the string, the method s = in.readLine() can be used. This reads all the characters from the current position to the line marker as the characters of the string. The line marker is read and discarded. There is no line marker character in the string; rather, the string ends with the last character in the line. The corresponding method `out.writeLine(s)` writes the characters of the string `s` followed by a line marker.

In many cases, strings are used simply to represent information that is not going to be manipulated at all, but simply remembered. For example, in the `Student` class of Section 9.2, it might have been desirable to include the student's name as an instance variable. This could have been done by declaring the name as a `String`. It probably also makes sense to declare the student number as a string since we do not intend to use it arithmetically, even though we call it a number. In fact, this gets rid of the problem of the student number (as an `int`) being printed with commas inserted. As a `String`, the student number is printed "as is." The modified version of the `Student` class would look like the example of Figure 10.3. (Ellipses (⋮) indicate lines of code unchanged and not reproduced here. Changes and insertions are indicated in **bold**.)

```
import BasicIO.*;
      ⋮
public class Student {
      ⋮
   private String  stNum;                 // student number
   private String  name;                  // student's name
   private double  a1, a2, test, exam;    // marks
   private double  finalMark;             // final mark
      ⋮
   public Student ( ASCIIDataFile from ) {
      stNum = from.readString();
      if ( from.successful() ) {
         name = from.readString();
         a1 = from.readDouble();
            ⋮
      };
   };  // constructor
      ⋮
   public String getStNum ( ) {
      return stNum;
   };  // getStNum

   /** This method returns the student's name.
    **
    ** @return String  the student's name                  */

   public String getName ( ) {
      return name;
   };  // getName
      ⋮
}  // Student
```

FIGURE 10.3 Example—Revised `Student` class

```
111111→    John_Doe→       8.6→    9.5→    22.0→   85.0
222222→    Mary_Bright→    10.0→   10.0→   24.5→   95.0
```

FIGURE 10.4 Sample `Student` data

Note the use of `readString` and `writeString` for reading and writing the string fields of the student object. When a text data file is used, the student number and the name would be separated by a tab. The name could include a space between first and last name. All of the fields concerning a single student would likely be on a single line in the file. Figure 10.4 shows the first two lines of a sample input file. (Underscores (_) mark spaces and arrows (→) mark tabs.)

The first `readString`, for the student number, would read up to the first tab (`111111`). Assuming this read was successful and had not reached end-of-file, the next `readString` would read to the next tab (i.e., `John_Doe`). Three `readDoubles` would read the next three fields (`8.6`, `9.5`, and `22.0`), up to tabs. Finally, the last `readDouble` would read the last field (`85.0`), up to the end-of-line. The next time student information is read, the same process would begin at the beginning of the next line.

As another example, a program that produces a copy of a text file might be written as in Figure 10.5. Here, repeatedly, lines of text are read and then written until end-of-file. To preserve the layout of the text, the entire line is read, including the white space, using `readLine`, and then written using `writeLine`. Since `readLine` strips off the end of line marker and `writeLine` writes an end-of-line marker, there is no problem ensuring that the correct marker for the platform is written. The lines are counted as processed and a happiness message is produced.

```
import BasicIO.*;

/** This program uses Strings to produce a copy of a text
  ** file.
  **
  ** @author D. Hughes
  **
  ** @version    1.0 (Mar. 2001)                                        */

public class CopyFile {

    private ASCIIDataFile       in;     // file to copy from
    private ASCIIOutputFile     out;    // file to copy to
    private ASCIIDisplayer      msg;    // happiness messages
```

(Continued)

```
    /** The constructor copies a text file line by line.          */

    public CopyFile ( ) {

        in = new ASCIIDataFile();
        out = new ASCIIOutputFile();
        msg = new ASCIIDisplayer();
        copy();
        in.close();
        out.close();
        msg.close();

    };  // constructor


    /** This method copies a text file creating a new one.        */

    private void copy ( ) {

        String  line;        // line being copied
        int     numLines;    // number of lines copied

        numLines = 0;
        msg.writeLabel("Processing...");
        msg.writeEOL();
        while ( true ) {
            line = in.readLine();
        if ( ! in.successful() ) break;
            numLines = numLines + 1;
            out.writeLine(line);
        };
        msg.writeLabel("Processing complete");
        msg.writeEOL();
        msg.writeInt(numLines);
        msg.writeLabel(" lines copied");
        msg.writeEOL();

    };  // copy


    public static void main ( String args[] ) { new CopyFile(); };


}   // CopyFile
```

FIGURE 10.5 Example—Copy a text file

10.3 THE String CLASS

The `String` class of the standard library (`java.lang`) defines the reference type `String` and methods that can be applied to strings. A partial list of methods is given in Table 10.2. A complete list can be found on the Web at the Sun Java site (see Appendix G for the reference). Methods returning `String` results create new `String` objects and the original `String` object is unchanged. Methods returning other values do not alter the original `String` object.

The methods `equals`, `equalsIgnoreCase`, and `compareTo` are used for `String` comparisons. Remember `==` and `!=` compare references. `s.equals(t)` returns `true` if every character from first to last in `s` exactly matches the corresponding character in `t`. `s.equalsIgnoreCase(t)` also compares corresponding characters in `s` and `t`; however, it ignores case differences. Characters in one string can be uppercase and correspon-

TABLE 10.2 `String` **methods**

Method	Result	Interpretation
`charAt ( int i )`	char	Character at position `i`
`compareTo ( String t )`	`int`	Compare with `t`
`concat ( String t )`	`String`	Concatenation with `t`
`equals ( String t )`	`boolean`	Same characters as `t`
`equalsIgnoreCase ( String t )`	`boolean`	Same characters as `t` (ignoring case differences)
`indexOf ( char c )`	`int`	Position of first occurrence of `c`
`indexOf ( String t )`	`int`	Position of first occurrence of `t`
`length ( )`	`int`	Number of characters in string
`replace ( char c, char d )`	`String`	Equivalent string with each occurrence of `c` replaced by `d`
`substring ( int f, int t )`	`String`	Substring from position `f` up to but not including `t`
`substring ( int f )`	`String`	Substring from position `f` to end
`toLowerCase ( )`	`String`	Equivalent string in all lowercase
`toUpperCase ( )`	`String`	Equivalent string in all uppercase
`trim ( )`	`String`	Equivalent string without leading and trailing white space

TABLE 10.3	String comparison
Comparison	**Meaning**
`s.compareTo(t) < 0`	`true` when `s` precedes `t` alphabetically
`s.compareTo(t) == 0`	`true` when `s` and `t` have the same characters
`s.compareTo(t) > 0`	`true` when `s` follows `t` alphabetically

ding characters in the other string can be lowercase and still be considered equal. The method call `s.compareTo(t)` returns an `int` value. It compares the corresponding characters in `s` and `t` until it either has compared all characters as equal or finds a pair that is different. If they are all equal, `compareTo` returns `0`. When they are not equal, if the character in `s` comes before the corresponding character in `t` in the Unicode coding scheme, it returns a negative number; otherwise, it returns a positive number. The result is essentially alphabetic (dictionary) ordering. When `s` comes before `t` alphabetically, `s.compareTo(t)` returns a negative number. In normal usage, the result of `compareTo` is in turn compared to zero to yield the relationship between `s` and `t`, as summarized in Table 10.3.

The method call `s.length()` returns the number of characters in the string `s`. A string may have no characters (null string), in which case `length` will return `0`. The call `s.charAt(i)` returns the character at position `i` in the string. The first character is at position `0` and the last is at position `s.length()-1`. If the actual parameter of `charAt` is outside the range `0–s.length()-1`, the program will fail with a `StringIndexOutOfBoundsException` error.

Example—Detecting Palindromes

As an example of string processing, consider the following problem. A **palindrome** is a word or phrase that reads the same forwards and backwards. The word "ewe" is a palindrome, as is the phrase "Able was I ere I saw Elba," supposedly uttered by Napoleon when he was exiled to the island of Elba. To determine whether a string is a palindrome, we could first create a new string that is the original with the letters reversed, and then compare this to the original string. If they are equal, the original string was a palindrome. Figure 10.6 is a program that reads phrases from a prompter and displays whether or not each phrase is a palindrome. The phrases are read using `readString` since we aren't worrying about anything but the words and the spaces between them. The method `reverse` returns a new string with the same characters in reverse order. This can be compared with the original string using `equalsIgnoreCase` to handle possible case differences.

A **PALINDROME** is a word or phrase that reads the same forwards and backwards.

```
import BasicIO.*;

/** This program determines whether strings are
 ** palindromes.
 **
 ** @author D. Hughes
 **
 ** @version    1.0 (Mar. 2001)                                    */

public class Palindrome {


    private ASCIIPrompter       in;      // prompter for input
    private ASCIIDisplayer      out;     // displayer for output

    /** The constructor determines whether strings are palindromes.  */

    public Palindrome ( ) {

        in = new ASCIIPrompter();
        out = new ASCIIDisplayer();
        checkPalindromes();
        in.close();
        out.close();

    };  // constructor


    /** This method reads strings and checks if they are
     ** palindromes.                                               */

    private void checkPalindromes ( ) {

        String  str;         // string to be checked as palindrome
        String  reversed;    // reversed version of str

        while ( true ) {
            in.setLabel("Enter string");
            str = in.readString();
```

(Continued)

```
        if ( ! in.successful() ) break;
            out.writeLabel("\"");
            out.writeString(str);
            reversed = reverse(str);
            if ( str.equalsIgnoreCase(reversed) ) {
                out.writeLabel("\" is a palindrome");
            }
            else {
                out.writeLabel("\" is not a palindrome");
            };
            out.writeEOL();
        };

    };  // checkPalindromes


    /** This method returns a string in which the characters
     ** of the parameter are in reverse order.
     **
     ** @param  str string to be reversed
     **
     ** @return String  string in reverse order.                    */

    private String reverse ( String str ) {

        String result;  // reversed string
        int i;

        result = "";
        for ( i=0 ; i<str.length() ; i++ ) {
            result = str.charAt(i) + result;
        };
        return result;

    };  // reverse


    public static void main ( String args[] ) { new Palindrome(); };


}   // Palindrome
```

FIGURE 10.6 Example—Determine whether string is a palindrome

TABLE 10.4	Reversing a string		
result before	**i**	**str.charAt(i)**	**result after**
""	0	'f'	"f"
"f"	1	'r'	"rf"
"rf"	2	'e'	"erf"
"erf"	3	'd'	"derf"

The method `reverse` uses `charAt` to index through the characters of the original string. As `i` is incremented from `0` to the string length minus `1` (`i<str.length()`), the characters of the string from first to last are accessed. Starting with a null string (`""`), the reversed string is built up by concatenating the characters, one by one, to the front of the result string so far. When the loop is complete, the resultant string is returned as the result of the method. This process is demonstrated in Table 10.4 with `str` being "`fred`".

Note that we are concatenating a `char` (`str.charAt(i)`) to a `String` (`result`). For the concatenation operator (+), Java considers that all types have a string representation and performs automatic conversion of the character into a string consisting of one character.

This process for reversing a string is not very efficient, as it repeatedly creates new string objects at every concatenation and discards them. The number of strings created is equal to the number of characters in the original string. There is another, more efficient, way of accomplishing this task; it requires arrays and will be discussed in Chapter 11.

Other String Methods

The method call `s.concat(t)` returns a new string that has the characters of `s` and `t` joined end-to-end. This is the same operation as the + operator when used with strings, except automatic conversion to string occurs for + but not for `concat`. The methods `indexOf` locate the index position of a character or string within the string. In the case of a `char` parameter, the result is the index, within the string, starting from `0`, of the first occurrence of the parameter. For a `String` parameter, the result is the index, within the string, of the character at the start of a sequence of characters that exactly matches the parameter. If the character or string does not occur within the string, the result is `-1`. Examples of concatenation and index are shown in Table 10.5.

The `substring` methods return a new string, which is the same as a portion (substring) of the string. In the first form (`s.substring(f,t)`), the first parameter (`f`) is the starting index position and the second (`t`) is the ending position. The result is a string containing the sequence of characters from position `f` to position `t-1`, inclusive of `f` but exclusive of `t`. In the second form (`s.substring(f)`), the substring starts at `f` and includes the rest of the string. `s.substring(f)` produces the same result as

TABLE 10.5 `String` **method examples**

```
String s;
String t;
s = "sing ring string";
t = "ring";
```

Method call	Result	Interpretation
`t.concat("ing")`	`"ringing"`	End-to-end, no spaces added
`s.indexOf('r')`	`5`	Spaces count, `r` is at position `5` (sixth character)
`s.indexOf('i')`	`1`	First occurrence of `i`
`s.indexOf('z')`	`-1`	`z` isn't in the string
`s.indexOf(t)`	`5`	`ring` begins at position 5 (with the `r`)
`s.indexOf("ing")`	`1`	First occurrence
`s.indexOf("ringing")`	`-1`	`ringing` doesn't occur
`s.substring(5,9)`	`"ring"`	Includes `5`, excludes `9`
`s.substring(10)`	`"string"`	From `10` to end
`s.substring(9,5)`		Exception (error) at run time

`s.substring(f,s.length())`. If `t <= f` or either `f` or `t` is `>= s.length()`, a `StringIndexOutOfBoundsException` occurs. Table 10.5 also shows examples of substrings.

The method `replace(c,d)` returns a new string that is the same as the original, except that each occurrence of the character `c` is replaced by the character `d`. If `c` doesn't occur in the string, the result is the same as the original. The methods `toLowerCase` and `toUpperCase` return a new string that is identical to the original, except that each character that is lowercase (uppercase) is replaced by its uppercase (lowercase) equivalent. The method `trim` returns a string equivalent to the original, except that leading and trailing white-space characters have been removed. If the original string consisted solely of white-space characters, the result is a null string.

Example—Formatting a Name

Let's consider an example. Often names are written in the form: `last, first`—so that the surname is easily seen, especially if the names are to be listed in sorted order, such as in a telephone book. However, when used in normal text or as a salutation in a letter, it is desirable to have the name in the form: `first last`. Figure 10.7 uses a method `format` that reformats a name from the form `last, first` into the form `first last`. The program simply reads a list of names from a file and lists them in the other form. The method `format` would more likely be part of a program that worked with names; for example, a form letter generator.

```
import BasicIO.*;

/** This program uses inputs name in form: last, first and
 ** lists them in form: first last.
 **
 ** @author D. Hughes
 **
 ** @version    1.0 (Mar. 2001)                               */

public class FormatName {

    private ASCIIDataFile       in;       // file of names
    private ASCIIDisplayer      out;      // display for formatted names

    /** The constructor reads names and reformats them.          */

    public FormatName ( ) {

        in = new ASCIIDataFile();
        out = new ASCIIDisplayer();
        display();
        in.close();
        out.close();

    };  // constructor


    /** This method reads names, reformats, and displays them.               */

    private void display ( ) {

        String name;     // name to be formatted
```

(Continued)

```
        while ( true ) {
            name = in.readString();
        if ( ! in.successful() ) break;
            out.writeString(format(name));
            out.writeEOL();
        };

    };  // display


    /** This method takes a name of form: last, first and
     ** reformats it in the form: first last.
     **
     ** @param  name     the name to be formatted
     **
     ** @return String  the reformatted name.                  */

    private String format ( String name ) {

        String  result;      // result name
        String  first;       // first name
        String  last;        // last name
        int     pos;         // position of comma

        pos = name.indexOf(',');
        last = name.substring(0,pos);
        first = name.substring(pos+1).trim();
        result = first.concat(" ");
        result = result.concat(last);
        return result;

    };  // format


    public static void main ( String args[] ) { new FormatName(); };


}   // FormatName
```

FIGURE 10.7 Example—Formatting a name

The method format takes a name (String) as a parameter and returns a new string representing the name in the other format. First it locates the comma (,) in the name string. It then breaks the string into two substrings (last and first) at the comma. The characters up to but not including the comma are the last name, and the characters after the comma are the first name plus any initials, etc. Note that the comma is eliminated by starting the second substring at `pos+1`. Since there could be more than one space after the comma, the `trim` method is used on the substring to get rid of the leading and possibly trailing white space. The final result is produced by first concatenating a space on the end of the first name. Note the use of the string literal `" "` and not the `char` literal `' '`. Automatic conversion to `String` occurs only for the concatenate (+) operator, not for a method parameter. Finally, the last name is concatenated to the end. This string is returned as the result of the function.

*10.4 StringTokenizer CLASS

> A **TOKEN** is a single, indivisible symbol from a language (particularly a programming language) such as a word, punctuation symbol, or literal.
>
> **LEXICAL ANALYSIS** is the process of separating a piece of text in some language (especially a programming language) into its individual tokens.

A common operation in text processing is breaking a string down into its individual components (for example, words). A word processor does this to achieve **word wrap**—placing a word that doesn't completely fit on one line at the beginning of the next line. A compiler does this to isolate the keywords such as `class` and `while`, identifiers, literals such as `123` and `"abc"`, operators like + and ==, and other punctuation such as `;` and `,`. These individual symbols are called **tokens** of the language (Java) and are isolated during a process called **lexical analysis**.

String Tokenizer

Any program that has to break an input string down into component parts must perform a kind of lexical analysis. The Java utility library `java.util` provides a class called `StringTokenizer` that makes this task much easier. The `StringTokenizer` class considers a string to consist of a number of tokens separated by one or more delimiters (specific characters not part of any token). When a `StringTokenizer` is established on a string, it is possible to access the tokens as strings in the order they occur in the string.

To establish a `StringTokenizer` on a string, the string and a string containing the delimiter characters is passed to the `StringTokenizer` constructor. Then, through the method `nextElement`, the next token can repeatedly be obtained until there are no more tokens. The method `hasMoreElements` returns `true` if there are any tokens remaining to be accessed. The tokenizer is normally used in code similar to that in Figure 10.8.

Delimiters

The string `delimiters` is just a list of the characters that serve as delimiters. For example, if we wished to tokenize a line of text in a word processor, the **delimiters** might include each punctuation symbol and the space character as in the string `"!():\";,.? "`. Note

```
String          str;
String          delimiters;
StringTokenizer tokens;
String          aToken;

get the string and set the delimiters
tokens = new StringTokenizer(str,delimiters);
while ( tokens.hasMoreElements() ) {
   aToken = tokens.nextElement();
   process the token
};
```

FIGURE 10.8 Example—Getting the tokens from a string

the escape to include the double quote. When the string is tokenized, any sequence of characters that are not delimiters, separated from another such sequence by one or more delimiters, is considered a token. For example, if the string to be tokenized and the delimiters are:

```
str = "This string, containing some words, will be tokenized!";
delimiters = "!():\";,.? ";
```

and the tokenizer is created as:

```
tokens = new StringTokenizer(str,delimiters);
```

The tokens accessed, in order, will be:

```
This
string
containing
some
words
will
be
tokenized
```

Note that the tokenizer is actually established on a copy of the string. This means that the string does not change as the tokens are accessed and that any change of the string referenced by `str` will not affect the action of the tokenizer.

Example—Analyzing Text

Figure 10.9 shows a program using a `StringTokenizer` to analyze some English language text. The analysis includes a count of the number of lines, the number of words, and the average length of the words in the text. Until end-of-file, it reads a line of text, using `readLine` to get the entire line including white space. It then establishes a `StringTokenizer` (`words`) on the line with the punctuation characters of English plus a space as delimiters (`punct`). It then proceeds to iterate through the words of the line until there are no more. With each word (`aWord`), it increments the word count (`nWords`) and accumulates the lengths of the words (`totLength`). Just so that you can see what is happening, the words are displayed as processed.

```
import BasicIO.*;
import java.util.*;

/** This program determines the average length of words
 ** in a text file.
 **
 ** @author D. Hughes
 **
 ** @version    1.0 (Mar. 2001)                                  */

public class WordLength {

    private ASCIIDataFile       in;      // text file to be analyzed
    private ASCIIDisplayer      out;     // displayer for results

    /** The constructor determines the average word length.        */

    public WordLength ( ) {

        in = new ASCIIDataFile();
        out = new ASCIIDisplayer();
        display();
        in.close();
        out.close();

    };  // constructor
```

(Continued)

```
/** This method reads words form a text file and displays
 ** the average length of the words found.                    */

private void display ( ) {

    String          line;        // line of text
    StringTokenizer words;       // tokenized words
    String          punct;       // punctuation (word separators)
    String          aWord;       // one word
    int             nLines;      // number of lines
    int             totLength;   // total length of words
    int             nWords;      // number of words

    punct = "!():\";,.? ";
    nLines = 0;
    nWords = 0;
    totLength = 0;
    out.writeLabel("The words");
    out.writeEOL();
    while ( true ) {
        line = in.readLine();
    if ( ! in.successful() ) break;
        nLines = nLines + 1;
        words = new StringTokenizer(line,punct);
        while ( words.hasMoreElements() ) {
            nWords = nWords + 1;
            aWord = (String)words.nextElement();
            out.writeString(aWord);
            out.writeEOL();
            totLength = totLength + aWord.length();
        };
    };
    out.writeEOL();
    writeDetails(nLines,nWords,(double)totLength/nWords);

}; // display


/** This method writes the results of the text analysis.
 **
 ** @param  lines      number of lines
 ** @param  words      number of words
 ** @param  aveLength  average word length.              */
```

(Continued)

```
    private void writeDetails ( int lines, int words, double aveLength ) {

        out.writeLabel("Number of lines: ");
        out.writeInt(lines);
        out.writeEOL();
        out.writeLabel("Number of words: ");
        out.writeInt(words);
        out.writeEOL();
        out.writeLabel("Average word length: ");
        out.writeDouble(aveLength);
        out.writeEOL();

    };  // writeDetails


    public static void main ( String args[] ) { new WordLength(); };


}   // WordLength
```

FIGURE 10.9 Example—Analyzing English text

Since the delimiter string doesn't include the apostrophe (') or hyphen (-), contractions and hyphenated words are considered as a single word and the apostrophe or hyphen is counted in the length of the word. If this were not desired, special processing would be required.

■ SUMMARY

A string is a sequence of text characters that is processed as a unit. In Java, a string is represented by the `String` class, which is one of the standard library classes. Strings are immutable objects; operations do not change existing strings, but rather produce new ones. Therefore, strings can essentially be treated as values, except that the equality operator (==) tests for object equality when what is usually desired is value equality, as provided by the method `equals`.

String literals are sequences of characters, including escapes enclosed in double quotes ("). A sequence of zero characters—called a null string—is represented by `""`. The only operator for strings is the concatenation operator (+), which joins two strings end-to-end. The `BasicIO` library supports string I/O via `readString`, `readLine`, `writeString`, and `writeLine`. All other operations come from the library class `String`.

The `String` class defines, among other operations, operations for determining the length of a string, selecting characters and substrings from a string, searching for characters or substrings in a string, and comparing strings. Index positions within a string begin at `0`. String comparison is based on alphabetic order, except that upper- and lowercase characters are distinct.

REVIEW QUESTIONS

1. T F Like other read methods in `BasicIO`, `readString` skips white space.
2. T F The first character in a string is numbered `1`.
3. T F If `s="wxyz"` and `n=s.length()`, then `s.charAt(n)` returns `'z'`.
4. T F If `s="sing  string  ring"`, then `s.trim()` returns `"sing string ring"`.
5. T F A null string is a string that has not yet been created by `new`.
6. T F A string is an example of an immutable object.
7. T F `s.replace(c,d)` creates an equivalent string, with every occurrence of `c` replaced with `d`.
8. In Java the notation `""` represents:
   a) a null string. b) a string of length `0`.
   c) a string literal. d) all of the above.
9. When an object's state can never change, it is called:
   a) constant. b) consistent.
   c) immutable. d) none of the above.
10. If `s="wxyz"` and `t="wxy"`, `s.compareTo(t)<0` evaluates to:
    a) `true`. b) `0`.
    c) a positive number. d) none of the above.
11. If `s="Ho Ho Ho, hope you have a good Xmas"` and `t="ho"`, then `s.indexOf(t)` returns:
    a) `-1`. b) `0`.
    c) `10`. d) none of the above.
12. Which of the following is considered a string separator in `BasicIO`?
    a) space b) tab
    c) end of line d) both b and c
13. What are the contents of `c` after executing the following?

```
a = "hello";
b = 'o';
c = a.concat(b);
```

    a) `"helloo"` b) `"hello o"`
    c) There is an error. d) `"ohello"`

14. What are the contents of b after executing the following?

```
a = "bonjour";
b = a.substring(1,5);
```

a) "onjo"
b) "bonjo"
c) "onjou"
d) "bonj"

15. If s="ABC" and t="Abc", what will be the result of s.compareTo(t)?

a) 0
b) a nonzero number
c) true
d) false

EXERCISES

1. Write a function:

```
private int occurrencesOf ( String s, char c ) {
```

that returns the number of occurrences of the character c within the string s. Write a main class to test this method on a number of strings.

2. Write a function:

```
private String remove ( String s, char c ) {
```

that removes each occurrence of the character c from the string s, returning the resulting string. Write a main class to test this method on a number of strings.

3. Modify the example in Figure 10.7 to handle middle names. Consider that a person can have any number of middle names (including none) and that the original format of the name is:

```
last, first middle middle . . .
```

You may assume that there is a comma and exactly one space after the last name, and exactly one space between each other name. There are no spaces within a name. The reformatted name should include middle initials only, each followed by a period.

4. Write a program that censors a text document. The program should read the document from an ASCIIDataFile and produce an equivalent document to an ASCIIOutputFile, except that all four-letter words are replaced by four asterisks (*). Treat as a word any sequence of alphabetic

characters separated from other words by a sequence of nonalphabetic characters, as in the word count program of Figure 7.6.

5 The Broccoli University Security Service (BUSS) is concerned about the security of messages that it transmits via e-mail between its agents. In order to ensure that unauthorized people cannot read the messages, they want to translate all messages into Pig-latin. You are to write the translation program.

In Pig-latin, English words are transformed by taking the leading consonants (that is, the letters up to the first vowel) from the front of the word and appending them to the end of the word, followed by the letters "ay". If there are no leading consonants, the letters "ay" are simply appended. For example:

English	**Pig-latin**
pig	igpay
string	ingstray
append	appenday

The program is to input an `ASCIIDataFile` containing the original document and produce a translated version to an `ASCIIOutputFile`. A count of the number of lines processed should be generated as happiness messages (to an `ASCIIDisplayer`).

The translated version is to be identical to the original except that all words have been translated into Pig-latin. You may assume that the original document has exactly one space between words, no punctuation, and no uppercase letters. For the purposes of the assignment, a word is considered to be a sequence of nonblank characters and vowels are the letters: a, e, i, o, u. You may assume that every word contains at least one vowel.

Hints:

Since exactly one space character exists between words, the end of a word can be located using `indexOf` as long as the last word also has a space behind it. (The program can append a space to the end of the input text line to ensure the presence of this space.) If each word is removed from the front of the line as it is located, a loop can be used to extract each word.

If there is a method that returns the index position of the first vowel in a word, the Pig-latin version of the word can be constructed by breaking the word into two substrings at the vowel and appending it back together in a different order.

The index position of the first vowel in a word can be found as the minimum index position of each of the letters a, e, i, o, and u.

11 Arrays

CHAPTER OBJECTIVES

- To know how to represent collections of information as arrays.
- To know when arrays are and are not appropriate for representing information.
- To be able to declare, create, and manipulate arrays.
- To understand the process of array assignment and comparison.
- To recognize two techniques for storing information in arrays—right-sized and variable-sized.
- To be able to use array traversal and recognize its various forms.
- To understand how arrays may be parameters to and results from methods.
- To be able to perform random processing of arrays.
- To know the difference between one-dimensional, two-dimensional, and higher dimensional arrays.
- To recognize the two standard traversal patterns for two-dimensional arrays—row-major and column-major.

Previously, all of our variables have represented a single value—integer, character, student, string—at any one time. Assigning a new value to the variable changed the value represented. It is common, however, to need to represent collections of things within a program. For example, you might want to consider all students in a class, or all lines of text in a document. If this collection cannot be processed in sequential order from first to last—as we have done when the information is in a file—we will need a way to store the entire collection in memory. For this we need what are called aggregates or arrays.

11.1 CREATING ARRAYS

> An **ARRAY** is a collection of items (values, objects) all of the same type, stored under a single name.
>
> An **ELEMENT** is an individual item within an array.
>
> The **ELEMENT TYPE** of an array is the type of the individual elements.

In Java, an **array** is a collection of items (values, objects) all of the same type, stored under a single name. The individual items are called **elements**, and the type is known as the **element type**. An array is declared using the second form of a `VariableDeclaratorId`, as in the syntax in Figure 11.1.

Declaration

This syntax indicates that, in a declaration, a variable identifier may be followed by one or more sets of brackets (`[]`), indicating that the identifier represents an array. A `VariableDeclaratorId` is actually used in field declarations (see Section 2.3), in local variable declarations (Section 3.3), and in formal parameter lists (Section 4.2) where we have previously indicated only `Identifier`. This means that arrays may be declared as fields (instance variables), local variables, and/or method parameters. As we will see later, they may also be returned as the result of a function method. An example of an array declaration that declares a local variable `a` to reference an array of `int` would be:

```
int     a[];
```

SYNTAX

```
VariableDeclaratorId:
      Identifier
      VariableDeclaratorId [ ]
```

FIGURE 11.1 Array declaration syntax

Array Creation

Arrays are classified as reference types (like object references). This means that the array variable is a reference to the actual array, just as an object variable is a reference to the actual object. Like objects, arrays must be constructed before they can be used. Figure 11.2 shows the syntax for an `ArrayCreationExpression`.

> The **DIMENSION** of an array is the number of subscripts needed to select an individual element of the array.
>
> A **ONE-DIMENSIONAL ARRAY** is one in which elements are selected by a single subscript. Such an array is sometimes called a vector or list.

Like object creation, array creation is initiated by the keyword `new`. This is followed by the element type and then one or more expressions, called the **dimensions** of the array, in brackets. For the time being, we will consider only **one-dimensional arrays**, those having only one dimension expression. An array can be constructed and assigned to the array variable `a` via:

```
a = new int[10];
```

Memory Model

This expression creates a new array of integers and stores its reference in `a`. The memory model is shown in Figure 11.3. Storage capable of storing 10 `int` values is allocated and then its reference is stored in `a`. The value of each individual element (`int`s) is not specified.

Array Operations

Assignment compatibility for arrays requires that the array being assigned (right-hand side) have the same number of dimensions and the same element type as the variable

SYNTAX

```
ArrayCreationExpression:
        new Type DimExprs

DimExprs:
        DimExpr
        DimExprs DimExpr

DimExpr:
        [ Expression ]
```

FIGURE 11.2 Array creation expression syntax

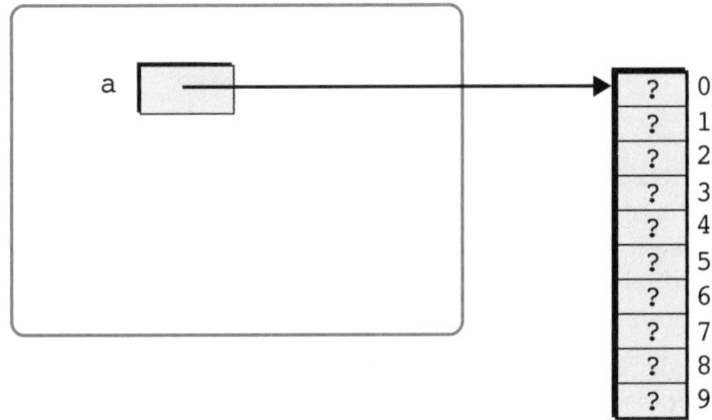

FIGURE 11.3 Array memory model

The **LENGTH** of a dimension of an array is the number of elements in that dimension of the array. For a one-dimensional array, the length of its only dimension is called the length of the array.

(left-hand side). Note that the **length** (number of elements) of the array is irrelevant, meaning that an array variable may reference arrays of various lengths; however, the number of dimensions and the element type are fixed by the declaration. This makes arrays in Java a bit more flexible than in many languages where even the number of elements is fixed by the declaration. As with reference variables, it is the reference that is assigned—no copy of the array is produced.

There are few operations available for arrays. Arrays may be compared for equality. Again, this is reference equality, not equality of the elements. Arrays are also considered to have a single attribute representing the length of the array. This attribute is accessed via the notation:

```
ArrayIdentifier.length
```

which is an expression resulting in the number of elements in the array referenced by the identifier. For example, with the array `a` declared and created above, we get `a.length`⇒`10`. In other words, there are `10` elements in the array referenced by `a`.

A **SUBSCRIPTED VARIABLE** is an array name followed by one or more subscripts, and is used to access an element of sub-portion of an array.

Subscripting

Since arrays represent collections of things, their primary purpose is to group the elements together so they can be conveniently processed. Most of the actual processing involves the individual elements of the array. To access the individual elements of the array, a **subscripted variable** is used. Figure 11.4 shows array subscripting.

The array identifier must be an array variable to which an array reference has been assigned, or else a `NullPointerException` occurs. The `Expression` must be an integer expression that evaluates to a value between `0` and `a.length-1` (for an array `a`),

SYNTAX

```
ArrayAccess:
        ArrayIdentifier [ Expression ]
        ArrayAccess [ Expression ]
```

FIGURE 11.4 Array subscripting syntax

A **SUBSCRIPT** is a notation written after an array name to access an element or sub-portion of an array in a subscripted variable. In Java, a subscript is an integer expression enclosed in brackets ([]).

ZERO-BASED SUBSCRIPTING refers to the specification in a language that the subscript 0 references the first element or sub-portion in a dimension of an array. Java uses zero-based subscripting.

ONE-BASED SUBSCRIPTING refers to the specification in a language that the subscript 1 references the first element or sub-portion in a dimension of an array.

or else an `ArrayIndexOutOfBoundsException` occurs. The expression is known as the **subscript** and indicates a particular element within the array, with `0` being the first element, `1` being the second, and `a.length-1` being the last element. Java uses **zero-based subscripting**; in other words, `0` is the first element. Many languages use **one-based subscripting** where the first element is numbered `1`.

An `ArrayAccess` may be used anywhere a simple variable identifier may be used. When used as an expression, either on the right-hand side of an assignment or as an actual parameter, the value is the value of the element designated by the subscript. When used in a variable context as the left-hand side of an assignment, the value of the element designated by the subscript is replaced. The type of a subscripted array reference is the element type of the array—`int` in this case. For example, the code:

```
a[3] = 5;
a[7] = a[3] + 4;
```

results in a change to elements `3` and `7` of the array `a`, as shown in Figure 11.5. Note that the values of the other elements are unaffected.

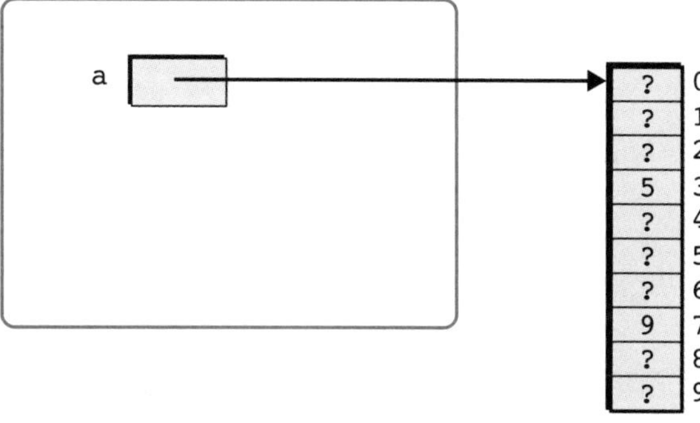

FIGURE 11.5 Accessing array elements

11.2 ARRAY PROCESSING

Arrays are necessary whenever a collection of items (values, objects) must be processed in nonsequential order. This is the case when all of the processing required cannot be done when the item is first encountered, but must wait until later items of the collection have been processed. Array processing involves: (1) the declaration of an array variable, (2) the creation of the array, (3) initialization of some elements, and (4) processing of some elements. To declare the array, all we need to know is the type of the elements. To create the array, however, we need to know the number of elements involved. Sometimes we know this *a priori*. Either the number is fixed or can be computed from information available when the array is created. Sometimes we do not know the number of elements involved, as when the amount of data is unknown until it has all been read. This gives rise to two different ways of using arrays; we designate them as **right-sized arrays** (when the size is known) and **variable-sized arrays** (when the size is unknown). Both ways will be discussed in the following sections.

> **RIGHT-SIZED ARRAY** definition to come.
>
> **VARIABLE-SIZED ARRAY** definition to come.
>
> A **TRAVERSAL** of a data structure (such as an array) is a process in which some operation is performed on each element of the structure.

The most common form of processing an array is to perform some set of operations on each element of the array. This process is called **traversal**. Regardless of the kind of array, array traversal is defined by the programming pattern of Figure 11.6.

Processing Right-sized Arrays

Above-average-rainfall program. Right-sized arrays can be used whenever we know, *a priori*, how many elements are involved. For example, consider a program that determines which months of the year have more than average rainfall for that year. The data would consist of 12 values, indicating the rainfall for the months of the year. The data cannot be processed sequentially, since it is impossible to determine whether a month's rainfall is above average unless the yearly average is known, and the average cannot be

Programming Pattern

```
for all elements (i) of the array (a)
    process a[i]
```

FIGURE 11.6 General array-traversal programming pattern

determined until the rainfall for all months has been accessed. The solution is to use an array to store the rainfall values. Since there are always 12 months in the year, we know that the array will have 12 elements, so a right-sized array can be used. Figure 11.7 shows the program.

```
import BasicIO.*;

/** This program lists the months of the year with above-
 ** average rainfall.
 **
 ** @author D. Hughes
 **
 ** @version    1.0 (Mar. 2001)                          */

public class Rainfall {

    private ASCIIDataFile      in;         // file with rainfall data
    private ASCIIDisplayer     out;        // displayer for output

    private String       month[] = {"Jan","Feb","Mar","Apr","May","June",
                                    "July","Aug","Sept","Oct","Nov","Dec"};

    /** The constructor reads the rainfall data, computes the
     ** average rainfall and lists the months with above-
     ** average rainfall.                                    */

    public Rainfall ( ) {

        in = new ASCIIDataFile();
        out = new ASCIIDisplayer();
        display();
        in.close();
        out.close();

    };  // constructor
```

(Continued)

```
    /** This method displays the months with above-average
     ** rainfall.                                              */

    private void display ( ) {

        double  rainfall[]; // rainfall for each month
        double  totRain;    // total rainfall for the year
        double  aveRain;    // average monthly rainfall
        int     i;

        rainfall = new double[12];
        totRain = 0;
        for ( i=0 ; i<rainfall.length ; i++ ) {
            rainfall[i] = in.readDouble();
            totRain = totRain + rainfall[i];
        };
        aveRain = totRain / rainfall.length;
        writeHeader(aveRain);
        for ( i=0 ; i<rainfall.length ; i++ ) {
            if ( rainfall[i] > aveRain ) {
                writeDetail(month[i],rainfall[i]);
            };
        };

    };  // display


    /** This method writes the header for the rainfall report.
     **
     ** @param  aveRain average rainfall.                      */

    private void writeHeader ( double aveRain ) {

        out.writeLabel("Average rainfall: ");
        out.writeDouble(aveRain,0,1);
        out.writeEOL();
        out.writeEOL();
        out.writeLabel("Months with above average rainfall");
        out.writeEOL();
        out.writeLabel("Month  Rainfall");
        out.writeEOL();

    };  // writeHeader
```

(Continued)

```
    /** This method writes the detail line for the rainfall
     ** report.
     **
     ** @param  String      month name
     ** @param  rainfall    rainfall amount.          */

    private void writeDetail ( String month, double rainfall ) {

        out.writeLabel(" ");
        out.writeString(month,4);
        out.writeDouble(rainfall,8,1);
        out.writeEOL();

    };  // writeDetail

    public static void main ( String args[] ) { new Rainfall(); };

}   // Rainfall
```

FIGURE 11.7 Example—Above-average rainfall

The rainfall data (`rainfall`) is declared as a one-dimensional array of `doubles`, in which the month is the dimension. Before the data can be read into the array, the array must be created. Since we know the size, the array creation can use the constant `12`.

Array traversal. Loading the rainfall data is an example of array traversal—processing each element to load a value. For right-sized arrays, the specific pattern is given as the programming pattern in Figure 11.8.

The loop index variable (`i`) is used as the array subscript and must range over all the elements of the array. This means that the initial value for `i` must be `0` and, the last time through the loop, `i` must be `a.length-1` (hence `i<a.length`).

STYLE TIP

In this case, we could have used `12` instead of `a.length` since there will always be 12 months in a year. However, it is good practice to use the `length` attribute of a right-sized array as the loop bound instead of a constant, since even quantities considered as constant at the time the program is written might change.

Programming Pattern

```
for ( i=0 ; i<a.length ; i++ ) {
    process a[i]
};
```

FIGURE 11.8 Right-sized array-traversal programming pattern

The array traversal pattern is merged with a summation pattern to sum the data as it is being read. The merging of patterns is, as we have seen, quite common. Note the use of the subscripted array reference as a destination (left-hand side) to store the value in the array element and then as an expression (right-hand side) to accumulate the value into the sum. When the rainfall data has been read and the average computed, a second array traversal is used to determine which months have above-average rainfall.

Array initializer. Note the second array used in this example (`month`). For the purposes of the program, the months are represented by the indices into the rainfall array (that is, `0` is January, `1` is February, etc.). Although this representation is convenient for the program, it is not as appropriate for the human reader of the output. What we would like to do is print out the *name* of the corresponding month instead of the month number. The array `month` provides exactly that transformation. `month` is an array of strings—each element is a `String` object. Corresponding to index `i` is the string representing the `i`th month. For example, corresponding to `0` is `"Jan"`. We can simply index into `month` to get the appropriate month name string for output.

At the end of the declaration of `month` we see something new—an array initializer. On a variable declaration, it is possible to initialize the variable, establishing a first value. We have chosen to do this explicitly in an assignment statement in programs so far as an element of good style. However, there are some instances in which using an initializer is a good idea. When an array is to contain a set of specific values—not when every element is to be initialized to the same value, such as `0`—an array initializer is considerably more compact and easier to read. An **array initializer** is a sequence of values all of the same type, separated by commas and enclosed in braces (`{}`). The effect is to create a new array whose element type is the type of the values. In this case the type is `String` since the values are `String` literals. The new array has length equal to the number of values, in this case `12`. A reference to this array is then assigned to the identifier being declared, here `month`. Array initializers can only be used in a declaration. They are *not* an expression.

> An **ARRAY INITIALIZER** is a notation that specifies the initial value of each element in an array. In Java, an array initializer is enclosed in braces ({}) and can only be used in an array declaration.

Processing Variable-sized Arrays

More often than not, the number of elements that we need in an array is unknown when the program is being written and cannot even be computed before the array must be created. This requires another approach to array processing—what we call variable-sized arrays. Note that this technique is the only one possible in languages where the length of an array must be specified in the declaration.

Above-average-marks program. For example, say we have a file containing marks students have received in their courses and we wish to list those students whose marks are above average. This is essentially the same problem as in the previous section. The data file contains the student information but, unfortunately, it does not contain the

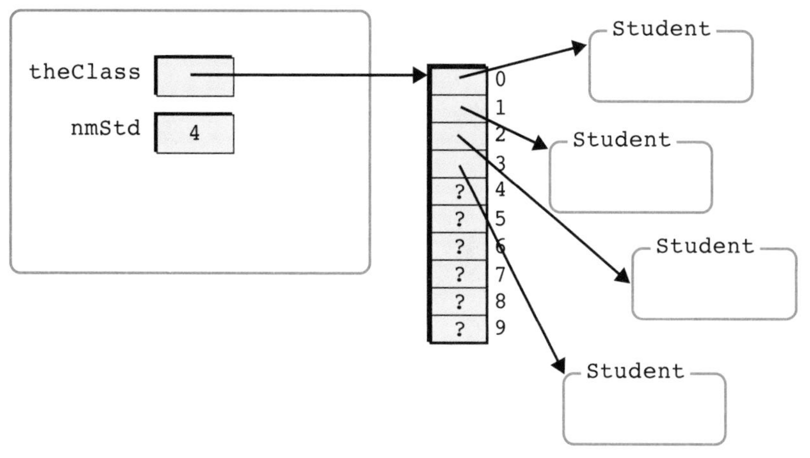

FIGURE 11.9 Variable-sized array

university average, nor a count of the number of students. As in the previous example, we cannot determine whether an individual student is above average until we have computed the overall university average; this computation requires input of all student information. We don't even know how many students there are until we have read them all, so how can we create the array? The only answer to this is to create an array (`theClass`) of arbitrary size. We choose a size when we write the program that we believe to be reasonable—not so small that a class won't fit and not so large as to waste space.

Since the number of students is unlikely to match the size of the array, only some of the elements of the array will contain relevant data. We need a scheme to determine which elements are relevant. The usual convention is to place the relevant items at the front of the array, starting at index `0` and continuing consecutively. Since the entire array isn't used, the array `length` attribute will not help us in processing, so we will need a variable (`numStd`) to keep track of the number of relevant values in the array. Figure 11.9 shows the situation if the array of students is created with `10` elements and there are only `4` students in the university.

Note that `theClass` references an array of `Student` references. This is appropriate since a `Student` variable is a reference to a `Student` object, and an element of a `Student` array is also a reference to a `Student` object.

Figure 11.10 shows the program, and the class specification for the `Student` class is given in Figure 11.11. Note that this is a different `Student` class than in Chapters 9 and 10 since this is the University's view of a student, whereas the previous class is a course instructor's view. It is not uncommon for different views of the same entity to produce different classes because a class is an abstraction of an entity, capturing only the information of interest in the view.

```
import BasicIO.*;

/** This program lists the students of the university that
 ** have above-average marks.
 **
 ** @author D. Hughes
 **
 ** @version    1.0 (Apr. 2001)                              */

public class AboveAverage {

    private final int   MAX_STD = 100;  // maximum number of students

    private ASCIIDataFile       in;     // file with student data
    private ASCIIDisplayer      out;    // displayer for output


    /** The constructor reads the student information, computes
     ** the university average, and displays the students that
     ** have above-average marks.                                */

    public AboveAverage ( ) {

        in = new ASCIIDataFile();
        out = new ASCIIDisplayer();
        display();
        in.close();
        out.close();

    };  // constructor


    /** This method displays the students with above-average
     ** marks.                                                   */

    private void display ( ) {

        Student theClass[]; // students in the university
        Student aStudent;   // one student
        int     numStd;     // number of students
```

(Continued)

```
    double  totMark;     // total of marks
    double  aveMark;     // average mark
    int     i;

    theClass = new Student[MAX_STD];
    numStd = 0;
    totMark = 0;
    while ( true ) {
        aStudent = new Student(in);
    if ( ! in.successful() | numStd >= MAX_STD ) break;
        theClass[numStd] = aStudent;
        totMark = totMark + theClass[numStd].getAverage();
        numStd = numStd + 1;
    };
    aveMark = totMark / numStd;
    writeHeader(aveMark);
    for ( i=0 ; i<numStd ; i++ ) {
        if ( theClass[i].getAverage() > aveMark ) {
            writeDetail(theClass[i].getStNum(), theClass[i].getAverage());
        };
    };

};  // display


/** This method writes the header for the mark report.
 **
 ** @param  ave average mark over all students.              */

private void writeHeader ( double ave ) {

    out.writeLabel("Average mark: ");
    out.writeDouble(ave,0,2);
    out.writeEOL();
    out.writeEOL();
    out.writeLabel("Students with above average mark");
    out.writeEOL();
    out.writeLabel(" St #   Mark");
    out.writeEOL();

};  // writeHeader
```

(Continued)

```
    /** This method writes a detail line for the mark report.
     **
     ** @param  stNum   the student number
     ** @param  ave     the student's average mark.          */

    private void writeDetail ( String stNum, double ave ) {

        out.writeString(stNum,6);
        out.writeDouble(ave,5,1);
        out.writeEOL();

    };  // writeDetail


    public static void main ( String args[] ) { new AboveAverage(); };


}   // AboveAverage
```

FIGURE 11.10 Example—Display above-average students

```
public class Student {
    public Student ( SimpleDataInput from ) ;
    public String getStNum ( ) ;
    public String getName ( ) ;
    public boolean registeredIn ( String course, String year ) ;
    public double getMark ( String course, String year ) ;
    public void setMark ( String course, String year, double mark ) ;
    public double getAverage ( ) ;
    public void writeTranscript ( SimpleDataOutput to ) ;
}   // Student
```

FIGURE 11.11 Example—`Student` class specification

Since the choice of the upper limit on class size—the size of the array—is arbitrary, it should be able to be easily changed. The declaration of `MAX_CLASS` and its consistent use throughout the program achieves this flexibility. Note the modifiers for `MAX_CLASS`. When declared `final`, an identifier's value may not be changed; it is constant. We have seen constant identifiers previously (in particular, `Math.PI`). A constant declaration must have an initializer to set the initial (only) value for the identifier.

STYLE TIP

It is a convention in Java to write constant identifiers in all uppercase letters and separate the words with underscores (_).

A constant identifier can be written anywhere a literal of the same type can be written. To change the maximum size of class the program can handle, the constant declaration is the only statement that must be modified. (Of course, the class will have to be recompiled.)

The array to hold the class is created using `MAX_CLASS` as the length. Note the subtle difference between creating an array of `Student` references using brackets and creating a single `Student` object using parentheses:

`new Student[MAX_CLASS]`	`new Student(in)`
array of `Student` *references*	*single* `Student` *object*

The loops. The loop to read the students and place them into the array is a modification of the process to EOF pattern. Clearly, we stop when we reach end-of-file. However, there is one other reason to stop—when we run out of space in the array. This requires the compound condition for loop termination. Since `numStd` is the number of students in the array so far, it is initialized to `0`. When we read a new student, we place the student into the next available position in the array, as designated by `numStd`, and then we increase `numStd` by `1`. Essentially, `numStd` always refers to the first *vacant* position in the array; positions `0`–`numStd-1` contain students. When we try to read the next student, we do so into a temporary variable (`aStudent`). This is done since we haven't yet checked to see if there is room for another student, so trying to read into `theClass[numStd]` could yield an error. Only after the program verifies that a student was actually read and that there is room in the array, is the reference stored into the array.

The input loop is also used to perform the summation, merging the read to EOF and summation patterns. The construct:

```
theClass[numStd].getAverage()
```

results in the execution of the `getAverage` method of the student object referenced by element `numStd` of the array `theClass`. Remember, a subscripted variable (`theClass[numStd]`) can be used wherever a variable of the same type (`Student`) can be used and even as the reference to the object to perform a method. The `Student` object is, of course, the student that was just read. The method call returns the student's overall average and is added to the total (`totMark`). Note that this statement was carefully placed before the increment of `numStd` (why?).

The loop determining the students who are above average is the version of the array traversal pattern for variable-sized arrays as given in the programming pattern of Figure 11.12. Here the variable indicating the number of relevant elements in the array is used in the test for loop termination.

Programming Pattern

```
for ( i=0 ; i<numberOfElements ; i++ ) {
    process a[i]
};
```

FIGURE 11.12 Variable-sized array-traversal programming pattern

11.3 ARRAYS AND METHODS

Like any other type, arrays may be passed as parameters to a method. Since array variables are reference variables, what is passed is the reference to the array. The formal parameter becomes another reference to the *same* array. Within the method, the array elements can be modified, but the array itself remains the same.

Examples

As an example, consider a modification to the example of Figure 11.7 to use a method to read the rainfall data. The modified code might look like Figure 11.13. Here ellipses (⋮) indicate lines of code unchanged and not reproduced, and changes and additions are noted in **bold**.

Arrays as method parameters. The array is passed as an actual parameter by giving its name without a subscript to indicate that the array reference is being passed. If the array name is followed by a subscript, just the value of the indicated element would be passed. The corresponding formal parameter specifies an array by including the brackets after the name. The situation just before the first statement of the method is executed is shown in Figure 11.14.

Note that the reference to the array is copied to the formal parameter. Both `rainfall` (in the constructor) and `rain` (in `readRain`) refer to the same array. Within the method, the `length` attribute of the array can be used to control the loop. Note that `length` is an attribute of the array that the variable `rain` is referencing, not an attribute of the variable `rain` itself. As values are read, they are placed into the array. When the method returns, the elements of the array referenced by `rainfall` have been modified.

This mechanism can also be used for variable-sized arrays, with slight modification. The method will also have to determine the number of elements placed in the array. Since a method is working with a copy of the actual parameter, attempting to return a value by changing the formal parameter won't have any effect. The answer is for the method to return the number of elements read as its result. The example in Figure 11.15 shows the input method for reading the student data for a modified version of Figure 11.10. The method would be called in the following statement:

```
numStd = readClass(theClass);
```

As before, the formal parameter is a copy of the reference to the array provided as the actual parameter, so the method modifies the elements of the array. The `length` attribute of the formal parameter can be used to determine the physical length of the array—the limit on the number of students that can be read. When the data has been read and the students counted, the count is returned as the result of the method and assigned to `numStd`. This gives the desired result.

The technique of passing an array as a parameter can be used whenever a method requires access to an array, not just for reading values into the array. When the array is

```
import BasicIO.*;
        ⋮
public class Rainfall {
        ⋮
        ⋮
    private void display ( ) {

        double  rainfall[]; // rainfall for each month
        double  totRain;    // total rainfall for the year
        double  aveRain;    // average monthly rainfall
        int     i;
        ⋮
        ⋮
        rainfall = new double[12];
        readRain(rainfall);
        totRain = 0;
        for ( i=0 ; i<rainfall.length ; i++ ) {
            totRain = totRain + rainfall[i];
        };
        aveRain = totRain / rainfall.length;
        ⋮
        ⋮
        in.close();
        out.close();

    };  // constructor


    /** This method reads the rainfall data.
     **
     ** @param  rainrainfall for year                                */

    private void readRain ( double rain[] ) {

        int     i;

        for ( i=0 ; i<rain.length ; i++ ) {
            rain[i] = in.readDouble();
        };

    };  // readRain
        ⋮
        ⋮
}   // Rainfall
```

FIGURE 11.13 Example—Above-average rainfall with input method

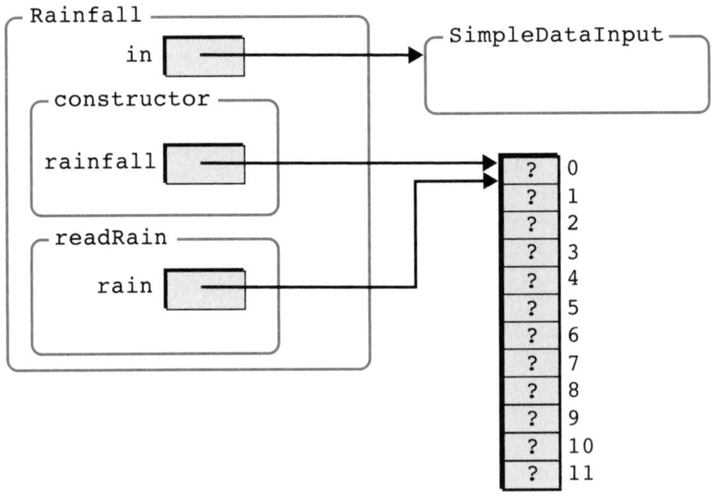

FIGURE 11.14 Array parameter

```
private int readClass ( Student theClass[] ) {

    int count;  // number of students

    count = 0;
    while ( true ) {
        aStudent = new Student(in);
    if ( ! in.successful() | count >= theClass.length ) break;
        theClass[count] = aStudent;
        count = count + 1;
    };
    return count;

};  // readClass
```

FIGURE 11.15 Example—Method reading data into variable-sized array

right-sized, it is sufficient to simply pass the array since the length of the array can be determined from the `length` attribute. When the array is variable-sized, although the physical length can be determined from the `length` attribute, the actual number of relevant elements needs to be known, so this must be passed as an additional parameter in a method header such as:

```
private void processStudents ( Student theClass, int numStd ) {
```

Arrays as results of function methods. Arrays may also be returned as the result of a method. When an array is passed as a parameter, the method is working with a copy of the reference to the array and so cannot replace it with a new array. The only way a method can produce a new array is to return it as the method result. The data input method from Figure 11.13 could be rewritten, once more, as in Figure 11.16 and called by the statement:

```
rainfall = readRain();
```

Note the unusual notation in the method header. The notation:

```
Type [ ]
```

is used as the result type when the result is an array of *Type*. This is essentially an array declaration with the identifier omitted. In Figure 11.16, the method `readRain` returns a reference to an array of `double`.

Within the method, a new array is created with reference stored in the local variable `rain`. This array is then filled with data as before. When the method is complete, the array referenced by the local variable is returned; that is, the reference to the array is returned. This reference is then stored in the variable `rainfall` in the invoking statement, producing the desired result. This technique cannot be used for variable-sized arrays since the method would have to return two values (the array and the number of relevant elements), and this is not possible.

```
private double[] readRain ( ) {

    double  rain[];
    int     i;

    rain = new double[12];
    for ( i=0 ; i<rain.length ; i++ ) {
        rain[i] = in.readDouble();
    };
    return rain;

};  // readRain
```

FIGURE 11.16 Example—Method returning an array

11.4 RANDOM PROCESSING OF ARRAYS

Previously, all of our examples have processed the arrays in sequential order, from element 0 through one less than the length of the array. One of the advantages of arrays is the ability they give us to process the elements in any order necessary. When there is no particular order to the processing of the elements, we call the processing **random access**.

> **RANDOM ACCESS** refers to the processing of a collection of items, in an array for example, in unpredictable order.

If we consider the syntax for array subscripting (Figure 11.4), we see that the subscript may be any expression that evaluates to a valid index. Our examples have simply used a variable (such as i) that is incremented from 0 to the length of the array minus 1 (**sequential access**). For random access, an expression that computes the element in which we are interested would be used.

Consider Figure 11.17. This program counts the frequency of occurrence of the letters within the input text. Such a program might be useful in **cryptography**, the study of encryption or "secret codes," where such frequencies can be used as a guide for letter substitution in breaking a code.

```
import BasicIO.*;

/** This class reads a text file and counts the number of
 ** occurrences of each letter (ignoring case).
 **
 ** @author D. Hughes
 **
 ** @version    1.0 (Apr. 2001)                              */

public class LetterCount {

    private ASCIIDataFile       in;      // file for text file
    private ASCIIDisplayer      out;     // displayer for statistics

    /** The constructor counts the frequency of occurrence of
     ** each letter.                                          */

    public LetterCount ( ) {

        in = new ASCIIDataFile();
```

(Continued)

```
        out = new ASCIIDisplayer();
        display();
        in.close();
        out.close();

    };  // constructor


    /** This method displays the letter count statistics for the
     ** text.                                                  */

    private void display ( ) {

        int     letCount[];      // letter frequency counts
        int     nLines;          // number of lines in text
        char    c;               // the character
        int     i;

        letCount = new int[26];
        for ( i=0 ; i<letCount.length ; i++ ) {
            letCount[i] = 0;
        };
        nLines = 0;
        while ( true ) {
            c = in.readC();
        if ( ! in.successful() ) break;
            if ( c == '\n' ) {
                nLines = nLines + 1;
            }
            else {
                if ( Character.isLetter(c) ) {
                    i = Character.toLowerCase(c) - 'a';
                    letCount[i] = letCount[i] + 1;
                };
            }
        };
        writeHeader(nLines);
        for ( i=0 ; i<letCount.length ; i++ ) {
            writeDetail((char)(i+'a'),letCount[i]);
        };

    };  // display
```

(Continued)

```
    /** This method writes the report header.
     **
     ** @param  lines   number of lines processed.              */

    private void writeHeader ( int lines ) {

        out.writeInt(lines);
        out.writeLabel(" lines of text processed.");
        out.writeEOL();
        out.writeEOL();
        out.writeLabel("Letter Frequency");
        out.writeEOL();

    };  // writeHeader


    /** This method writes a detail line of the report.
     **
     ** @param  letter  the letter
     ** @param  freq    the frequency of occurrence.            */

    private void writeDetail ( char letter, int freq ) {

        out.writeLabel("  ");
        out.writeChar(letter);
        out.writeLabel("      ");
        out.writeInt(freq);
        out.writeEOL();

    };  // writeDetail


    public static void main ( String args[] ) { new LetterCount(); };


}   // LetterCount
```

FIGURE 11.17 Example—Counting letter frequencies

The program uses an array of `int` (`letCount`) as counters of the number of occurrences of each of the alphabetic characters. Since the number of letters (26) is known beforehand, a right-sized array can be used. `letCount[0]` will be the count of the `a`s, `letCount[1]` the `b`s, and so on. Since this is essentially a summation problem with 26 different sums, all 26 elements are initialized to `0` using a right-sized array traversal. The characters of the text are then processed until end-of-file, using the process line-oriented text pattern, which also serves as the loop of a summation pattern. The number of lines is incremented whenever a line separator is encountered. If the character is a letter of either case, the appropriate letter count is incremented. By converting the letter to lowercase and then subtracting `'a'`, the letters are mapped onto the integers from `0` to `25` with `'a'` mapped to `0`, `'b'` to `1`, etc. This value is then used to subscript the array of counters (`letCount`), to increment the correct count.

When the file has been processed, a table is generated displaying the counts for each letter; in other words, the elements of `letCount`. To make the table look better, the first column is the letter itself. This is produced by adding `'a'` to the index (`i = 0, 1, ...`) and casting the result to `char`, producing the characters `'a'`, `'b'`, etc., consecutively.

In general, random processing of arrays involves a computation on some data value (such as `c`, the letter input). The computation yields an index into an array (`letCount`), and then the selected array element is processed. Often results are reported using a subsequent sequential traversal of the array.

*11.5 PROCESSING `String` DATA AS ARRAY OF `char`

In Section 10.3 we considered processing `String` data. In situations in which considerable character-by-character modification of the string is required, it is often inefficient to use the `String` methods. Consider the palindrome example (Figure 10.6). In the method `reverse`, the characters of the string are accessed one-by-one using `charAt`, and then “glued” back together, in reverse order, using concatenation (+). Since `String` objects are immutable, the concatenation operation produces a new `String` object each time. This means that, for a string of length `n` (with `n` characters), `n + 1` `String` objects are created and only the last one ultimately used. Since object creation involves considerable overhead of processing time and storage space, this approach is quite inefficient.

The `String` class provides a method `toCharArray` that returns a new array of characters of the same length as the string and containing each of the characters of the string. Since arrays are *not* immutable, we can manipulate this array more efficiently than the original string and then convert it back to a new string using the version of the `String` constructor that takes an array of characters as a parameter. This constructor results in a string containing the characters from the array.

Figure 10.6 can be modified by simply replacing the method `reverse` with the new version given in the example in Figure 11.18. The method first obtains an array of

```
private String reverse ( String str ) {

    char    theString[];// string as array of characters
    char    c;
    int     i;

    theString = str.toCharArray();
    for ( i=0 ; i<theString.length/2 ; i++ ) {
        c = theString[i];
        theString[i] = theString[theString.length-1-i];
        theString[theString.length-1-i] = c;
    };
    return new String(theString);

};  // reverse
```

FIGURE 11.18 Example—Reversing a string

characters, `theString`, from the parameter `str`. This array is right-sized; it has exactly the same number of elements as the original string has characters. The method goes through a loop exchanging the `i`th character with the `i`th character from the end of the string. It exchanges the character at index `0` with the character at index `theString.length-1`, the character at index `1` with the character at index `theString.length-2`, etc. This exchange has to be done only to the halfway point of the string (`<theString.length/2`), since each time through the loop two characters of the string are moved.

Note how the characters are exchanged. First the character at one position is saved in a temporary variable (`c`). The other character is stored in the array, replacing the first. Finally, the saved character is stored, replacing the second. This effects the exchange. It cannot be done without the temporary variable, or both positions will wind up with the same value. This is an example of a programming pattern for exchanging values as shown in Figure 11.19.

When the exchange loop is complete, the characters in the array are in reverse order. The array of characters is used to produce a new string using the appropriate `String` constructor. Note that this version of `reverse` creates only two new objects—an array of characters and a `String`—regardless of the number of characters in the original string; it is much more efficient than the original.

Programming Pattern

```
temp = firstVar;
firstVar = secondVar;
secondVar = temp;
```

FIGURE 11.19 Exchanging-values programming pattern

CASE STUDY Grade-Reporting System Revisited

Problem

Now that we have seen strings and arrays, it is a good time to revisit the grade-reporting system developed in Chapter 9. We have already seen (in Section 10.2) that we could modify the `Student` class to store the student's name. We also saw how storing the student number as a string would improve the report by removing the commas. We will now look at how the system can be generalized to allow for any number of pieces of work completed by students in the course.

As originally written, the system allowed four pieces of work specifically identified as assignments 1 and 2, a test, and an exam. In the `Student` class (Figure 9.17), the marks in these pieces of work were stored in specific variables (`a1`, `a2`, `test`, and `exam`). Similarly, in the `MarkingScheme` class (Figure 9.16), the bases and weights were stored in `a1Base`, `a1Weight`, and so on. Although the values were specifically identified as being an assignment, test, or exam, there was no difference in the way these values were processed. In each case, to compute the final mark, the mark was divided by the base and multiplied by the weight.

Analysis and Design

We can extend the system by using arrays to hold the student's marks (`marks`, in `Student`) and the bases and weights (`bases`, `weights`, in `MarkingScheme`). We need to ensure that the corresponding elements in the three arrays contain the information about the same piece of work. That is, we need to know that `marks[i]` is the mark for the piece of work whose base mark is `bases[i]` and whose weight is `weights[i]`. Then the final mark can be calculated by dividing the element from the `mark` array by the corresponding element in the `bases` array and multiplying by the corresponding element in the `weights` array.

The remaining issues consist of knowing how many pieces of work exist and deciding which class has responsibility for this information. Clearly, if the number of pieces of work is likely to change from year to year, we don't want to constrain the program to a particular value, so this value will have to be read from the data file. Since the number of pieces of work pertains to the course as a whole, it probably wouldn't reside with the student. However, it could be argued that it is really part of the marking scheme because the marking scheme defines what pieces of work there are and their bases and weights. This is the choice we will make.

The arrays for the bases and weights in `MarkingScheme` can be made right-sized. Assuming the data stream has the count of the number of pieces of work before the bases and weights, the count can be known before we have to create the arrays. What about the array for the marks in the `Student` class? The `Student` class can know of the number of pieces of work in two ways: (1) if it is informed by supplying this value as a parameter on the constructor, or (2) if it can inquire of some other class by using an accessor method.

Since the `MarkingScheme` class knows the information, but the `Student` doesn't know about the marking scheme (except within its `calcFinalMark` method), the only choice is for the value to be passed as a parameter to the constructor. Since the `Course` object creates the `Student` objects, it will have to pass this value. For the `Course` object to know the number of pieces of work, it will have to inquire of the `MarkingScheme` object (of which it does know).

To make a long story short, the `MarkingScheme` object will be responsible for reading and keeping track of the number of pieces of work. It will supply an accessor method (`getNumWork`) to access this value. The `Course` object will, when creating a `Student` object, pass this value to the `Student` constructor, which can then create the `mark` array as a right-sized array and use this to input the correct number of marks.

To make the system a bit nicer, a couple of other changes are made. As described in Section 10.2, the student's name is included as an attribute of `Student` and the student number is processed as a string. The report is augmented to include the student's name in the detail line. To allow the program to be used for any course, the course name is included in the data file and used in the report heading.

The course name is clearly an attribute of the course, so the `Course` takes responsibility and provides an accessor method (`getCourseName`). Since the `Report` needs the course name to generate the report header, the main class passes this information to the `Report` constructor. The course name is provided as a string as the first data item in the data file.

A sample input file is shown in Figure 11.20. The first line is the course name, the second is the number of pieces of work. This is followed with the appropriate number of pairs: (`base`, `weight`) defining the marking scheme. Following this is the student data. For each student (until EOF) there is a student number, a name, and marks for each of the pieces of work.

Figure 11.21 shows a sample report produced by the system, with page size of 12 lines. The header, which is repeated at the top of each page, includes the page number and the course name. The detail lines include the student number, name, and final mark. The summary includes the course average.

```
COSC 1P02
4
10   10
10   10
50   30
100  50
111111    Doe, John         10  10  50  100
222222    Average, Joe5     5   25  50
333333    Missing, Im 0     0   0   0
444444    Student, Jane     8   7   37  75
```

FIGURE 11.20 Sample data file for `GradeReport2`

```
Final Mark Report                    page:  1

                COSC 1P02

 ST #             Name                  Mark
------------------------------------------------

111111   Doe, John                     100.0
222222   Average, Joe                   50.0
333333   Missing, Im                     0.0

Final Mark Report                    page:  2

                COSC 1P02

 ST #             Name                  Mark
------------------------------------------------

444444   Student, Jane                  74.7

------------------------------------------------

                        Average:        56.2
```

FIGURE 11.21 Sample report from `GradeReport2`

Implementation

The only change to the main class (`GradeReport`, Figure 9.20), is in the creation of the `Report` object. To provide the course name for the report header, the main class must pass the course name (obtained from the course object) to the `Report` constructor as follows:

```
aReport = new Report(reportFile,aCourse.getCourseName(),12);
```

The first parameter is the file for the report, the second the course name, and the third the page size.

Figure 11.22 shows the modified version (from Figure 9.18) of the `Course` class. The course name (`courseName`) becomes an additional instance variable, which is read in the constructor. An additional accessor method (`getCourseName`) provides access to this name. In the `doReport` method, the number of pieces of work (`numWork`) is accessed from the `MarkingScheme` and passed to the `Student` constructor.

```
import BasicIO.*;
    ⋮
public class Course {

    private SimpleDataInput courseData;     // input stream for data
    private String          courseName;     // name of the course
    private MarkingScheme   scheme;         // marking scheme for course
        ⋮
    public Course ( SimpleDataInput from ) {

        courseData = from;
        courseName = courseData.readString();
        scheme = new MarkingScheme(courseData);

    };  // constructor


    /** This method returns the name of the course.
      **
      ** @return String  the course name.                          */

     public String getCourseName ( ) {

        return courseName;

     }; // getCourseName
        ⋮
        ⋮
    public void doReport ( Report theReport ) {

        Student aStudent;               // one student
        int     numWork;                // number of pieces of work
        double  totMark;                // total of students' marks
        int     numStd;                 // number of students in course

        numWork = scheme.getNumWork();
        numStd = 0;
        totMark = 0;
        while ( true ) {
            aStudent = new Student(courseData,numWork);
```

(Continued)

```
        if ( ! courseData.successful() ) break;
            numStd = numStd + 1;
            aStudent.calcFinalMark(scheme);
            totMark = totMark + aStudent.getFinalMark();
            theReport.writeDetailLine(aStudent);
        };
        theReport.writeSummary(totMark/numStd);
        return numStd;

    };  // doReport


}   // Course
```

FIGURE 11.22 Example—Modified Course class

Figure 11.23 shows the modified version (from Figure 9.17) of the `Student` class. The student number (`stNum`) is now a `String`, and a new instance variable (`name`) for the name has been added. The marks for the pieces of work are now represented by an array (`marks`). The constructor includes an extra parameter (`numWork`), which is used to create the right-sized `marks` array. The constructor reads the student number as a `String` and reads the name. It then reads the appropriate number of marks into the `marks` array. The `getStNum` accessor method returns a `String` and there is an accessor method for the name (`getName`). The accessor methods for the individual pieces of work have been replaced by the method `getMark` that takes, as an additional parameter, the index (`work`) of the mark field to be accessed. `calcFinalMark` passes the entire `marks` array to the `MarkingScheme` to compute the final mark.

```
import BasicIO.*;
   ⋮
public class Student {


    private String  stNum;              // student number
    private String  name;               // name
    private double  marks[];            // marks
    private double  finalMark;          // final mark
        ⋮
        ⋮
    public Student ( ASCIIDataFile from, int numWork ) {

        int      i;
```

(Continued)

```
        stNum = from.readString();
        if ( from.successful() ) {
            name = from.readString();
            marks = new double[numWork];
            for ( i=0 ; i<marks.length ; i++ ) {
                marks[i] = from.readDouble();
            };
            finalMark = -1;
        };

    };  // constructor
        :
        :
    public String getStNum ( ) {

        return stNum;

    };  // getStNum


    /** This method returns the student's name.
      **
      ** @return String  the student's name                         */

    public String getName ( ) {

        return name;

    };  // getName


    /** This method returns the student's mark in a specified
      ** piece of work.
      **
      ** @param  work    the piece of work number
      **
      ** @return double  the student's mark                         */

    public double getMark ( int work ) {
```

(Continued)

```
        return marks[work];

    };  // getMark
        :
        :
    public void calcFinalMark( MarkingScheme ms ) {

        finalMark = ms.apply(marks);

    };  // calcFinalMark


}   // Student
```

FIGURE 11.23 Example—Modified Student class

Figure 11.24 shows the MarkingScheme class as modified (from Figure 9.16). Considerable code has been changed since the entire representation of the marking scheme data has changed. The eight instance variables for bases and weights have been replaced by the two arrays: bases and weights. An additional instance variable representing the number of pieces of work (numPow) is included, although it is not strictly necessary; it could be determined from the length attribute of the arrays. The constructor reads the number of pieces of work, creates the arrays, and then reads the bases and weights in pairs. Since the class is responsible for the number of pieces of work, it provides an accessor method for this information. Finally, the apply method has been modified to take an array of double representing the marks (marks). It now uses an array traversal and summation loop to compute the scaled, weighted sum of the marks, producing the final mark.

```
import BasicIO.*;
   :
public class MarkingScheme {

    private int     numWork;          // number of pieces of work
    private double  bases[];          // base marks for pieces of work
    private double  weights[];        // weights for pieces of work
        :
        :
    public MarkingScheme ( ASCIIDataFile from ) {

        int     i;
        numWork = from.readInt();
```

(Continued)

```
        bases = new double[numWork];
        weights = new double[numWork];
        for ( i=0 ; i<bases.length ; i++ ) {
            bases[i] = from.readDouble();
            weights[i] = from.readDouble();
        };

    };  // constructor

    /** This method returns the number of pieces of work
      ** contributing to the final mark.
      **
      ** @return int number of pieces of work

    public int getNumWork ( ) {

        return numWork;

    };  // getNumWork
        :
        :
    public double apply ( double marks[] ) {

        double  result;      // computed final mark
        int     i;

        result = 0;
        for ( i=0 ; i<bases.length ; i++ ) {
            result = result + marks[i] / bases[i] * weights[i];
        };
        return result;

    };  // apply

}   // MarkingScheme
```

FIGURE 11.24 Example—Modified `MarkingScheme` class

Finally, Figure 11.25 shows the modified `Report` class. The modifications here are a result of the inclusion of the student's name in the report and the generalization to allow the course name to be supplied in the data instead of being fixed. To accommodate the addition of the student's name, the `writeHeader` and `writeFooter` methods are slightly modified to provide for a wider report and to include a header for the student name column. The `writeDetailLine` method is modified to display the student name (using the `getName` accessor method). To accommodate the generalization for course name, an instance variable for the course name (`courseName`) is defined; the constructor takes the course name as a parameter and saves it; and the `writeHeader` method displays this value instead of a literal.

```
import BasicIO.*;
   :
public class Report {

    private ASCIIReportFile report;      // output stream for report
    private String          courseName; // name of the course
       :
       :
    public Report ( SimpleDataOutput to, String cn, int ps ) {

        report = to;
        courseName = cn;
        pageSize = ps;
            :
    };  // constructor
        :
        :
    public void writeDetailLine ( Student std ) {
        :
        report.writeString(std.getStNum(),6);
        report.writeLabel("  ");
        report.writeString(std.getName(),20);
        report.writeDouble(std.getFinalMark(),7,1);
        :
    };  // writeDetailLine
        :
        :
    public void writeSummary ( double ave ) {
        :
        report.writeEOL();
        report.writeLabel("-------------------------------------");
        report.writeEOL();
        report.writeEOL();
        report.writeLabel("                           Average:");
        :
```

(Continued)

```
    };  // writeSummary
      :
      :
    private void writeHeader ( ) {

        pageNum = pageNum + 1;
        report.writeLabel("Final Mark Report                  page: ");
        report.writeInt(pageNum,2);
        report.writeEOL();
        report.writeEOL();
        report.writeLabel("                    ");
        report.writeString(courseName);
        report.writeEOL();
        report.writeEOL();
        report.writeLabel(" ST #            Name                Mark");
        report.writeEOL();
        report.writeLabel("------------------------------------------");
        report.writeEOL();
          :
    };  // writeHeader
          :
}   // Report
```

FIGURE 11.25 Example—Modified Report class

Although these changes seem extensive, consider that they were caused by a change in the problem specification—to the analysis phase. The higher in the development process the change occurs, the more far-reaching the changes are likely to be, since they affect decisions made in *all* subsequent phases. This is why the early phases are so important. In this example, the system design was quite resilient to change and the changes were fairly easily implemented.

Testing and Debugging

As described in Section 9.2, the various classes should be tested individually and then in conjunction with collaborating classes until a complete system integration test is performed. As this is a new version of a previously released project, the test sets that were developed, and archived, for the original project should be re-run. Of course, since the input specifications have been modified, the data files will also have to be modified. The data files must now include the course name and the number of pieces of work, and each student record must include the student's name. Otherwise, the data values would be the same.

New tests must be devised to test the new functionality. The significant change in the specification is that the number of pieces of work may vary. This means that a new test with only one piece of work should be included as a boundary condition. The existing test will test multiple pieces of work.

11.6 MULTIDIMENSIONAL ARRAYS

Often data is presented in tabular form; see, for example, university enrollment statistics across universities and departments (Figure 11.26) or rainfall by month and year. In these cases, the data is said to have two dimensions because each piece of data has two attributes: university and department, or month and year. Sometimes there can be additional dimensions as well. For example, we might consider the university enrollments over years, as well as universities and departments. If we wish to represent such information as a whole, as opposed to processing the individual values sequentially, we need arrays of higher dimension, or **multidimensional arrays**.

A **MULTIDIMENSIONAL ARRAY** is an array whose items are selected by two or more subscripts.

The syntax shown in Figures 11.1 and 11.2 allow any number of dimensions for an array, as indicated by multiple sets of brackets (`[]`) in the declaration and multiple `DimExpr` in the array creation expression. A two-dimensional array can be viewed as a table of rows and columns.

Example—University Enrollment Report

For example, an array to represent the enrollment statistics for five departments at four universities is declared and created via the following statements:

```
int     enrol[][];
    :
enrol = new int[5][4];
```

The array `enrol` consists of five rows (the departments) and four columns (the universities), each element at the intersection of a row and column being an integer: the enrollment for the department at the university. The arrangement representing the data of Figure 11.26 looks like Figure 11.27.

	Adams	Beacon	Madison	Lexington	Total
Math.	162	15	237	35	449
Business	836	182	987	243	2,248
Comp. Sci.	263	91	321	110	785
Biology	743	432	648	0	1,823
French	42	59	117	57	275
Total	2,046	779	2,310	445	5,580

FIGURE 11.26 Enrollment statistics

	0	1	2	3
0	162	15	237	35
1	836	182	987	243
2	263	91	321	110
3	743	432	648	0
4	42	59	117	57

FIGURE 11.27 Array of enrollment data

In Java, the numbering of both the rows and columns begins at `0`, as for one-dimensional arrays. An individual element of the array is referenced via an array access (Figure 11.4) with two subscripts; for example, the reference:

```
enrol[3][2]
```

indexes the element in the fourth row, third column, which is the enrollment in Biology at Madison University (648 students).

Like one-dimensional arrays, multidimensional arrays can be processed as right-sized arrays or variable-sized arrays. When a right-sized two-dimensional array is used (like `enrol` above), the number of rows in the array is given by the `length` attribute (`enrol.length`⇒`5`). For any row, the number of columns in the row is given by the `length` attribute for that row (`enrol[2].length`⇒`4`).

STYLE TIP

Note: The way the `enrol` array was created ensures that each row has the same number of columns, as we would expect for a table, so it doesn't really matter which row we use to determine the number of columns. However, in Java, it is possible to have arrays in which the rows have different numbers of columns. In this case, it is critical to reference the `length` attribute for the correct row. We will be careful to write the code so that the correct `length` attribute is accessed to ensure correctness in all cases.

If a two-dimensional array is to be variable-sized, we would fill elements in the first rows and the first columns of each row—the top-left corner of the array. We would maintain two auxiliary variables: one indicating the number of rows that contain data and the other indicating the number of columns of those rows containing data. Processing would be similar to the one-dimensional case; the auxiliary variables would be used to bound the loops used in accessing the array instead of the `length` attribute.

Processing Two-dimensional Arrays

Like one-dimensional arrays, two-dimensional arrays are processed in either a sequential or a random manner. Random access is typically used when the array is a lookup table. For example, we use a lookup table to answer the question, "What is the enrollment in Biology at Madison University?" Here the row index (3) and column index (4) are known since they are obtained from input or they can be directly determined. Sequential access usually occurs when the entire array must be processed. Since the array is two-dimensional, there are two natural orders for sequential processing: row-by-row or column-by-column.

> A LOOKUP TABLE is a two-dimensional array in which a value in one column is used to locate (look up) the value in the other column(s).
>
> ROW-MAJOR ORDER refers to the storage or processing of a multi-dimensional array row-by-row.
>
> LEXICOGRAPHIC ORDER is when the elements of an array are stored or processed in such an order that, when the subscripts are concatenated, the resulting numbers are in numeric order. Row-major order is a lexicographic ordering.

The programming pattern of Figure 11.28 describes row-by-row (row-major) processing. The index `i` sequences through the rows while `j` sequences through the columns. The order of access is: `a[0][0]`, `a[0][1]`, `a[0][2]`, ..., `a[1][0]`, `a[1][1]`, `a[1][2]`, ..., `a[2][0]`, `a[2][1]`, `a[2][2]`.... Note that, if we look at the subscripts as digits of a number, the resulting numbers: `00`, `01`, `02`,... `10`, `11`, `12`, ... `20`, `21`, `22`,... are in numeric order. When information is processed in such an order, we say it is processed in lexicographic order.

Depending on the use of the pattern, there may be processing required before or after each row, or both. If the rows have no particular significance in the algorithm, those steps are omitted.

Programming Pattern

```
for ( i=0 ; i<a.length ; i++ ) {
    preprocessing for row i
    for ( j=0 ; j<a[i].length ; j++ ) {
        process a[i][j]
    };
    postprocessing for row i
};
```

FIGURE 11.28 Row-major array-processing programming pattern

Programming Pattern

```
for ( j=0 ; j<a[0].length ; j++ ) {
    preprocessing for column j
    for ( i=0 ; i<a.length ; i++ ) {
        process a[i][j]
    };
    postprocessing for column j
};
```

FIGURE 11.29 Column-major array-processing programming pattern

COLUMN-MAJOR ORDER refers to the storage or processing of a multi-dimensional array column-by-column.

An array is said to be **REGULAR** if all the rows have the same number of columns, all the planes have the same number of rows, and so on.

The programming pattern of Figure 11.29 describes column-by-column (**column-major**) processing. Again, the index `i` sequences through the rows and `j` through the columns. However, since `j` is in the outer loop, `i` sequences through all values for each value of `j`, giving the order of access: `a[0][0]`, `a[1][0]`, `a[2][0]`, ..., `a[0][1]`, `a[1][1]`, `a[2][1]`, ..., `a[0][2]`, `a[1][2]`, `a[2][2]`.... Note the use of `a[0].length` as limit on the outer loop. The pattern assumes the array is **regular**; in other words, that each row has the same number of columns. Only regular arrays can be processed in column-major order. If the array were not regular, it would be impossible to know how many columns to process. For this reason, row-major processing is preferred unless the array is known to be regular and the data *must* be processed column-by-column.

The example of Figure 11.30 demonstrates array processing. It reads a file containing university enrollment data and produces the summary table of Figure 11.26. The program creates a right-sized array (`enrol`) to hold the raw statistics (Figure 11.27). The two one-dimensional arrays `DEPTS` and `UNIVS`, created as constant arrays of strings, are the names of the departments and universities, respectively, and serve to define the number of departments and universities.

```
import BasicIO.*;

/** This class inputs enrollment statistics from a number of
 ** departments at a number of universities and produces a
 ** summary table with row, sum, and grand totals.
 **
 ** @author D. Hughes
 **
 ** @version    1.0 (Jan. 2001)                          */
```

(Continued)

```
public class UStats {

    private final String    UNIVS[] = {"   Adams","     Beacon",
                                        "  Madison","Lexington"};
    private final String    DEPTS[] = {"Math.","Business",
                                        "Comp. Sci.","Biology","French"};

    private ASCIIDataFile       dataFile;    // file for input
    private ASCIIReportFile     report;      // file for report
    private ASCIIDisplayer      msg;         // displayer for messages


    /** The constructor reads the enrollment table, computes the
     ** summary statistics, and prints them.                  */

     public UStats ( ) {

        dataFile = new ASCIIDataFile();
        report = new ASCIIReportFile();
        msg = new ASCIIDisplayer();
        display();
        dataFile.close();
        report.close();
        msg.close();

    };  // constructor


    /** This method reads the enrollment stats and generates and
     ** displays the summaries.                                            */

    private void display ( ) {

        int enrol[][];        // enrollment stats
        int uTotals[];        // University totals
        int dTotals[];        // Department totals
        int total;            // grand total

        msg.writeLabel("Processing.....");
        enrol = new int[DEPTS.length][UNIVS.length];
        readStats(enrol);
        uTotals = sumRows(enrol);
        dTotals = sumCols(enrol);
        total = sumAll(enrol);
```

(Continued)

```
        writeStats(enrol,uTotals,dTotals,total);
        msg.writeLabel(".....complete");
        msg.writeEOL();

    };  // display

    /** This method reads the enrollment statistics for the
     ** universities and departments.
     **
     ** @param  enrol   the array to read into.                    */

    private void readStats ( int stats[][] ) {

        int i, j;

        for ( i=0 ; i<stats.length ; i++ ) {
            for ( j=0 ; j<stats[i].length ; j++ ) {
                stats[i][j] = dataFile.readInt();
            };
        };

    };  // readStats

    /** This method sums the enrollments by row.
     **
     ** @param  stats   the enrollment statistics.
     **
     ** @return int[]   the row sums.                              */

    private int[] sumRows ( int stats[][] ) {

        int sums[];
        int i, j;

        sums = new int[stats.length];
        for ( i=0 ; i<stats.length ; i++ ) {
            sums[i] = 0;
            for ( j=0 ; j<stats[i].length ; j++ ) {
                sums[i] = sums[i] + stats[i][j];
            };
        };
        return sums;

    };  // sumRows
```

(Continued)

```
/** This method sums the enrollments by column.
 **
 ** @param  stats   the enrollment statistics.
 **
 ** @return int[]   the column sums.                             */

private int[] sumCols ( int stats[][] ) {

    int sums[];
    int i, j;

    sums = new int[stats[0].length];
    for ( j=0 ; j<stats[0].length ; j++ ) {
        sums[j] = 0;
        for ( i=0 ; i<stats.length ; i++ ) {
            sums[j] = sums[j] + stats[i][j];
        };
    };
    return sums;

};  // sumCols

/** This method computes the grand sum of the enrollment
 ** statistics.
 **
 ** @param  stats   the enrollment statistics.
 **
 ** @return int     the grand sum                                */

private int sumAll ( int stats[][] ) {

    int sum;
    int i, j;

    sum = 0;
    for ( i=0 ; i<stats.length ; i++ ) {
        for ( j=0 ; j<stats[i].length ; j++ ) {
            sum = sum + stats[i][j];
        };
    };
    return sum;

};  // sumAll
```

(Continued)

```
    /** This method displays the enrollment stats in a tabular
     ** format with labels and totals for each row and column, and
     ** a grand total.
     **
     ** @param  stats   the enrollment statistics.
     ** @param  rSums   the row sums.
     ** @param  cSums   the column sums.
     ** @param  sum     the grand sum.                          */

    private void writeStats( int stats[][], int rSums[], int cSums[], int sum ) {

        int i, j;

        report.writeLabel("            ");
        for ( i=0 ; i<UNIVS.length ; i++ ) {
            report.writeString(UNIVS[i],10);
        };
        report.writeLabel("      Total");
        report.writeEOL();
        report.writeEOL();
        for ( i=0 ; i<stats.length ; i++ ) {
            report.writeString(DEPTS[i],10);
            for ( j=0 ; j<stats[i].length ; j++ ) {
                report.writeInt(stats[i][j],10);
            };
            report.writeInt(rSums[i],10);
            report.writeEOL();
        };
        report.writeEOL();
        report.writeLabel("     Total ");
        for ( j=0 ; j<cSums.length ; j++ ) {
            report.writeInt(cSums[j],10);
        };
        report.writeInt(sum,10);
        report.writeEOL();

    };  // writeStats


    public static void main ( String args[] ) { new UStats(); };


}   // UStats
```

FIGURE 11.30 Example—Producing enrollment statistics

The method readStats is used to read the enrollment data. The previously created array enrol is passed as a parameter. Since the array is right-sized, no other parameters are necessary. The method uses the row-major array processing pattern to read the enrollment statistics since the data file contains the data in row-major order, by department.

The department totals require row-major processing of the array to produce a new array (dTotals). The method sumRows provides this processing. It creates a right-sized array (sums) and, using the row-major pattern, computes the sums for each row. The row preprocessing involves the initialization of the current row sum (sums[i]) to zero. The element processing involves accumulating the element into the current row sum. The method then returns the resulting one-dimensional array.

The sumCols method produces the university totals. The array is assumed to be regular and the column sum array is created right-sized, as the number of columns in the first row. The algorithm is an implementation of the column-major pattern. The current column sum (sums[j]) is initialized to zero as the column preprocessing. The element is accumulated into the column sum as the element processing. Again, the sums are returned by the method as an array.

The method sumAll produces the total enrollment in all departments at all universities. The order of processing makes no difference because all elements must be accumulated into the sum, so the row-major pattern is used. This pattern doesn't require the regularity assumption. The sum is initialized prior to the pattern because we only want to do it once. The elements are accumulated into the sum, which is returned by the method.

The table is produced by the method writeStats. This method is a merger of the report generation pattern (Figure 5.14) and the row-major pattern, since the report must be printed row-by-row. The headings are a listing of the universities (UNIVS). As row preprocessing, the department name (DEPTS[i]) is displayed. The element processing displays the element value. Finally, the row postprocessing involves displaying the row total (dTotals[i]). As in the report summary, the column totals (uTotals) are displayed.

This example is a bit contrived since it would be possible to read, produce all the row, column, and grand totals and display the table in a single pass over the array (after initialization). In fact, since the processing is sequential, it was not even necessary to use arrays (except for the column totals—why?). Also, the readStats method could have returned the two-dimensional array as a result, or the row and column sum methods could have been passed an array to fill. If the number of universities and departments were not known in advance, variable-sized arrays could have been used, passing the number of departments (rows) and number of universities (columns) as parameters as necessary.

■ SUMMARY

Arrays are a basic data structure provided in most programming languages. An array represents a collection of data values or object references. The individual values are accessed via subscripting, and a subscripted variable may be used wherever a variable of the element type of the array may be used. Arrays allow a program to collect the data to be processed in one place and then to process the data in nonsequential order. Arrays may be one-dimensional (e.g., a sequence, list, or vector), two-dimensional (a table), or of even higher dimension.

In Java, an array is similar to an object in that an array variable is a reference variable, pointing to the actual array. Like objects, an array must be created using `new` and the size of the array may be supplied at creation time. Once created, an array's size is fixed. Array elements are indexed by integers; the first element is element `0`.

Two styles of array processing arise: right-sized arrays and variable-sized arrays. For right-sized arrays, the size must be known *a priori* or must be computable at the time of creation. In this case, the array is created with the required number of elements and processing uses the length attribute (`a.length`). If the size is not known at creation time, an array of "large enough" size is created and only the first part—elements from `0`—is used to store data. An additional variable is used to record the number of elements in use in the array, and array processing is based on this variable. Arrays may be passed as method parameters and returned as method results, just like any object type.

For two-dimensional arrays, two processing patterns occur: row-major and column-major. In row-major processing, the elements of the array are processed row-wise, processing across row `0`, then row `1`, etc. In column-major processing, the elements are processed column-wise, down column `0`, then column `1`, etc.

REVIEW QUESTIONS

1. T F In Java, the elements of the array must all be of the same type.
2. T F Summing the elements of an array is a traversal.
3. T F The following initializes `a` to an array of the five `int` values `1` through `5`:

```
int a[];
a = {1,2,3,4,5};
```

4. T F A variable-sized array changes length to suit the amount of data being processed.

5. T F Array variables are reference variables.
6. T F Processing in row-major order is possible only in regular arrays.
7. T F An array may not be returned by a function method.
8. In the following code, what is the last element of the array?

```
int a[];
a = new int[5];
```

   a) `a[1]` b) `a[5]`
   c) `a[a.length]` d) `a[4]`

9. In processing a right-sized array:
   a) every element should contain data.
   b) the `length` attribute should be used for traversal.
   c) the length of the array must be known.
   d) all of the above are true.

10. What is the value of `s` after the following code?

```
int i, a[];
make(a,5);
s = 0;
for ( i=0 ; i<a.length ; i++ ) {
   s = s + a[i];
};
⋮
private void make ( int a[], int s ) {
   int  i;
   a = new int[s];
   for ( i=0 ; i<a.length ; i++ ) {
         a[i] = i;
   };
}; // make
```

   a) 0 b) 5
   c) 15 d) none of the above

11. Which of the following is the access pattern for lexicographic order?
   a) `a[1][2], a[1][1], a[1][0], a[0][2], a[0][1], a[0][0]`
   b) `a[0][0], a[0][1], a[0][2], a[1][0], a[1][1], a[1][2]`
   c) `a[0][0], a[1][1], a[2][2], a[3][3], a[4][4], a[5][5]`
   d) `a[0][0], a[1][0], a[0][1], a[1][1], a[0][2], a[1][2]`

12. What is the value of the variable `s` after the following code?

```
int i, s;
int a[][] = {{1,2,3},{2,3,4},{3,4,5}};
s = 0;
for ( i=0 ; i<a[0].length ; i++ ) {
   s = s + a[i,i];
};
```

a) 0 b) 6
c) 9 d) 27

13. A variable declared `final`:
    a) is an instance variable.
    b) may not be changed (assigned to).
    c) must have an initializer.
    d) may not be changed and must have an initializer; b and c are true.
14. When passing a variable-sized array as a parameter:
    a) the formal parameter must indicate the array length.
    b) the array length is passed as an additional parameter.
    c) the array length can be determined using the `length` attribute of the formal parameter.
    d) none of the above is true.
15. When performing random processing of an array:
    a) the elements are processed in arbitrary order.
    b) the array must be regular.
    c) the array must be right-sized.
    d) all of the above are true.

EXERCISES

1. Write a method that computes the dot product of two vectors stored in right-sized arrays. The method would have header:

```
private double dotProd ( double a[], double b[] )
```

   The dot-product is the sum of the products of the corresponding elements of the vectors. For example, if `a = {1,2,3,4}` and `b = {2,4,6,8}`, the dot product would be `60 = 1*2 + 2*4 + 3*6 + 4*8`. You may assume that the two arrays are the same size. Write a main class to test this method.

2. The sieve of Erostosthenes is an efficient process for determining all the prime numbers up to a specific limit. The process uses an array of `boolean` values, each indicating whether or not the element's index is a prime. For example, if the array is called `sieve`, then `sieve[2]` would be `true` since `2` is a prime, while `sieve[4]` would be `false` since `4` is not a prime. The array is initialized so all elements are `true`. Then, starting at position `2`, the next `true` element is located. Now, the element at each multiple of this index value is set to `false`. Then the next `true` element is located and the multiples are set to `false`. This process continues until the search for `true` values reaches the halfway point in the array. The `true` elements indicate the primes.

   Write a program that uses the sieve method to find and list (to an `ASCIIDisplayer`) all primes up to the limit entered by the user from an `ASCIIPrompter`.

3. Often more important in code-breaking than the frequency of occurrence of single letters is the frequency of occurrence of letter pairs (or digraphs). In a manner similar to that shown in Figure 11.17, write a program that reads a text document (`ASCIIDataFile`) and produces a table representing the frequency of occurrence of each letter pair. The rows of the table will indicate the first letter of the pair, and the columns will indicate the second letter of the pair. Be sure to record every pair. A four-letter word has three pairs; for example, the pairs in `week` are: `we`, `ee` and `ek`.

4. At Broccoli University, many departments use multiple-choice tests for evaluation of students. Marking these by hand is tedious and error-prone, so a computer program to perform this task is desired. The Computation Center has purchased a mark-sense form reader that will read answer sheets and produce a data file containing the students' answers. You have been contracted to produce the program that marks the tests and generates a report.

   A multiple-choice test consists of a number of questions for which responses are a choice from five possible answers (denoted: `A`, `B`, `C`, `D`, `E`). There is an answer key giving the correct responses. A student's mark is computed as the number correct minus 25% of the number incorrect and reported as a percentage by dividing by the number of questions.

   The mark-sense reader produces an `ASCIIDataFile` file consisting of one line for each student containing a student number followed by the letters corresponding to the responses on the form in tab-delimited format. For example, if there were five questions on the test, the line for one student from this file might be:

```
1111    A    B    C    D    E
```

   corresponding to student `1111` answering `A` to question `1`, `B` to question `2`, etc. At the beginning of the file is a line giving the number of questions on the test followed by the correct answers, again in tab-delimited format. For example,

```
5       A    B    C    D    E
```

   indicates that there are five questions and the correct answer for question `1` is `A`, for `2` is `B`, etc. You may assume that the responses are always one of `A`, `B`, `C`, `D`, or `E` and the number of responses given for the key and each student are correct.

   The program is to produce a report (to an `ASCIIReportFile`) that gives, for each student, the student number, the answers, and the mark. The mark is a percentage, but note that it could be negative. In addition, the report is to give a summary indicating the number of correct responses for each question—the number of students who answered correctly. The report is to also give the percentage correct—the number correct divided by the number of students. For example, the report might look like the following:

```
St #  1   2   3   4   5  Mark(%)

1111  A   B   C   D   E   100.0

2222  A   E   C   E   E    50.0

3333  B   C   D   E   A   -25.0


#Cor  2   1   2   1   2

%Cor 66% 33% 66% 33% 66%
```

5. Using the classes from the modified grade reporting system (Section 11.6), write a program that allows a marker to enter marks for a particular piece of work. The program should prompt for the piece of work number and then sequence through the students of the course (read from an `ASCIIDataFile`), prompting for the students' grades. The grade entered should be verified against the base mark. When a student's mark in the piece of work has been entered, the program should write the updated student information to a new `ASCIIOutputFile`. The program should produce a happiness message indicating the number of student records processed. Clearly, the `Student` class will have to be modified to provide an updater method for the marks and an output method for the student information (see, for example, Sections 8.4 and 8.5).

6. Arrays are commonly used to allow access to objects that are to be processed in random order. Consider, for example, an order-processing application for Widgets-R-Us. (See Chapter 5, Exercise 3 and Chapter 6, Exercise 2 and their modified versions as Chapter 8, Exercises 1 and 2.) A clerk would receive the order and use the system to process the order, producing a shipping request and updating the inventory. Since the orders do not occur in the same order as the items in the inventory file, the inventory items would have to be read and stored in an array. When the clerk wants to process an order, s/he must enter the item number, and the program must locate the desired inventory object, that is, the one with the specified item number. This process is called *searching*, and is a fundamental operation in computer science. The simplest form of a search is to start with the first item in the array, and check whether it is the desired

one and has the matching item number. If it does, the search is over; otherwise, the next item in the array is checked, and so on until the item is located.

As described in the exercises in Chapters 5 and 6, for each inventory item, the inventory number (use `String`), quantity on hand (`int`), unit value (`double`), reorder point (`int`), and reorder amount (`int`) are recorded. In addition, there is an item description (`String`). The file of inventory information (`ASCIIDataFile`) contains one line per item, preceded by a line containing the number items in the inventory.

The program should read the items into an array and then begin processing orders. It should prompt for the item number (terminating on end-of-file) and search the array for the appropriate `Inventory` object. Here you may assume that the item number entered is a valid item number. The program should then prompt for the number ordered, indicating the quantity of that item on hand. The clerk will enter the number requested. You may assume that this is no larger than the quantity on hand. The program will prompt for customer name (`String`) and write a shipping request (a line of text) to a shipping report file (`ASCIIReportFile`) indicating the item number, description, quantity ordered, and customer name. It will then decrease the quantity on hand of the item.

When the clerk enters end-of-file, the program will produce a new inventory file (`ASCIIOutputFile`), writing the number of items in the inventory followed by the updated inventory object records.

A Instruction Processing

Remember that computers also store the program itself in memory. This means that the individual program instructions must be represented as sequences of binary digits. Since the instructions are the way in which we communicate the algorithm to the computer, they form a language. This binary language (the language of the machine) is called **machine language**.

Basically, each different operation, such as adding together two numbers, is assigned a binary number called the operation code (or **opcode**). Since we must specify what values are to be added, there is also an address part to the instruction, indicating where, in memory, the value(s) resides. A sample machine language instruction is given in Figure A.1. The first eight bits are the opcode and the next 24 bits are the address. It might represent "add the contents of memory location `107` to the current value in the ALU".

As part of the design of a computer processor, the kinds of instructions to provide and the numbers for the opcodes must be chosen. Different processors use different codes so processors' machine languages are different. This is why, when we buy software, we must be sure we are buying it for the correct processor. To make life a bit easier, processor designers (e.g., Intel, Motorola) maintain a level of consistency within processor families so all Intel Pentium chips have basically the same language, although later chips might have a larger vocabulary. This is called **upward compatibility**, that is, later

```
01011010000000000000000001110101
| opcode |         address        |
```

FIGURE A.1 Machine language instruction

processors can understand the machine language of earlier processors in the same family, but not necessarily vice versa.

As was described in Chapter 1, the control unit is responsible for following the computer program and directing the other components. Since the CPU must remember some things temporarily, it contains a few special pieces of memory called **registers**. One of these registers (called the **instruction address register**—IAR), is used by the control unit to sequence through the instructions of the program and another (the **instruction register**—IR) is used to hold the current instruction. Typically, the arithmetic/logic unit also has a number of registers to hold intermediate results. The CPU is connected to memory by a set of wires called a **bus** along which data, in the form of electrical current, can flow. The control unit also has a set of control wires to each of the other components to direct them. This organization is shown in Figure A.2 (the memory addresses and contents are written in decimal for convenience).

The basic process that the control unit follows is called the **machine cycle**. The machine cycle consists of three phases: fetch, decode, and execute, which the control unit repeats from the time the power is turned on until the system is shut down.

The instruction **fetch** begins with the control unit consulting the IAR and directing the memory to send the contents of the indicated memory location (`148`) along the bus.

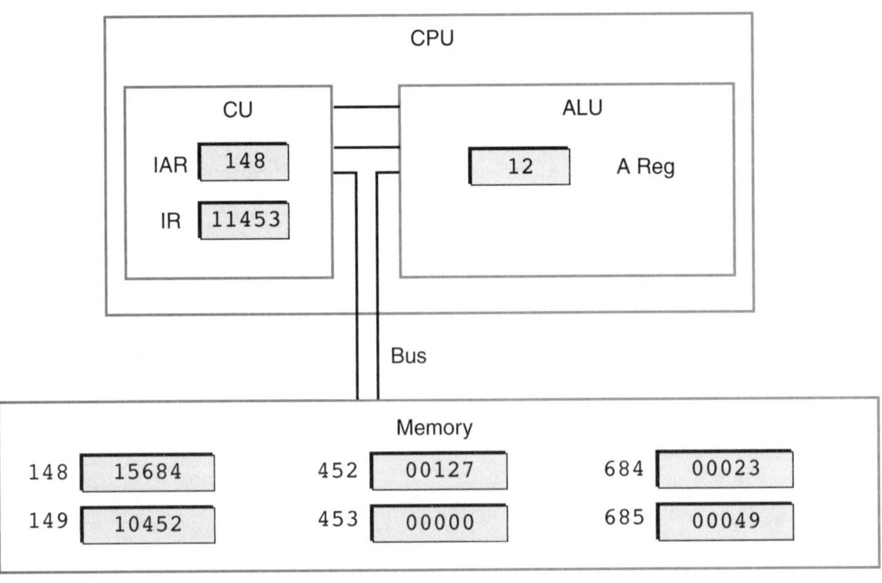

FIGURE A.2 Instruction processing

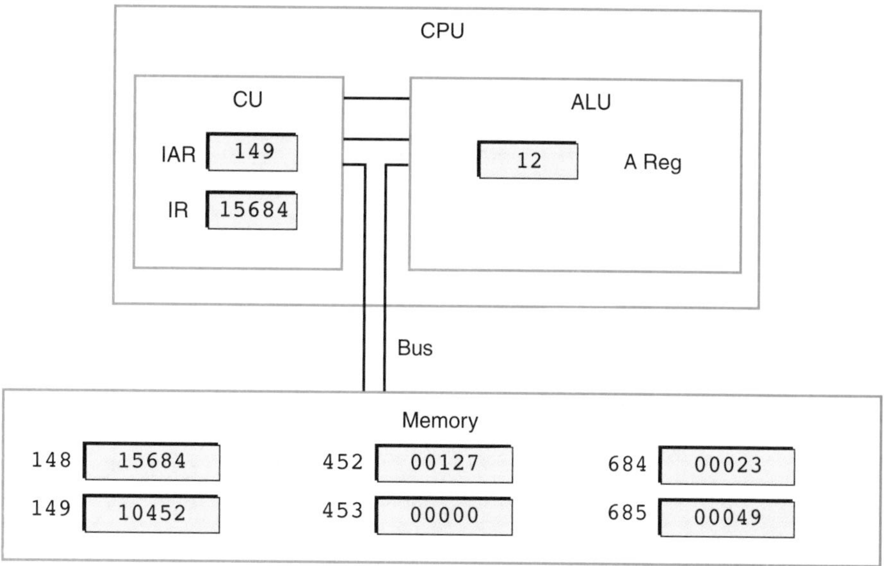

FIGURE A.3 Instruction fetch

The control unit then saves this instruction in the IR and increases the value of the IAR by one, to sequence to the next instruction. The result of the fetch is shown in Figure A.3.

Now the control unit performs the instruction **decode**. Basically, within the IR, it divides the instruction up into its opcode (here we will consider the first two decimal digits) and address (the next three digits) parts. It then sends the appropriate signal to other components to tell them what to do next. In this case, let's assume that `15` is the opcode for add. The control unit sends a signal to the ALU indicating an `add` operation and a signal to the memory to send the contents of the indicated address (`684`) along the bus. This is shown in Figure A.4.

The final phase is the **execute** phase. Here the components perform the operations indicated by the control unit. In this case, the memory sends the content (`23`) of address `684` along the bus. As the ALU receives this value, it adds it to the contents of the register giving the value `35`. The result is shown in Figure A.5. Now the cycle begins again with the fetch of the instruction at address `149`.

To ensure that all of the hardware components work together (that is, know when to look for an instruction from the control unit), they are synchronized by the system clock, much as we humans use a clock to synchronize our activity when we agree to meet at a restaurant at 7:00. The **system clock** is a crystal that emits electrical pulses at a specific

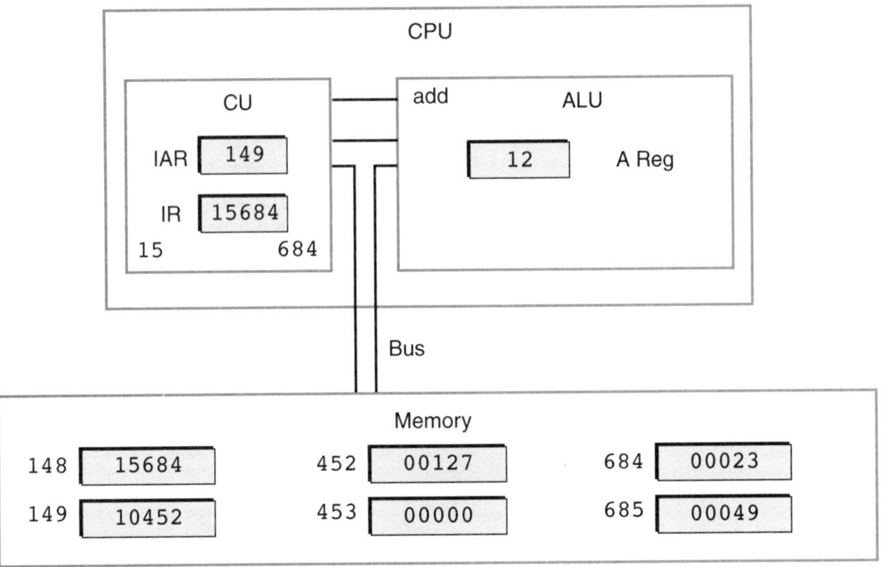

FIGURE A.4 Instruction decode

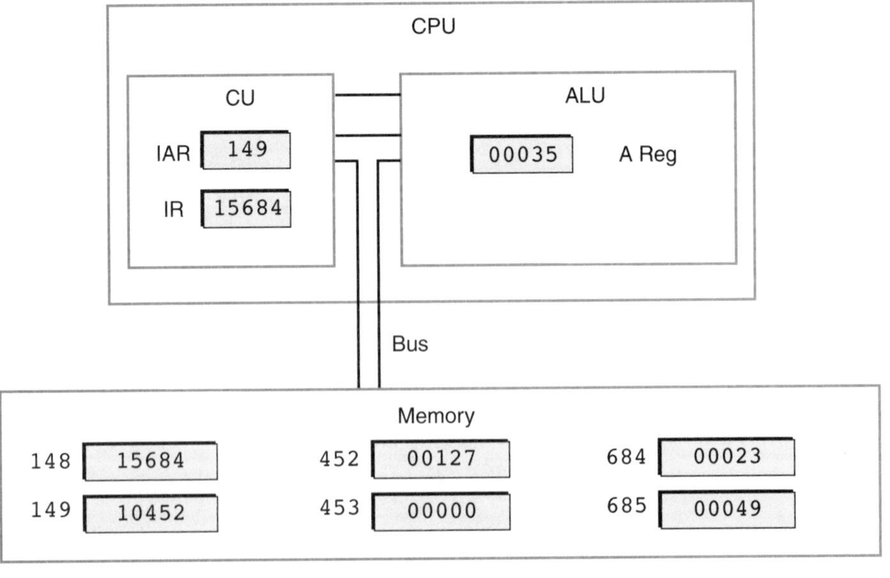

FIGURE A.5 Instruction execute

frequency. Each component counts the pulses and knows when to look for control signals. The clock speed thus controls the timing (the speed) of the machine cycle (some specific number of pulses per cycle), and ultimately the speed of the computer itself. Clock speeds are measured in **megahertz** (MHz, million cycles per second) and so CPU speeds are described in megahertz (e.g., a 400MHz Pentium II). Actually, the clock speed is only useful in comparing chips of the same model such as two Pentium IIs, but it doesn't tell the entire story when comparing different models or different chip families.

B

Java Syntax[1]

B.1 NOTATION

The grammar of Java is expressed (in *The Java Language Specification*[2]) using a formal notation for describing LALR(1) (programming language) grammars. In this notation, the grammar is described by a set of rules of the form:

```
SyntacticUnit:
        alternative1
        alternative2
```

At the beginning of the rule there is a word (formally called a nonterminal symbol), which is the name of the rule, followed by a colon. Following this line are one or more lines (called right-hand sides or rhs) representing alternative ways of writing the syntactic unit (i.e., piece of a program) defined by the left-hand side (or lhs—the word before the colon). Each alternative consists of a sequence of words and symbols that are to be written in order. Words written in italics are nonterminal symbols (i.e., names of other rules), which are to be written according to the specification of the rule with that name. Words and symbols written in plain font (called terminal symbols) are to be written as-is (e.g., `class` and `;`).

[1] Reproduced with permission from *The Java Language Specification.*

[2] Gosling, J., Joy, B. & Steele, G.; *The Java™ Language Specification*; Addison-Wesley; Reading, MA; 1996.

To make the rules a little easier to write (and read), a few notational conveniences are used. A rule of the form:

```
noun-phrase:
    article noun
    noun
```

can be written as:

```
noun-phrase:
    article opt noun
```

where the subscript *opt* on the nonterminal `article` means that the inclusion of `article` is optional. A rule of the form:

```
noun:
    John
    Mary
    book
    Java
```

can be written as:

```
noun: one of
    John Mary book Java
```

where the special phrase `one of` written on the first line of a rule means that the terminal symbols on the following lines are really alternatives. Finally, a very long alternative can be written on more than one line with the subsequent lines indented substantially.

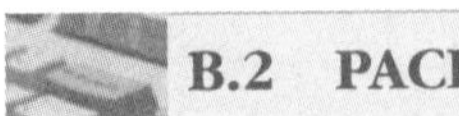

B.2 PACKAGES

```
CompilationUnit:
    PackageDeclarationopt ImportDeclarationsopt
    TypeDeclarationsopt

PackageDeclaration:
    package PackageName ;
```

```
ImportDeclarations:
    ImportDeclaration
    ImportDeclarations ImportDeclaration

TypeDeclarations:
    TypeDeclaration
    TypeDeclarations TypeDeclaration

ImportDeclaration:
    SingleTypeImportDeclaration
    TypeImportOnDemandDeclaration

SingleTypeImportDeclaration:
    import TypeName ;

TypeImportOnDemandDeclaration:
    import PackageOrTypeName . * ;

TypeDeclaration:
    ClassDeclaration
    InterfaceDeclaration
    ;
```

B.3 CLASSES

```
ClassDeclaration:
    ClassModifiers_opt class Identifier Super_opt Interfaces_opt
        ClassBody

ClassModifiers:
    ClassModifier
    ClassModifiers ClassModifier

ClassModifier: one of
    public protected private
    abstract static final strictfp

Super:
    extends ClassType

Interfaces:
    implements InterfaceTypeList
```

```
InterfaceTypeList:
    InterfaceType
    InterfaceTypeList , InterfaceType

ClassBody:
    { ClassBodyDeclarations_opt }

ClassBodyDeclarations:
    ClassBodyDeclaration
    ClassBodyDeclarations ClassBodyDeclaration

ClassBodyDeclaration:
    ClassMemberDeclaration
    InstanceInitializer
    StaticInitializer
    ConstructorDeclaration

ClassMemberDeclaration:
    FieldDeclaration
    MethodDeclaration
    ClassDeclaration
    InterfaceDeclaration
    ;

InstanceInitializer:
    Block

StaticInitializer:
    static Block
```

B.4 FIELDS AND VARIABLES

```
FieldDeclaration:
    FieldModifiers_opt Type VariableDeclarators ;

FieldModifiers:
    FieldModifier
    FieldModifiers FieldModifier

FieldModifier: one of
    public protected private
    static final transient volatile
```

VariableDeclarators:
    VariableDeclarator
    VariableDeclarators , *VariableDeclarator*

VariableDeclarator:
    VariableDeclaratorId
    VariableDeclaratorId = *VariableInitializer*

VariableDeclaratorId:
    Identifier
    VariableDeclaratorId [ ]

VariableInitializer:
    Expression
    ArrayInitializer

ArrayInitializer:
    { $VariableInitializers_{opt}$ $,_{opt}$ }

VariableInitializers:
    VariableInitializer
    VariableInitializers , *VariableInitializer*

B.5 METHODS

MethodDeclaration:
    MethodHeader MethodBody

MethodHeader:
    $MethodModifiers_{opt}$ *ResultType MethodDeclarator* $Throws_{opt}$

MethodModifiers:
    MethodModifier
    MethodModifiers MethodModifier

MethodModifier: one of
    public protected private abstract static
    final synchronized native strictfp

ResultType:
    Type
    void

```
MethodDeclarator:
    Identifer ( FormalParameterList_opt )

FormalParameterList:
    FormalParameter
    FormalParameterList , FormalParameter

FormalParameter:
    final_opt Type VariableDeclaratorId

Throws:
    throws ClassTypeList

ClassTypeList:
    ClassType
    ClassTypeList , ClassType

MethodBody:
    Block
    ;
```

B.6 CONSTRUCTORS

```
ConstructorDeclaration:
    ConstructorModifiers_opt ConstructorDeclarator Throws_opt
        ConstructorBody

ConstructorModifiers:
    ConstructorModifier
    ConstructorModifiers ConstructorModifier

ConstructorModifier: one of
    public protected private

ConstructorDeclarator:
    SimpleTypeName ( FormalParameterList_opt )

ConstructorBody:
    { ExplicitConstructorInvocation_opt BlockStatements_opt }

ExplicitConstructorInvocation:
    this ( ArgumentList_opt ) ;
    super ( ArgumentList_opt ) ;
    Primary . super ( ArgumentList_opt ) ;
```

B.7 INTERFACES

InterfaceDeclaration:
    InterfaceModifiers$_{opt}$ interface *Identifier*
        ExtendsInterfaces$_{opt}$ *InterfaceBody*

InterfaceModifiers:
    InterfaceModifier
    InterfaceModifiers InterfaceModifier

InterfaceModifier: one of
    public protected private
    abstract static strictfp

ExtendsInterfaces:
    extends *InterfaceType*
    ExtendsInterfaces , *InterfaceType*

InterfaceBody:
    { *InterfaceMemberDeclarations*$_{opt}$ }

InterfaceMemberDeclarations:
    InterfaceMemberDeclaration
    InterfaceMemberDeclarations InterfaceMemberDeclaration

InterfaceMemberDeclaration:
    ConstantDeclaration
    AbstractMethodDeclaration
    ClassDeclaration
    InterfaceDeclaration
    ;

ConstantDeclaration:
    ConstantModifiers$_{opt}$ *Type VariableDeclarators*

ConstantModifiers:
    ConstantModifier
    ConstantModifier ConstantModifers

ConstantModifier: one of
    public static final

AbstractMethodDeclaration:
    AbstractMethodModifiers$_{opt}$ *ResultType MethodDeclarator*
        Throws$_{opt}$;

```
AbstractMethodModifiers:
    AbstractMethodModifier
    AbstractMethodModifiers AbstractMethodModifier

AbstractMethodModifier: one of
    public abstract
```

B.8 TYPES

```
Type:
    PrimitiveType
    ReferenceType

PrimitiveType:
    NumericType
    boolean

NumericType:
    IntegralType
    FloatingPointType

IntegralType: one of
    byte short int long char

FloatingPointType: one of
    float double

ReferenceType:
    ClassOrInterfaceType
    ArrayType

ClassOrInterfaceType:
    ClassType
    InterfaceType

ClassType:
    TypeName

InterfaceType:
    TypeName

ArrayType:
    Type [ ]
```

B.9 NAMES

```
PackageName:
    Identifier
    PackageName . Identifier

TypeName:
    Identifier
    PackageOrTypeName . Identifier

SimpleTypeName:
    Identifier

ExpressionName:
    Identifier
    AmbiguousName . Identifier

MethodName:
    Identifier
    AmbiguousName . Identifier

ClassName:
    Identifier
    AmbiguousName . Identifier

PackageOrTypeName:
    Identifier
    PackageOrTypeName . Identifier

AmbiguousName:
    Identifier
    AmbiguousName . Identifier
```

B.10 BLOCKS AND STATEMENTS

```
Block:
    { BlockStatements_opt }

BlockStatements:
    BlockStatement
    BlockStatements BlockStatement
```

BlockStatement:
    LocalVariableDeclarationStatement
    ClassDeclaration
    Statement

LocalVariableDeclarationStatement:
    LocalVariableDeclaration ;

LocalVariableDeclaration:
    final$_{opt}$ *Type VariableDeclarators*

Statement:
    StatementWithoutTrailingSubstatement
    LabeledStatement
    IfThenStatement
    IfThenElseStatement
    WhileStatement
    ForStatement

StatementNoShortIf:
    StatementWithoutTrailingSubstatement
    LabeledStatementNoShortIf
    IfThenElseStatementNoShortIf
    WhileStatementNoShortIf
    ForStatementNoShortIf

StatementWithoutTrailingSubstatement:
    Block
    EmptyStatement
    ExpressionStatement
    SwitchStatement
    DoStatement
    BreakStatement
    ContinueStatement
    ReturnStatement
    SynchronizedStatement
    ThrowStatement
    TryStatement

EmptyStatement:
    ;

LabeledStatement:
    Identifier : *Statement*

```
LabeledStatementNoShortIf:
    Identifier : StatementNoShortIf

ExpressionStatement:
    StatementExpression ;

StatementExpression:
    Assignment
    PreIncrementExpression
    PreDecrementExpression
    PostIncrementExpression
    PostDecrementExpression
    MethodInvocation
    ClassInstanceCreationExpression

IfThenStatement:
    if ( Expression ) Statement

IfThenElseStatement:
    if ( Expression ) StatementNoShortIf else
        Statement

IfThenElseStatementNoShortIf:
    if ( Expression ) StatementNoShortIf else
        StatementNoShortIf

SwitchStatement:
    switch ( Expression ) SwitchBlock

SwitchBlock:
    { SwitchBlockStatementGroups_opt SwitchLabels_opt }

SwitchBlockStatementGroups:
    SwitchBlockStatementGroup
    SwitchBlockStatementGroups SwitchBlockStatementGroup

SwitchBlockStatementGroup:
    SwitchLabels BlockStatements

SwitchLabels:
    SwitchLabel
    SwitchLabels SwitchLabel

SwitchLabel:
    case ConstantExpression :
    default :
```

```
WhileStatement:
    while ( Expression ) Statement

WhileStatementNoShortIf:
    while ( Expression ) StatementNoShortIf

DoStatement:
    do Statement while ( Expression ) ;

ForStatement:
    for ( ForInit_opt ; Expression_opt ; ForUpdate_opt )
        Statement

ForStatementNoShortIf:
    for ( ForInit_opt ; Expression_opt ; ForUpdate_opt )
        StatementNoShortIf

ForInit:
    StatementExpressionList
    LocalVariableDeclaration

ForUpdate:
    StatementExpressionList

StatementExpressionList:
    StatementExpression
    StatementExpressionList , StatementExpression

BreakStatement:
    break Identifier_opt ;

ContinueStatement:
    continue Identifier_opt ;

ReturnStatement:
    return Expression_opt ;

ThrowStatement:
    throw Expression ;

SynchronizedStatement:
    synchronized ( Expression ) Block
```

```
TryStatement:
    try Block Catches
    try Block Catches_opt Finally

Catches:
    CatchClause
    Catches CatchClause

CatchClause:
    catch ( FormalParameter ) Block

Finally:
    finally Block
```

B.11 EXPRESSIONS

```
Primary:
    PrimaryNoNewArray
    ArrayCreationExpression

PrimaryNoNewArray:
    Literal
    Type . class
    void . class
    this
    ClassName . this
    ( Expression )
    ClassInstanceCreationExpression
    FieldAccess
    MethodInvocation
    ArrayAccess

Literal:
    IntegerLiteral
    FloatingPointLiteral
    BooleanLiteral
    CharacterLiteral
    StringLiteral
    NullLiteral

ClassInstanceCreationExpression:
    new ClassOrInterfaceType ( ArgumentList_opt ) ClassBody_opt
    Primary . new Identifier ( ArgumentList_opt ) ClassBody_opt
```

```
ArgumentList:
    Expression
    ArgumentList , Expression

ArrayCreationExpression:
    new PrimitiveType DimExprs Dims_opt
    new TypeName DimExprs Dims_opt
    new PrimitiveType Dims ArrayInitializer
    new TypeName Dims ArrayInitializer

DimExprs:
    DimExpr
    DimExprs DimExpr

DimExpr:
    [ Expression ]

Dims:
    [ ]
    Dims [ ]

FieldAccess:
    Primary . Identifier
    super . Identifier
    ClassName . super . Identifier

MethodInvocation:
    MethodName ( ArgumentList_opt )
    Primary . Identifier ( ArgumentList_opt )
    super . Identifier ( ArgumentList_opt )
    ClassName . super . Identifier ( ArgumentList_opt )

ArrayAccess:
    ExpressionName [ Expression ]
    PrimaryNoNewArray [ Expression ]

PostfixExpression:
    Primary
    ExpressionName
    PostIncrementExpression
    PostDecrementExpression

PostIncrementExpression:
    PostfixExpression ++
```

PostDecrementExpression:
    PostfixExpression -

UnaryExpression:
    PreIncrementExpression
    PreDecrementExpression
    + *UnaryExpression*
    - *UnaryExpression*
    UnaryExpressionNotPlusMinus

PreIncrementExpression:
    ++ *UnaryExpression*

PreDecrementExpression:
    — *UnaryExpression*

UnaryExpressionNotPlusMinus:
    PostfixExpression
    ~ *UnaryExpression*
    ! *UnaryExpression*
    CastExpression

CastExpression:
    (*PrimitiveType* $Dims_{opt}$) *UnaryExpression*
    (*ReferenceType*) *UnaryExpressionNotPlusMinus*

MultiplicativeExpression:
    UnaryExpression
    MultiplicativeExpression * *UnaryExpression*
    MultiplicativeExpression / *UnaryExpression*
    MultiplicativeExpression % *UnaryExpression*

AdditiveExpression:
    MultiplicativeExpression
    AdditiveExpression + *MultiplicativeExpression*
    AdditiveExpression - *MultiplicativeExpression*

ShiftExpression:
    AdditiveExpression
    ShiftExpression << *AdditiveExpression*
    ShiftExpression >> *AdditiveExpression*
    ShiftExpression >>> *AdditiveExpression*

```
RelationalExpression:
    ShiftExpression
    RelationalExpression < ShiftExpression
    RelationalExpression > ShiftExpression
    RelationalExpression <= ShiftExpression
    RelationalExpression >= ShiftExpression
    RelationalExpression instanceof ReferenceType

EqualityExpression:
    RelationalExpression
    EqualityExpression == RelationalExpression
    EqualityExpression != RelationalExpression

AndExpression:
    EqualityExpression
    AndExpression & EqualityExpression

ExclusiveOrExpression:
    AndExpression
    ExclusiveOrExpression ^ AndExpression

InclusiveOrExpression:
    ExclusiveOrExpression
    InclusiveOrExpression | ExclusiveOrExpression

ConditionalAndExpression:
    InclusiveOrExpression
    ConditionalAndExpression && InclusiveOrExpression

ConditionalOrExpression:
    ConditionalAndExpression
    ConditionalOrExpression || ConditionalAndExpression

ConditionalExpression:
    ConditionalOrExpression
    ConditionalOrExpression ? Expression :
        ConditionalExpression

AssignmentExpression:
    ConditionalExpression
    Assignment

Assignment:
    LeftHandSide AssignmentOperator AssignmentExpression
```

```
LeftHandSide:
    ExpressionName
    FieldAccess
    ArrayAccess

AssignmentOperator: one of
    = *= /= %= += -= <<= >>= >>>= &= ^= |=

Expression:
    AssignmentExpression

ConstantExpression:
    Expression
```

B.12 RESERVED WORDS

The following words are reserved in Java and may not be used as identifiers.

```
abstract    default    if           private        this
boolean     do         implements   protected      throw
break       double     import       public         throws
byte        else       instanceof   return         transient
case        extends    int          short          try
catch       final      interface    static         void
char        finally    long         strictfp       volatile
class       float      native       super          while
const       for        new          switch
continue    goto       package      synchronized
```

C Programming Patterns

This appendix collects together and summarizes the programming patterns described in the chapters of the text. Programming patterns describe groupings of program statements that commonly occur in computer programs. They were inspired by the landmark book describing design patterns[1] although programming patterns are much simpler and are intended for use in the coding phase rather than the design phase.

C.1 DESCRIPTION OF PATTERNS

Each pattern is described using a number of sections:

- **Name**—Describes the pattern in a few words.
- **Intent**—Describes the situations in which the pattern might be used.
- **Motivation**—Describes a typical scenario in which the pattern might be used.
- **Structure**—Describes the structure of the pattern, typically as a pseudocode algorithm.
- **Example**—Gives an example of the pattern in Java.
- **Related Patterns**—Lists other patterns often used in conjunction with the pattern.

The patterns are organized into related groups—looping, I/O, data synthesis, and array traversal. Some patterns may be included in a number of categories.

[1] Gamma, E., et al.; *Design Patterns–Elements of Reusable Object-Oriented Software*, Addison-Wesley, Reading, MA; 1994

C.2 USE OF PATTERNS

The pseudocode descriptions of the patterns include phrases and words in italics. These are replaced by appropriate code or statements from the programming language as described in the Structure sections. Patterns can be combined with other patterns in two ways—nesting and merging—to produce solutions to coding problems.

Nesting Patterns

One pattern may be nested within another. Typically, the nested pattern is substituted for one or more pseudocode statements within the other pattern. The result is the product of the two patterns. For example, the Process to EOF pattern may be nested within the Stream I/O pattern (Figure C.1), producing a piece of code that processes a stream from beginning to end.

Merging Patterns

Patterns may be merged together. Typically, this involves using the looping structure of one pattern to drive both patterns. The result is the composite of the two patterns. For example, the Process to EOF pattern may be merged with the Summation pattern producing a pattern that sums the data in the file. The loop construct of the Process to EOF pattern used as the loop for the Summation pattern is shown in Figure C.2.

```
open stream
while not at EOF
    read data value
    process data value
close stream
```

FIGURE C.1 Nesting patterns

```
sum = 0;
while not at EOF
    read data value
    sum = sum + data value
```

FIGURE C.2 Merging patterns

C.3 LOOPING PATTERNS

Looping patterns provide control of repetition of a sequence of operations or another pattern. They are commonly merged with other patterns, providing the control of the loop while the other pattern provides the processing. For example, the Countable Repetition pattern can be merged with the Summation pattern to sum over a known number of items or the Process to EOF pattern can be merged with the Summation Pattern to sum all data within a file.

Countable Repetition

Intent. This pattern is used whenever a sequence of operations must be performed a specific number of times.

Motivation. If an operation is to be repeated and the number of repetitions can be computed prior to the repetition, this pattern can be applied. For example, it could be used to produce an interest table (see Figure 5.7) where the number of years for the table was predefined. It could also be used to compute the average of the marks in a class when the number of students can be read from the input stream (see Figure 5.10).

Structure. The basic structure of the pattern is shown in Figure C.3. *times* is replaced by either a constant representing the specific number of times to repeat the operations or an expression from which the number of repetitions can be computed. *statementList* is replaced by the statements representing the operations that are to be repeated.

Expressed in Java, the pattern uses a `for` statement to control the loop, as shown in Figure C.4. The Java implementation requires a loop index variable be declared, usually

```
repeat times times
    statementList
```

FIGURE C.3 Countable repetition

```
for ( index=1 ; index<=times ; index++ ) {
    statementList
};
```

FIGURE C.4 Countable repetition in Java

```
int     numStd;     // number of students
double  aMark;      // one student's mark
double  totMark;    // total of marks
double  aveMark;    // average mark
int i;

numStd = in.readInt();
totMark = 0;
for ( i=1 ; i<=numStd ; i++ ) {
    aMark = in.readDouble();
    totMark = totMark + aMark;
};
aveMark = totMark / numStd;
```

FIGURE C.5 Example—Computing class average

as a local variable within the method, with its name substituted for *index*. *times* and *statementList* are replaced as for the general pattern.

Example. The program segment shown in Figure C.5 reads the number of students in the class (`numStd`) and then computes the average mark for these students by reading and summing the individual marks. The code is a merger of the Countable Repetition and Summation patterns.

Related Patterns. The Countable Repetition pattern is often merged with other patterns providing the looping construct when the number of repetitions is known in advance. The Right-sized Array Traversal and the Variable-sized Array Traversal patterns are special cases of the Countable Repetition pattern and the Row-major Array Processing and Column-major Array Processing patterns are special cases of nested Countable Repetition patterns.

Process to EOF

Intent. This pattern is used whenever a sequence of operations must be performed for all data in a file.

Motivation. Often a set of operations must be performed for every data value in a file. The number of values is unknown until the entire file is processed. For example, it could be used to compute the average of the marks in a class when the number of students is unknown and there is one data value per student in the file (see Figure 6.12).

Structure. The basic structure of the pattern is shown in Figure C.6. The first line in the body of the pattern is replaced by code that obtains a data value from the file. The second line is replaced by statements that process that value.

```
while not at EOF
    read data value
    process data value
```

FIGURE C.6 Process to EOF

```
while ( true ) {
    try to read data value
if ( unable to read ) break;
    process data value
}
```

FIGURE C.7 Process to EOF in Java

Expressed in Java, the pattern uses a `while` statement with a `true` condition to provide an infinite loop and an `if` statement and a `break` statement to perform conditional exit at EOF, as shown in Figure C.7. When the `BasicIO` package is used for stream input from a file (*in*), the condition *unable to read* is replaced by `! in.successful()`.

Example. The program segment shown in Figure C.8 reads student marks from an input stream (in), counts and sums them, and then computes the average mark for these students. The code is a merger of the Process to EOF and Summation patterns.

```
int     numStd;      // number of students
double  aMark;       // one student's mark
double  totMark;     // total of marks
double  aveMark;     // average mark

numStd = 0;
totMark = 0;
while ( true ) {
    aMark = in.readDouble();
if ( ! in.successful() ) break;
    numStd = numStd + 1;
    totMark = totMark + aMark;
};
aveMark = totMark / numStd;
```

FIGURE C.8 Example—Computing class average

Related Patterns. The Process to EOF pattern is often merged with other patterns, providing the looping construct when all the data in a file is to be processed. The Process Records to EOF pattern is a special case of the Process to EOF pattern.

Process Records to EOF

Intent. This pattern is used whenever the data in a file is grouped into records of related information and a sequence of operations must be performed for all records in a file.

Motivation. Often a set of operations must be performed for every entity represented by a record in a file. The number of records is unknown until the entire file is processed. For example, it could be used to produce the Dean's List when the number of students is unknown and there is one record per student (see Figure 6.17).

Structure. The basic structure of the pattern is shown in Figure C.9. The first line in the body of the pattern is replaced by code that obtains a data record from the file. The second line is replaced by statements that process that record.

Expressed in Java, the pattern uses a `while` statement with a `true` condition to provide an infinite loop and an `if` statement and a `break` statement to perform conditional exit at EOF, as shown in Figure C.10. Since the fields of the record must be read by separate method calls, the first field is read before the test, and the remaining fields are read after the test. When the `BasicIO` package is used for stream input from a file (*`in`*), the condition *`unable to read`* is replaced by `!` *`in`*`.successful()`.

Example. The program segment shown in Figure C.11 reads records containing the student number and average from an input stream (`in`) and displays those students who made the Dean's List. The code is a merger of the Process Records to EOF and Report Generation patterns.

```
while not at EOF
    read record
    process record
```

FIGURE C.9 Process to EOF

```
while ( true ) {
    try to read first field of record
if ( unable to read ) break;
    read remaining fields of record
    process record
}
```

FIGURE C.10 Process Records to EOF in Java

```
int      numStd;      // number of students
int      numList;     // number on the list
int      aStdNum;     // one student's student number
double   aMark;       // one student's mark

numStd = 0;
numList = 0;
writeHeader();
while ( true ) {
    aStdNum = in.readInt();
if ( ! in.successful() ) break;
    aMark = in.readDouble();
    if ( aMark >= 80 ) {
        numList = numList + 1;
        writeDetail(aStdNum,aMark);
    };
    numStd = numStd + 1;
};
writeSummary(numList);
```

FIGURE C.11 Example—Producing the Dean's List

Related Patterns. Process Records to EOF is a special case of the Process to EOF pattern. The Process Records to EOF pattern is often merged with other patterns, especially the Report Generation pattern, providing the looping construct when all the records in a file are to be processed.

Convergence

Intent. This pattern is used whenever a computation must be performed repeatedly until the result approaches some target value.

Motivation. A computation sometimes consists of an initial approximation of the result with subsequent refinement of the approximation, until the approximation is close enough to the desired value. For example, it could be used to compute a root of an equation using the secant method, where each time through the loop, the approximation is refined until its functional value is close enough to zero (see Figure 6.6). Another variant would be a guessing game where the computer (or player) guesses values until the value is the desired one. Here, "close enough" means exactly correct.

Structure. The basic structure of the pattern is shown in Figure C.12.

The first line is replaced by code that determines an initial approximation. This might be a constant value, might be obtained via input, or might be computed. The test for convergence typically compares some function of the approximation with a target

```
compute initial approximation
while approximation hasn't converged
    refine approximation
```

FIGURE C.12 Convergence

value. Often this comparison involves a tolerance—a maximum amount the approximation can differ from the desired value (*goal*)—for convergence to occur. In this case, the condition for the loop would be something like:

```
while abs(f(approximation) - goal) > tolerance
```

The line in the body of the loop is replaced by statements that compute the next approximation. If the computation of the initial approximation and the computation of the subsequent approximations are the same code, the pattern can be refined, as shown in Figure C.13.

Expressed in Java, the pattern uses a `while` statement with a condition that determines when convergence has *not* occurred, as shown in Figure C.14. The variant is expressed using a `do while` loop with the same condition.

Example. The program segment shown in Figure C.15 computes an approximation to a root of the equation represented by the function `f` using the secant method (see Section 6.1). It starts with two initial values (`a` and `b`) input by the user and refines the approximation (`b`) until the function value at `b` (`f(b)`) is within a tolerance of `0.0001` of `0`.

Related Patterns. The Convergence pattern is typically used on its own; however, it can be merged with other patterns when the other pattern is to be repeated until some value computed by that pattern converges.

```
repeat
    compute approximation
until approximation has converged
```

FIGURE C.13 Convergence (variant form)

```
compute initial approximation
while ( approximation hasn't converged ) {
    compute next approximation
}
```

FIGURE C.14 Convergence in Java

```
double  a;  // first bound for root
double  b;  // second bound for root

a = in.readDouble();
b = in.readDouble();
while ( Math.abs(f(b)) > 0.0001) {
    b = (a * f(b) - b * f(a)) / (f(b) - f(a));
};
```

FIGURE C.15 Example—Computing a root of an equation

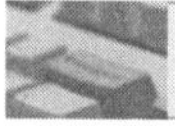

C.4 INPUT/OUTPUT PATTERNS

The input/output patterns involve special processing concerned with input and output from/to files or other sources/destinations. They include special processing for line-oriented text files and patterns for table and report generation. Closely related are the Process to EOF and Process Records to EOF patterns described in Section C.3. I/O patterns are commonly merged or nested with other patterns in order to provide a source of input or destination for output within other processing.

Stream I/O

Intent. This pattern is used whenever I/O has to be done to or from some I/O device that is abstracted as a stream.

Motivation. The stream abstraction is a generalization of I/O devices, including file I/O. A stream must be opened which, for example, connects the stream to the physical file. Once opened, I/O may be performed from/to the stream. Finally the stream must be closed to complete the processing, for example, by writing the last buffer and disconnection from the file. The Stream I/O pattern is used whenever a stream is being used.

Structure. The basic structure of the pattern is shown in Figure C.16. The first line is replaced by whatever statements are required to open the stream. The second line represents all processing involving the stream, which may be extensive, and is often placed in a method to simplify the code. The third line is replaced by whatever statements are required to close the stream.

```
open stream
statements involving I/O to/from the stream
close stream
```

FIGURE C.16 Stream I/O

```
stream = new StreamClass();
statements involving I/O to/from the stream
stream.close()
```

FIGURE C.17 Stream I/O in Java using BasicIO

Expressed in Java using the BasicIO package, opening the stream involves creation of an appropriate stream object selected from the BasicIO stream classes (see Table 5.1). Closing the stream involves an invocation of the close method of the stream object. This technique is shown in Figure C.17, where *stream* is replaced by the stream object reference variable and *StreamClass* by the appropriate class from Table 5.1.

Example. The program segment shown in Figure C.18 reads an employee's hours worked and rate of pay and prints the employee's gross pay. The example involves nested Stream I/O patterns, the one for the output stream nested within the one for the input stream.

Related Patterns. The Stream I/O pattern is used with most other patterns since most programs involve the input/output of data. Typically, the other patterns are nested within the Stream I/O pattern (often indirectly via a method invocation). Programs often use multiple streams, in which case the Stream I/O patterns are nested when the streams are to be

```
private ASCIIPrompter   in;      // prompter for input
private ASCIIDisplayer  out;     // displayer for output
      :
    double  hours;  // hours worked
    double  rate;   // hourly pay rate
    double  pay;    // amount paid out

    in = new ASCIIPrompter();
    out = new ASCIIDisplayer();

    rate = in.readDouble();
    hours = in.readDouble();
    pay = rate * hours;
    out.writeDouble(pay);
    out.writeEOL();

    out.close();
    in.close();
```

FIGURE C.18 Example—Computing pay

used at the same time, or they are used one after the other when one stream is to be completely processed before processing of the next is begun. This later case is also commonly used when a file is used for temporary storage and an output stream is opened to the file, the data written, the file closed, and subsequently an input stream opened to the same file so that the data can be read back.

Process Line-oriented Text File

Intent. This pattern is used whenever a line-oriented text file must be processed character-by-character.

Motivation. A line-oriented text file is a stream of characters, some of which are line-separator characters. When such a file must be processed, character-by-character, the line-breaks typically have significance and must be treated specially. For example, a program that reads a file containing text incorrectly typed in uppercase and produces a new file in which all uppercase characters have been replaced by their lowercase equivalents, would use this pattern. The presence of a line-break character in the input requires that the corresponding output line be terminated at the same place (see Figure 7.4).

Structure. The basic structure of the pattern is shown in Figure C.19. The pattern is really an extension of the Process to EOF pattern. The first line in the body of the pattern obtains the next character from the input. The `then-part` of the `if` does the special processing required at end of line while the `else-part` does the normal processing. In some cases, the normal processing (or part thereof) must also be done at end of line, in which case the normal processing (or part thereof) is placed after the `if` rather than as the `else-part`. The pattern is nested (directly or indirectly) within a Stream I/O pattern for the stream from which the text is read.

Expressed in Java using the `BasicIO` package, the pattern is as shown in Figure C.20. The pattern would be nested within a Stream I/O pattern for the input stream *in*. Since all characters, including the line markers, are being processed, the `readC` method is used for input. The test for end of line involves comparing the character that

```
while not at EOF
    get next character
    if at end of line
        handle end of line
    else
        handle other characters
```

FIGURE C.19 Process line-oriented text file

```
while ( true ) {
    chr = in.readC();
if ( ! in.successful()) break;
    if ( chr == '\n' ) {
        handle end of line
    }
    else {
        handle other characters
    };
};
```

FIGURE C.20 Processing line-oriented text file in Java

```
char    c;  // a text character

while ( true ) {
    c = in.readC();
if ( ! in.successful() ) break;
    if ( c == '\n' ) {
        out.writeEOL();
    }
    else {
        out.writeC(Character.toLowerCase(c));
    };
};
```

FIGURE C.21 Example—Converting uppercase to lowercase

is read with the newline character (`'\n'`), which is returned by `readC` when a line marker is read.

Example. The program segment shown in Figure C.21 reads a text file and converts all uppercase characters into lowercase, producing a new text file. The segment is nested within Stream I/O patterns for the input (`in`) and output (`out`) streams.

Related Patterns. The Process Line-oriented Text File pattern is always nested within a Stream I/O pattern for the input stream. Other patterns may be nested within it to perform the processing of the individual characters. In some cases, another pattern may be merged with this one, using the loop of the Process Line-oriented Text File pattern to control the processing in the other pattern. In that case, the body of the other pattern is usually within the `else-part` of the end of line test as processing of the regular characters. The Process Line-oriented Text File pattern is a special case of the Process to EOF pattern.

Table Generation

Intent. This pattern is used whenever processed data is to be presented in a two-dimensional table of rows and columns.

Motivation. Often, processed data is best presented in tabular form consisting of a number of rows each containing information in a number of columns. A table typically has a title and headings for each column. For example, a compound interest table might consist of a title indicating the principal and interest rate, and the body of the table would consist of a number of rows, one for each year, giving the year number, interest earned in the year, and balance after the year (see Figure 5.13).

Structure. The basic structure of the pattern is shown in Figure C.22. The first two lines of the pattern are replaced by the code required to produce the table title and headings. Often, this code is placed within a method to simplify the code. The table body is produced by a loop through all the lines of the table. This loop is typically provided via merging with an appropriate looping pattern. Each row of the table is generated by a loop through all columns, again via merging with a looping pattern. The body of the innermost loop is replaced by the code to generate and display the individual table entry. Finally, after the inner loop (i.e., after the row has been generated) the appropriate code for marking the end of the table row is produced. A table is generated to an output stream so the Table Generation pattern is typically nested within a Stream I/O pattern.

When the code for the generation of each column in a row is not the same, the inner loop is replaced by a sequence of code to produce the column entries sequentially. This produces the variant of the pattern shown in Figure C.23. The code for generating the table row is often placed in a method to simplify the code.

When expressed in Java using `BasicIO`, the code for marking the end of the line includes an invocation of the method `writeEOL`. In the variant, this invocation is usually placed in the method that generates the table row.

Example. The program segment shown in Figure C.24 produces a compound interest table. The segment is nested within a Stream I/O pattern for the output (`out`) stream

```
generate title line(s)
generate heading line(s)
for each line of the table
    for each entry in the line
        generate entry
    mark end of line
```

FIGURE C.22 Table generation

```
generate title line(s)
generate heading line(s)
for each line of the table
    generate table row
    mark end of line
```

FIGURE C.23 Table generation (variant)

```
double  b;  // balance
double  r;  // rate
double  i;  // interest
int     ny; // number of years
int     n;  // year number
   ⋮
writeHeader(b,r);
for ( n=1 ; n<=ny ; n++ ) {
    i = b * r;
    b = b + i;
    writeDetail(n,i,b);
};
```

FIGURE C.24 Example—Producing a compound interest table

and merged with a Countable Repetition pattern since the number of table rows is computable. Since the entries in the columns of a row are not computed in the same way, the program uses the variant of the pattern. The code for writing the table title and headings is abstracted to the method `writeHeader` and the code for writing a table row, including writing the end of line marker, is abstracted to the method `writeDetail`.

Related Patterns. The Table Generation pattern is always nested within a Stream I/O pattern for the output stream. It is merged with a looping pattern to control the number of rows. Typically, this is a Countable Repetition pattern since the number of rows is usually known or computable. Similarly, the pattern is merged with a looping pattern in order to control the number of columns, again often a Countable Repetition pattern. Of course, this second merger is unnecessary in the variant.

Report Generation

Intent. This pattern is used whenever processed data is to be presented as a report consisting of a number of rows each containing related information in the columns of the row.

```
generate report title line(s)
generate report heading line(s)
for each line(entry) in the report
    obtain data for entry
    produce report line for entry
    mark end of line
produce report summary
```

FIGURE C.25 Report generation

Motivation. Often, processed data is best presented as a report in a tabular form consisting of a number of rows each containing related information in a number of columns. A report typically has a title and headings for each column and the report body is followed by some summary information. For example, a marks report (see Figure 5.14) could be produced consisting of a title indicating the course and headings for the student number and mark. The report body would list, for each student, the student number and mark. Finally, as summary information, the average mark for the class would be displayed (see Figure 5.13).

Structure. The basic structure of the pattern is shown in Figure C.25. The first two lines of the pattern are replaced by the code required to produce the report title and column headings. Often, this code is placed within a method to simplify the code. The report body is produced by a loop through all the report entries (lines) of the table. This loop is typically provided via merging with an appropriate looping pattern such as the Process Records to EOF pattern. The first line of the loop body is replaced by the code to obtain the data for the row, often by reading a record. This may be placed in a method to simplify the code. The second line is replaced by the code to produce a report line, which is often called a detail line. Again this is often placed in a method. The last line is replaced by whatever code is necessary to handle the end of the report line. The line after the loop is replaced by whatever code is necessary to produce the report summary. This is also typically placed in a method. A report is generated to an output stream, so the Report Generation pattern is typically nested within a Stream I/O pattern.

When expressed in Java using `BasicIO`, the code for marking the end of the line includes an invocation of the method `writeEOL`. This is usually included in the method that produces the detail line.

Example. The program segment shown in Figure C.26 produces a marks report consisting of a title giving the course name, headings on the report for student number and mark, detail lines giving the student number and mark, and a summary giving the class

```
int     numStd;      // number of students
int     aStdNum;     // one student's student number
double  aMark;       // one student's mark
double  totMark;     // total of marks
double  aveMark;     // average mark

writeHeader();
numStd = 0;
totMark = 0;
while (true) {
    aStdNum = in.readInt();
if ( !in.successful() ) break;
    numStd = numStd + 1;
    aMark = in.readDouble();
    writeDetail(aStdNum,aMark);
    totMark = totMark + aMark;
};
aveMark = totMark / numStd;
writeSummary(aveMark);
```

FIGURE C.26 Example—Producing a marks report

average. The segment is nested within Stream I/O patterns for the input (`in`) and output (`out`) streams and merged with a Process Records to EOF pattern since the data is record-oriented. The code for writing the report title and headings is abstracted to the method `writeHeader`. The code for writing a detail line, including writing the end of line marker, is abstracted to the method `writeDetail`. Finally, the code for writing the summary information is abstracted to the method `writeSummary`.

Related Patterns. The Report Generation is actually an extension of the Table Generation pattern. The pattern is always nested within a Stream I/O pattern for the output stream. It is merged with a looping pattern to control the number of rows. Typically, this is a Process Records to EOF pattern since the row data is usually synthesized from the data within the records of a file.

C.5 DATA SYNTHESIS PATTERNS

Data synthesis patterns are patterns that manipulate data to produce specific results. They are usually merged with a looping pattern to process all of the data in some collection.

Exchange Values

Intent. This pattern is used whenever the value in two variables needs to be exchanged.

Motivation. Many applications require reorganizing information. In these cases, it is often necessary to exchange the values in two variables, or more commonly, in two elements of an array. This has to be done carefully so as not to lose either of the original values. For example, to reverse a string represented as an array of characters, the values at the front and end can be exchanged, then the second and second to the last, and so on (see Figure 11.8).

Structure. The structure of the Exchange Values pattern is found in Figure C.27. *firstVar* and *secondVar* are replaced by the two variables or array elements whose values are to be exchanged. The pattern requires an auxiliary variable (here called *temp*), of the same type as the values being exchanged, that is typically declared as a local variable. The auxiliary variable is necessary to avoid losing the value of one of the variables.

Example. The program segment shown in Figure C.28 reverses the string represented by the array of characters `theString`. The first value is exchanged with the last value, the second with the second last, and so on, until the middle of the string is reached. The Exchange Values pattern is nested within a Countable Repetition pattern since a computable number of pairs must be exchanged.

Related Patterns. The Exchange Values pattern is usually nested within a looping pattern since applications usually call for repeated exchanges.

```
temp = firstVar;
firstVar = secondVar;
secondVar = temp;
```

FIGURE C.27 Exchanging values

```
char    theString[];     // string as array of characters
char    temp;
int     i;
  ⋮
for ( i=0 ; i<theString.length/2 ; i++ ) {
    temp = theString[i];
    theString[i] = theString[theString.length-1-i];
    theString[theString.length-1-i] = temp;
};
```

FIGURE C.28 Example—Reversing a string

Summation

Intent. This pattern is used to produce the sum of a set of data values.

Motivation. One of the most common data synthesis operations is producing a sum of a set of data values. This is often done prior to computing an average. The data values typically come from a data file or are stored in an array. For example, the pattern can be used to compute the average mark achieved by students on a test when the test marks are stored in a file (see Figure 5.13).

Structure. The structure of the Summation pattern is found in Figure C.29. A variable to hold the sum must be declared appropriately and substituted for *sum*. The first line within the loop body is replaced by code that accesses the next value from the set of values. *datavalue* is replaced by the variable, which may be a subscripted variable if the data values are in an array, that holds the next data value obtained. The two lines are often merged into one if the values are already in the array.

Example. The program segment shown in Figure C.30 computes the average of the student marks stored in a file. The variable `totMark` is the *sum* and the variable `aMark`

```
sum = 0;
for all data values
    obtain next datavalue
    sum = sum + datavalue
```

FIGURE C.29 Summation

```
int     numStd;       // number of students
double  aMark;        // one student's mark
double  totMark;      // total of marks
double  aveMark;      // average mark

numStd = 0;
totMark = 0;
while ( true ) {
    aMark = in.readDouble();
if ( ! in.successful() ) break;
    numStd = numStd + 1;
    totMark = totMark + aMark;
};
aveMark = totMark / numStd;
```

FIGURE C.30 Example—Computing class average

```
count = 0;
for all data values
    count = count + 1
```

FIGURE C.31 Count

is the *datavalue*. The code is nested within a Stream I/O pattern for the input stream (`in`). The looping structure is provided via a merger with the Process to EOF pattern since there is an unknown amount of data in the file. The average is computed from the sum and the number of students.

The code requires that the number of students be counted as they are read since this number is not known. The process to count data values is a pattern that is derived from the Summation pattern. In counting, we are summing `1`s as many times as we have data items. This leads to the Count pattern shown in Figure C.31. Here the variable that is to store the count replaces *count*. Note in the above example, that `numStd` is the *count*, and the Summation and Count patterns are merged with each other and the Process to EOF pattern.

Related Patterns. The Count pattern is a derivative of the Summation pattern and the two are often merged. They are usually merged with a looping pattern that provides the repetition for the sum or count.

Find Maximum (Minimum)

Intent. This pattern is used when it is necessary to find the highest (or lowest) value from a collection of data values.

Motivation. Often it is necessary to determine the highest (or lowest) value from a set of data values. The data values typically come from a data file or are stored in an array. For example, the pattern can be used to compute the highest mark and lowest mark achieved by students on a test, when the test marks are stored in a file (see Figure 6.20).

Structure. The structure of the Find Maximum pattern is found in Figure C.32. *maximum* is replaced by an appropriately declared variable that will store the maximum value of the collection. The right-hand side of the first line is replaced by an expression that yields the smallest possible value for the type of data being processed. Within the

```
maximum = smallest possible value;
for all data values
    if datavalue > maximum
        maximum = datavalue;
```

FIGURE C.32 Find maximum

```
minimum = largest possible value;
for all data values
    if datavalue < minimum
        minimum = datavalue;
```

FIGURE C.33 Find minimum

```
maximum = first data value;
for all data values after the first
    if datavalue > maximum
        maximum = datavalue;
```

FIGURE C.34 Find maximum (variant)

loop, whenever a data value is obtained that exceeds the maximum so far, the maximum is updated.

The Find Minimum pattern is the same as the Find Maximum pattern except that *minimum* is used instead of *maximum*, the initial value is the largest possible value for the data type being processed, and the operator in the test is inverted. The Find Minimum pattern is shown in Figure C.33.

There is a variant of the patterns that is often used. Instead of initializing *maximum* (*minimum*) to the smallest (largest) value, *maximum* or *minimum* is initialized to the first value in the set. The loop then processes the remaining values. The variant for finding the maximum is shown in Figure C.34. This variant is used when the largest (or smallest) value for the type could naturally occur in the data set and when it is easy to access the first data value, such as when the values are stored in an array.

Example. The program segment shown in Figure C.35 determines the maximum mark achieved by students in the class where the marks are stored in a file. The variable

```
double  highMark;     // highest mark
double  aMark;        // one student's mark

highMark = - Double.MAX_VALUE;
while ( true ) {
    aMark = in.readDouble();
if ( ! in.successful() ) break;
    if ( aMark > highMark ) {
        highMark = aMark;
    };
};
```

FIGURE C.35 Example—Finding highest mark

`highMark` is the *`maximum`* and the variable `aMark` is the data value. `Double.MAX_VALUE` is a Java constant that is the `double` value with greatest magnitude. The negative of this is the smallest possible `double` value. The code is nested within a Stream I/O pattern for the input stream (`in`). The looping structure is provided via a merger with the Process to EOF pattern since there is an unknown amount of data in the file.

Related Patterns. The Find Maximum and Find Minimum patterns are merged with a looping pattern that provides the repetition over all data values in the set. This looping pattern is an array traversal pattern when the values are stored in an array.

C.6 ARRAY TRAVERSAL PATTERNS

Array traversal patterns are used when processing all of the elements of an array. They are special cases of the Countable Repetition pattern and nested Countable Repetition patterns and thus could be considered looping patterns. They are usually merged with other patterns to provide the looping structure and access to the elements of the array in sequence.

One-dimensional Array Traversal

Intent. This pattern is used when it is necessary to process all of the elements of a one-dimensional array.

Motivation. When data is stored in an array it is common to have to process each of the elements of the array in turn. This is called a traversal. For example, if rainfall data is stored in an array and it is desired to produce a list of the months that had above-average rainfall for the year, the One-Dimensional Array Traversal pattern could be used (see Figure 11.7).

Structure. The general structure of the One-dimensional Array Traversal pattern is found in Figure C.36. The line in the body of the loop is replaced by the processing of the individual element using the subscripted variable `a[i]`.

Expressed in Java there are two versions of the pattern, one for right-sized arrays and one for variable-sized arrays. The pattern uses a `for` statement to provide the loop indexing *`i`* through the required values. The pattern for right-sized arrays is shown in

```
for all elements of the array a
    process a[i]
```

FIGURE C.36 One-dimensional array traversal

```
for ( i=0 ; i<a.length ; i++ ) {
    process a[i]
};
```

FIGURE C.37 Right-sized array traversal

```
for ( i=0 ; i<numberOfElements ; i++ ) {
    process a[i]
};
```

FIGURE C.38 Variable-sized array traversal

Figure C.37. The physical length of the array is used as the limit on the loop. A loop index variable is declared and substituted for *i* and the array name is substituted for *a*.

The pattern for variable-sized arrays is shown in Figure C.38. Here the variable representing the number of values stored in the array is used as the loop limit. A loop index variable is declared and substituted for *i*, the variable representing the number of values in the array is substituted for *numberOfElements*, and the array name is substituted for *a*.

Example. The program segment shown in Figure C.39 finds the average of the values stored in the right-sized array `rainfall`. The segment is a merger of the Right-sized Array Traversal and the Summation patterns. The loop index is `i`, and the right-sized array is `rainfall`.

Related Patterns. The One-Dimensional Array Traversal patterns are actually special cases of the Countable Repetition pattern. They are usually merged with other patterns providing the looping over the elements of the array while the element processing is defined by the other pattern.

```
double  rainfall[]; // rainfall for each month
double  totRain;    // total rainfall for the year
double  aveRain;    // average monthly rainfall
int i;
  :
totRain = 0;
for ( i=0 ; i<rainfall.length ; i++ ) {
    totRain = totRain + rainfall[i];
};
aveRain = totRain / rainfall.length;
```

FIGURE C.39 Example—Finding average rainfall

Two-Dimensional Array Traversal

Intent. This pattern is used when it is necessary to process all of the elements of a two-dimensional array.

Motivation. When data is stored in an array it is common to have to process each of the elements of the array in turn. This is called a traversal. For example, if enrollment data is stored in a two-dimensional array by university and department within university, and it is desired to produce the total enrollment in the system, the Two-Dimensional Array Traversal pattern could be used (see Figure 11.30).

Structure. The general structure of the Two-dimensional Array Traversal pattern is found in Figure C.40. The first line in the body of the first loop is replaced by any processing required before the processing of the first dimension. The line in the body of the second loop is replaced by the code for the processing of the individual element using the subscripted variable *a[i][j]*. Finally, the last line of the outer loop is replaced by any processing required after processing the first dimension.

There are two possible traversal orders—row by row, called row-major processing, and column by column, called column-major processing. For row-major processing, the outer loop uses the index `i`, indexing it through the row indices, and the inner loop uses `j`, indexing it through the column indices. For column-major processing, the outer loop uses the index `j`, indexing it through the column indices, and the inner loop uses the index `i`, indexing it through the row indices.

Expressed in Java, the Row-major Array Traversal pattern uses nested `for` statements to provide the looping structure. The outer loop indexes `i` through the row indices, and the inner loop indexes `j` through the column indices. The pattern for right-sized arrays is shown in Figure C.41. The physical number of rows in the array (`a.length`) is used as the limit on the outer loop and the physical size of the appropriate row (`a[i].length`) is used as the limit on the inner loop. Loop index variables are declared and substituted for `i` and `j`, and the array name is substituted for `a`.

The Column-major Array Traversal pattern uses nested `for` statements to provide the looping structure. The outer loop indexes `j` through the column indices, and the inner loop indexes `i` through the row indices. The pattern for right-sized arrays is shown in Figure C.42. The number of columns in the first row of the array (`a[0].length`) is used as the limit on the outer loop and the number of rows in the array (`a.length`) is

```
for all elements in one dimension of array a
    preprocessing for this dimension
    for all elements in the other dimension of the array a
        process a[i][j]
    postprocessing for this dimension
```

FIGURE C.40 Two-dimensional array traversal

```
for ( i=0 ; i<a.length ; i++ ) {
    preprocessing for row i
    for ( j=0 ; j<a[i].length ; j++ ) {
        process a[i][j]
    };
    postprocessing for row i
};
```

FIGURE C.41 Row-major array traversal

```
for ( j=0 ; j<a[0].length ; j++ ) {
    preprocessing for column j
    for ( i=0 ; i<a.length ; i++ ) {
        process a[i][j]
    };
    postprocessing for column j
};
```

FIGURE C.42 Column-major array traversal

used as the limit on the inner loop. The pattern is only valid when all rows are the same length. Loop index variables are declared and substituted for `i` and `j`, and the array name is substituted for *a*.

Example. The program segment shown in Figure C.43 finds the total enrollment over each university and each department within the university, where the enrollment data is stored in the array `stats`. The segment is a merger of the Row-major Array Traversal and the Summation patterns. The loop indices are `i` and `j`, and the right-sized array is `stats`.

```
double  stats[][];  // enrollment stats
int sum;            // total enrollment
int i, j;
  ⋮
sum = 0;
for ( i=0 ; i<stats.length ; i++ ) {
    for ( j=0 ; j<stats[i].length ; j++ ) {
        sum = sum + stats[i][j];
    };
};
```

FIGURE C.43 Example—Finding average rainfall

Related Patterns. The Two-Dimensional Array Traversal patterns are actually special cases of nested Countable Repetition patterns. They are usually merged with other patterns providing the looping over the elements of the array while the element processing is defined by the other pattern.

D

Glossary

abacus (§1.1)

An **abacus** is a wooden frame around rods strung with beads. The beads can be moved up and down to perform complex calculations. (In essence, it was the first hand-held calculator.)

abstraction (§4)

Abstraction is the method of dealing with complexity by ignoring the details and differences and emphasizing similarities.

accept (parameter) (§4.2)

If a method is defined with a formal parameter list, it is said to **accept parameters.**

accessor method (§8.4)

An **accessor method** is a method that serves to return the value of an attribute, usually an instance variable, of an object.

actual parameter (§4.2)

An argument (**actual parameter**) is the expression in a method call that provides a value for a formal parameter.

Ada Augusta King (Countess of Lovelace) (§1.1)

Ada Augusta King, daughter of the poet Lord Byron and Countess of Lovelace, was an amateur mathematician and avid handicapper of horses. She wrote programs for the Analytical Engine and is regarded as the first programmer. The programming language Ada is named in her honor.

address (§1.2)

An **address** is a number identifying a location in memory. Information in memory is accessed by specifying the address at which it is stored (its address).

algorithm (§1)

An **algorithm** is a well-defined sequence of steps to achieve a specific task. A computer program is an algorithm written in a programming language.

analysis (§9.1)

In software development, **analysis** is the process of determining what is actually required of a proposed software system.

Analytical Engine (§1.1)

The **Analytical Engine** was designed by Charles Babbage in the 1840s. This machine was the mechanical forerunner of modern computers. Just like computers of today, there was a means of entering data (input) and receiving results (output) via dials, a place to store intermediate results (memory), an arithmetic mill (the part that did the computations, what we call the processor) and a mechanism for programming the machine.

anti-virus software (§1.5)

Anti-virus software are programs that check to see if a computer (or disk) is infected with a virus and then remove it.

applet (§2.1)

An **applet** is a special kind of Java program that runs within a browser (e.g., Internet Explorer) and provides the executable content to a web page. This is why Java was described as the "programming language for the Web."

application software (§1.3)

Application software are programs (e.g., Word 2000) that allow the computer to be applied to a specific task (e.g., word processing).

architectural plan (§9.1)

An **architectural plan** is the specification describing how the classes in the implementation of a system work together to produce the desired result.

arithmetic/logic unit (ALU) (§1.2)

As part of the CPU, the **arithmetic/logic unit** (ALU) performs the arithmetic (e.g., addition) and logical (e.g., comparison of numbers) functions of the computer.

array (§11.1)

An **array** is a collection of items (values, objects) all of the same type, stored under a single name.

array initializer (§11.2)

An **array initializer** is a notation that specifies the initial value of each element in an array. In Java, an array initializer is enclosed in braces (`{}`) and can only be used in an array declaration.

ASCII (§7.2)

ASCII (American Standard Code for Information Interchange) is a coding scheme that is the current standard for text storage and transmission on computer networks.

assembler (§1.4)

An **assembler** is the program that reads an assembly language program and produces and stores an equivalent machine language program.

assembly (§1.4)

Assembly is the process of translating the assembly language instructions into machine language prior to execution.

assembly language (§1.4)

In a second-generation language or **assembly language** each operation (opcode) is represented by a name and the operands (addresses) are expressed as a combination of names and simple arithmetic operations. Each assembly language instruction still corresponds to one machine operation.

assignment statement (§3.4)

An **assignment statement** is a statement through which the value of a variable is changed or set.

assignment-compatible (§3.4)

Assignment compatibility are the rules, in a language such as Java, that determine whether a value computed by an expression may be assigned to a variable. In Java, an expression of type `B` is **assignment-compatible** with a variable of type `A` if: (1) `A` and `B` are the same, (2) if `B` is a subtype of `A`, or (3) `A` can be converted to `B` using a widening conversion.

auxiliary storage devices (§1.2)

Auxiliary (secondary) **storage devices** are nonvolatile storage devices, such as a disk, used to store information (i.e., programs and data) for long periods of time, since main memory is volatile.

Charles Babbage (§1.1)

Charles Babbage was a mathematician and inventor who was very interested in automating calculations. He developed a machine called the Difference Engine (1822–42), which was able to automatically calculate difference tables (important for preparing trajectory tables for artillery pieces); he also designed the Analytical Engine, which was the mechanical forerunner of modern computers.

behavior (§8.2)

The **behavior** of an object is the effect of its methods. The behavior can depend on the state of the object.

binary I/O (§5.1)

Binary I/O is intended for consumption by another computer program and recorded in binary form (sequences of bytes).

binary (base-2) number system (§1.2)

In mathematics, the number system that has only two digits is called the **binary** (or base-2) **number system**. The two digits are `0` and `1`. This corresponds to the situation in computer memory (which is made up of bi-stable devices), so the binary number system has been adopted by computers as their basic number representation.

binary operator (§7.1)

A **binary operator** is any operator that takes exactly two operands. Most operators in Java are binary operators.

bi-stable device (§1.2)

A **bi-stable device** is an electronic component that has two states: open (no current flowing) or closed (current flowing) and that thus serves as a switch. Vacuum tubes and transistors are bi-stable devices.

bit (§1.2)

A **bit** is a single *b*inary dig*it*. The term is used to differentiate them from the decimal digits. Each switch (transistor) in computer memory represents one bit, and thus the bit is the smallest unit of measure for storage.

body (of a constructor or method) (§2.3)

The **body** of a constructor or method is the sequence of statements that defines the action of the constructor or method.

body (of a loop) (§6.1)

The **body** of a loop is the sequence of statements that is repeated as controlled by the loop statement.

boolean expression (§6.1)

A **boolean** expression is an expression that evaluates to a truth, or boolean, value: `true` or `false`.

boolean function (§7.1)

A **boolean function** (or predicate) is a function that returns a boolean result.

boolean literal (§7.1)

The **boolean literals** in Java are the keywords `true` and `false`, which represent the two possible boolean values.

boolean operator (§7.1)

A **boolean operator** is one of the three operations *and* (`&` or `&&` in Java), *or* (`|` or `||` in Java), and *not* (`!` in Java). These operators take boolean operands and produce a boolean result.

boolean variable (§7.1)

A **boolean variable** is a value variable that stores one of the two boolean values, `true` or `false`.

bootstrap loader (§1.3)

The **bootstrap loader** is a simple program that starts loading the operating system from the hard disk into RAM and then instructs the control unit to start fetching the instructions of the operating system.

bug (§1.4)

A **bug** occurs when the program tries to do something that is unreasonable (e.g., divide a number by zero) or doesn't produce the desired result. These errors are sometimes called execution or logic errors.

bus (§A)

The CPU is connected to memory by a set of wires called a **bus** along which data (in the form of electrical current) can flow. This is how information is fetched and stored.

byte (§1.2)

A group of eight bits is called a **byte**; it is the basic unit of storage on computers. In many coding schemes, a byte can represent a single text character.

calling (a method) (§4)

Calling or invoking a method occurs through the execution of a method invocation statement. The actual parameters are evaluated and passed to the formal parameters, the calling method is suspended and the called method begins execution at the first statement of its body.

carpal tunnel syndrome (§1.5)

Carpal tunnel syndrome is an inflammation in the carpal tunnel (the small opening in the wrist through which the ligaments, blood vessels and nerves serving the hand pass). This inflammation places pressure on the nerves causing tingling in the fingers and, in extreme cases, severe and unrelieved pain in the hand and wrist.

cast (§3.2)

A **cast** is an explicit direction to the compiler to cause a conversion. A cast, in Java, is written by writing the desired type in parentheses in front of an operand.

central processing unit (CPU) (§1.2)

The **central processing unit** (CPU) contains the circuitry that allows the computer to do the calculations and follow the instructions of the program. The CPU is divided into two main parts: the control unit and the arithmetic/logic unit.

character set (§7.2)

A **character set** is the set of characters, including both graphic and control characters, that are represented by a coding scheme.

class (§2.3)

Classes are the fundamental building blocks in object-oriented programming. A **class** is a specification of a set of possible objects in a computer system modeling a set of potential real-world entities such as tellers or students.

class declaration (§2.3)

A **class declaration** is the specification of a class in a Java program that defines a set of possible objects.

class specification (§9.1)

A **class specification** is a semi-formal specification of a class as a part of the implementation of a software system that defines the responsibilities of the class.

class stub (§9.2)

A **class stub** is a substitute for a supplier class used in the testing of a client class. It contains method stubs for each of the public methods of the real supplier class.

client class (§9.2)

A **client class** is a class that makes use of services provided by another class and thus depends on the supplier class's specification.

close (§5.1)

The disconnection of a stream from a source/destination is called **closing** the stream.

code reuse (§8.5)

Code reuse is one of the major advantages of object-oriented programming. It involves the use of the same code in a variety of locations in a project or in multiple projects, without the need to duplicate the code.

coding (§9.1)

Coding is the phase of software development in which the classes defined in the design phase are implemented in a programming language.

coding scheme (§7.2)

A **coding scheme** is a convention that associates each character from a character set with a unique bit pattern—a binary representation of the integers from 0. The common coding schemes are ASCII, EBCDIC, and Unicode.

cohesive (§8.3)

A class is **cohesive** if its instance variables represent information logically associated with the entity that the class represents and the methods represent operations the entity would logically perform.

column-major order (§11.7)

Column-major order refers to the storage or processing of a multi-dimensional array, column-by-column.

comment (§2.1)

A **comment** is a piece of commentary text included within the program text that is not processed by the compiler but serves to help a reader understand the program segment.

communications devices (§1.2)

Communications devices are devices that allow computers to exchange information using communications systems (e.g., telephone, cable). Communications devices unite computers into networks (including the Internet).

compile (§1.4)

Compiling is the process of translating a high-level language program into machine language as carried out by a compiler.

compiler (§1.4)

A **compiler** is a program that translates (compiles) a program written in a high-level language into machine language.

composition (§2.4)

Composition, or nesting, is a method of programming in which one piece of code (e.g., a loop) is placed within the body of another to achieve the combined effect of both.

computer programming language (§1.4)

A **computer programming language** is a notation (language) for expressing algorithms for computer operation.

computer science (§1)

Computer science is the study of computer hardware, algorithms, and data structures and how they fit together to provide information systems.

computer vision syndrome (§1.5)

Computer vision syndrome occurs from extended viewing of a computer monitor. Computer monitors, like television screens, actually flicker or pulse at a fairly high frequency. This places considerable strain on the eyes and, after time, leads to eye fatigue and headaches.

condition (§6.1)

A **condition** is a boolean expression that serves as the test in a loop or decision structure.

conditional loop (§6)

An indefinite loop or **conditional loop** is a loop that is repeated until (or as long as) some condition occurs.

constructor (§2.3)

A **constructor** a sequence of steps to be performed when a new object is created to initialize the object to a valid state.

constructor declaration (§2.3)

A **constructor declaration** is the specification of the set of steps for a constructor.

control character (§7.2)

A **control character** is a nongraphic character from a character set that is used to control a display, printer, or network connection.

control structure (statement) (§6)

A **control structure** (statement) is a statement that either controls a loop or makes a decision.

control unit (CU) (§1.2)

As part of the CPU, the **control unit** (CU) controls the components of the computer and follows the instructions of the program.

conversion (§3.2)

A **conversion** is a change in the type of a value—often implying a change in representation—within an expression.

CRC card (§9.2)

A **CRC** (Class Responsibilities Collaborators) **card** is a device used during design to help flesh out the classes discovered during analysis by assigning responsibilities to each class. Each class is represented by an index card on which the responsibilities of the class and the classes with which it collaborates in fulfilling its responsibilities are recorded.

cryptography (§11.4)

Cryptography is the study of encryption or coding and decoding messages using "secret codes."

data (§1)

Data are items (e.g., facts, figures, and ideas) that can be processed by a computer system.

data abstraction (§8.3)

Data abstraction is a technique for dealing with complexity in which a set of data values and the operations upon them are abstracted, as a class in an object-oriented language, defining a type. The abstraction can then be used without concern for the representation of the values or implementation of the operations.

database (§1.3)

A **database** (system) is application software that organizes collections of interrelated data such as student registration and marks information at a university.

debugging (§9.1)

When a class or program doesn't perform according to specification it is said to contain a bug. **Debugging** is the phase of software development in which it is determined why the class(es) fail and the problem is corrected.

decision (§6)

A **decision** is a set of sequences of statements in which one sequence is chosen to be executed based on a condition or expression.

declaration (of a variable) (§3.3)

A **declaration** is a construct in a programming language through which a variable's type and scope are defined.

decode (§A)

Instruction **decode** is the second phase of the machine cycle in which the control unit divides the instruction up into its opcode and operands. It then sends the appropriate signal to other components to tell them what to do next.

definite loop (§6.4)

A **definite loop** is one in which the number of times the loop body will be repeated is computable before the execution of the loop is begun.

derive (§2.1)

A program is **derived** (composed) from a grammar by writing sequences of symbols, starting with the goal symbol, and substituting, for some nonterminal symbol, one of the alternatives on the right-hand side of its rule, until only terminal symbols are left.

design (§9.1)

Design is the phase in software development in which decisions are made about how the software system will be implemented in a programming language.

desktop (§1.3)

The **desktop** is a representation of an office desktop, consisting of symbols called icons, that represent things like the hard drive, file folders containing programs or data, and programs themselves. The desktop is part of the graphical user interface.

desktop computer (§1.2)

A **desktop** (desk-side) **computer** is a traditional PC in which the system unit is small enough to fit on or immediately beside a desk.

detailed design (§9.2)

Detailed design is the second subphase of design in which detailed class specifications are produced. A detailed class specification includes all public variables and methods with their types and parameters.

Difference Engine (§1.1)

Charles Babbage developed, under contract to the British Government, a machine called the **Difference Engine** (1822–42) that was able to automatically calculate difference tables (important for preparing trajectory tables for artillery pieces).

digitization (§1.2)

Digitization is the process of encoding data (e.g., a picture or sound) as sequences of binary digits. For example, music can be coded as a sequence of binary numbers, each representing the height of the sound wave measured at particular sampling intervals. This is the way music is stored on audio CDs.

dimension (of an array) (§11.1)

The **dimension** of an array is the number of subscripts needed to select an individual element of the array.

dirty data (§1.5)

Dirty data refers to errors in data introduced through manual entry of data (usually from a keyboard).

documentation (§1.2)

Documentation is instructions (either as a printed book or online documentation that is read on the computer) for the user that describes how to make use of the software.

documentation (§9.1)

Documentation is a collection of descriptions and other information about a software system to support training and use by users (user documentation) or support the maintenance phase (technical documentation).

domain knowledge (§1.3)

Domain knowledge is knowledge of the area to which application software is applied. Application software is written to require little knowledge of computer science but it does expect the user to have domain knowledge.

EBCDIC (§7.2)

EBCDIC (Extended Binary Coded Decimal Interchange Code) is a coding scheme used primarily on mainframe (especially IBM) computers.

edit (§1.4)

Editing is the first phase in program preparation in which a special program, called a program editor (similar to a word processor, but designed for programming languages instead of natural languages) is used to type in, correct, and save a source (high-level language) program.

edit-compile-link-execute cycle (§1.4)

Producing executable code during program development involves a repeating sequence of operations—edit, compile, link, execute—called the **edit-compile-link-execute cycle**.

editor (§1.4)

A program **editor** is a program, similar to a word processor but designed for programming languages instead of natural languages, that allows the user (programmer) to enter, modify, and save source program text.

element (§11.1)

An **element** is an individual item within an array.

element type (of an array) (§11.1)

The **element type** of an array is the type of the individual elements.

else-part (§6.3)

The **else-part** is the second of the nested sequences of statements in an `if` statement and is executed when the condition is `false`.

embedded system (§2.1)

An **embedded system** is a system in which the software is part of a larger hardware system. Examples are missile guidance systems, the ignition system in an automobile, and the control system in a microwave oven.

end-of-file (EOF) (§5.1)

When reading, since the amount of information contained in a stream is finite, there will be a situation in which there are no more (or not enough) byte(s)/character(s) remaining in the stream. This situation is called reaching **end-of-file** (**EOF**) since, traditionally, files have been the usual source for a stream.

end-of-line (EOL) (§5.2)

An **end-of-line** (**EOL**) marker is actually a character(s) that the display device treats as a signal to start the following text on a new line.

e-notation (§3.1)

E-notation is a notation for floating-point values in Java where the literal is followed by the letter `e` (or `E`) and a second number that represents a power of `10` by which the first number is multiplied. For example, `1.2E+8` represents the value 120000000.0 (i.e., 1.2×10^8).

escape sequence (§7.2)

An **escape sequence** is a representation of a character (usually a nongraphic character) by a sequence of graphic characters. In Java, escape sequences begin with a `\`.

execute (§1.4)

When the machine language version of a program is being executed by the processor, we say that the program is being **executed** (is in execution).

execute (§A)

Instruction **execute** is the final phase of the machine cycle in which the components perform the operations indicated by the control unit.

execution error (§1.4)

An **execution error** occurs when the program tries to do something that is unreasonable (e.g., divide a number by zero). These errors are also called logic errors or bugs.

expression (§3.2)

An **expression** is a sequence of operands (variables and literals) and operations (operators and method calls) that describe a computation.

fetch (§A)

Instruction **fetch** is the first phase of the machine cycle in which the control unit, consulting the IAR, directs the memory to send the contents of the indicated memory location along the bus into the IR.

fetching (§A)

Reading (sometimes called **fetching**) information is obtaining the settings of the bits at a particular address in main memory.

field (of class or object) (§2.3)

A **field** is a named memory location in which an object can store information. Typically, it is an instance variable.

field (of a record) (§5.2)

A **field** is a single piece of information (e.g., a name) that is part of the collection of related information about an entity (e.g., an employee) that makes up a record. A field is written by a single call to a `write` method or it is read by a single call to a `read` method.

field declaration (§2.3)

A **field declaration** is the specification of a field within a class, giving its name and type.

field width (§5.2)

The **field width** is the number of characters an output data value is to occupy in formatted output.

finite state machine (§7.2)

A **finite state machine** is one representation of a computation defined by Alan Turing through which properties of computability can be derived.

first-generation computer (§1.1)

The **first-generation computers** used vacuum tubes as their primary switching device. Since vacuum tubes had a high failure rate, these computers were not reliable.

first-generation language (§1.4)

In a **first-generation language** (machine language) each operation that the computer is to perform is written as a separate instruction as a sequence of binary digits.

fixed-point (§3.1)

Fixed-point numbers are exact whole number values that roughly correspond to the integer domain in mathematics.

floating-point (§3.1)

Floating-point numbers are approximations to mixed-fractions that correspond roughly to the rational numbers in mathematics.

formal parameter (§4.2)

A parameter (**formal parameter**) is a variable name declared in the method header that receives a value when a method is called.

formal parameter declaration (§4.2)

A **formal parameter declaration** is the specification in a method header of the types of parameters that a method accepts and their local names.

formatted output (§5.2)

Formatted output is a form of text output allowing control over layout of the information and insertion of headings and titles, and so on.

fourth-generation computer (§1.1)

The **fourth-generation computers** use VLSI (very large scale integration), in which it is possible to place many millions of transistors and the accompanying circuitry on a single IC chip.

function (§4.3)

A method that, like functions in mathematics, computes a value is called a function method or simply a **function**.

function method (§4.3)

A method that, like functions in mathematics, computes a value is called a **function method** or simply a function.

garbage (§8.3)

In Java, objects that have been created but are no longer accessible, not being referenced by any variable, are termed **garbage**.

garbage collection (§8.3)

In Java, storage for objects that are no longer accessible (called garbage) is periodically recovered and made available for reuse in a process called **garbage collection**.

gigabyte (GB) (§1.2)

A **gigabyte** (GB) is a thousand megabytes (actually 2^{30} or 1,073,741,824 bytes). Auxiliary storage is often measured in gigabytes, so a hard drive might have 20GB of storage.

grammar (§2.1)

The **grammar** (or syntax rules) of a programming language is the set of rules defining the syntax of the language.

graphic character (§7.2)

A **graphic character** is a character from the character set that is graphically displayed on the display or printer. These include the letters of the alphabet, numerals, punctuation, and other special characters.

graphical user interface (GUI) (§1.1)

A **GUI** (graphical user interface) is an interface between the user and the computer that makes use of a graphical display on which symbols (called icons) can be displayed and a pointing device (e.g., mouse) that the user uses to point out actions to be performed.

green PC (§1.5)

So called **green PCs** are designed to reduce environmental effects primarily by reducing electrical consumption. This is accomplished by, among other things, putting the monitor into a low-power stand-by mode when the computer display hasn't changed for a period and only rotating the disk drive when files are actually being accessed.

hacker (§1.5)

Hackers are individuals who attempt to break into computer systems by guessing passwords to accounts and, once connected, can cause all manner of damage from simply stealing data to deleting or modifying it.

happiness message (§5.3)

A **happiness message** is a message displayed by a program that informs the user when something is happening or when the program finishes correctly.

hardware (§1.2)

Hardware are the physical components (e.g., processor, monitor, mouse) of the computer itself.

hidden (§4.5)

An instance variable of a class is **hidden** (i.e., not visible within) by a local variable of the same name declared in a constructor or method of that class.

high-level language (HLL) (§1.4)

A problem-oriented language or **high-level language** is a language that expresses the algorithm in a notation close to natural language (e.g., more English-like). However, the language is more formalized than natural language (to remove ambiguities).

I/O (§5.1)

I/O (input/output) is the operation of obtaining data from outside the computer (input, using input devices) or presenting information to the environment of the computer (output, using output devices).

icon (§1.3)

Icons are small symbols that represent things such as the hard drive, file folders containing programs or data, and programs themselves on the desktop as part of the graphical user interface.

identifier (§2.1)

In programming languages, **identifiers** are words coined by the programmer to identify entities (e.g., classes, methods, variables) but that have no predefined meaning in the language.

if-then statement (§6.3)

The **if-then statement** is a decision structure in which the nested sequence of statements is executed or not. It is represented by the if-then form of the `if` statement in Java.

if-then-else statement (§6.3)

The **if-then-else statement** is a decision structure in which one of a pair of nested sequences of statements is executed. It is represented by the if-then-else form of the `if` statement in Java.

if-then-elsif statement (§6.3)

The **if-then-elsif statement** is a decision structure in which one of a set of three or more nested sequences of statements is executed based on consecutive tests of conditions. There is no if-then-elsif statement in Java; however, one can be simulated using nested `if` statements.

immutable (§10.1)

Objects of a class are **immutable** if their state (value) cannot be changed. `String` objects are immutable in Java.

increment (§3.4)

Increment is an operation in which a variable's value is increased by a set amount (often 1).

increment (in a `for` loop) (§6.4)

The **increment** (decrement) in a `for` loop is the amount by which the loop index is increased (decreased) each time through the loop.

indefinite loop (§6)

An **indefinite loop** or conditional loop is a loop that is repeated until (or as long as) some condition occurs.

(loop) index (§6.4)

A loop index variable, or **index** for short, is the variable used within a `for` loop to count through the repeated executions of the loop.

infinite loop (§6.1)

An **infinite loop** is a loop that doesn't terminate; in other words, it runs forever. Usually this is a logic error or bug in a program.

information (§1)

Information is processed data (e.g., reports, summaries, animations) produced by a computer system through computation, summary, or synthesis.

information hiding (§8.3)

Information hiding is a method of abstraction in which only select information is made visible to a client. In data abstraction, this usually involves hiding the variables (the representation) and exposing certain methods (the operations).

input device (§1.2)

Input devices are the components that the computer uses to access data that is present outside the computer system. Input devices perform a conversion from the form in which the data exists in the real world to the form that the computer can process.

instance variable (§2.3)

An **instance variable** is a field of a class that is declared without the modifier `static`. It represents a storage location that the object uses to remember information. Each object has its own memory for instance variables.

instruction address register (IAR) (§A)

The **instruction address register** (IAR) is a register used by the control unit to sequence through the instructions of the program. It contains the address of the next instruction to be fetched.

instruction register (IR) (§A)

The **instruction register** (IR) is a register used by the control unit to hold the instruction currently being decoded.

integer division (§3.2)

Integer division is division of integral (fixed-point) values producing an integral result without remainder.

integrated circuit (§1.1)

An **integrated circuit** (IC) is a solid-state device on which an entire circuit (i.e., transistors and the connections between them) can be created (etched). They are the main circuitry of third generation computers.

interactive development environment (IDE) (§1.4)

Software development environments (sometimes called **interactive development environments** (IDE)) are programs that are used by programmers to write other programs. From one point of view, they are application programs because they apply the computer to the task of writing computer software. On the other hand, the users are computer scientists and the programming task is not the end in itself, but rather a means to apply the computer to other tasks. Often software development environments are grouped under the category of systems software.

internationalization (§7.2)

Internationalization is the ability of a program to operate correctly when used in different locales where different languages and numeric representations are used.

Internet addiction (§1.5)

Internet addiction occurs when an individual has established a dependency on surfing the web. Like any other addict, these individuals suffer withdrawal if deprived of access and typically allow the rest of their lives (e.g., family, employment) to suffer in pursuit of their habit.

in-test loop (§6.2)

An **in-test** loop is a loop in which the test for loop termination (or continuation) occurs within the loop body. There is no in-test loop in Java although one can be manufactured using a `while` statement, an `if` statement, and a `break` statement.

invoking (a method) (§4)

Calling or **invoking** a method occurs through the execution of a method invocation statement. The actual parameters are evaluated and passed to the formal parameters, the calling method is suspended and the called method begins execution at the first statement of its body.

Jacquard (Jacquard's loom) (§1.1)

Jacquard was a French inventor who developed an automated weaving loom that used wooden cards with punched holes to control the pattern in the weaving process. This idea was borrowed by Babbage for input in his Analytical Engine.

Java (§1)

Java is a modern (1990s) object-oriented programming language developed by James Gosling et al. at Sun Microsystems.

Java bytecode (§2.5)

Java bytecode is a platform-independent binary language similar to machine language that it generated by a Java compiler. This code must be executed by a Java interpreter.

Java interpreter (§2.5)

A **Java interpreter** is a program (i.e., machine language) that inputs and executes Java bytecode program code. This is how a Java program is executed and how Java achieves platform-independence.

keyword (§2.1)

In programming languages **keywords** are words that have a specific meaning and are defined by the language (e.g., `class`).

laptop computer (§1.2)

A **laptop computer** is a PC that is small and light enough to be used on the lap while sitting on an airplane or commuter train seat.

lazy evaluation (§7.1)

Lazy evaluation is a process by which operands in an expression are evaluated only as needed. It was first used in the language LISP. The short-circuit operators in Java use lazy evaluation.

length (of an array) (§11.1)

The **length** of a dimension of an array is the number of elements in that dimension of the array. For a one-dimensional array, the length of its only dimension is called the length of the array.

lexical analysis (§10.4)

Lexical analysis is the process of separating a piece of text in some language (especially a programming language) into its individual tokens.

lexicographic order (§11.7)

Lexicographic order is when the elements of an array are stored or processed in such an order that, when the subscripts are concatenated, the resulting numbers are in numeric order. Row-major order is a lexicographic ordering.

library (§1.4)

A **library** is a collection of pieces of previously written (and previously compiled) code, saved on disk, that can be used in building a program.

link (§1.4)

Linking is the third phase in program preparation where pieces of machine language code produced by a compiler or assembler are combined with machine code from libraries.

link error (§1.4)

Link errors occur during linking when the linker cannot find the desired pieces of library code (typically because the programmer mistyped a name somewhere).

linker (§1.4)

A **linker** is a program that combines pieces of machine language code produced by a compiler or assembler with machine code from libraries.

local method (§4.1)

A **local method** is a method of the same object (i.e., one whose declaration is in the same class as the code we are writing) written with the `private` qualifier.

local variable (§3.3)

A **local variable** is a variable used to temporarily store a value within a method or constructor. In Java, its scope is the body of the method or constructor.

logic error (§1.4)

A **logic error** occurs when the program tries to do something that is unreasonable (e.g., divide a number by zero) or doesn't produce the desired result. These errors are sometimes called execution errors or bugs.

lookup table (§11.7)

A **lookup table** is a two-dimensional array in which a value in one column is used to locate (lookup) the value in the other column(s).

loop (§6)

A **loop** is a sequence of statements that is repeated either a specific number of times or until some condition occurs.

loop index variable (§6.4)

A **loop index variable**, or index for short, is the variable used within a `for` loop to count through the repeated executions of the loop.

machine cycle (§A)

The basic process that the control unit follows is called the **machine cycle**. The machine cycle consists of three phases: fetch, decode, and execute, which the control unit repeats from the time the power is turned on until the system is shut down.

machine language (§A)

Machine language is a binary representation of the instructions understood by the control unit. Since the instructions are the way in which we communicate the algorithm to the computer, they form a language.

main class (§4.1)

One class in each Java program (called the **main class**) must have a method called `main` (the main method) where execution begins.

main memory (§1.2)

The **main memory** (or RAM—Random Access Memory) is (as the name implies) the place where the computer remembers things (much like our own short-term memory). Everything that the computer is working on (including data being processed, the results or information produced, and the program instructions themselves) must be present in memory while it is being used.

main method (§4.1)

One class in each Java program (called the main class) must have a method called `main` (the **main method**) where execution begins.

mainframe (§1.2)

A **mainframe** computer is larger and more powerful than a minicomputer. These are the traditional kinds of computers that typically occupy an entire room and are the mainstay of big business. These machines can handle hundreds of users at a time and are used in applications such as airline reservations and banking.

maintenance (§9.1)

Maintenance is the phase of software development in which bugs detected in the field are corrected and new features are analyzed and implemented.

McCarthy operator (§7.1)

A short-circuit (or **McCarthy**) **operator** is an operator that does not always evaluate both of its operands to produce a result. The short-circuit operators in Java include

`&&` (*and-then*) and `||` (*or-else*). They are used in special cases in place of the usual *and* (`&`) and *or* (`|`) operators.

megabyte (MB) (§1.2)

A **megabyte** (MB) is a million bytes (actually 2_{20} or `1,048,576` bytes). Main memory size is usually measured in megabytes, so a microcomputer might have 256MB of RAM.

megahertz (MHz) (§A)

System clock speeds are measured in **megahertz** (MHz). One megahertz is one million cycles (pulses) per second.

memory model (§3.4)

A **memory model** is a model (notation) of the behavior of the program with respect to memory.

method (§4)

A **method** (procedure) is a named sequence of instructions that can be referenced (invoked, called) in other places in the program through the use of a method (procedure) invocation statement.

method body (§4.2)

The **method body** is the sequence of statements that is performed when the method is invoked.

method declaration (§4.2)

A **method declaration** is the specification of the method giving its result type, name, parameter list, and body.

method header (§4.2)

The **method header** specifies what the method defines by specifying its result type, name, and its list of (formal) parameters.

method invocation (§4)

Calling or **invoking** a **method** occurs through the execution of a method invocation statement. The actual parameters are evaluated and passed to the formal parameters, the calling method is suspended, and the called method begins execution at the first statement of its body.

method stub (§4.4)

A **method stub** is a replacement for a method not yet written that displays a message to the console for testing and debugging purposes.

microcomputer (§1.1)

By the mid-'70s, it was possible to put the complete circuitry for the processor of a simple computer on a single chip (called a microprocessor). Such a computer is called a **microcomputer**.

microprocessor (§1.1)

A **microprocessor** is a single VLSI chip containing the complete circuitry of a computer processor. It is the basis for a microcomputer.

minicomputer (§1.2)

A **minicomputer** is a refrigerator-sized computer that can handle between twenty and fifty users at one time. They are typically used in mid-sized businesses or branch offices.

mixed mode (§3.2)

A **mixed-mode** expression is one in which the sub-expressions are not of the same mode (type).

mode (§3.2)

The **mode** of an expression is the type of the value that the expression produces (e.g., an integer mode expression is one that produces an integral result).

Mohammed ibn Musa Al-Kowarizmi (§1.1)

Mohammed ibn Musa Al-Kowarizmi (ca. 850) was an Arab philosopher who wrote at length about arithmetic processes and lent his name to the subject (algorithm from Al-Kowarizmi).

multidimensional array (§11.7)

A **multidimensional array** is an array whose items are selected by two or more subscripts.

mutable (§10.1)

Objects of a class are **mutable** if their state (value) can be changed. Most objects are mutable.

John Napier (Napier's bones) (§1.1)

The English mathematician **John Napier** developed (1617) a tool (called **Napier's bones**) based on the logarithmic tables, which allowed the user to multiply and divide easily. This evolved into the slide rule (Edmund Gunther, 1621), which was the mainstay of scientists and engineers until the recent development of the hand-held calculator.

narrowing conversion (§3.2)

A **narrowing conversion** is one where the value is converted into another ("smaller") type with potential loss of information (e.g., converting `double` to `int` in Java).

nesting (§2.4)

Nesting or composition is a method of programming in which one piece of code (e.g., loop) is placed within the body of another to achieve the combined effect of both.

not (§6.2)
The boolean operator ***not*** produces the logical negation of its operand, that is, it produces `true` from `false` and `false` from `true`. *Not* is represented by the `!` operator in Java.

notebook computer (§1.2)
A **notebook computer** is a PC that is small enough (about the size of a typical notebook) to be carried in a briefcase and used on the lap or desktop.

null string (§10.1)
A string consisting of zero characters is called the **null string**.

numeric literal (§3.1)
A **numeric literal** is a notation (token) in a programming language that represents a numeric value.

numeric type (§3.1)
A **numeric type** is a type that represents numeric values (fixed or floating point). In Java this includes the types `byte`, `short`, `int`, `long`, `float`, and `double`.

Numerical Analysis (§6.1)
Numerical Analysis is that branch of mathematics and computer science that determines numerical but approximate solutions of mathematical problems that are analytically intractable.

object (§2.1)
An **object** is an instance of a class that exists at execution time. It has a state and behavior and typically models a real-world entity such as a customer or a report.

object code (§1.4)
Object code is the machine language code produced by compiling a high-level language program.

object reference variable (§7)
An **object reference variable** (or reference variable) is a variable that references an object and is declared using a class name as the type.

object-oriented programming (§2.1)
In **object-oriented programming**, a program is designed to be a model of the real-world system it is replacing. The program contains objects that represent real-world entities (e.g., customers, students, reports, financial transactions, etc.), which interact with (make use of) each other.

one-based subscripting (§11.1)
One-based subscripting refers to the specification in a language that the subscript 1 references the first element or sub-portion in a dimension of an array.

one-dimensional array (§11.1)

A **one-dimensional array** is one in which elements are selected by a single subscript. Such an array is sometimes called a vector or list.

opcode (§A)

In the machine language, each different operation that can be performed by the processor is assigned a (binary) number called the operation code (or **opcode**).

open (§5.1)

The connection of a stream to a source/destination is called **opening** the stream.

operand (§3.2)

An **operand** is a component of an expression that represents a value in a computation. Operands include literals and variables.

operand (§A)

In a machine language instruction, the part(s) of the instruction (as binary digits) that represents the data being processed (usually an address of data in memory) is called an **operand**.

operating system (§1.3)

The **operating system** (OS) is a set of programs that manage the resources of the computer. When the computer is first turned on, it is the operating system that gets things started and presents the user interface that allows the user to choose what s/he wishes to do.

operator (§3.2)

An **operator** is a token (symbol or word) in a programming language used to represent an operation, such as addition, within an expression

operator precedence (§3.2)

Each **operator** in a language has a **precedence** that defines how the operators bind (are applied to) the operands. Operators with higher precedence bind to the operands before operators of lower precedence. Operator precedence defines a partial ordering for the operations in the expression.

output device (§1.2)

Output devices are the components of the computer that present results from the computer to the outside environment. They perform the conversion from the computer representation to the real-world representation.

palindrome (§10.3)

A **palindrome** is a word or phrase that reads the same forwards and backwards.

parameter (§4.2)

A **parameter** (formal parameter) is a variable name declared in the method header that receives a value when a method is called.

Blaise Pascal (§1.1)

Blaise Pascal, after whom the programming language Pascal is named, developed a fully mechanical adding machine in 1642; the user didn't have to perform the algorithm, the machine did.

passing a parameter (§4.2)

Passing a parameter is the process that occurs during a method call, by which actual parameter values are computed and assigned to formal parameters.

personal computer (PC) (§1.1)

A **personal computer** is a computer that is simple and inexpensive enough to be purchased and used by a nontechnical individual. Personal computers (PCs) were made possible by the development of microprocessors and began with the Apple II in 1977.

Plankalkül (§1.1)

Plankalkül was a notation for expressing programs developed by Zuse for his Z3 computer. It is regarded as the first programming language.

platform independence (§2.1)

Platform independence is the property that the code generated by a compiler can run on any processor. This feature is also called "write-once-run-anywhere" and allows Java code to be written on a Macintosh or PC (or other machine) and then run on whatever machine is desired.

pocket PC (§1.2)

A **pocket PC** is a microcomputer small enough to be carried in a pocket. It typically uses a stylus or alternative input device instead of a traditional typewriter-style keyboard.

positional number system (§1.2)

A **positional number system** is a notation for writing numbers in which a number is written as a sequence of digits (`0` through `9` for base ten, `0` or `1` for base two), with digits in different positions having different values. Both our usual decimal number system and the binary number system are positional number systems while Roman numerals are not.

post-test loop (§6.2)

A **post-test loop** is a loop in which the test for loop termination (or continuation) occurs after the last statement of the loop body. This is represented by the `do` statement in Java.

predicate (§7.2)

A boolean function (or **predicate**) is a function that returns a boolean result.

pre-test loop (§6.2)

A **pre-test loop** is a loop in which the test for loop termination (or continuation) occurs before the first statement of the loop body. This is represented by the `while` statement in Java.

primitive type (§7)

A **primitive type** is a type that is fundamental to the programming language. It is not represented in terms of other types. In Java, the primitive types are `byte`, `short`, `int`, `long`, `float`, `double`, `char`, and `boolean`.

problem statement (§9.1)

A **problem statement** is a loose specification of the requirements for a software system, usually written by a user (or user group). It serves as the starting point for analysis.

problem-oriented language (§1.4)

A **problem-oriented language** or high-level language is a language that expresses the algorithm in a notation close to natural language (e.g., more English-like). However, the language is more formalized than natural language (to remove ambiguities).

procedural abstraction (§4)

Procedural abstraction is the technique whereby we ignore the details of the procedure (i.e., the way it accomplishes its task) and emphasize the task itself.

procedure (§4)

A method (**procedure**) is a named sequence of instructions that can be referenced (invoked, called) in other places in the program through the use of a method (procedure) invocation statement.

procedures (§1.2)

Procedures are the steps that the user must follow to use the software as described in the documentation.

production (§9.1)

Production is the phase of software development in which the developed system has been tested and debugged and is made available to the user community.

programmable (§1)

A device (such as a computer) is **programmable** if it can be instructed (programmed) to perform different tasks.

programmer (§9.1)

A **programmer** is a computer scientist whose primary responsibility is to develop code according to specifications laid out in the design phase.

programmer/analyst (§9.1)

A **programmer/analyst** is a computer scientist who is involved in analysis, design, and coding.

programming pattern (§2.4)

A **programming pattern** is a commonly used pattern of programming language statements that solves some particular kind of problem. It serves as a guide to writing some part of a program.

prompt (§5.3)
A **prompt** is text displayed during an input operation to identify, to the user, what information is being requested.

pseudocode (§4)
Pseudocode is an informal English-like notation for expressing algorithms.

punctuation (§2.1)
In programming languages, **punctuation** (e.g., ;) are symbols that separate, group, or terminate (mark the end of) other symbols.

random access (§11.4)
Random access refers to the processing of a collection of items, in an array for example, in unpredictable order.

random access memory (RAM) (§1.2)
The main memory or **RAM** (Random Access Memory) is (as the name implies) the place where the computer remembers things (much like our own short-term memory). Everything that the computer is working on (including data being processed, the results or information produced, and the program instructions themselves) must be present in memory while it is being used. Information in RAM can be processed in any (random) order.

read (§1.2)
Reading (sometimes called fetching) information is obtaining the settings of the bits at a particular address in main memory.

read (§5.1)
The act of obtaining information from an input stream is called **reading**.

read-only memory (ROM) (§1.3)
Read-only memory (ROM) is nonvolatile memory that comes from the computer manufacturer loaded with a program called the bootstrap loader.

record (§6.3)
A **record** is a set of related pieces of information, or fields, about a single entity stored in a file.

reference equality (§7.1)
The equality operators (== and !=), when used on reference variables, indicate equality if the variables reference the *same* object. This is called **reference equality**.

reference variable (§7)
An object reference variable (or **reference variable**) is a variable that references an object and is declared using a class name as the type.

register (§A)

Since the CPU must remember some things temporarily, it contains a few special pieces of memory called **registers**. The registers are part of the CPU itself (i.e., on the processor chip in a microprocessor), not part of main memory.

regular array (§11.7)

An array is said to be **regular** if all the rows have the same number of columns, all the planes, the same number of rows, and so on.

relational operator (§7.1)

A **relational operator** is one of six operators (in Java: `<`, `<=`, `==`, `>=`, `>`, `!=`) that can be used to compare values, producing a `boolean` result.

release (§9.1)

A **release** of a software system is a minor upgrade to the system, primarily to fix bugs. It does not usually involve a change in functionality.

requirements specification (§9.1)

A **requirements specification** is a formal specification of the requirements of a software system and is one of the products of the analysis phase of software development.

return (§4.1)

When the statements of a method are completed (or a `return` statement is executed), the method is said to **return** to the place from which it was called (i.e., execution continues at the statement where the method was originally invoked).

row-major order (§11.7)

Row-major order refers to the storage or processing of a multi-dimensional array, row-by-row.

scope rules (§4.5)

The rules that sort out the (unique) meaning of a name (e.g., a variable name) within a program are called **scope rules**.

secant method (§6.1)

The **secant method** is a method of numerical analysis that may find a numerical solution of the root of a function.

second generation (§1.1)

The **second-generation** electronic computers used transistors as their primary switching device. Using solid state technology made second-generation computers faster and more reliable.

second-generation language (§1.4)

In a **second-generation language,** or assembly language, each operation (opcode) is represented by a name and the operands (addresses) are expressed as a combination of names and simple arithmetic operations. Each assembly language instruction still corresponds to one machine operation.

secondary storage devices (§1.2)
Auxiliary (**secondary**) **storage devices** are nonvolatile storage devices, such as a disk, used to store information (i.e., programs and data) for long periods of time since main memory is volatile.

semantics (§2.1)
The **semantics** (of a programming language) specifies the meaning (i.e., effect of executing the program) of correctly composed programs.

senior programmer (§9.1)
A **senior programmer** is a more experienced programmer who may be called upon to do design, or lead a programming team.

sequential access (§11.4)
Sequential access refers to the processing of a collection of items, in an array for example, in order from first to last.

sequential execution (§6)
In **sequential execution**, execution begins at the start of the first method (`main`) and, as each method is called, the calling method is suspended. The called method executes and then returns to the place from which it was called; execution then continues in the calling method, and so on, until execution reaches the end of the `main` method, at which point the program terminates.

sequential file processing architecture (§9.2)
In the **sequential file processing architecture**, each entity for which processing is to be performed is represented by a record on a sequential file. The records are read and processed, one at a time, to produce the result.

short-circuit operator (§7.1)
A **short-circuit** (or McCarthy) **operator** is an operator that does not always evaluate both of its operands to produce a result. The short-circuit operators in Java include `&&` (*and-then*) and `||` (*or-else*). They are used in special cases in place of the usual *and* (`&`) and *or* (`|`) operators.

software (§1.2)
Software are the computer programs (algorithms expressed in a computer language) that allow the computer to be applied to a particular task.

software analyst (§9.1)
A **software** (or system) **analyst** is a senior computer scientist who performs the analysis phase of software development.

software development environments (§1.3)

Software development environments (sometimes called interactive development environments (IDE)) are programs that are used by programmers to write other programs. From one point of view, they are application programs because they apply the computer to the task of writing computer software. On the other hand, the users are computer scientists and the programming task is not the end in itself, but rather a means to apply the computer to other tasks. Often, software development environments are grouped under the category of systems software.

software piracy (§1.5)

Software piracy is the illegal copying of software. The copyright laws protect intellectual property (including software); however, they are not easily enforceable in an age when a perfect copy can be produced in seconds.

software system (§9.1)

A **software system** is a set of programs and related files that provides support for some user activity.

source code (§1.4)

A source program (**source code**) is the original program written in a high-level language that is being compiled.

source program (§1.4)

A **source program** (source code) is the original program written in a high-level language that is being compiled.

spreadsheets (§1.3)

Spreadsheets are a type of common application software for doing numerical calculations, such as balancing a checkbook.

state (§8.2)

The **state** of an object is represented by the set of values stored in each of its instance variables. The effect of a method call to an object can depend on its state.

state diagram (§8.2)

A **state diagram** is a form of a state transition diagram used to describe the possible states of an object and the transitions between the states.

state transition diagram (§7.2)

A **state transition diagram** is a diagram that represents the possible changes of state in a finite state machine. It consists of ovals representing states and arcs representing transitions. A version of state transition diagrams, called statecharts or state diagrams, can be used to represent the possible states and transitions of an object in an object-oriented program.

statement (§2.3)

A **statement** is the specification of a single action within a program.

store (§1.2)

Storing (sometimes called writing) information is recording the information into main memory at a specified address by changing the settings of the bits at that address.

stored program concept (§1.1)

The mathematician John von Neumann defined the **stored program concept**—that a computer must have a memory in which instructions are stored and which can be modified by the program itself.

stream (§5.1)

A **stream** is a sequence of information (either bytes for binary information or characters for text information) from/to which information (i.e., bytes/characters) may be obtained or appended.

string (§10.1)

A **string** is a sequence of zero or more characters from a character set. In Java, a string is an object of the `String` class and the characters are from the Unicode character set.

string literal (§10.1)

A **string literal** is a representation for a string value within the program text. In Java, a string literal is a sequence of zero or more graphic characters from the Unicode character set or escape sequences, enclosed in double-quotes (`"`).

subscript (§11.1)

A **subscript** is a notation written after an array name to access an element or subportion of an array in a subscripted variable. In Java, a subscript is an integer expression enclosed in brackets (`[]`).

subscripted variable (§11.1)

A **subscripted variable** is an array name followed by one or more subscripts, used to access an element or subportion of an array.

substring (§10.3)

A **substring** is a sequence of zero or more consecutive characters within a string.

subtype (§3.4)

A type `B` is a **subtype** of another type `A` if `B` is a specialization ("special kind of") of `A`. In Java, a class is a subtype of any class it (directly or indirectly) extends or any interface it (directly or indirectly) implements.

supercomputer (§1.2)

Supercomputers are the most powerful computers. Although similar in size to mainframes, these very expensive computers can perform complex arithmetic computations very quickly. They are commonly used in research and areas involving large amounts of computation, such as weather forecasting.

syntax (§2.1)
The **syntax** (of a programming language) specifies how the basic elements of the language (e.g., identifiers, keywords, and punctuation) are used to compose programs. It is described by a set of rules (syntax rules or grammar).

syntax error (§1.4)
A **syntax error** is a grammatical error in the expression of an algorithm in a high-level language. Syntax errors are detected by the compiler.

syntax rules (§2.1)
The **syntax rules** (or grammar) of a programming language are the set of rules defining the syntax of the language.

system analyst (§9.1)
A software (or **system**) **analyst** is a senior computer scientist who performs the analysis phase of software development.

system clock (§A)
To ensure that all of the hardware components work together (i.e., know when to look for an instruction from the control unit), they are synchronized by the system clock. The **system clock** is a crystal that emits electrical pulses at a specific frequency. Each component counts the pulses and knows when to look for control signals.

system designer (§9.1)
A **system designer** is a senior computer scientist who performs the design phase of software development.

system software (§1.3)
System software are software that manage the computer system and consists primarily of the operating system (e.g., Windows 2000).

system testing (§9.1)
System testing is the part of testing that involves the complete set of classes that makes up the system. It is the last phase of testing.

tab-delimited format (§5.3)
A file in **tab-delimited format** contains text fields separated by tabs or new lines.

technical documentation (§9.1)
Technical documentation includes specifications, architectural plans, implementation notes, and other documentation to support the maintenance phase.

technical support (§9.1)
Technical support staff provide assistance to users when they encounter problems with a software system.

technical writer (§9.1)

A **technical writer** is a computer scientist whose role in software development is to write documentation, primarily user documentation.

terminate (§2.1)

A software system (program) **terminates** when it is no longer executing (i.e., being executed by the CPU). This can happen by the program terminating normally (i.e., by reaching the normal end of its execution) or due to an execution error (in which case we say the program crashed).

test harness (§9.2)

A **test harness** is a substitute main class used to drive the testing of a class or set of classes.

tester (§9.1)

A **tester** is a computer scientist that carries out testing of system components, usually groups of classes that must work together.

testing (§9.1)

Testing is the phase of software development in which the implemented classes are executed, individually and in groups, to determine if they meet the specifications.

text I/O (§5.1)

I/O intended for human consumption is presented as **text** (sequences of characters typically represented according to the ASCII coding scheme).

then-part (§6.3)

The **then-part** is the first of the nested sequences of statements in an `if` statement and is executed when the condition is `true`.

third generation (§1.1)

The **third generation** of computers used integrated circuits as their main circuitry. An integrated circuit is a solid-state device on which an entire circuit (i.e., transistors and the connections between them) can be created (etched).

token (§10.4)

A **token** is a single, indivisible symbol from a language (particularly a programming language) such as a word, punctuation symbol, or literal.

tolerance (§6.1)

The **tolerance** is a specification of how close an approximation should be in finding an algorithmic solution to a numerical problem.

trainer (§9.1)

A **trainer** is a computer scientist whose role is to train users in the use of the developed software system.

transistor (§1.1)

A **transistor** is a solid-state device that provides the same capabilities as a vacuum tube (i.e., an electronic switch). However, unlike vacuum tubes, which were large and very prone to failure, transistors were small and lasted indefinitely.

traversal (§11.2)

A **traversal** of a data structure (such as an array) is a process in which some operation is performed on each element of the structure.

truth table (§7.1)

A **truth table** is a table, similar to an addition table, which shows the results of a boolean operation or expression for each operand value.

unary operator (§7.1)

A **unary operator** is an operator that takes exactly one operand.

Unicode (§7.2)

Unicode (UNIversal CODE) is a coding scheme that is the new ANSI standard. It supports most of the world's languages and is becoming the Internet standard. Java uses the Unicode coding scheme for `char` values.

updater method (§8.4)

An **updater** (or mutator) **method** is a method that serves to modify the value of an attribute, usually an instance variable, of an object.

upward compatible (§A)

A processor family (e.g., the Intel x86/Pentium family) is said to be **upward compatible** if later processors in the family can understand the machine language of earlier processors in the same family (but not necessarily *vice versa*).

user (§1.2)

A **user** is an individual that uses a computing system to produce a result (e.g., produce an essay). Typically, this is not someone trained in computer science; however, s/he most likely is trained in computer use.

user documentation (§9.1)

User documentation includes user guides, tutorials, reference manuals, and help systems that support user training and use of a software system.

vacuum tube (§1.1)

A **vacuum tube** (much like a light bulb) is an evacuated tube of glass with a coil of wire as a heater, which causes electrons to be emitted (emitter) and flow across the vacuum to a plate called the collector. A gate can be charged (or discharged) to block (or allow) the flow of electrons. Vacuum tubes were the primary switching device in first-generation computers.

value equality (§7.1)

The equality operators (== and !=), when used on values of a primitive type, indicate equality if the values are equivalent. This is called **value equality**.

value variable (§7)

A **value variable** is a variable that stores a value and is declared using a primitive type name as the type.

variable (§3.3)

A **variable** is a name (identifier) associated with some cells in memory into which a value may be stored.

variable dictionary (§3.3)

A **variable dictionary** is a (set of) comment describing the purpose of a variable identifier within the program.

version (§9.1)

A **version** of a software system is a major upgrade of the system, usually to provide new functionality.

very large scale integration (VLSI) (§1.1)

VLSI (very large scale integration) characterizes integrated circuits (ICs), which contain many millions of transistors and the accompanying circuitry. Fourth-generation computers use VLSI circuitry.

virus (§1.5)

A **virus** is a program that has been written by someone with considerable knowledge of an operating system. It can make copies of itself onto a floppy disk inserted into an infected machine or transmit itself along with a file being downloaded from another computer. Once on the machine, the effect of the virus can range from fairly benign (e.g., displaying a message on a particular date) to malicious (such as erasing the contents of the hard disk).

visibility rules (§4.5)

The rules defining where a variable (or for that matter a method) declared in some declaration can be used (referenced) within the program are called the **visibility rules** (essentially the converse of scope).

visible (§4.1)

An entity (class, method, or variable) that is declared is said to be **visible** at some point in the program if its use has meaning at that point in the program.

volatile (§1.2)

Volatile means subject to change. Main memory is volatile since, after power is lost (e.g., the computer is shut down), the contents of memory cannot be relied upon. This means that main memory can only be used for short-term storage.

John von Neumann (§1.1)

The mathematician **John von Neumann** defined the stored program concept—that a computer must have a memory in which instructions are stored and that can be modified by the program itself.

white space (§2.1)

White space, in a Java program, are sequences of spaces, tabs, new lines, and comments that serve only to separate symbols in the program and are otherwise ignored by the compiler. They are inserted to make it easier for the human reader to understand the program.

widening conversion (§3.2)

A **widening conversion** is one where the value can be converted into another ("larger") type without loss of information (e.g., converting `int` to `double` in Java).

word processing (§1.3)

Word processing is one type of common application software designed primarily for creating and editing text documents.

word wrap (§10.4)

Word wrap is a feature of word processing programs in which, in the layout of a line of a paragraph, if a word will not completely fit on a line, it is moved to the beginning of the next line.

workstation (§1.2)

A **workstation** is a powerful microcomputer typically used in scientific, engineering, and animation applications.

write (§5.1)

The act of appending information to an output stream is called **writing**.

zero-based subscripting (§11.1)

Zero-based subscripting refers to the specification in a language that the subscript `0` references the first element or subportion in a dimension of an array. Java uses zero-based subscripting.

Konrad Zuse (§1.1)

Konrad Zuse was a German inventor who worked on a series of computing devices culminating in the Z3 (about 1941), an electronic and programmable computer. Zuse also developed a notation for programs called Plankalkül, which is regarded as the first programming language.

E

Custom Packages

This appendix describes the nonstandard packages used in the text. The description consists of a reproduction of the JavaDoc output for the packages.

E.1 BasicIO

Class BasicIO.SimpleDataInput

```
java.lang.Object
   |
   +----BasicIO.SimpleDataInput
```

public abstract class SimpleDataInput
extends java.lang.Object

This class provides a uniform interface to I/O streams for input and output of the primitive java types, the String type and object types (where supported by the class). It specifies the operations supported by input stream classes: ASCIIPrompter, ASCIIDataFile, and BinaryDataFile.

Each operation (including the constructors), is either successful or unsuccessful (as indicated by a subsequent call to the method: successful).

The input stream is considered to be separated into fields (each data item being considered a field). The input operations for the standard types (primitive, String, and object) read one field. Some streams (i.e., ASCIIDataFile) are separated into lines (by an end-of-line marker), which are then separated into fields. A label, such as the prompt in ASCIIPrompters, may be associated with an input request.

The following stream types are supported:

ASCIIPrompter—Input from the keyboard via a dialog box with prompt.

ASCIIDataFile—Input from a file of text with white space separating values and tabs and line separators terminating strings.

BinaryDataFile—Input from a file containing values in Java internal representation.

Constructors

ASCIIPrompter ( );

This constructs a prompter that will display a dialog box containing the prompt, a text box for data input, and two buttons:

OK: indicating that the input should be accepted.

End: indicating that the operation should be unsuccessful (i.e., emulating EOF).

A field is the contents of the text box.

ASCIIPrompter (boolean logIt);

This constructs a prompter as above. If the parameter is true, the I/O activity is logged to a file. That is, for each prompt, a line is produced containing the current prompt value followed by the contents of the text box entered. The default constructor does not do logging.

ASCIIDataFile ( );

This constructs a stream to access an ASCII text file for input. It displays the standard file open dialog box. Fields are separated by field separators (tabs or EOL markers).

BinaryDataFile ( );

This constructs a stream to access a binary data file for input. It displays the standard file open dialog box. Each object is considered to be a field.

Version:

3.1 (08/00)

v1 original implementation

v2 rewrite for Java 1.1

v2.1 add raw character I/O (readC, ReadLine)

v2.2 use Java 1.2 print model

v3 bring in line with TurtleGraphics

v3.1 recompile with new VM

Author:

Dave Hughes

Dept. of Computer Science

Brock University

St. Catharines, Ontario

Canada

See Also:

SimpleDataOutput

Constructor Index

- **SimpleDataInput**()

Method Index

- **close**()
  This method closes the input stream, releasing resources as necessary.
- **readBoolean**()
  This method inputs a boolean value from the stream.
- **readByte**()
  This method inputs a byte value from the stream.
- **readC**()
  This method inputs the next character from the stream.
- **readChar**()
  This method inputs a char value from the stream.
- **readDouble**()
  This method inputs a double value from the stream.
- **readFloat**()
  This method inputs a float value from the stream.
- **readInt**()
  This method inputs an int value from the stream.
- **readLine**()
  This method inputs a line as a String value from the stream.

- **readLong**()
  This method inputs a long value from the stream.
- **readObject**()
  This method inputs an Object value from the stream.
- **readShort**()
  This method inputs a short value from the stream.
- **readString**()
  This method inputs a String value from the stream.
- **setLabel**(String)
  This method sets the label for the next read operation.
- **skipToEOL**()
  This method repositions the stream to the point after the next line marker, if there is one.
- **successful**()
  This method indicates whether or not the previous operation was successful.

Constructors

- **SimpleDataInput**

```
public SimpleDataInput()
```

Methods

- **close**

```
public abstract void close()
```

This method closes the input stream, releasing resources as necessary. It should be invoked when the stream is no longer being used.

- **successful**

```
public boolean successful()
```

This method indicates whether or not the previous operation was successful. If the operation was the the constructor, failure indicates that the stream could not be opened for some reason. If it was a read operation, failure indicates the read was not possible (usually EOF or bad data format). If it was the close, failure indicates that the stream could not be closed and may subsequently be inaccessible.

Returns:
boolean: whether last operation was successful

- **skipToEOL**

  `public void skipToEOL()`

  This method repositions the stream to the point after the next line marker, if there is one. Subsequent input will come from the next stream line.

  ASCIIPrompter—This stream does not have stream lines. skipToEOL has no effect.

  ASCIIDataFile—A stream line is one line (i.e., to the next line separator). skipToEOL skips to the beginning of the next line.

  BinaryDataFile—This stream does not have stream lines. skipToEOL has no effect.

- **readBoolean**

  `public boolean readBoolean()`

  This method inputs a boolean value from the stream. The operation fails at end of the stream or if the input does not match boolean format.

  Returns:
  boolean: value read

- **readByte**

  `public byte readByte()`

  This method inputs a byte value from the stream. The operation fails at end of the stream or if the input does not match byte format.

  Returns:
  byte: value read

- **readC**

  `public char readC()`

  This method inputs the next character from the stream. The operation fails at end of the stream.

  ASCIIDataFile—A single ASCII character (1 byte) is read. This may include line separator or field separator characters.

  ASCIIPrompter—Same result as readChar (readChar is preferred).

  Binary Streams—Same result as readChar (readChar is preferred).

  Returns:
  char: value read

- **readChar**

  `public char readChar()`

  This method inputs a char value from the stream. The operation fails at end of the stream.

  Returns:
  char: value read

- **readDouble**

  `public double readDouble()`

  This method inputs a double value from the stream. The operation fails at end of the stream or if the input does not match double format.

  Returns:
  double: value read

- **readFloat**

  `public float readFloat()`

  This method inputs a float value from the stream. The operation fails at end of the stream or if the input does not match float format.

  Returns:
  float: value read

- **readInt**

  `public int readInt()`

  This method inputs an int value from the stream. The operation fails at end of the stream or if the input does not match int format.

  Returns:
  int: value read

- **readLine**

  `public java.lang.String readLine()`

  This method inputs a line as a String value from the stream. The operation fails at end of the stream.

  ASCIIPrompter—Same result as readString (readString is preferred).

  ASCIIDataFile—The ASCII characters from the current stream position to the next line separator or eof are returned as a string (possibly an empty string).

  Binary Streams—Same result as readString (readString is preferred).

  Returns:
  String: string read

- **readLong**

```
public long readLong()
```

This method inputs a long value from the stream. The operation fails at end of the stream or if the input does not match long format.

Returns:
long: value read

- **readObject**

```
public java.lang.Object readObject()
```

This method inputs an Object value from the stream. The operation fails at end of the stream.

ASCII Streams—This method is not supported for ASCII input streams. Result is null.

Binary Streams—An object in Java internal format is read. The object must be Serializable.

Returns:
Object: object read

- **readShort**

```
public short readShort()
```

This method inputs a short value from the stream. The operation fails at end of the stream or if the input does not match short format.

Returns:
short: value read

- **readString**

```
public java.lang.String readString()
```

This method inputs a String value from the stream. The operation fails at end of the stream.

ASCIIPrompter—The contents of the text box are returned as a String (possibly an empty string).

ASCIIDataFile—The ASCII characters from the current stream position to the next tab, line separator, or eof are returned as a string (possibly an empty string).

Binary Streams—A string of Unicode characters in Java internal format is read.

Returns:
String: string read

■ **setLabel**

```
public void setLabel(java.lang.String label)
```

This method sets the label for the next read operation.

ASCIIPrompter—The label is displayed as the prompt on subsequent dialog boxes.

ASCIIDataFile—The label is ignored. setLabel has no effect.

BinaryDataFile—The label is ignored. setLabel has no effect.

Parameters:
label: - the label for the read.

Class BasicIO.SimpleDataOutput

```
java.lang.Object
   |
   +----BasicIO.SimpleDataOutput
```

public abstract class **SimpleDataOutput** extends java.lang.Object

This class provides a uniform interface to I/O streams for input and output of the primitive Java types, the String type, and object types if they are supported by the class. It specifies the operations supported by output stream classes: ASCIIDisplayer, ASCIIReportFile, ASCIIOutputFile, and BinaryOutputFile.

Each operation (including the constructors), is either successful or unsuccessful (as indicated by a subsequent call to the method: successful).

Some output streams are considered to be separated into lines by line markers (e.g., EOLs in ASCIIDisplayers and ASCIIReportFiles). A label is nondata text (e.g., headings, titles, formatting controls) that is inserted into a stream (i.e., ASCIIDisplayer and ASCIIReportFile) for human consumption. ASCIIDisplayer and ASCIIReport files include a single space or label between consecutive values in the same line. ASCIIDataFiles are tab delimited within a line.

The following stream types are supported:

ASCIIDisplayer—Output to the screen displayed in a scrollable window.

ASCIIReportFile—Output to a file which is intended to be printed.

ASCIIOutputFile—Output to a file of the data values in their text form (suitable for input via ASCIIDataFile). Values are tab-delimited.

BinaryOutputFile—Output to a file of values in Java internal representation (suitable for input via BinaryDataFile).

Constructors

ASCIIDisplayer ( );

This constructs a window containing a scrollable text area to which values can be written, and three buttons:

Close: closes the window. Subsequent writes will have no effect.

Print: prints the contents of the displayer. Displays the standard print dialog.

Save: saves the contents of the window to a text file. Displays the standard save dialog box.

ASCIIReportFile ( );

This constructs a stream to access an ASCII text file for output. It displays the standard save dialog box.

ASCIIOutputFile ( );

This constructs a stream to access an ASCII text file for output. It displays the standard save dialog box.

BinaryOutputFile ( );

This constructs a stream to access an binary data file for output. It displays the standard save dialog box.

Version:

3.1 (08/00)

1.0 initial version

2.0 rewrite for Java 1.1

2.1 add raw character I/O (writeC, writeLine)

2.2 add 1.2 print model support

3 bring into line with TurtleGraphics

3.1 recompile with most recent VM

Author:

Dave Hughes

Dept. of Computer Science

Brock University

St. Catharines, Ontario

Canada

See Also:

SimpleDataInput

Constructor Index

- **SimpleDataOutput**()

Method Index

- **close**()
  This method closes the output stream, releasing resources as necessary.
- **successful**()
  This method indicates whether or not the previous operation was successful.
- **writeBoolean**(boolean)
  This method outputs a boolean value to the stream.
- **writeBoolean**(boolean, int)
  This method outputs a boolean value to the stream using w character positions.
- **writeByte**(byte)
  This method outputs a byte value to the stream.
- **writeByte**(byte, int)
  This method outputs a byte value to the stream using w character positions.
- **writeC**(char)
  This method outputs a char value to the stream.
- **writeChar**(char)
  This method outputs a char value to the stream.
- **writeChar**(char, int)
  This method outputs a char value to the stream using w character positions.
- **writeDouble**(double)
  This method outputs a double value to the stream.
- **writeDouble**(double, int, int)
  This method outputs a double value to the stream using w character positions and d decimal places.
- **writeEOL**()
  This method writes an end-of-line marker to the stream.
- **writeFloat**(float)
  This method outputs a float value to the stream.
- **writeFloat**(float, int, int)
  This method outputs a float value to the stream using w character positions and d decimal places.

- **writeInt**(int)
  This method outputs a int value to the stream.
- **writeInt**(int, int)
  This method outputs an int value to the stream using w character positions.
- **writeLabel**(String)
  This method outputs a sequence of nondata characters to the stream.
- **writeLine**(String)
  This method outputs a string value as a line to the stream.
- **writeLong**(long)
  This method outputs a long value to the stream.
- **writeLong**(long, int)
  This method outputs a long value to the stream using w character positions.
- **writeObject**(Object)
  This method outputs an object to the stream.
- **writeObject**(Object, int)
  This method outputs an object value to the stream using w character positions.
- **writeShort**(short)
  This method outputs a short value to the stream.
- **writeShort**(short, int)
  This method outputs a short value to the stream using w character positions.
- **writeString**(String)
  This method outputs a string to the stream.
- **writeString**(String, int)
  This method outputs a String value to the stream using w character positions.

Constructors

- **SimpleDataOutput**

```
public SimpleDataOutput()
```

Methods

- **close**

```
public abstract void close()
```

This method closes the output stream, releasing resources as necessary. It should be invoked when the stream is no longer being used.

■ **successful**

`public boolean successful()`

This method indicates whether or not the previous operation was successful. If the operation was the constructor, failure indicates that the stream could not be opened for some reason. If it was a write operation, failure indicates the write was not possible (usually some I/O error). If it was a close operation, failure indicates inability to close the stream. The stream subsequently may be inaccessible.

Returns:
boolean: whether last operation was successful

■ **writeEOL**

`public void writeEOL()`

This method writes an end of line marker to the stream.

ASCIIDisplayer—The marker is a line separator character.

ASCIIReportFile—The marker in a line separator marker.

ASCIIOutputFile—The marker is a line separator marker.

BinaryOutputFile—Binary streams are not considered to have lines. `writeEOL` has no effect.

■ **writeBoolean**

`public void writeBoolean(boolean b)`

This method outputs a boolean value to the stream. The operation fails on an I/O error.

Parameters:
b - the value to be written

■ **writeBoolean**

`public void writeBoolean(boolean b, int w)`

This method outputs a boolean value to the stream using w character positions. The operation fails on an I/O error.

ASCII streams—The value is written in w character positions.

Binary streams—Has the same effect as writeBoolean above.

Parameters:
b - the value to be written.
w - character positions to use for value.

- **writeByte**

```
public void writeByte(byte b)
```

This method outputs a byte value to the stream. The operation fails on an I/O error.

Parameters:
b - the value to be written.

- **writeByte**

```
public void writeByte(byte b, int w)
```

This method outputs a byte value to the stream using w character positions. The operation fails on an I/O error.

ASCII streams—The value is written in w character positions.

Binary streams—Has the same effect as writeByte above.

Parameters:
b - the value to be written.
w - character positions to use for value.

- **writeC**

```
public void writeC(char c)
```

This method outputs a char value to the stream. The operation fails on an I/O error.

ASCIIOutputFile—A single ASCII character (1 byte) is written without separator.

Other Streams—Same result as writeChar (writeChar is preferred).

Parameters:
c - the value to be written.

- **writeChar**

```
public void writeChar(char c)
```

This method outputs a char value to the stream. The operation fails on an I/O error.

Parameters:
c - the value to be written.

- **writeChar**

```
public void writeChar(char c, int w)
```

This method outputs a char value to the stream using w character positions. The operation fails on an I/O error.

ASCII streams—The value is written in w character positions.

Binary streams—Has the same effect as writeChar above.

Parameters:
c - the value to be written.
w - character positions to use for value.

- **writeDouble**

```
public void writeDouble(double d)
```

This method outputs a double value to the stream. The operation fails on an I/O error.

Parameters:
d - the value to be written.

- **writeDouble**

```
public void writeDouble(double d, int w, int p)
```

This method outputs a double value to the stream using w character positions and d decimal places. The operation fails on an I/O error.

ASCII streams—The value is written in w character positions with p decimal places.

Binary streams—Has the same effect as writeDouble above.

Parameters:
d - the value to be written.
w - character positions to use for value.
p - decimal places to use for value.

- **writeFloat**

```
public void writeFloat(float f)
```

This method outputs a float value to the stream. The operation fails on an I/O error.

Parameters:
f - the value to be written.

- **writeFloat**

```
public void writeFloat(float f, int w, int p)
```

This method outputs a float value to the stream using w character positions and d decimal places. The operation fails on an I/O error.

ASCII streams—The value is written in w character positions with d decimal places.

Binary streams—Has the same effect as writeFloat above.

Parameters:
f - the value to be written.
w - character positions to use for value.
d - decimal places to use for value.

- **writeInt**

```
public void writeInt(int i)
```

This method outputs an int value to the stream. The operation fails on an I/O error.

Parameters:
i - the value to be written.

- **writeInt**

```
public void writeInt(int i, int w)
```

This method outputs an int value to the stream using w character positions. The operation fails on an I/O error.

ASCII streams—The value is written in w character positions.

Binary streams—Has the same effect as writeInt above.

Parameters:
i - the value to be written.
w - character positions to use for value.

- **writeLabel**

```
public void writeLabel(java.lang.String s)
```

This method outputs a sequence of nondata characters to the stream. The sequence usually consists of identifying information (e.g., headings, titles) or layout (e.g., tabs, spaces, form feeds) intended for human reading. The operation fails on an I/O error.

ASCIIReportFile—The label replaces separators between values on the same line.

ASCIIDisplayer—The label replaces separators between values on the same line.

ASCIIOutputFile—Data file streams are not intended for human reading. writeLabel has no effect.

BinaryOutputFile—Binary streams are not intended for human reading. writeLabel has no effect.

- **writeLine**

`public void writeLine(java.lang.String s)`

This method outputs a string value as a line to the stream. The operation fails on an I/O error.

ASCIIOutputFile—The string is written followed by a line separator.

Other Streams—Same result as writeString (writeString is preferred).

Parameters:
s - the value to be written.

- **writeLong**

`public void writeLong(long l)`

This method outputs a long value to the stream. The operation fails on an I/O error.

Parameters:
l - the value to be written.

- **writeLong**

`public void writeLong(long l, int w)`

This method outputs a long value to the stream using w character positions. The operation fails on an I/O error.

ASCII streams—The value is written in w character positions.

Binary streams—Has the same effect as writeLong above.

Parameters:
l - the value to be written
w - character positions to use for value.

- **writeObject**

`public void writeObject(java.lang.Object o)`

This method outputs an object to the stream. The operation fails on an I/O error.

ASCII streams—The object must implement toString.

Binary streams—The object must be Serializable.

Parameters:
o - the object to be written.

- **writeObject**

```
public void writeObject(java.lang.Object o, int w)
```

This method outputs an object value to the stream using w character positions. The operation fails on an I/O error.

ASCII streams—The value is written in w character positions. The object must implement toString.

Binary streams—Has the same effect as `writeObject` above. The object must be Serializable.

Parameters:
o - the value to be written.
w - character positions to use for value.

- **writeShort**

```
public void writeShort(short s)
```

This method outputs a short value to the stream. The operation fails on an I/O error.

Parameters:
s - the value to be written.

- **writeShort**

```
public void writeShort(short s, int w)
```

This method outputs a short value to the stream using w character positions. The operation fails on an I/O error.

ASCII streams—The value is written in w character positions.

Binary streams—Has the same effect as writeShort above.

Parameters:
s - the value to be written.
w - character positions to use for value.

- **writeString**

```
public void writeString(java.lang.String s)
```

This method outputs a string to the stream. The operation fails on an I/O error.

Parameters:
s - the value to be written.

- **writeString**

  `public void writeString(java.lang.String s, int w)`

  This method outputs a String value to the stream using w character positions. The operation fails on an I/O error.

  ASCII streams—The value is written in w character positions.

  Binary streams—Has the same effect as writeString above.

  Parameters:
  s - the value to be written.
  w - character positions to use for value.

E.2 TurtleGraphics

Class TurtleGraphics.Turtle

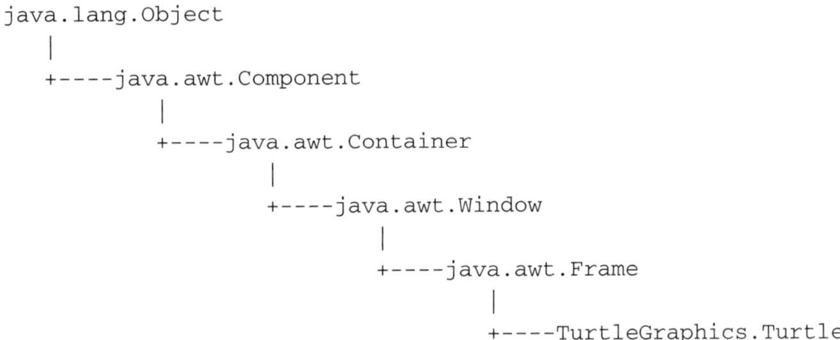

```
java.lang.Object
   |
   +----java.awt.Component
           |
           +----java.awt.Container
                   |
                   +----java.awt.Window
                           |
                           +----java.awt.Frame
                                   |
                                   +----TurtleGraphics.Turtle
```

public class **Turtle**
extends java.awt.Frame
implements java.awt.print.Printable

This class provides a simple line-drawing tool called a Turtle, based on Turtle Graphics of the Logo language. A Turtle presents a window on the screen in which line drawing can be done using the drawing primitives. The size of the drawing area and the speed of drawing may be specified at creation. It is also possible to create a log file that records the sequence of drawing operations (including parameters) that occurred during a session. The units for drawing are pixels.

Version:

3.1 (08/00)

v2 Rewrite for Java 1.1.

v3 add absolute line drawing.

v3.1 add 1.2 print model.

Author:

Dave Hughes

Dept. of Computer Science

Brock University

St. Catharines, Ontario

Canada

Variable Index

- **FAST**
- **MEDIUM**
- **SLOW**

Constructor Index

- **Turtle**()
  The default constructor creates an unlogged turtle with a drawing area 200 × 200 drawing at SLOW speed.
- **Turtle**(boolean)
  This constructor creates an optionally logged turtle with a drawing area of 200 × 200, drawing at SLOW speed.
- **Turtle**(int, int)
  This constructor creates an unlogged turtle with a drawing area of specified size, drawing at SLOW speed.
- **Turtle**(int, int, long, boolean)
  This constructor creates a Turtle with a logging facility, a drawing area of the width and height specified, and a specific drawing speed.
- **Turtle**(long)
  This constructor creates an unlogged turtle with a drawing area of 200 × 200, drawing at a specified speed.

Method Index

- **backward**(double)
  This method moves the pen distance, drawing units in the opposite direction to the turtle's current heading.
- **forward**(double)
  This method moves the pen distance, drawing units in the turtle's current heading.
- **left**(double)
  This method rotates the heading of the turtle theta radians to the left of its current heading.
- **moveTo**(double, double)
  This method moves the pen to the specified coordinates.
- **penColor**(Color)
  This method changes the color that the pen will draw when drawing lines.
- **penDown**()
  This method puts the pen to paper.
- **penUp**()
  This method raises the pen from the paper.
- **penWidth**(int)
  This method changes the width of the line that the pen draws.
- **right**(double)
  This method rotates the heading of the turtle theta radians to the right of its current heading.

Variables

- SLOW
  `public static final long SLOW`
- MEDIUM
  `public static final long MEDIUM`
- FAST
  `public static final long FAST`

Constructors

- **Turtle**

```
public Turtle(int width, int height,
              long speed, boolean logIt)
```

This constructor creates a Turtle with a logging facility, a drawing area of the width and height specified, and a specific drawing speed.

Parameters:
logIt - log the operations?
width - width of drawing area (pixels)
height - height of drawing area (pixels)
speed - speed of drawing (SLOW, MEDIUM, FAST).

- **Turtle**

```
public Turtle()
```

The default constructor creates an unlogged turtle with a drawing area 200 × 200 drawing at SLOW speed.

- **Turtle**

```
public Turtle(int width, int height)
```

This constructor creates an unlogged turtle with a drawing area of specified size, drawing at SLOW speed.

Parameters:
width - width of drawing area (in pixels)
height - height of drawing area (in pixels)

- **Turtle**

```
public Turtle(long speed)
```

This constructor creates an unlogged turtle with a drawing area of 200 × 200, drawing at a specified speed.

Parameters:
speed - drawing speed (see constants)

- **Turtle**

  `public Turtle(boolean logIt)`

  This constructor creates an optionally logged turtle with a drawing area of 200 × 200, drawing at SLOW speed.

  Parameters:
  logIt - log the operations

Methods

- **penUp**

  `public void penUp()`

  This method raises the pen from the paper. Subsequent drawing actions will not draw lines.

- **penDown**

  `public void penDown()`

  This method puts the pen to paper. Subsequent drawing actions will draw lines.

- **left**

  `public void left(double theta)`

  This method rotates the heading of the turtle theta radians to the left of its current heading. No drawing is done.

  Parameters:
  theta - number of radians to rotate.

- **right**

  `public void right(double theta)`

  This method rotates the heading of the turtle theta radians to the right of its current heading. No drawing is done.

  Parameters:
  theta - number of radians to rotate.

- **forward**

  `public void forward(double distance)`

  This method moves the pen distance, drawing units in the turtle's current heading. If the pen is down, drawing will occur. If the pen is up, only the turtle's current position will be affected.

  Parameters:
  distance - the distance to move.

- **backward**

```
public void backward(double distance)
```

This method moves the pen distance, drawing units in the opposite direction to the turtle's current heading. The heading is not affected. If the pen is down, drawing will occur. If the pen is up, only the turtle's current position will be affected.

Parameters:
distance - the distance to move.

- **moveTo**

```
public void moveTo(double x, double y)
```

This method moves the pen to the specified coordinates. If the pen is down, drawing will occur. If the pen is up, only the turtle's current position will be affected. The turtle's current heading remains unchanged.

Parameters:
x - the x-coordinate to move to
y - the y-coordinate to move to

- **penColor**

```
public void penColor(java.awt.Color c)
```

This method changes the color that the pen will draw when drawing lines. The default color is Color.black. The standard class Color provides color constants and constructors and can be imported from the java.awt package.

Parameters:
c - the color to draw with.

- **penWidth**

```
public void penWidth(int width)
```

This method changes the width of the line that the pen draws. The default width is 1.

Parameters:
width - the width for the pen (pixels).

F

Answers to Review Questions

Chapter 1

1. F
2. T
3. F
4. T
5. F
6. T
7. F
8. T
9. F
10. F
11. b
12. b
13. b
14. b
15. d
16. c
17. c
18. a

Chapter 2

1. F
2. T
3. T
4. T
5. F
6. F
7. T
8. b
9. c
10. d
11. c
12. c
13. d
14. d
15. a

Chapter 3

1. F
2. T
3. F
4. T
5. T
6. T
7. F
8. T
9. d
10. b
11. c
12. d
13. b
14. d
15. c

Chapter 4

1. T
2. T
3. F
4. F
5. T
6. F
7. T
8. F
9. b
10. d
11. c
12. b
13. b
14. c
15. d

Chapter 5

1. T
2. T
3. F
4. T
5. F
6. F
7. F
8. T
9. b
10. c
11. c
12. d
13. a
14. d
15. a

Chapter 6

1. T
2. F
3. T
4. T
5. T
6. T
7. F
8. F
9. a
10. b
11. c
12. c
13. b
14. b
15. d

Chapter 7

1. T
2. F
3. F
4. T
5. F
6. d
7. b
8. d
9. d
10. c

Chapter 8

1. T
2. T
3. T
4. F
5. F
6. T
7. T
8. c
9. d
10. d
11. d
12. d
13. c
14. b
15. b

Chapter 9

1. T
2. F
3. F
4. F
5. T
6. F
7. F
8. b
9. d
10. c
11. b
12. c
13. a
14. a
15. c

Chapter 10

1. F
2. F
3. F
4. T
5. F
6. T
7. T
8. d
9. c
10. d
11. c
12. d
13. a
14. a
15. b

Chapter 11

1. T
2. T
3. F
4. F
5. T
6. F
7. F
8. d
9. d
10. d
11. b
12. c
13. d
14. b
15. a

G

Additional Reading

For more on the history of computing devices, see:

Williams, M.R.; *A History of Computing Technology*; IEEE Computer Society Press, Los Alamitos, CA; 1997.

For brief biographies of pioneers of computing and references to more detailed biographies, see:

Lee, J.A.N.; *Computer Pioneers*; IEEE Computer Society Press, Los Alamitos, CA; 1995.

For the specification of the Java syntax and semantics see:

Gosling, J., Joy, B., & Steele, G.; *The Java™ Language Specification*; Addison-Wesley, Reading, MA; 1996.

or for the second edition, online, see:

http://java.sun.com/docs/books/jls/second_edition/html/jTOC.doc.html

For the complete specification of Java including all API libraries, news, new releases of the language specification, and downloadable JDK (Java Development Kit), see online at:

http://java.sun.com/

For more about Turtle geometry, see:

Abelson, H. & diSessa, A.A.; *Turtle Geometry*, MIT Press, Cambridge, MA; 1980.

For a complete description of Design Patterns, see:

Gamma, E., et al.; *Design Patterns–Elements of Reusable Object-Oriented Software*; Addison-Wesley, Reading, MA; 1994.

For a description of Responsibility-based Design and CRC cards, see:

Beck, K. & Cunningham, W.; "A Laboratory for Teaching Object-Oriented Thinking"; Proc. OOPSLA '89 (New Orleans, LA Oct. 1989); SIGPLAN Notices v24, n10 (Oct. 1989), pp. 1–6; ACM Press (1989).

and

Wirfs-Brock, R. & Wilkerson, B.; "Object-Oriented Design: A Responsibility Approach"; Proc. OOPSLA '89 (New Orleans, LA Oct. 1989); SIGPLAN Notices v24, n10 (Oct. 1989), pp 71–76; ACM Press (1989).

Index

Note: Italicized page locators indicate figures/tables.

D